Consumer Capitalism

Human life is in experiencing time-space by generating knowledge. Through division of labour we increase our knowledge-generating capacity, economize on our effort and embody economically relevant knowledge in collectively produced commodities. Then, we compete against each other trying to make it private, through consumption. But as the time-space we perceive (the cosmos) is always frightfully greater than the time-space we can experience, we end up consuming insatiably, vainly trying to soothe our existential anxiety.

Consumer Capitalism departs from the standard economic approach which fails to take into account the ontological and psychological substratum of behaviour, thus ignoring the accountability of consumers, concealing the nature of their motive, the wastefulness of capitalistic growth and its consequences. Motivational uniformity propounded in *Consumer Capitalism* provides a cohesive framework, which controls individualistic disruption and allows markets to promote variety. System growth, price and structure changes obtain fluently from individual agency. The inwardly coercive nature and vanity of the driving motive explain aggressiveness, distress and rapacity that characterize life under capitalism. Scarcity, utility and self-interest acquire content.

This volume demonstrates how consumers scramble to foresee market conditions, generate use-type knowledge and gain positional advantage by purchasing commodities which embody more human time-space through capital-intensive production. Along with production innovations, these knowledge increments change prices, adjust demand to the technological structure and promote growth through increased roundaboutness. *Consumer Capitalism* explores how capitalistic growth surveys existential distress rather than welfare, but consumers' innovative capacity must be kept high, sustaining their illusion that by owning capital-embodying commodities they can experience life. In this sense, consumers are capitalists, although the capital appropriated through consumption is not further productive.

Anastasios S. Korkotsides is Assistant Professor, Faculty of Economics, University of Athens, Greece.

Routledge Frontiers of Political Economy

Consumer Capitalism

Anastasios S. Korkotsides

Routledge
Taylor & Francis Group

LONDON AND NEW YORK

First published 2007
by Routledge
2 Park Square, Milton Park, Abingdon, Oxon OX14 4RN

Simultaneously published in the USA and Canada
by Routledge
270 Madison Ave, New York, NY 10016

Routledge is an imprint of the Taylor & Francis Group, an informa business

Transferred to Digital Printing 2009

© 2007 Anastasios S. Korkotsides

Typeset in Times New Roman by
Newgen Imaging Systems (P) Ltd, Chennai, India

British Library Cataloguing in Publication Data
A catalogue record for this book is available
from the British Library

Library of Congress Cataloging in Publication Data
A catalog record for this book has been requested

ISBN10: 0–415–37518–5 (hbk)
ISBN10: 0–415–54780–6 (pbk)

ISBN13: 978–0–415–37518–4 (hbk)
ISBN13: 978–0–415–54780–2 (pbk)

For Alexis and Stelios

Der Muthigste unter uns hat nicht Muth genug zu dem, was er eigentlich weiß…

(The Bravest amongst us is not Brave enough for that which he, literally, knows…)

(Friedrich Nietzsche, *Nietzsche Werke. Kritische Gesamtausgabe*, 8. Abteilung, 2. Band. Nachgelassene Fragmente Herbst 1887 bis März 1888. Verse 9 [52] (41) 20, 25)

Contents

Illustrations

Figures

Tables

Preface

This is an infidel book. It is about fear, not faith, and about aggression that comes with fear. It is about existential anxiety that brings us into society, within which we seek to expand our time-space by generating knowledge that is useful for the practical conduct of life. Economically relevant knowledge is produced faster through division of labour. Distribution of such valuable output, however, poses a challenge. It sets each one against all others, in a vortex of conflict that climaxes in capitalism, where life is reduced to inventing ways of selfishly appropriating socially produced value. The primitive urge for day-to-day survival is transfigured into a quest for a particular type of knowledge, which provides its possessor control over humans through control over the product of their toil. The consumption activity constitutes a vital component of this act of expropriation, complementing and meshing inseparably with production and income distribution. This contest sets the context and content of self-interest and constitutes the rationalization of capitalism, developing into a modern type of slavery, where animalish aggression and violence are channelled into a sophisticated, culturally fabricated and institutionally fostered game of wits.

Complacency impedes wisdom. Social science cannot be evangelical, announce good news, make promises, adulate or appease the crowds. It must interrogate about the type of history they create, based on their social and self-awareness. Self-awareness is hard to get at, not only because one must see through a diffracting introspect glass, but because one must first see the glass, which is one and the same with what it shows. When reality is depressing and prospects are gloomy, we avert our eyes from it. We get acclimatized to it, evade it by twisting of language, abstract from it or simply ignore it in order to get by. When violence is rife and Manichaeistic divisions into 'we' and 'they' prevail, some take heart from traces of altruism or other noble expressions. This perpetuates delusion. The more we repulse a fear the more repulsive it grows, and the most repulsed fear is the fear of death: the fear of ourselves.

Economics, for its part, may not shirk from what falls in its share. To become social, it must promote understanding of brute facts about society and its prospects; not cope out, deny the obvious or festoon a deplorable situation. To the deceptively impartial methodological individualism of mainstream theory, social economics must juxtapose an honest account of acquisitive aggressiveness promoted by capitalism and corroding ethics, cultures and individual conscience. Widening gaps between rich and poor notwithstanding, we all share in an emotional desolateness that stems from existential anxiety and seeks relief in paroxysmic consumption. The plight of mankind has become deeper and more intricate than the old agony to stay alive.

This book treads an unorthodox, controversial, often quarrelsome path in its content and writing style. It grants that real economics is mundane, violent and alien to savoir excursions through the scenic pages of scientific economic journals or books. Science is about ideas, and the fate of a theory depends on the acceptance of its conceptual code. Before the knowledge landscape is cleared and truth can be told apart from flight of fancy, the avant-garde mixes with the absurd and daring with preposterousness. But novelty depends on context, and a book's audience constitutes a vital part of its context. The kind of competence asked of this book's readers is perseverance in the face of an unflattering self-view and an inquisitive spirit not thwarted by artificially erected discipline boundaries.

Although a gravely felt condition permeates its writing, this is not a pessimist book. Pessimist is what finds reality gloomier than it really is and gives no glimmer of hope. Refusing to see what is actually gloomy is hopeless. So, before dismissing a theory such as the one submitted here, one should consider David Hume's advice: 'When any opinion leads into absurdities, 'tis certainly false; but 'tis not certain an opinion is false, because 'tis of dangerous consequences.'

Anastasios S. Korkotsides
Athens
September 2006

Acknowledgements

It is doubtful that this book would have been written if it were not for Yanis Varoufakis, a good colleague of mine in the Faculty of Economics at the University of Athens, and for Terentianus Maurus, a Latin grammarian and writer, *c.* second century AD. Yanis found more in my drafts than I thought was there. Terentianus Maurus maintained that '*Pro captu lectoris habent sua fata libelli*'. (The fate of a book depends on the competence of its readers.) So, the usual disclaimer applies for Maurus (and for those acknowledged next), but not for Yanis. If it is all nonsense, he carries a negligible part of the blame. If there is any value in it, he deserves a good part of the credit.

Kostis Vaitsos, of the same Faculty, also supplied constructive criticism on an earlier draft. His contribution is acknowledged, as is that of Costas Roumanias, a former student of mine, who offered a critical eye from a considerably different point of view, while defending his dissertation for a PhD at Oxford University, and then again at the late stages in my writing, while being a Lecturer at the University of Macedonia. Svetoslav Danchev, a student at the UADPhilEcon (the Doctor of Philosophy programme in Economics at the University of Athens) also provided very helpful comments. Given the unorthodox content and style of the book, a sample of readers' reactions was much needed. Such generosity, coming from students, I take as great honour. Speaking of students, I tested the reactions of exposure to the venomous radiation of these ideas on those who attended an advanced undergraduate course titled 'Dynamical Economic Systems' and also on those in the UADPhilEcon. My impression is that they have come through, with better humour and greater enthusiasm about this discipline, not with less, as I feared.

To Kenneth Ted Wallenius, my dear friend and former PhD advisor at Clemson University, I owe an intellectual debt because he taught me the value of parsimony and of outlying observations in statistical data analysis. But, whether he meant it or not, he also solidified my faith in outlying observation outposts: Nothing is outlying, except from a viewpoint.

I am thankful to the obliging people at the Library of my Faculty, as well as those at other Libraries where I searched for material. I also thank the people at Routledge, who promptly provided their expertise and assistance. Financial support for this research was provided by the Special Account for Research Grants of the National and Kapodistrian University of Athens, and it is gratefully acknowledged.

But great as all these debts may be, this book was written for my sons, Alexis and Stelios, who became interested in the project, stood by me throughout and gave me heart. May their world be less aggressive and wasteful than was ours! May their world disprove my theory!

Part I

1 Theory, society and consumption

While the Athenian democracy of Pericles was declining, Socrates aggravated its citizens with his teaching that the worst thing about ignorance is that those who are neither wise nor virtuous are pleased with themselves; they are self-complacent. So, he made a plea for self-awareness: *Gnothi seauton*! The Athenians accused him of impiety and sentenced him to death by drinking hemlock. Socrates, a democrat, declined his students' offer to help him escape, submitting to the institutions of a degenerate democracy.

In his *Nicomachean Ethics* (I. v. 3), Aristotle averred that 'The generality of mankind ... show themselves to be utterly slavish, by preferring what is only a life for cattle; but they get a hearing for their view as reasonable because many persons of high position share the feelings of Sardanapallus.'[1] The Athenians went after him also, prosecuting him for impiety. Being not an avowed democrat, Aristotle refused to let Athens 'sin twice against philosophy' and fled to Chalkis, where he died soon after.

Nietzsche did not meet with much better fate, for maintaining that 'The Bravest amongst us is not Brave enough ...'

Adam Smith admonished, somewhat more guardedly: 'He is a bold surgeon, they say, whose hand does not tremble when he performs an operation upon his own person; and he is often equally bold who does not hesitate to pull off the mysterious veil of self-delusion, which covers from his view the deformities of his own conduct' (Smith, 1869: 138). And: 'If we saw ourselves in the light in which others see us, or in which they would see us if they knew all, a reformation would generally be unavoidable' (ibid.: 139).

In his Introduction to *Leviathan*, Hobbes (1991: 10, original emphases) noted:

> But there is another saying not of late understood, by which they might learn truly to read one another, if they would take the pains; and that is, *Nosce teipsum, Read thy self:* which was not meant, as it is now used, to countenance, either the barbarous state of men in power, towards their inferiors; or to encourage men of low degree, to a sawcie behaviour towards their betters; But to teach us, that for the similitude of the thoughts, and Passions of one man, to the thoughts, and Passions of another, whosoever looketh into himself, and considereth what he doth, when he does *think*,

opine, reason, hope, feare, &c, and upon what grounds; he shall thereby read and know, what are the thoughts, and Passions of all other men, upon the like occasions.

Self-awareness is an ideal; a feat of extreme difficulty, a noblest pursuit. But our aggressiveness, which protrudes conspicuously behind a thin civilized veneer, leaves little room for it, as we are preoccupied with concealing our violence from ourselves and from others, covering up its motives and goals. So, the above thinkers were not admired for what they really taught, but for watered-down versions of their ideas. Yet, the lesson to be drawn from them is that they did not cop out of their duty to speak as they saw right. They took it as their moral obligation to revolt against moral decay, resisting siding with the underprivileged and finding malice only in the privileged. They knew that all can do harm and that anonymous masses can do the greatest.

A good part of the said deception is done by twisting of language. For example, car 'accidents' are not accidental, neither is their calling them so. Such doing away with one's own guilt or responsibility should normally be seen as ludicrous, but normal or ludicrous, decent or indecent are socially defined, according to prevailing standards. This is how it *is*, if this is how many *think* it is. Nothing practically exists unless it is seen by the many, and what the many see is hard to dispute. Seeing what they don't is being paranoid. Not believing in what they believe is being impious. All value is social, and sanity is by consensus. Outside consensus, there is insanity. Socrates was insane. Nietzsche was insane. Boltzmann was insane and *We* are sane. The fence keeps us safe from those inside, 'inside' being always the 'smaller' part.

Ignorance is never imposed, so it is not an excuse. The right to be thinking cannot be deprived. It can only be voluntarily surrendered. In the darkest of instances, those who meant to keep their spirit alive did so. To be base, one must take pride in it and enjoy it. Those who choose to be base and ignorant enjoy their ignorance and despise anyone who is noble or wise. Baseness and servility feed ignorant veneration and pretentious admiration of great work, without the slightest of understanding or true appreciation. Most would poke fun at Einstein or Beethoven and they would tear the Parthenon down, if they could; what they left standing of it, that is, for being too big to fit in private marble collections or in museums, and too removed from Dresden, to be pulverized in a single air raid.

As Feuerbach (1957) contended, in his Preface to the second edition of *The Essence of Christianity*, modern society prefers the picture to the object, the counterfeit to the authentic; the reproduction of reality to reality itself; what appears, to what is really there. Delusion is its sanctity, truth is its profanity. And the climax of its delusion is the pinnacle of its sacredness. Fromm (2004: 69) maintained that 'most people prefer to think in fictions, rather than in realities, and to deceive themselves and others about the facts underlying individual and social life'. It may be more arguable to say that they deliberately *select* interpretations of reality or actively *construct* impressions of it that allow them to perpetuate their delusion.

Motivating observations

With its mainstream branch sailing clear of emotions through entertainment of the *Homo economicus* caricature that obliges to no motives and can be accused of no evil sentiments, and with Marxists siding with the underdogs, economic theorizing appeased and adulated the crowds, avoided to interrogate them, deluding itself and the crowds in the process and missing much interpretative substance. It largely ignored the wisdom of its own patron saints, picking selectively from their ideas. Marx and Smith condemned disgrace, aggression and avarice in such harsh terms, that any theory honestly founded upon their complete spectrum of ideas should pay particular attention to the intrinsic aggressiveness of the economic conduct of laymen. In their philosophies, which were expressed conclusively in the *Wealth of Nations* and in *Capital*, but which should be read against the background of the *Theory of Moral Sentiments*, the *Economic and Philosophical Manuscripts* and their other writings, they drew economic activity in less bright colours than their followers painted it. They unmistakably sketched it as strife. Urbane Smith argued: 'The pride of man makes him love to domineer, and nothing mortifies him so much as to be obliged to condescend to persuade his inferiors. Wherever the law allows it, and the nature of the work can afford it, therefore, he will generally prefer the service of slaves to that of freeman' (Smith, 1937: 365). And: 'For though management and persuasion are always the easiest and safest instruments of government, as force and violence are the worst and the most dangerous, yet such, it seems, is the natural insolence of man, that he almost always disdains to use the good instrument, except when he cannot or dare not use the bad one' (ibid.: 751).

But vile or not, the psychological underpinnings of economic activity have not escaped notice. Pareto (1916/35, Sec. 2078) insisted that 'All human conduct is psychological and, from that standpoint, not only the study of economics but the study of every other branch of human activity is a psychological study and the facts of all such branches are psychological facts.' Duesenberry (1967: 18) contended that

> we have to face up to the problems of the psychological bases of consumer choice. But as soon as one considers that problem one sees why economists have tried to avoid it. At first glance every conceivable motivation seems to be involved in consumer choices. If we wish to explain in detail every purchase by every individual we are in a hopeless position. We certainly cannot create a useful analytical scheme on the basis of detailed individual psychology.
>
> This consideration need not detain us very long. We are, after all, primarily concerned with the central tendencies of the relations between economic variables and consumer choices. If it can be shown that one set of forces dominates the behavior of most individuals, we can center our attention on the operation of those forces.

In the present investigation, we look precisely for that 'one set of forces' in the terra incognita of existential consumer ontology, wherein lies the unique motivational factor involved ultimately in all economic objects and choices: ANGST. Thus, we divorce with all those brands of political economy which confuse knavish materialism with tastes that appear variegated on the surface, but always converge on some kind of 'utility' that has historically taken on a multitude of forms: usefulness, pleasure, associated with positive experiences or with the avoiding of negative ones, or just as content-free preference orderings entertained by neoclassical theory. Whatever nuances these may take in the lasting debate over what *utility* implies (classical, Benthamite, neoclassical, etc.), none carries any distressful existential connotations. So, for economy, since a precise distinction would matter little for our argument, we will house them under a utilitarian roof, without meaning to smooth out any real differences between them.

Returning to the classical economists, they had neither expelled psychology from their considerations, nor had they cleared the crowds of envious emotions. Marx had not portrayed the many as victims, with all wrongdoing being done by a small class of capitalists seized by greed. His fundamental idea was that humans live their lives in full consciousness of themselves, in conscious relation to each other and to nature. It is *thus* that they create their own history, which evolves along with the mode of production, itself determined by the stage of development of social forces. So, he expected workers to emancipate themselves and society on their own accord, rebuking those who argued that the masses were poorly educated for this task and that they should be freed from above, by the bourgeois humanists. He held individuals accountable for the history they created, for their own alienation and dehumanization. But by failing to address individual psychological motivators, he helped others draw a gleaming picture of the proletariat.

Analogously, a fragrance of impeccable common welfare was artificially made to emerge from the sludge of avarice that was condemned unequivocally by Smith, setting his economic theory apart from his *Theory of Moral Sentiments*. Mainstream economics adopted uncritically the hypothesis that economic activity promoted some common good, as a self-evident hypothesis, digging no deeper. This evades that humans covet most what belongs to others, as there is little else to long for after satisfying their basic needs. But Smith (1869: 55) argued: 'And thus, place, that great object which divides the wives of aldermen, is the end of half the labours of human life; and is the cause of all the tumult and bustle, all the rapine and injustice, which avarice and ambition have introduced into the world.' But *place* implies conflict, since there is no such thing as first place for everyone, or an unstratified society where all occupy the same place (except for an ideally anarchic one), and what is a pleasure for one may be displeasure for others. Place is relative.

In his *Economic and Philosophical Manuscripts* Marx insisted on two things. First, 'the history of *industry* and industry as it *objectively* exists is an *open* book of the *human faculties*, and a human *psychology* which can be sensuously apprehended. ... No psychology for which this book, i.e., the most sensibly present and accessible part of history, remains closed, can become a *real* science with a genuine content' (Fromm, op. cit.: 109, original emphases). Second, the only thing that truly belongs to social humans and constitutes their personality is their labour, their personal time-space registered in the knowledge amassed through their productive and general attainments. This, Marx maintained, is social man's nature and, referring to science in general, he argued that 'One basis for life and another for science is *a priori* a falsehood. Nature, as it develops in human history, in the act of genesis of human society, is the *actual* nature of man; thus nature, as it develops through industry, though in an *alienated* form, is truly *anthropological* nature' (ibid.: 110, original emphases).

In spite of these, theory brushed aside motivation and meticulously avoided basing its argument on human psychology. Mainstream agents lack ontology, 'existing' in social vacuum, simply acting as vehicles of preferences. The shallowness of all utility-based explanations is plain to the fact that one could come up with the same theory by hypothesizing that people seek anything whatsoever, suffice it that it is non-intersubjective. This could well be forgetfulness, for example, so that, by consuming, people seek to forget their troubles, such forgetfulness being as easy as any other kind of utility to map onto a hypersurface. Such explanation could even fit better with solipsistic social anaesthesia that characterizes modern life, and it could explain better a number of other phenomena, such as that the distracting effect of commodities wanes soon after they are bought, prompting people to keep purchasing. Pleasure could be satiable (few can stand too much bliss without going crazy), but the need to distract oneself never diminishes, because there is no end to the troubles or worries people want to forget about. So, around Christmas, suicides surge as depression becomes deeper, due to disappointment of high expectations and due to one's impression that others are happy, while those who stay behind consume even more frantically. Similarly, one can offer a present on Valentine's Day either to show affection, or to suggest that . . . bygones are bygones.

It is widely agreed by now that utility maximizing does not avail for constructing a meaningful theory of consumer behaviour. The ferociousness with which people go after consumables betrays some coercive emotional driver, which speaks loud and clear of existence: of continuing to experience time-space. And experiencing speaks of knowledge. *Cogito, ergo sum*, declared Descartes, and Shackle (1972: 156, original emphases) added: 'So far as men are concerned, *being* consists in continual and endless fresh *knowing*.' Fresh knowing ascribes duration to time, and through this we experience our lives, as we will discuss in more detail. In this lies all that social complexity which theory evades by assuming tastes to be exogenous. The relevance of social standing – a psychological desideratum that appears under various guises such as status, distinction, identity seeking, demonstration or bandwagon effects, norm-guided behaviour, etc., as reviewed by Kahneman *et al.* (1999), Kasser (2002) and others – cannot be denied. What may escape notice, though, is that this is a manifestation of some underlying compulsion, which explains aggressive acquisitiveness that finds expression through consumption.

Once a knowledge prism is adopted, concepts such as those of welfare, rational self-interest, scarcity, etc. emerge with new meanings that help explain much which remained obstinately opaque under a conventional light. It is also made possible to meet what may be called an 'additivity requirement', avoiding an embarrassing inconsistency: It is reasonable to expect that if all agents pursue a certain goal with some degree of success, some expression of it must be visible at every higher level. Individual attainments must be quasi-additive, in some meaningful sense. For example, if people drew pleasure from consuming commodities, one should see pleasure hewed on their faces, social welfare to be really improving not just in the growth statistics and society to be happier. If they found relief by consuming, this should show in their behaviour. But if inexorable angst drives them, distress should be expected to show on their faces and aggression to mark their conduct. All indications are that the latter is the case. People's faces are tense, carved with anxiety, aggressive. Instead of observing a rising Gross Domestic Product (GDP) to ease tensions, as the usual argument goes, the collective situation in affluent societies is patently violent, depression mars life and despondent human debris adorns the outskirts of the cities. There is little gratifying in a day's news, most of which is about violence for some kind of gain. There is little of what we might properly call 'collective utility'. Rather, cynically aggressive, acquisitive national strategies emerge as collective outcomes of similarly motivated individual behaviour.

Explanation of economic behaviour must meet two requirements: First, its basic motivation and its goal must be clearly spelled out and they must be uniform across agents and activities. Second, there must emerge from it some consistent property at every higher level. That is, it must be possible to reconstruct the *mechanism* which produced and let develop the higher-order entity, in terms of *principles* that are operative at lower levels. This does not mean that macroeconomics must – or can be – micro-founded in the way of simple aggregation of individual outcomes, since the structure feeds back onto its constituting agency. (Aggregate demand relationships are meaningless, if preferences are interdependent.) But it means that economic theory must be firmly founded upon agency in such a way that what obtains at every higher level will not contradict in any significant way what the theory asserts about individual behaviour. Outcomes at the level of the economy must be somehow deducible from individual conduct and, conversely, individual conduct must be reconciled with the social structure, in reciprocal fashion.

Where one deals with outcomes of human initiation, where things could always have been otherwise, one should not vow for precise conclusions or exact proofs, but for rules of general validity and for underlying principles muddled by contingencies, for mechanisms removed from the observable realm, for universal constructions that can help organize thought, explain stylized facts and condense the description of any individual coherence or regularity there is to be found. Proof, in a strict sense, is of propositions in logic, not for assertions about the real world. As Shackle (op. cit.: 255) noted: 'In order to achieve demonstrative proof, the economic theoretician must reject time.' So, in order not to lose contact with reality, the validity, relevance and efficacy of theories should be judged on the basis of explanatory power and consistency with facts. According to Aristotle (1934: I. vii. 20–3, original emphasis):

> Nor again must we in all matters alike demand an explanation of the reason why things are what they are; in some cases it is enough if the fact that they

are so is satisfactorily established. This is the case with first principles; and the fact is the primary thing – it *is* a first principle. And principles are studied – some by induction, others by perception, others by some form of habituation, and also others otherwise; so we must endeavour to arrive at the principles of each kind in their natural manner, and must also be careful to define them correctly, since they are of great importance for the subsequent course of the enquiry.

And, as concerns the attainable degree of certitude, he warned against exaggerated promises:

> We must therefore be content if, in dealing with subjects and starting from premises thus uncertain, we succeed in presenting a broad outline of the truth: when our subjects and our premises are merely generalities, it is enough if we arrive at generally valid conclusions. Accordingly we may ask the student also to accept the various views we put forward in the same spirit; for it is the mark of an educated mind to expect that amount of exactness in each kind which the nature of the particular subject admits. It is equally unreasonable to accept merely probable conclusions from a mathematician and to demand strict demonstration from an orator.
>
> (Ibid.: I. iii. 4)

Indeed, it would be naïve to demand event-predictive accuracy of an economic theory, or evidence that acting agents are discursively aware of the psychological mechanism that motivates their behaviour. Moreover, no single theory can explain all aspects and shades of conduct. Instances where a theory may fail, or appears to fail, can always be found. The question is whether a particular theory can explain a prevailing situation meaningfully, or better than others, which melts down to how robustly it can explain outcomes on the basis of underlying mechanisms. The relevance of conclusions depends on the clarity of stated motives. As stated by Shackle (op. cit.: 355): 'Theory ... is not right or wrong but less or more powerful in affording "a good state of mind" to men confronted with an unfathomable universe.'

An ontological lead, as *coming with* the individual, conceivably *before* the emergence of social structure, gives precedence to agency over structure and shows the latter to obtain from some need the individual *intends* to serve, some goal he tries to achieve. If the need is uniform (and there is no reason why it should not be, given that we are all human), this can supply every higher-level structure with a quasi-Will, which looks as if it were of its own, making it appear as a self-sufficient, quasi-vital entity. At the same time, structure feeds back and encroaches on the individual, but only according to design by the constituting agents, who can always re-evaluate the situation, *their* situation, modifying the structure along the way as they find appropriate. So, although Hodgson's (2002: 168) 'reconstitutive downward causation' rightly implies that 'it is impossible to take the parts as given and then explain the whole ... because the whole, to some extent, reconstitutes the parts', it must also not escape that the underlying cause of which these parts are carriers is immutable. Therefore, a less rigid distinction between agency and structure is warranted than is usually made, given their common underlying immutable exigency, which for us is *Existence*. And as Hargreaves Heap (2004) advises, 'economics needs a better understanding of individual agency if the problem of the squirrel wheel is ever to be seriously addressed'.

Real agents as consumers

The most crucial component of agency is the one most neglected by theory. It is the knowledge generated by consumers, which decides the way in which they make choices, which in turn determines the structure of consumption demand and, along with production-related knowledge, the structure of the entire system. To implicate consumers as active participants in the economics debate should be as obvious as daylight. Smith (1937: 625) claimed that 'Consumption is the sole end and purpose of all production.' Keynes (1936: 46) argued: 'All production is for the purpose of ultimately satisfying a consumer.' And: 'Consumption – to repeat the obvious – is the sole end and object of all economic activity' (ibid.: 104). Further: 'the expectation of consumption is the only *raison d'être* of employment' (ibid.: 211). Finally: 'the more significant change, of which we have to take account, is the effect of changes in *demand* both on costs and on volume. It is on the side of demand that we have to introduce quite new ideas' (ibid.: 294, original emphasis).

Implicating the consumer, however, would raise not only analytical difficulties but also embarrassing social issues that would become hard to evade. So, theory chose to neglect the above obvious facts, laying out a task and a plan for itself that would be more amenable to ideological (and methodological) manipulation. The historical circumstances of the Industrial Revolution, when modern economics was born, helped downplay the role of consumers. Focusing on the mechanisms of industrial production and income distribution drew Marx's attention away from individual motivation, towards the forces that arise from material conditions relating to these two components of capitalistic development. To be fair, speaking of a 'mode of consumption' would have made little sense then, as masses struggled to survive and contributed little in the way of that type of knowledge upon which discretionary consumption expenditures are made. Alienation was due to the industrial production mode only, since there can be no discretion or alienation in consuming for survival. Such consumption is largely dictated by nature. But, as Smith (1937: 734) noted: 'The man whose whole life is spent in performing a few simple operations...generally becomes as stupid and ignorant as it is possible for a human creature to become.' The question then is: Can it really be claimed that in today's capitalism consumption is innocent of debilitating potential?

The answer to this is obviously negative, and in this may be found a contradiction that haunts *and guides* life under capitalism: A debilitating generativeness taking place in the sphere of consumption. Within limits imposed by nature, all economics is endogenous and reducible to a single factor: the creative capacity of the human brain, debilitated or alert, lofty or base. All human performance depends on the action of this *sublime agent*, which is put to the service of psychological motives, incessantly expanding the stock of knowledge upon which human calculations are based. This agent performs what Loasby (1999: 71) calls 'active but incremental experimentation at the margins of knowledge'. Such was the basis of Keynes's explanation of investment behaviour, as he held that

> human decisions affecting the future, whether personal or political or eco-
> nomic, cannot depend on strict mathematical expectation, since the basis for
> making such calculations does not exist; ... it is our innate urge to activity
> which makes the wheels go round, our rational selves choosing between the
> alternatives as best we are able, calculating where we can, but often falling
> back for our motive on whim or sentiment or chance.
>
> (Keynes, 1936: 162–3)

This generative activity becomes more effective through division of mental and physical labour, as is well known about production, a division which is itself a result of this very same creativity. But the kind of self-interest served by dividing labour and abandoning production in autarky – a self-interest which is reflected ultimately in the social kind of consumption that characterizes modern capitalism – is not as obvious as economic textbooks imply. Self-interest and scarcity need to be given pragmatic content, since it makes great difference whether self-interest is in seeking pleasure, relief from some distress, pain, or fear, or some other. In particular, it matters in what sense, in what ways and to what extent self-interest is other-disregarding.

These require getting to the root of concepts. In his *Introduction to the Critique of Hegel's Philosophy*, Marx noted: 'To be radical is to grasp something at its roots. But for man the root is man himself.' Therefore, we must look into our-selves for finding root explanations. Barring this, much of what passes as political radicalism is radical illusion: a proclivity to project the critics' own goodwill on society, hampering the search for meaningful explanations, letting capitalism pass either as an unqualified accomplishment or as anathema. It impedes understanding of its achievements, its resilience and its consequences, or even events such as the present protracted regress in working conditions in the West, as capital breaks through barriers in search for cheap labour against which Western workers have to compete, working longer hours for less pay and reduced benefits. Old dogmas inhibit self-awareness and set obstacles to addressing causes. Social critics must recognize that the best service they can provide to suffering masses is to help them understand *why* they support the conditions of their own exploitation, *why* they have become their own greatest enemies. Ignorance constitutes no explanation. The question is: What is it that made them choose to be ignorant?

To claim that capitalism is not supported by the masses is wishful thinking. In today's capitalism one sees crowds rushing furiously to make the best out of it, grabbing as much from the commons as they can, their faces scarred by avarice.

Their only disgruntlement is for failing in this; not for realizing its baseness. If one cannot read faces, one can eavesdrop on conversations to find out that the single topic which monopolizes people's interests and in which they are most conversant is money: how to make and how to expend more of it. Day and night they are out looking for a steal. After a catastrophic forest fire in a resort area, the single issue bothering people living in it is loss of tourist income. Let's put it straight: Capitalists and non-capitalists in the conventional sense share much more in common than critics are willing to admit, opting to side with the losers even in stock markets. In this has come down the alienation of both workers and capitalists from their activity, from the product of this activity, from nature, from other humans and, consequently, from their own selves.

People seem eager to 'seize the opportunity' and 'make it big', through consumption, if all else fails. There is little awareness among workers that their relative affluence may be at some others' expense, or temporary. Under normal circumstances they have little fear of any grim prospects and little zest to create the history of their own and everyone else's emancipation. They do create history, albeit a history of losing but sanguine gamblers beaten in a race which they hope to win next time. Capitalism provides hope and solace. There is always one more opportunity, always some who are worse off to compare with, and always a long way remaining to the top. Today, it is not at all clear who is more staunchly for capitalism and who is more aware of its consequences: Is it those who ride the crest of it, or those who have not yet enjoyed its fruits? Distribution of dignity is fuzzy. Lines are blurred, not as crisp as drawn by Marx. Workers' revolt seems far too remote. Capitalism has changed the way people see things, face life and act, by acting on their conscience. Understanding, therefore, what motivates people is *sine qua non* for explaining capitalism and for understanding whatever rationalization there is to it and to people's intentions within it. What is needed is a measure of reference for individual success.

In an ocean of animus, one may seek refuge on islands of humanism. In everyday life, people are capable of noble conduct, showing occasional generosity, altruism, solidarity, etc. Without these, life would be a miserable excursion into solitude. Actually, there could be no society then, which is a precondition for accomplishing individual pursuits. So, one might wonder: 'Why not look at the bright side of things and take heart?' Well, we should certainly look at both the bright and the dark sides, drawing from each what can be drawn, but not more, by wishful thinking. By closing our eyes on the dark sides of ourselves we do not promote the bright ones. Life is an asymmetry that gives rise to many other asymmetries. Of the wealth of emotions and thoughts, normal social conduct requires that we expose more of the nice half of the spectrum, and this is not considered hypocrisy. So, one should be cautious not to rush into interpreting conduct as other-regarding. We cannot advance our personal goals outside society, or against it, so we tolerate each other and maintain bonds. Hobbes (op. cit.: 106, original emphases) named this 'COMPLEASANCE; that is to say, *That every man strive to accommodate himselfe to the rest*'. In this sense, self-regard underlies all our actions, including those occasions where noble sentiments seem to take over. True compassion is rare, coming in calculated doses as by a doctor's prescription, whereas aggression and violence are never in short supply. What helps perpetuate these is a delusion that it is not us, but someone else that is always to blame. The same carries over to all higher levels. Thus, no nation will admit to being an aggressor, and many societies which are racially tolerant when all is well will turn racist when things take a bad turn (such as when immigrants 'take jobs'). But no society will ever admit to its being racist.

In order to conceal the rivalry that marks capitalism, mainstream theory discovered an amazing association between base selfishness and common welfare, by extracting out of its context a passage of Smith's about a butcher and a baker. This association was later exploited to promote a neo-liberal ideology. But we know more about human passions from other fields. Hume (2000: 316) maintained that 'whether the passion of self-interest be esteem'd vicious or virtuous, 'tis all a case; since itself alone restrains it: So that if it be virtuous, men become social by their virtue; if vicious, their vice has the same effect', but: 'Nothing is more certain, than that men are, in a great measure, govern'd by interest, and that even when they extend their concern beyond themselves, 'tis not to any great distance' (ibid.: 342). And in discussing what he called the 'principle of comparison', Hume argued: '*The direct survey of another's pleasure naturally gives us pleasure, and therefore produces pain when compar'd with our own. His pain, consider'd in itself, is painful to us, but augments the idea of our own happiness, and gives us pleasure*' (ibid.: 379, original emphases). Along similar lines, Shackle (1972: 240) warned: 'The world...is economic only subject to unappeasable greeds and rivalries and implacable enmities.'

Passions do not always shine through public behaviour, so they must be deduced from what avails. For the same reason, it is precarious to draw separating lines between agents and erect theoretical edifices upon divisions that obtain from visible aspects of conduct. The picture is further blurred by our reluctance to be critical of ourselves. We declare ourselves to be rational, defining tautologically as rational what we do and make ourselves infallible by refusing to admit our mistakes. In our own minds, we were made in the image of an omniscient God, ascribing circuitously omniscience to ourselves. We also see God as a guarantor of life after death, which is, incidentally, eternal. Religion always gave promises of a 'life after'. Our desperate quest for immortality reveals our fear of death, as do stately graves, mummification, funeral gifts, aspiring for posthumous fame, various myths, etc. This fear seeks to be relieved in metaphysical ways, as well as through material ones.

The road to a realistic theory of behaviour is sown with obstacles and contradictions that leave room for counter-arguments to every argument that one might make. Therefore, it is only on the basis of unifying principles that specific issues can be dealt with. Having not achieved consensus on principles, having premised its methodological individualism on exogenous tastes that expel the consumer as an energetically participating and accountable entity, having ignored intersubjectivity that bears the mark of rivalry, economic theory turned a blind eye to facts that are visible upon a minimum of impartiality. Thus, it failed to identify causes and confined itself to outcomes. It promoted an uncritical, unqualified faith in the meritoriousness of economic activity in general, taking for granted that the more energetically we engage in it the more we benefit ourselves and others, fulfilling in a sense God's Will. Not of Schumacher's old-fashioned, *Small-is-Beautiful* type of God (who was Buddhist, anyway!), but of a Western, progressive God of creative destruction. Growth was glorified and equated with progress, while physical ramifications induced by the two thermodynamic laws and disturbing effects on social cohesion, personal constitution and culture were downplayed to such an extent that pointing out such prejudice submits one to the charge of advocating a pastoral life in idyllic idleness.

Science is not neutral, and social science is ideological. But the way things stand with neoclassical hegemony, dissenting honesty amounts to defiance. Still, defiance cannot harm economics more than it has harmed itself with its pretentious sombreness and parochial positivism. The first task, from the angle we visit things here, is to revoke the little man's licence to collude without being held accountable. Only then will it be possible to discover the rationalization induced by capitalism in human affairs, as this rationalization finds expression through agent action. To this end must be produced theories which, as Keynes (op. cit.: 297) advised, must not aim

> to provide a machine, or method of blind manipulation, which will furnish an infallible answer, but to provide ourselves with an organized and orderly method of thinking out particular problems; and, after we have reached a provisional conclusion by isolating the complicating factors one by one, we then have to go back on ourselves and allow, as well as we can, for the probable interactions of the factors amongst themselves. This is the nature of economic thinking. Any other way of applying our formal principles of thought (without which, however, we shall be lost in the wood) will lead us to error. It is the great fault of symbolic pseudo-mathematical methods of formalizing a system of economic analysis...that they expressly assume strict independence between the factors involved and lose all their cogency and authority if this hypothesis is disallowed;...Too large a proportion of recent 'mathematical' economics are mere concoctions, as imprecise as the initial assumptions they rest on, which allow the author to lose sight of the complexities and interdependencies of the real world in a maze of pretentious and unhelpful symbols.

Heeding these means to search for underlying motives, explaining self-interest as a socially arbitrated concept. If one inspects everyday reality, one cannot help noticing the uniform relentlessness with which people pursue some obscure objective on a round-the-clock basis. This alludes to some underlying cause or mechanism that is capable of accommodating all the observed expressional diversity. Causal reduction must be down to a single source, avoiding dichotomies and raising distinctions only when necessary. In particular, the distinctions between workers and capitalists, producers and consumers and profits and utility must be reassessed because, as Shackle (1972: 61, original italics) put it,

> The real question is, what ultimate building-blocks of conduct, if any, are elemental enough, are sufficiently part of the nature of things and of human

nature, to be indispensable to all human endeavours to cope with their essential circumstances, their 'predicament', and are thus the ultimately reliable stuff of theories? A theory will only be efficient if it uses ideas which are elemental in this sense, the irreducible *tesserae* out of which any mosaic of human affairs must be composed. Large-scale formal structures, by contrast, are fragile.

Endogeneity, knowledge and openness

Such fragile structures are not what economic theorizing is in short supply of, but a theory can reach no farther than the agents that it entertains. The depth of explanation it can provide depends on the degree of endogeneity these agents can generate, and this depends on their acknowledged ontology. *Homo economicus* is the most stripped-down, non-ontological caricature of an agent, being omniscient in a world where there is no knowledge. Perfectly human actors are too complex to account for in detail, so some trimming is necessary. Too much trimming, however, can make a theory pointless. *Homo economicus* has no history, no future, no feelings or sentiments, he is not capable of generating newness or making speculative choices, whence he is totally unaccountable, which is not as fortuitous as it appears. He is asocial, in the sense that his tastes are unaffected by choices made by others. Thus, he cannot be envious. He is perfectly malleable, so one can model any imaginable situation by imposing appropriate behavioural assumptions on him. But as different situations call for different sets of assumptions, everything can be 'explained' and nothing is really explained this way.

Confusing models with theory has helped hijack the notion of endogeneity, which must be at the root of economic explanation if economics is to be social. For this, however, a robust theory must underlie modelling, whereas in mainstream economics models substitute largely for theory. As real endogeneity is impossible to derive from the said caricature agent, it is sometimes thought that tastes are made endogenous by relating them functionally with other variables in a model. In other cases, tastes are thought to have been made endogenous by making them depend on the behaviour of other agents, as with Leibenstein's (1950) bandwagon or snob effects, or to obtain from imitation, status seeking, etc., or to be affected by institutions such as markets, as in Bowles (1998). These are self-referential situations, the burden of endogeneity being thus placed upon those other elements on which tastes are made to depend. This cannot be resolved unless some reliable ontology is entertained that is capable of generating novelty. Endogenous means born to the system, by self-motivated agents, and the only gamete that can give birth to anything is the sublime agent, which fertilizes knowledge. Imitation, status, recognition and other such notions need themselves to be explained, endogenously.

If the agents entertained by a theory cannot generate tastes in meaningful ways, nothing can. *Homo economicus* is totally incapable of this. Presumably, a modeller can observe such *homos* as they reveal their preferences over bundles of commodities and model their behaviour. But all substance lies in preference *changes* that reflect taste changes, and if these are not explained, then nothing really is. Only by explaining the process whereby tastes are formed can one hope to obtain explanatory endogeneity, and this requires understanding agent motivation, which comes with agent psychology and a well-specified goal. The dynamics generated by such a self-interested and generative ontology cannot be the dynamics of mechanisms, whose time is extensive and which are pulled passively through least action towards some low potential state. In contrast, life is tonality that fights such natural gravity, the etymology of which is same as that of 'grave'. At issue is the emergence of pieces of knowledge that keep tonality up, shaping tastes, among other things.

Marx's initiating entity, *homo faber*, possesses a partial and rather developed ontology, not a developing one. He is effectively censored of evolving components by his particular set-up, which is the industrial production mode. *Homo faber* has material needs and produces with his labour the conditions of his material existence. Thus emerge social forces that determine the way social structures evolve, setting norms, determining values, and back to the conditions of material survival, which are updated according to the level of industrial progress. What remains to be resolved is an issue of income distribution. But in spite of its relative realism, this purely natural character accommodates no non-material motivation, and his social space is exhausted in the spheres of production and income distribution. At least, this is how the pedestrian version of the ideas put forward by Marx goes, paying less than due attention to his other writings besides *Capital*.

The actors entertained in the present report possess an evolving human ontology. They are born, learn by experience that they will die, are filled with angst and try to postpone death by using their intellect to generate life-expanding knowledge, thus affecting the conditions under which such knowledge is generated and, hence, the kind of knowledge that agents will mainly pursue and are likely to produce. Agents actively develop the conditions within which they perceive and interpret their existence and the world in which they exist. In this sense, the systems they develop differ from inert systems, since the latter may be changed by physical matter/energy flows to which they may be open, but do not purposively act on their environment, on those inputs or on themselves.

Man-made systems are inexorably open to mental flows from their own agents. It is through such flows that they were created in the first place, through such flows they are changed, and changes are extremely fast and impressive in capitalism. Therefore, to model such systems as complete and closed ones sacrifices almost all that is worth studying in them. As Loasby (op. cit.: 14) explained: 'all closures apply to representations; the phenomena themselves cannot be isolated. In attempting such isolation we may even abstract away from rather than towards the essential features that we wish to study. ... Thus all closures are in some degree false.'

The failure of all attempts to convincingly close the price system even in its most rudimentary form attests also to the practical vanity and analytical impossibility of closure, with a bare minimum of credence. No price system could be found that would explain how the overall system could be driven to rest stably at some market-clearing state. Even after reducing its degrees of freedom down to the absolute minimum of one by assuming a uniform profit rate and a uniform wage rate, so that there would be only one distributive variable to be determined, closure proved sticky. The Cambridge Growth Equation approach or various ways of setting the interest rate have stumbled on the non-negotiable openness to an endless flow of knowledge generated by the sublime agent. The situation reminds of the Earth's being showered by a continuous energy flow from the Sun, barring which all other inputs would be useless. If the Earth is assumed closed on this flow, nothing remains to talk meaningfully about. Although analogues are used here with caution, similarities in this case go beyond. The rate at which the Sun's energy can be captured seems negligible, if one ignores its ubiquity. But it is immense on the aggregate and immensely useful. If we assume it out, there goes life. Such is also the case with consumer creativity, which is difficult to represent in a formal way or measure its effect as it comes, in little, inconspicuous pieces, as a continuous, low-density flow intricately interwoven with other system elements. Assume it out, though, and there goes capitalism. The sublime agent is a non-quantifiable initiator and driver of all the activity described as *life*, and it is supplied generously by nature in a way that no cost can be ascribed to it. Part of this life, hence, offshoot of this agent, is economics. Whatever cost we may associate with 'labour', it will not bear any kind of stable relationship with the innovative output of this factor. (This takes most of the steam out of what have become known as 'new growth theories', as we will discuss further.)

Stoppage of knowledge generation means stoppage of time. For the individual, this comes with death. The 'intrinsic powers of human inventiveness', as Polanyi (1966/83: 81) referred to them, cannot be quantitatively accounted for, or put to rest. Since what the mind produces cannot be known before it is produced, the associated fundamental uncertainty obliges agents to exercise choice. This bears on all theories. Fundamental to Marx were the concepts of value and surplus. To fix the notion of value and make it measurable needs a concept as yardstick, from outside the system proper: a reference system and a unit of measurement. According to Shackle (1972: 46): 'In the world of natural or practical sciences, a unit is ideally required to be invariant against changes of the identity of the observer, and against changes of place or date, or of any circumstance whatever. Value cannot meet any one of these requirements.' In a quest for analytical concreteness, however, choices made at this junction were aimed at making value objective. Marx took its material base to be labour-power expended during production and reproduced through consumption of commodities. Labour, understood as quantifiable in some physical way (time, energy, etc.) allowed a materialistic theory of value whose relevance depended on the degree to which measurable facets of labour reflected its economic worthiness. Under conditions of hand-to-mouth survival, this was a reasonable assumption to make, in the sense that raw energy constituted the bulk of labour's contribution and there was little in the way of creative contributions on its part, either in production or in consumption. Speculative innovativeness, which associates with accumulation beyond the bare minima for survival, did not interfere decisively with stable relations.

The system could be treated as quasi-closed and a labour theory of value was meaningful.

But speculative innovativeness, which has none of these simple characteristics, has taken over as determinant of the performance of a capitalist economy by engagement of the entire population in consumption, through new institutional set-ups. The relationship of humans to the product of their toil proved more intricate than in Marx's account, which lacked psychological grounding. Capitalism encouraged a fleeting relationship to develop between humans and the commodities they produced through their alienated industry, which they consumed in an equally alienated way. Brainpower was put monolithically to the service of this selfish relationship, engaging all in a race for value creation and expropriation, including the workers who were thus exploited further, precisely as the conditions of accelerated growth allowed many of them to expend beyond subsistence. This enslaved them in the consumption sphere as well, numbing their social reflexes. They all tried to exploit each other, as they fought to snatch the product of socially contributed toil. This served the interests of capitalists, since the value workers appropriated by purchasing consumables could produce no more value, while productive capital kept accruing to capitalists. All scrambled to reap where everyone had anonymously sown, at the expense of each other, thus deciding value, surplus and the intensity of their own exploitation.

The time asymmetry is present in these. Technological advance reduces dependence on direct labour by embodying socially accumulated knowledge in capital items. This can be paralleled with packing up energy in a battery cell for use in the future. (And as batteries discharge naturally, capital depreciates.) Consumption commodities produced by means of such capital absorb direct human inputs plus capital services, and consumption is a creative activity aimed at claiming back both types of value. Consumption-related knowledge is needed in order to absorb the expanding output of production-related ingenuity and in order to enhance the efficiency of the system. But consumption is the final stage of the process of economically transforming materials and ascribing value to them, and the process cannot be reversed. So, consumer commodities embody past knowledge, for being produced by capital items and labour, plus knowledge infused to them at the stage of consumption, but this is not 'reusable knowledge', in the sense that it cannot produce more commodities. So, consumer commodities cannot be used for expropriating more time-space, in the future. Thus, a non-capitalist (in the conventional sense) consumer who is blinded by greed contributes knowledge at all stages, allowing capitalists to usurp the productive part of it while he is himself in position to claim back only forms that look no further into the future. Through this institutional stratagem of post-Marx capitalism, monumental changes were precipitated that had been hampered by previous arrangements that blocked workers from participating energetically in the socio-economic process and making discretionary expenditures.

So, knowledge is at the base of everything, and this is very well known. Marx's perspective to alienation confirms it, as also his thesis that labour is the essence of all wealth, since he made it clear in the *Economic and Philosophical*

Manuscripts that he did not refer to brute physical labour, but to creative labour, of skills and dexterities. And if labourers are creative in production, they cannot fail to be creative also in consumption. And if they are alienated during production, they must also be alienated as consumers, to the extent that their consumption reaches beyond bare essentials, over which there is little discretion. So, consumption must be included in the exploitation and alienation process, which are mental rather than physical conditions.

The basis of wealth (and of welfare, etc.) is in the human capacity to create an *idea* of value *objectified* in commodities, however stubbornly may have been defended a strict separation between objects and ideas. Economic value, as all value, is subjective and social. It exists only in the context of some valuation process that aims at some particular target. What is highly valued in one context may be valueless in another. Through subjective, relativist and speculative valuations of artefacts within a socially determined context, agents try to defeat each other in a race, getting trapped in this aspiration. This is not a race against natural desires in social void, but *a race against time-space, as perceived through the lens of society*. In this, producers have no final jurisdiction over anything, as standard theory maintains. The production process can determine nothing by itself, in oblivion to consumers' goal-seeking choices. In particular, value cannot be based on anything physical or external and it is foolish to see it as residing in commodities, since it is precisely to the effect of serving as value carriers that commodities are made by the agents themselves. Therefore, only consumers can decide value, through the choices they make.

As Lawson (1997) explained, 'the possibility of choice presupposes not only that events could have been different, but also that agents have some conception of what they are doing and wanting to achieve in their activity. That is, if choice is real then human actions must be intentional under some description.' So, making choice makes sense only over an open domain of intentions. And as we will explain, for a choice to be capitalistically meaningful it must produce further scarcity: a deeper, wider sense of deprivation, in final analysis a deprivation of life.

In human sciences, a perspective to human behaviour has been adopted that places emphasis on individuals affecting the conditions of their own development within an evolving social background, which reflects back and acts on those same individuals. The individual takes cognizance of its own self by its reflection on society. Choices are autonomous only to the extent that – and in the sense that – they reflect on society and society is reflected upon them. Autonomy and sovereignty make no sense in social isolation. In capitalism, even more so than in other systems, these take on the form of a contest for vital time-space, where the particulars that make up the individuality of each contestant are his or her ways of being effective in this contest, and the most relevant social component of this relationship is that the time-space claimed individually is socially contributed, through division of labour.

These imply a historicism to which Marx was reluctant to subscribe. He argued that social conditions obtain as outcomes of the interplay of forces developed historically in the sphere of production. Such forces, he maintained, should be interpreted in the light of antagonism between social classes. He considered basing explanation on individual action and psychology as disorienting, especially if emphasis were placed on the 'exceptional individual' as a driver of the socio-historic process. And Marx was right, as far as this went, but social dialectics involve also a good measure of mundane everyday behaviour, the basic components of which are banal consumerism and rampant individualism characterizing the capitalist culture. These have evolved into a general code of aggressive economism, tawdry aesthetic and brassy glamour that surreptitiously alienate society underneath the great events. It is a kind of alienation that largely escaped Marx, due to his concern with production and distribution. But it is in this *total* alienation that must be traced the internal contradictions of today's capitalism, which make its relationship with the masses precarious, an alienation that takes place in all spheres of activity. The masses change from ally to enemy, once in a while, not by revolt, or in any kind of real awareness, and not simply in their capacity as workers but, most alarmingly for the capitalists, in that their consuming behaviour may not resonate with the system's productive forces as these develop at a fast pace, causing demand slow-downs and sending the system to take anguished measurements of consumer sentiment. Then, banners are put up at shops in Brooklyn and Queens urging: 'Consume! It helps the economy *and it is patriotic.*'

Given these, the capitalists' greed for increased profits and low labour costs may go outsourcing, or it may force native labour to compete with underpaid, uninsured, imported slaves they cynically call immigrants. This, however, may backfire not so much due to reduced *volume* of spending, as the received view goes, as due to the fact that dispirited consumers may not be able *to keep innovative pace* with a capitalist technology that constantly expands its capacity to introduce fast *structural and qualitative* changes. Then, consumption may act like a gear-box with long gear ratios, which can choke an engine designed to rev at extremely high RPM (Revolutions Per Minute).

Marx's division into owners and non-owners of means of production could provide a reasonable basis for explaining capitalist dynamics only to the extent that, and as long as, a same partitioning of society could also be made in the consumption sphere: into owners and non-owners of 'means of consumption', according to their capacity to appropriate capital through consumption commodities. In Marx's time, this was the case. Social divisions induced by the mode of production held also in the consumption arena. Capitalism was going through expansionary growth, while structural changes were supported by growing native populations and by innovations in navigation and transportation that opened colonial markets, upsetting the balance of trade in favour of the colonists. This maintained home prices at levels that forced the native workers to mind about basics as they struggled to survive, with little chance for discretionary expenditures. Profits accrued to capitalists from exploitation of cheap home labour under high price schedules.

However, expansionary growth cannot last forever. As 'use-knowledge' and 'make-knowledge' go hand in hand, conquered markets tend to evolve into antagonists.[2] In fact, Kindleberger (1975) argued that expansion can even blunt the need for structural changes and make an economy lag behind. Sustained growth requires structure-increasing innovations, which only a society that participates wholeheartedly, in its entirety, in all spheres of activity can supply. So, before the potential for expansion to foreign markets was exhausted, young and vibrant capitalism managed to engage the entire native population in its perspective, instituting participatory political arrangements and blurring the class distinctions in the consumption arena. This helped accelerate production and consumption innovations, leading to impressive structural changes and escalating roundaboutness. Productive capital continued to be in the hands of the few, but ever greater numbers were made to think that they, too, could have a say in the political and economic processes and make their presence felt, *through universal suffrage and consumption.*

This required that the system should maintain a subtle balance between the profit incentive for producers, on one hand, and a distribution of income that would induce consumers to adapt their lifestyles to new commodities, on the other, engaging everyone in the production of value. Equitable distributions of income that would encourage innovative consumption could act as disincentive for entrepreneurship. Inequitable distributions could depress consumer sentiment, retarding not so much the consumers' urge to expend income (after all, there is little else they can do with it for any considerable length of time), but their generative enthusiasm and their capacity to improve the structural efficiency of the system by innovating uses for qualitatively new commodities. Consumption generativeness needs high consuming spirits. One's aggregate expenditures may even be increased when one is downcast, but such expenditures will probably be unimaginative. So, distribution of income has become even more critical for spearheading capitalism, as it must sustain a flame of hope in the masses by blurring in their minds the distinction between means of production and consumption commodities, but it must also not impair entrepreneurship.

Structure is critical, and this is why everything hinges ultimately on mental tonality and high spirits. Classical economists considered proportions to be more important than scale, and the distribution of wealth in an economy to be more important than its total volume. As Keynes (op. cit.: 4, original emphasis) noted: 'Ricardo expressly repudiated any interest in the *amount* of the national dividend, as distinct from its distribution.' Such interest on the part of the theorist was not just concern with justice. It was basically concern with economic performance. As there are differences between consumption patterns at different income levels, distribution of income is critically connected with the structure of consumption and, through this, with the structure and performance of the economy. And the relationship of the masses with the accumulation process is fragile. If consumers fall out of tune or become sluggish, the system faces a threat. And as the innovation process is better organized in controlled R&D environments, accelerated technical changes may wear thin the feeble innovative capacity of the general public. To compensate for this asymmetry in generative performance, large numbers of consumers are needed to channel their shrewdness single-mindedly into the project.

In contrast to classical economists, modern economists have played down the role of structure, focusing mainly on aggregate magnitudes. As Shackle (1972: 39) argued: 'Economics is the supremely ingenious device for eliciting scalar quantity from vast heterogeneous assemblies of qualitatively incommensurable things. But this trick only serves certain purposes. It submerges detail, not abolishes it.' And: 'Economics has concerned itself with quantities and proportions, rather than with shapes, structures and intricate compositions of richly various pieces. ... But this ... excludes very much that the business man and the human being in his full nature are deeply concerned with' (ibid.: 40).

So, culture feeds back on human agency, encouraging or discouraging natural urges, inducing people to act in some kind of harmony. Capitalism promotes acquisitiveness by distributing income in ways that incite people to pursue ever new wants, shifting expenditures from old commodities for which there has developed low income and price elasticities of demand, to new ones where, due to high such elasticities, cost-reducing innovations have greater impact. Lacking use-innovations, accelerated make-innovations, large-scale methods and capital-intensive production techniques would make no sense; they would be like blank shots, and they would not be coming about. Prompting consumers to pursue knowledge needed for taking advantage of what production cranks out adds an inexhaustible source of dynamic variety. Whereas for infant capitalism venture-some entrepreneurship and production innovations aided by brute force provided thrust, while expanding markets and growing native populations absorbed output, today it is the dreams of the masses that matter. These must be kept flaming, because if they start fading they may be hard to ignite again.

Evasive economics

Science is exploration. It takes excitement, even romance. Inspiration is often drawn from erratic phenomena, failures or incomplete calculations. Ideas appearing initially as flights of fancy are not rejected outright and taking risks is encouraged. But these hardly speak of economics, which has become about renovation of the same old ideas. Academic economists are prompted to take sure steps inside the orthodox stockyard of ideas, to process data and crank out models. Standing theoretical issues are treated as lesser objects of research. Ideological or methodological divergence is discouraged. One must steer clear of provocative ideas and avoid questioning sacrosanct axioms. Psychology, ethics, economic crime from petty theft and corporate fraud to the affectionate relationship between the heinous trafficker and the reputable banker, all these and many other fail to inform an economist, who would not consider it proper to interrogate whether much of what takes place within the law is in fact 'legal crime', by any other standard.

A tightly knit sociology of socially removed economists is thus reproduced who are fluent in a deceptively assertive jargon, but who possess little of the contemplative intellectuality of the discipline's forefathers, many of whom were not even economists by profession. Whereas the writings of the latter are a pleasure to read and a treasure to master, the gain from reading most of what is published today is in being kept informed about what ideas are marketable. Academic economists talk when they have nothing to say. One soon learns not to waste time with the difficult substance of serious issues, but to rush into publishing at bulk rate. Passing the publish-or-perish shibboleth is more important for an academic economist than the truth content or social value of his or her work. Today, lesser economists print in a couple of years more than the greatest thinkers of the past wrote in their entire lives. This cheapens knowledge and helps consolidate the hegemony of a narrow orthodox perspective, precisely as its *bona fide* acceptance declines.

Since economists lack no ingenuity, one must suspect that this smacks of ideology. The requirement for a misplaced rigour and pretentious objectivity made possible by calculated choice of assumptions helps brush aside everything that relates to the less amiable aspects of capitalism. What relates to passions and does not yield to easy quantification is ignored. This is supposed to make economic theorizing value free and impartial, but precisely the opposite is true. That social theorizing is ideological is obvious and unavoidable, but this need not imply intellectual blindness. So, the low scores economics receives are fair, as are derogatory remarks made by friend and foe alike. Suffice it to recall Keynes's bitter aphorism that 'Some day, economics may become a science' (quoted in Rymes, 1989: 83), or Friedman's indictive confession (in his speech at the annual meeting of the American Economic Association, in 1972): 'I believe that we economists in recent years have done vast harm – to society at large and our profession in particular – by claiming more than we can deliver.'

To find the cause of such malaise one must start from a theory's inception: from the external concept or idea upon which it is founded. The neoclassical launch pad made promises for a hard science precisely as it obliterated all chances of delivering on them. An *economicus homo* who is intellectually, morally and emotionally mutilated by exogenous tastes may help evade conceptual, methodological and analytical difficulties, but undermines all possibility of addressing real issues. Worst of all, he sweeps under the rug the motive of fierce consumer antagonism that keeps today's capitalism in motion, so as not to dent its image as a mechanism for satisfying the consumers' legitimate desires. Entertaining a more realistic agent would make it hard to hide its real nature. Thus, there is kickback and collusion: In return for their passive, enthusiastic consent, masses are cleared of blame for the choices they make and for their consequences, which are seen as being mostly environmental, but in truth go beyond, into human constitution. Thus, this collusion serves both the capitalist ideology and the masses.

In socially divided production, one wins what some other loses. In a zero-sum contest over a multi-dimensional state space with a large number of players, it is strategies and choices that matter. These induce structural changes by means of knowledge generated in pursuit of self-interest. Scale is less important. But knowledge generation is difficult to handle and requires that goals, intentions and psychological dispositions be spelled out, which calls for interdisciplinary approaches as it runs into taboos and into the dark folds of psychism. Evading these, orthodox economics drew attention away from anything that could mar the image of capitalism. But that came at a cost: the cost of failing to explain even such basic facts as GDP growth, letting silently pass that if there is more to divide amongst us, we will all climb higher on the happiness ladder *en masse*, and there will be less social friction. But such nice upshots are not true if the game is zero-sum, so there must be something else to the growth hysteria. Hushing that something else reduces GDP growth to ideology. Founding public *good* upon private *vice* is grossly erroneous Spinoza or Mandeville dogma. Capitalist growth is malignant, as it is based on conflict, and it has been legitimately challenged as a proper measure of welfare (e.g. see Easterlin, 1972; Hirsch, 1977; Ryan and Deci, 2001; Hargreaves Heap, 2004; Layard, 2005). As though we did not know, experiments came to document that if others climb up the social ladder as we do, then we are not happier than before. We prefer that others' incomes fall more than ours to seeing everyone's income rise by the same amount, or even in the same proportion. (See Solnick and Hemenway, 1998; Layard, 2003.) If the average lifespan in my milieu is 50 years, then I expect to live at least as much, and I might be content with eighty. But if it is 100, anything less than that will not do. Others give me a measure of practical possibilities, so that if I fall behind I am displeased more than I am pleased by improving my standing by the same measure.

Assuming antagonistic structural uncertainty out, the internal consistency of orthodox theory cannot be disputed. But this would assume time out, leaving us only with states or outcomes, in oblivion to inputs and to the dynamics of their transformation. The notion of state is a conceptual convenience (and the notion of steady-state is even more so). It is of a timeless, fixed-knowledge world, even if one considers, as in what is commonly called 'dynamic analysis', a succession of such states. As long as one knows the mechanism, real time does not really enter. Real time is in the next inescapable and unpredictable discovery on end, which changes the contours of response hypersurfaces and even the state space itself. Even if we tried, we would not be able to make the economic world stand still. As Schumpeter (1947: 82) put it: 'Capitalism then is by nature a form of economic change and not only never is but never can be stationary.' Capitalism makes every efficient state obsolete in a shorter and shorter time. Creative intellect never stops introducing changes that generate monopoly and monopsony conditions, which increase a particular type of efficiency relative to previously attained levels. Inefficiency typically associated with non-competitive conditions is only relative to a fictitiously optimal state that would result if all innovations up to some point were given time to be diffused, with no new ones added.

Superseding dominant paradigms in the course of a science's development attests to its vigour and neutrality. The equilibrium paradigm – a paradigm of states, not of processes – remained dominant long after it exhausted its contribution. It was already superseded by Menger's (1976 [1871]) Marshallian vision of an economy whose growth comes from within, as growth of knowledge. That economics is about knowledge was never disputed, but never seriously pursued. So, Boulding (1966) was right in protesting that 'economic development...is essentially a knowledge process ... but we are still too much obsessed by mechanical models, capital-income ratios, and even input–output tables, to the neglect of the study of the learning process which is the real key to development.'

Optimally equilibrated stimulus/response systems provide a first approximation and insight about the workings of economic society. But the former will return passively to a rest state through paths of least action after a shock, while the latter, which are subject to similar equilibrium-restoring forces, also generate forces that fight equilibrium. Any particular equilibrium that would correspond to any given body of knowledge is disturbed by new, endogenously generated knowledge. Seen from a different angle, the equilibrium towards which the system would tend under a fictitious no-new-knowledge condition is always renewed as endogenously generated knowledge keeps modifying the structure of the system. In the language of attractors, since these are conventionally associated with clustering, we may speak here of *repellents* instead, that is, of endogenous forces which push the system away from every attracting state, in no fixed *direction*, as if pulled by some *dome attractor*. The system evolves in the direction of conquering more time-space through increased roundaboutness, driven by a same urge of individual agents and by their calculative action.

Economic choice invokes purpose: the vision of a goal, whose standard is continuous improvement rather than approaching some preset optimum. According to Hodgson (1993: 23): 'The reality of human choice and purpose requires a notion of teleology or finalism rather than merely efficient cause. Explanation of economic phenomena requires reference to intentions, not just stochastic outcomes or mechanical cause and effect.' This agrees with Aristotle's thesis that organization may be meaningfully studied only in teleological terms. Concerning theory, Dobb (1972 [1937]: 71, original emphasis) maintained that if

> all that is postulated is simply that men '*choose*', without anything being stated even as to how they choose or what governs their choice, it would seem impossible for economics to provide us with any more than a sort of algebra of human choice, indicating certain rather obvious forms of interrelationship between choices, but telling us little as to the way in which any actual situation will behave.

Neoclassicism is indeed *algebra* of human pseudo-choice, while real systems are goal seeking, embedded within higher-level social systems that are in turn embedded in an outer environment which sets limits on their variables. According to Simon (1969: 6): 'If science is to encompass these objects and phenomena in which human purpose as well as natural law are embodied, it must have means for relating these two disparate components.' That is, it must explain the connection between the cosmic environment and human intentionality within it, which can be nothing else but to sustain this connection. The pursuit of pleasure as a purpose of life is the false view of the sophist Aristippus (fourth century BC) who propounded that absolute physical hedonism coincides with the noble and desirable, that the presence of a desire is adequate justification for its pursuit, and that knowledge should be judged according to how it promotes these. But this view does not explain what desire is and what it stems from. In contrast, Aristotle maintained that even *happiness*, as intentionally pursued, cannot be an end in itself, but a fulfilling *activity*. In activity then lies the origin, which means in life.

It needs to be repeated, apropos, that the term utility has been used to connote all kinds of arousals, including the absence of arousal, as in the neoclassical case where it is claimed to stand merely for preference orderings not explicitly linked to any human perceptives or sensations (of which *Homo economicus* is not capable of, anyway). But we will lump them all under the term *utility*, in the sense that none of them admits evil intentions or zero-sumness, and given that no finer distinction is needed for our basic argument.

Hodgson (1999: 143) notes that 'abstractions are essential but they always do some violence to the complex, changing reality. ... All acts of categorization and abstraction must, therefore, be provisional. All theoretical foundations must forever be under scrutiny.' The truth content of a theory depends critically on how well the basic situation is understood before an abstraction is attempted. Unlike classical economists, who spared no effort in trying to understand how things worked before submitting formal representations, modern economists place emphasis on falsely reassuring axiomatic modelling, rather than on understanding the underlying reality. This has induced a mentality that Loasby (op. cit.: 23) termed 'control without understanding', where mathematics is called upon to dress up the economist's arrogance.

As Paul Lafargue noted in his *Reminiscences of Marx*: '[Marx] held the view that a science is not really developed until it has learned to make use of mathematics' (Fromm, 2004: 175). But profligate use of mathematics cannot compensate for conceptual looseness. Economics rushed to adopt the deductive method of a science where theory making does not bow to usefulness, while its own task was to explain a world of practical human intentions and the dynamics deriving from those. This seemingly innocent pursuit of scientific rigour served also particular ideological purposes. As Di Ruzza and Halevi (2004: 135) argue: 'Economics... performs a central ideological role in shaping power relations. In this way, economics has eliminated the multiple array of moral values in our perceptions of what humanity is and of how to address humankind's existence.'

This 'ideological and political dimension of economics' makes it into a theological discipline. Few are happy with this state of affairs, although many capitalize on it through a system of rewards based on structures of intellectual power that impose a certain conduct on economists. But this is only part of the reason why neoclassicism remains dominant. The main reason is the lack of convincing alternatives. Aside from their pretentious call for disciplined reasoning (which supposedly goes only with the kind of closed-form modelling they sanction), mainstream economists are right in arguing, as critically noted by Strassmann (1994), that

> Claiming that a model is deficient is a minor feat – presumably anyone can do that. What is really valued is coming up with a better model, a better theory.

And so, goes the accumulated wisdom of properly taught economists, those who criticize without coming up with better models are only pedestrian snipers. Major scientific triumphs call for a better theory with a better model in recognizable form.

Ossification of Marxic theory helped neoclassicists draw attention away from what was crucial for capitalism's survival, namely, its convincing the labouring masses, with the lure of a vain hope, to adopt its cause and put their brains to work for it through consumption, without staking its essence. Capitalism was thus able to advertise their gains relative to the past and relative to the non-capitalist world, concealing their worsening social condition and prospects, as well as their intellectual and moral degradation, diverting thought away from those facts which show it to feed on and promote social malevolence.

Turning a blind eye on reality could not have been simple oversight. To ignore consumer participation is either of fools, which neoclassicists are certainly not, or intentional. Same with ignoring the economic relevance of surging, unspeakable crime, or with the abduction of politics by vested interests. To label neoclassicism autistic or irrelevant is misleading. Autism is not deliberate, while neoclassicism is perfectly in line with its cause. (If this were not so, neoclassicists would not be able to take what is thrown at them with such good humour.) It is false to attribute the refusal to accommodate consumer creativity into economic theory to 'a belief that any social processes determining consumer behaviour are the proper business not of economists but of other social scientists' (Mason, 2002: 100), or to 'a desire within the discipline itself to secure recognition as an exact science grounded in mathematics and econometrics, and capable of providing precise economic systems, models and measurements free from any "psychological" baggage' (ibid.).

The success of neoclassicism to promote its ideology is due to a lack of effective alternative theories. Coming up with such theories requires understanding human motives and goals and articulating the connection between economic conduct and agent ontology. This takes rediscovering some obvious facts. For example, in today's obsession with growth, it is largely forgotten that there was always a touch of vulgar, some pungent odour to the market, connoted in Greek by the word ἀγοραῖος (the adjective deriving from *agora*, which means market, or public place), meaning tradable, alluding to the fact that everything, *including humans*, could find a price in it. It also alludes to the fact that everyone weighs in the market his or her own interest *against* that of everyone else's, depriving others of rights on what he or she purchases and makes 'own'.

There are many obvious facts that need to be taken into account. Weisskopf (1971) argued that all value is socially contextualized and all scarcity is existential. All other scarcity derives from this. We are deprived of life to such deeply felt extent that we have historically used all imaginable ways in our effort to extend our stay. Some of these are inter-temporal, as is war, or taking the life of animals. Since mythical times, war has always been for some Golden Fleece: for *vital* space, resources and slaves. The first man-made artefacts were weapons, clothes and shelter, intended to support and extend human life prior to caring about comforts. Others change with culture, but there is a claim on vital space in every act of privatization or disrespect of a shared environment, such as when littering on public space or upsetting others' quiet by making noise. These display *power*, since only he who has power over something can do as he pleases with it. And the most dangerous forms of power are insidious. Time-space expropriation is a life-lasting occupation conducted in its greatest part without complete awareness, almost unintentionally, like breathing. Thus disguised it flourishes.

The case of athletics (from the Greek ἆθλος: achievement, labour) is informative. What was eventually disguised as noble sports competition, or just spectacle, used to be savage, Herculean Labours: a bout with the divine and eternal, in an attempt to prove man's powers and consequent rights on eternity. (Hercules was a demigod, by the way.) Outside myth, it was just brutal fight; bestial force of one contestant against another, ending with the death or incapacitation of one of them. In other games was expressed the desire for conquering time-space by running faster, jumping farther or higher, without physically harming some opponent, but there are still violent sports, not to mention bullfighting, dog fights, etc., where life is actually taken, or the violence done to the athletes' body through performance-enhancing substances. On certain occasions, war itself was conducted symbolically, through wrestlers or duellers. Truce was also sometimes agreed upon in equally allusive symbolism, while certain athletic events took place, such as during the Olympic Games. Finally, it is worth pondering over the fact that the summit of Olympian nobility was in the rewarding of victors not only with a mere laurel wreath but also with great recognition.

We tend to exaggerate our differences from 'uncivilized' peoples and from animals. It serves our vanity to think that we have overcome our bestial past, that we have travelled a long way from the death rows of slaves at the oars of galleys. One fails to see slaves or cannibals these days. But cannibalism (which, by the way, was practiced by more societies than we are willing to admit) was seldom, if ever, for feeding. It was ritualistic, as cannibals thought that by devouring humans they expropriated their powers, expanding their own. Thus was decided who got what part of those sacrificed, according to the tribe's hierarchy and prejudices.

In less primitive societies, control was exercised through ownership over slaves, who were deprived of control over their own bodies and lives, that is, of their own time-space. *Life* was what was taken from them, in the form of cheap labour, sexual abuse or otherwise. They were as objects, or animated property, as Aristotle pointed out, and could be exchanged. The important point again is that it was *life* that was owned through slaves, precisely as there is life in man-made commodities made private, effecting inanimated slavery through objectification. Those who were 'impious', and thought they would not need slaves after death, set them free with their will. (Aristotle was one of those.) Hume (op. cit.: 14) saw a master in him who 'has the power of directing in certain particulars the actions of another, whom we call servant'. The product of one's labour being a result of his accumulated skills, appropriating such product made one person master over another. Even poor men were masters of their wives and children, usurping the product of their toil. Indeed, in view of the slave's role imposed on women for such long periods in so many cultures, it is surprising that feminist economists have not come forward with an explanation of economics in life-taking terms, challenging the naïve 'male-chauvinist' explanations. But it does not strike as odd (actually, it supports our argument) that as soon as women became e-*man*-cipated they quickly picked up oppressive habits and expropriative tasks and tactics that were the supposedly shameful privilege of men. Cynical as this may sound, it must be clear by now what 'equal opportunities' was about.

Marx insisted that humans are effectively reflected in the product of their labour, which depends on the mode of production and social organization: 'As individuals express their life, so they are. What they are, therefore, coincides with their production, both with *what* they produce and with *how* they produce. The nature of individuals thus depends on the material conditions determining their production' (Marx and Engels, 1939: 7). In feudal society, direct slavery was instituted, as muscle power was the main human input to a mostly agricultural production. Ownership over the product of a slave's toil was to the effect of extending the slave-owner's personal time-space. Indeed, even literally, he often lived longer and commanded more space.

With the Industrial Revolution, machines (the satanic mills) replaced muscle power. They were the mechanical slaves against which the workers were obliged to compete. Their time was controlled by the pace of the machines, and whoever controlled those controlled the worker also. There was thus little need for the old kind of slavery. Then came the meta-industrial revolution, with a vital cybernetics component and general automation. Norbert Wiener, who helped lay the foundations of these developments, warned: 'Such mechanical labor has most of the economic properties of slave labor, although, unlike slave labor, it does not involve the direct demoralizing effects of human cruelty. However, any labor that accepts the conditions of competition with slave labor accepts the conditions of slave labor, and is essentially slave labor' (Wiener, 1948: 27). Working longer hours for less pay, accepting reduced benefits and making compromises on work conditions and terms of retirement, Western workers are painfully finding out these days that they were not immune to such competition. Knowledge embodied in capital can be dealt with only by countervailing humane knowledge, not by technocratic illusions.

Finally, with the information revolution the master became slave to the product of his own work, except that slavery was now indirect, invisible, mesmerizing. The mind came under the spell of commodities, becoming wasted in pursuit of mundane knowledge that served the meta-industrial system, letting atrophy other intellectual faculties. Neither Marx nor Wiener feared *economic* enslavement. Both raised for mankind an issue of Life: of the quality and purpose of life, which they feared could be scorched by technology and affluence. Indeed, we know already how to produce a lot and we can learn how to produce more. Besides, as long as man-made artefacts cannot replace humans as innovative consumers, we also know that, for the wheel to go round, workers must have a share of income not just enough to allow them to go by, but sufficient to keep their spirits high so as to consume innovatively. So, we could also deal with distribution better than in the past, if we so desired. Therefore, what matters these days is *what kind* of knowledge mankind will or should pursue.

Accountability

Before setting out to explain our main, time-space expropriation argument, we must clear up a certain popular fallacy that comes in various forms. Here, we will attack what may be named *fallacy of misplaced innocence*. Later, we will defend our theory against an *imperceptibility fallacy*. By fallacy of misplaced innocence we mean that self-complacent attitude of the many to find no fault in their own conduct and take no responsibility, always putting the blame elsewhere. [In a State where all governments have 'neglected' – in spite of the constitution's ordaining so – to record public forest land and have always legalized private seizure of such land, and where people routinely throw lit cigarette butts out of car windows, they all wonder who sets summer fires. I can show you around such a place.] We also mean to imply the attitude which always blames the powerful who abuse their power (after all, what good is power if you cannot abuse it?), and never those who *happened* to possess no such power, but promoted it, through submission or otherwise. It is precisely because of this reason that standing up against unjust power is praiseworthy, and Antigone (who in the legend defied the orders of King Creon that went against her conscience) is a perennial symbol of dignity. We mean, for example, to suggest that women have been historically *responsible* in part for male chauvinism, by fostering those relations within which it could flourish. If such reasoning seems to equate victims with victimizers, it is because blame is confused with responsibility and dichotomous reasoning puts all blame on one side, misplacing innocence on the other. In social matters, however, the issue is not one of blame but of shared responsibilities. After all, the notion of wrong that attaches to blame is context dependent, so that what appears *ex post* as wrong may well have been appropriate or decent conduct at the time. So, it is a holistic, participative co-determination kind of interpretation of history that sits at the base of our argument, not allocating guilt.

Distribution of value under industrial production poses a challenge. It places each one against all others, as all try to claim as much of socially produced value as they can. The difficulty is that this involves more than levels of income, which set only the *scale* of expenditures. The actual value that one appropriates is decided through rivalry in the consumption arena, according to the *structure* of such expenditures, that is, according to (a) the composition of the saving and consumption mix and (b) the composition of the current consumption vector for each individual, in relation to the totality of consumers. These are decided speculatively, in anticipation of the behaviour of others. To accomplish their goal, agents must not only exploit already available information, but they must also generate new knowledge that they will possess privately for a while, taking advantage of it only to the extent that others, too, will pick it up and make use of it, shortly after.

Knowledge then takes over as determinant of power over humans and over nature, providing an illusion of extending one's time-space at the expense of others, imposing an alien power over them, the power of one's wit and capacity to anticipate correctly the trends of general behaviour in the market. Seeking to snatch this single scarce elixir from each other through the products of socially contributed toil is what brings people together and divides them. This is the real tragedy of the commons, whereas anything else that goes under the same name is outward, material manifestation of it. Human time-space is in the man-made arte-facts that one owns privately, that is, deprives others from having access to. But as this is conflictive, laws are required to prevent by force, or by threat of force, the further expropriation of thus appropriated possessions.

This is radical departure from conventional wisdom and theory, casting economics in a light of malice rooted in apprehension over death. It does not visit it as a fulfilling activity, or as an act of necessity. It has conceptual, theoretical and methodological ramifications and turns many things upside down. For one thing, it reduces all apparent scarcities down to one, namely, the scarcity of life, interpreting economic activity as part of an aggressive campaign. It interprets *all* violence, both that which aims at meeting basic needs or pleasing basic desires *and* that which comes with culture, as being basically economic.

Monolithic as these may sound, the question is whether it is thus done injustice to reality, or whether reality has indeed become monolithic. But it would be a mistake to understand these as implying some kind of deterministic teleology, an inexorable dictate beyond human volition. On the contrary, our argument implicates every agent as fully responsible and accountable for his or her minutest thought, choice and action. In particular, our theory rests crucially upon the assumption that consump-tion above basics is an activity in discretion, which we take as obvious.

Note first that such explanation of individual conduct meets the additivity requirement we set from the outset. Individual acquisitiveness finds expression at the firm level, where firms compete against each other; big businesses try to devour smaller ones, etc. At the economy level, technologically advanced economies try to control resources, dominate other economies, penetrate cultures and markets and so on. Thus, capitalism has corroded cultures with a long history of frugality, tight social bonds and well-guarded codes, which gave way to an aggressive, market-dictated attitude towards life and towards people. Only in such light should be interpreted the various accounts such as the following one given by Adam Smith, for the promotion of the common good through pursuit of individual advantage:

> Every individual is continually exerting himself to find out the most advan-tageous employment for whatever capital he can command. It is his own advantage, indeed, and not that of the society, which he has in view. But the study of his own advantage naturally, or rather necessarily leads him to prefer that employment which is most advantageous to the society.
>
> (Smith, 1937: 421)

'Whatever capital' must be understood as just a single kind of capital, namely, knowledge capital, since this is the only one possessed naturally by agents. And 'advantageous' to the individual or to society must be understood as improving their position relative to others. If one thinks about it, there is no other generative capital that we possess, except our intellect. (Even just finding out what capital we possess needs thinking about it.) All tangible capital that may accrue to a person or to a society derives from this. Focusing on the tangible aspects of capital misleads one into setting production and consumption apart. If we focus instead on this generative capacity, then production and consumption merge as parts of a single cognitive approach to some goal pursued individually and finding collective expression through what is known one-sidedly as industrial production towards growth.

Starting from knowledge, instead of from natural desires, makes people account-able, because this admits that fundamental, not just derivative choices are made concerning the kind of life to be led and the ways about it. Thus, whether driven by fear of death or otherwise, it is up to the actors themselves to decide whether to get trapped in zero-sum contest for gain against each other, depriving them-selves of an option not to take part, or an escape route once in, since staying out will then mean falling behind: since what one refrains from claiming is snatched by others, as nothing is identified with some particular maker and the only way to decide about rights of ownership on the product of socially contributed toil is through the said contest. As Hirsch (1977: 109) put it, 'each individual consumer will come out worse himself unless he acts in what, collectively, is a self-defeating way'.

This is all *made* to be like a Roman treadmill, a rat race or squirrel wheel. Staying put when others run ensures that one contributes more time-space to the pool than he or she takes out. So, one needs to run ever faster to maintain his position, which makes capitalism a self-propelling culture, in which all know that if they do not compete others will take over. This way, the past, as labour fossilized in commodities, dominates the present (living each moment through emancipating work, leisure, etc.), the artefact overwhelms its creator and capital acquires inde-pendence to which humans become subordinate. People become possessed by possessions: One day, cell phones are attached on to humans. The next day humans are attached on to cell phones.

If one goes through Marx's argument about alienation not in the usual production-bound sense, but through the glass of his *Economic and Philosophical Manuscripts*, one can see that these update it to the present, which is marked by wasteful deprivation and in which people are alienated not only from the com-modities they make, but also from the commodities they purchase and use. That is, they are alienated from all aspects of collaborative human contribution, which ultimately means from humans. Alienation does not stop at the factory gate but continues with consumption, in the market for wants that have mushroomed since Marx's time into an all-permeating, uninterrupted life-preoccupation. Those who act in such a way, which may be called *capitalistically rational*, are more likely to succeed by this measure but also more likely to become depressed, as they realize more gravely that success is in vain. So, the wealthy are more prone to depression and other such illnesses. As Smith (1869: 163) observed: 'In ease of the body and peace of the mind, all the different ranks of life are nearly upon a level, and the beggar, who suns himself by the side of the high way, possesses that security which kings are fighting for.'

The alienating power of consumption and its economic significance may not be overemphasized, and it certainly cannot be ignored. The product of alienated labour cannot be an object of non-alienated discretion by workers as consumers, since alienated workers cannot be transformed, as they move from the factory floor to the shopping centre, into emancipated consumers. This reverses the position of thinkers like Guy Debord who argue that alienated consumption has become a task and an obligation of consumers towards capitalism. Causality runs in the opposite direction: It is alienated consumption that drives capitalism. This summons Jean-Claude Michéa's (1999) view that it matters not only what world we will leave to our children but, even more, to what children we will leave our world!

It is important to note that alienation on the consumption front starts earlier in one's life than alienation through production. It starts when a child acquires the skills and psychological disposition for aggressive, insatiable consumption that reflects the angst of the elders that surround it. SMS messaging has become their favourite pastime, to the joy of the communications industry. Parents take their offspring along when they go shopping, teaching them how to consume human time-space. The spectacle of life-taking violence has become as pervasive and marketable as to let our children grow up with life-taking video games, which dominate their lives as soon as they can handle a *joy*stick. Soon, life-taking becomes their virtual joy and actual reality. For fear of death, the joy of life becomes joy of life-taking. And at the street corner of unemployment, The Army is always 'a good opportunity' (to take life).

While alienated consumers try to outsmart each other and claim as big a chunk of the produced pie as they can, they carry no illusion that owning commodities can make them happy, as they are not happy while making those. Modern consumers do not develop any emotional relationship with the commodities they buy, any more than they develop one with those they produce. They simply use them as demonstration of their aptness in expropriating time-space; as measures of their *social displacement*. The way people approach the fruits of human toil they approach humans. Showing no respect for the former, feeling a sense of ownership and control over them reflects on how they feel about the latter. This is genuine choice, and conscious participation.

As Mill (1972 [1843]: 484) argued about a ruler's judgement and action, it reflects in one way or another 'the feelings, habits, and modes of thought which characterize the particular class in that community to which they themselves belong' and, by extension, of the entire community. This is even more so in democracies, where people elect their leaders according to their own measures of excellence, and there can be no misfit between the two. Neither can there be a misfit of daring Schumpeterian entrepreneurs, on one hand, and timid, non-adventurous consumers, on the other. *All* power is held by public approval, including the power of the capitalists. People are passive bystanders to nothing. They *create* the virtual reality in which they live. They do not just consent to changes. They impose them. Personal and collective liabilities are difficult to disentangle, as each is a condition and a consequence of the other. But language often falls short of acknowledging such facts, perpetuating confusion. Thus, Wiener (op. cit.: 160) claimed that

> A certain precise mixture of religion, pornography, and pseudo science will sell an illustrated newspaper. A certain blend of wheedling, bribery, and intimidation will induce a young scientist to work on guided missiles or the atomic bomb. To determine these, we have our machinery of radio fan ratings, straw votes, opinion samplings, and other psychological investigations, with the common man as their object; and there are always the statisticians, sociologists, and economists available to sell their services to these undertakings.

Yet, none is induced against his will, no man is an object, and trying to explain social reality without holding society accountable is disrespect for history. Democratic capitalism, in particular, has received wide approval and practical support by the masses. People take pride in their *having* much more than in their *being* and they appraise each other accordingly. When poor, they admire those who possess much in the way of wealth, asking not how huge fortunes were made. And whether poor or rich, they have much less respect for those who are noble or wise.

Any departures from these and any observed differences, class or other, are due to personal manners and to unavoidably different degrees of expropriative success. This is a more productive way of interpreting Marx's view that it is social forces that matter, not individuals. But social critics took their wishful thinking for real, discarded the market plebiscite as phoney, failed to understand the real situation and were overtaken by facts. No plebiscite is more genuine than that of the market, which is impossible to rig. People take pride in their capacity to function with success in the market, having little else to be proud of. They (which the reader is invited to replace with 'we') see capitalism as *their* (*our*) achievement, as much as of the capitalists'. They admire the college dropout who becomes mogul overnight, and they admire him even more when he is proven to be a crook, because he epitomizes their dreams. They reap benefits from capitalism at the expense of others, whose wealth is plundered. They benefit from global pillage, reaping low infant-mortality rates, longer life expectancy, flashy cars, flushing toilets, 'juicy hamburgers', high crime rates, air-conditioning appliances, pollution, depression and antidepressants, opting for the whole package. After defeating hunger, they *chose* to be obese, which means they enjoy becoming obese, complaining about being obese, and exercising in the gyms (breathing voluminously each other's exhalation) in order to fight obesity. And with half of mankind starving, they consider it indecorous to eat up all food and leave dishes empty. Thus, *they chose* genetically modified foodstuffs, toxic pesticides, chemical fertilizers, maltreatment and barbarous slaughtering of animals, etc., as they refused to buy pears with an occasional cute little worm in them, bought two pears, ate one and threw the other away, having chosen wastefulness as their prized lifestyle. Such consumption attitude needs a meaningful explanation; not frivolous mumbling about some hazy utility. In other words, *what is 'utility'?*

Concerning the apportioning of responsibilities, credit or fault, the question is this: If the cork floats, is this due only to its own specific gravity or to that of the liquid also? Clearing the masses for no reason other than their large numbers is quite common, but inferences drawn from this border on the ludicrous. If the most polluting States do not sign an environmental agreement, this is not against the will of their citizens, who refuse to put their affluence at stake. In pernicious optimism, people in general overestimate the capacity of the physical environment to forgive their insolence (much as they overestimate their own capacity to withstand each other's cruelty). They delude themselves into thinking that vital resources (oil, clean air, a protective atmospheric layer, etc.) come in unlimited amounts, so they remain undaunted by energy shortages, crises, or by man-made disasters, refusing to learn from those. *Solitudinem faciunt, pacem appellant.* (They, as conquerors, make desert and call it peace.) They make uninhabitable purgatories they call cities and enjoy living in them with their pets, while all other species desert them. They manage by twisting of language: They confuse democracy with suffrage in universal ignorance, and freedom with their right to apply force on others, or with their echoing back views that are submitted to them through the mass media.[3] Most relevant to our project is that they confuse consumption with welfare.

The point that concerns us here, however, is not whether people are wise or ignorant, well meaning or mean, emancipated, sensible or foolish, politically alert, naïve, or whatever, but that *they choose to be what they are*, and that *they choose not to undertake any responsibility for the consequences*. In short, they choose to be self-righteous and complacent, taking any measure of self-criticism or any attempt at self-awareness as sheer masochism. Thus, none will relinquish his or her right to drive because he or she is an incompetent driver, and none will even admit to being such.

Education and general cultivation are matters of personal choice, and therefore so is ignorance, because the former take exertion while ignorance does not. It just takes least action, of which anyone is capable, so one must opt for it, in full conscience of the enjoyment in lack of exertion, but also in full awareness of its consequences. This is a basic choice, in most cases made once in one's life, so that its memory wanes until it is eventually forgotten that a choice was actually made. To be precise, ignorance is not about inactivity of the brain, which is impossible anyway, but about monolithic, routinized, lowly brain activity. In such life, economic indicators may prosper and the level of consumption may be rising, but the *quality* of life will be that which Aristotle thought to be worthy of cattle.

Consumer Capitalism will hopefully be explained to no confusion. Productive capital will still be seen as being in the hands of a few, and there is still, as there was always, little chance that one born to a working-class family will make it big, as the North American tale goes. But theory must harbour questions and take note of the fact that, even though workers still do not own productive capital, their aspirations are different from the usual impression one may draw by reading Marx superficially. Social forces gather up from individual action, but structures thus formed feed back on individuals. Marx's thesis, that people create their own history, invokes self-determination. Any other reading of him is pedestrian.

Hume (op. cit.: 346) argued: 'Throw any considerable goods among men, they instantly fall a quarrelling, while each strives to get possession of what pleases him, without regard to the consequences.' Thus,

> The state of society without government is one of the most natural states of men, and may subsist with the conjunction of many families, and long after the first generation. Nothing but an encrease of riches and possessions cou'd oblige men to quit it; and so barbarous and uninstructed are all societies on their first formation, that many years must elapse before these cou'd encrease to such a degree, as to disturb men in the enjoyment of peace and concord.
>
> (Ibid.)

And capitalism immensely increased possessions and riches so that, instead of directing their efforts towards attaining excellence, people strove aggressively to acquire knowledge and dexterities only for promoting material advantage. Thus, it became that 'In ancient times the opulent and civilized found it difficult to defend themselves against the poor and barbarous nations. In modern times the poor and barbarous find it difficult to defend themselves against the opulent and civilized' (Smith, 1937: 669). Was Smith really speaking about his time, or about ours?

For gaining this advantage, people set up markets. This makes the market not a co-ordinating mechanism, but a domain for applying marginal knowledge that counters the natural forces which pull towards full diffusion of existing knowledge and thus towards equilibrium, these being the forces neoclassical theory is confined to. In capitalism, everything meets at the marketplace where the crest of knowledge finds ground to demonstrate its expropriative potential. Human values are reduced to market value and are expressed in monetary terms. Amongst masses, the dream of a mobile phone is more vivid, arousing and compelling, than the 'chore' of reading a book. Only what sells counts, and thus is born a bemusing antinomy between unabashed individualism and a general demise of personality, as individuality degenerates into market individualism and this into solipsism: *Ego solus ipse*! The social grid gets dissolved into a footloose society. For all their differences, people become increasingly same, like 'bricks in the wall', chasing and being haunted by a dream that is always receding. But the dream is not consumption, as standard theory asserts. Nothing less than existential anxiety can explain such an impelling pathology.

It was thought that mistrust could subside with material affluence. Yet, centuries after the Enlightenment people look even more enviously at each other. Immersed in selfish calculation, they turn a blind eye to all the aggression and violence that surround them, hoping that by doing so *they* will be spared. So, they choose to ignore that some are detained for years and tortured with no charges brought against them, or that suspects are treated as guilty and verdicts are announced by the most official lips on television upon their arrest, etc. But, against the received view, we contend that there is deliberate choice involved and general, all-out collusion. Human and civil rights are not just violated. They are surrendered, at various pretexts.[4] Personal communications are monitored and 'privacy' has become a very short joke. But people opt for these (as when they contend for hosting the Olympic Games after 'September 11, 2001') and the reason is always some acquisitive calculation.

Reality is replete with economically motivated brutality. Many children stand no chance of surviving, while many who do are brutally exploited, often forced to fight the wars of the grown-ups. But someone else is always to blame, never the church-going, respectable citizen with a wife, a mistress and three cars in the driveway. He belongs to a 'silent majority' that has few scruples for the cosiness it enjoys, pledges to charity, and has a reserved place in Heaven (*if* God proves to be forgiving enough or not too discriminating). Well-to-do citizens can lay couched in their sofas, gulping beer while watching their high-tech weapons burn, radiate, poison and kill with 'surgical precision' some 'things' that do not even show on the screen. 'Precision', to be accurate, means that the victims are in the precise proportions that each group (children, babies, etc.) is to be found in the general population. Amidst so much confused arrogance, these 'well-to-do' are slow getting the message of their own defeat, which comes with the shock, horror *and revolt* in the pictures of mutilated children. They keep thinking that it is all like those 'fantastic' computer war-games they raise their own children with, making provision for the perpetuation of their species. But the worst – which most critics refuse to recognize – is that many among the not-so-well-to-do envy such cosiness.

Wars are always, on either side, just, patriotic and blessed by God. (It is reassuring to have an almighty God back us up when we commit atrocities.) Brutal States always consider themselves to be guardians of freedom and civilization. People approve of their government's aggression against others, do not mind about who makes profits from 'the war effort' as long as others pay the cost, and withdraw their support only when things do not work out as scheduled. (The President's popularity took a dive again, recently.) Then they discover money-making companies to blame for the war. Those who have much, because they have usurped much, think highly of themselves and little of those who have nothing, because their vision of life is not in *being*, but in *having*. So, they take less-affluent people for flies that can be killed by the numbers, while the life of a single one of their own justifies starting a war and destroying an entire country. But, those who have nothing have nothing to lose, do not fear death and fight back. Then, waking up is quite painful! (Unfortunately, it does not last.)

Drugs offer one more example of misplaced collective innocence. There is hardly a single one of us that to a different extent and in different ways is not somehow responsible for the way things stand with drug use and addiction in general, and for the fact that they became overnight a significant part of our culture.

Yet, there is hardly anyone who would admit so, not even parents, which is obviously absolutely absurd. A whole population deceives itself into thinking that they can hide behind a few drug lords or traffickers. Such examples abound.

Cruelty one meets with among humans should shock every sane person, primitive or beast. (Even scarecrows are made to look like humans.) There is a macabre market for human organs and tissue from live and dead, and massive human trafficking. Private armies and bodyguards abound. One can find more uniformed and armed personnel in the big cities in 'peace time' than in a combat zone. Actually, big cities are combat zones of sorts and our supposedly free and democratic states have become police states. There is 'security' even in toilets and cemeteries. By letting fear to be raised inside them people allow walls to be raised around them, living under continuous surveillance, locking themselves up behind armoured doors and inside electromagnetic fields produced by security devices. Thus isolated, with social grids demolished, they talk *to* their cell phones instead of to the person they are supposed to communicate with. Yesterday's victims become today's victimizers. Yesterday's refugees become today's racists, as they fear their jobs will be lost to newly arrived ones. Note, however, as this is vital for our argument, that this is all 'in defence'.

Staying on a strict diet of televised manure, masses make national heroes of pop singers, football players and other celebrities. They 'love' the star system they have created, as their entire lives are lived through appropriative vanity. They hate to think in involved ways, degenerating mentally and echoing what the mass media dictate to them, proudly registering it through the polls as personal opinion, imposing it on the rest of society as utter wisdom. Supposedly sane people convince themselves that the more they buy the more they save. Thus, one meets the most cheerfully determined faces at shopping places, where people meet with the content of their lives. But cheerfulness quickly fades, letting show a gruesome distress.

Let us sum it all up: Whatever may obtain at any higher level, whether this is as we claim here or not, it is consequent upon individual choices, with the resulting structure reflecting back on individuals. And choosing makes one accountable.

Methodological requirements

The problem of economic theory is a problem of society. Therefore, Tony Lawson is right in claiming, in his *Economics and Reality*, that economic theorizing must be soundly based on the ontology of economic subjects. But what is 'ontology' other than 'existence'? Now, if one agrees with us that paroxysmic consumption is a transparent exhibition of such ontology, then one must also agree that what is revealed of the requisite ontology through consumption is a *grave* [*sic*] distress of amazing proportions. This, as noted by Lawson (1997: 180), who cites Giddens (1984), can supply 'continuity, stability and sameness in daily affairs' and 'at the level of the unconscious is a basic need for inner security grounding a generalised disposition towards the maintenance of trust in the natural world and the avoidance of anxiety'.

Once this connection is understood, it becomes clear that a down-to-earth perspective is required, not an evangelical one. However bleak the scientist's intuition may be, it must be reported honestly and evaluated impartially, against the forces of popular ignorance. The self-interested citizen must be interrogated about his motives and goals. Received views, orthodox methods and sacrosanct axioms such as those about noble, welfare-promoting competitiveness, unimpeded growth and boundless productivity, and concepts such as those of self-interest and scarcity must be put under scrutiny. Theory must wake up to facts which are long known to professionals in behavioural finance, or in investor and marketing psychology, the latter having discovered, for example, that a $499 price makes more sense than $500, as also that our eyes first land on the right hand pages as we browse through magazines and so ads have been placed there, feeding our consuming appetite. Economic theory must pick up from this vulturous appetite and move on to supply robust explanations for what remains. Since all that remains is somehow connected with consumption, it follows that economics is as good as its theory of consumer behaviour.

As Marshall (1920: 1) maintained, economics is the 'study of mankind in the ordinary business of life'. Therefore, theory must engage the lay people as active participants in the economic debate. It must be concerned with what ordinary people do; not what they ought to do or what they could do. It must walk with people on the sidewalk, looking through shop windows with one eye, fixing the other on the neighbour's new car. Because it is thus squinting that people walk in life, coveting each other's wealth. It must explain *why* they squint and *what* they squint at, adopting Marx's method: 'we set out from real, active men and on the basis of their real life process we demonstrate the development of the ideological reflexes and echoes of this life process' (Marx and Engels, 1939: 14); and his two-step materialist approach: The first premise of history is production of means to sustain life. 'The second fundamental point is that as soon as a need is satisfied, ... new needs are made; and this production of new needs is the first historical act' (ibid.). Therefore, legitimate explanation must be based on root causes. One can 'explain' anything by choosing to start from a later stage, as does orthodox theory which starts from revealed preferences. Here, we try to drive explanation as far back as it goes, explaining 'the first historical act' as an ontological, namely, existential one. We explain regular, enduring structures on the basis of a uniform and stable driving urge, trying to recover the simple behind the complex. The basic idea is simple, it verges on the obvious, and we delight, with Kierkegaard, in reflecting on what appears to be simple, and with what seems to be extremely complex but really isn't: Consumption is part of the quest for life, along with production. In thus expanding our experienced time-space we interpret our self-interest and gain self-esteem, as well as the (subservient) admiration of others.

In visiting these, we follow Lawson's (op. cit.: 176) advice concerning method, where two opposite errors must be avoided when studying emergence of structure from individual agency: (a) The structure must not be *reduced to* elements or governing principles operating at the lower level and (b) dependence of the structure upon the principles operating at the lower level must not be ignored. As he argues, reproduction/transformation of social structures is rarely intended, and individual agents are not consciously aware of the structures upon which they draw:

> Individuals draw upon existing social structure as a typically unacknowledged condition for acting, and through the action of all individuals taken in total, social structure is typically unintentionally reproduced. Social structure in general is neither created by, nor independent of, human agency, but rather is the unmotivated condition of all our motivated productions, the non-created but drawn upon and reproduced/transformed condition for our daily economic/ social activities.
>
> (Ibid.: 169)

The requisite awareness takes more than logical thinking. It takes also what Einstein (1954: 226 and 270) termed 'intuition, resting on sympathetic understanding of experience', to which Georgescu-Roegen (1966: 14) added 'a consummate intellectual phantasy. Logic helps us only present thought already thought out, but it does not help us think out thought.' Speaking about 'value theory, and especially in that branch of it known as the theory of production', Shackle (op. cit.: 116–17) argued that 'The search for such principles, the pursuit of useful hypotheses about threads of uniformity running through ostensibly diverse sectors of production, might call for audacious ingenuity, but it would open fresh fields of suggestion where at present economic theory seems to be running into the sands of over-refined logic.'

Economics as activity is a felt and experienced condition. Therefore, its theory cannot be real, if it is abstract and remote. On the other hand, making theory with too much involvement runs the risk of being partisan, emotional and off the mark. Empathy and logic need to be balanced so that risks can be taken, but also analysis should not get strayed into futile speculation. Enthusiasm must be informed with Joel Mokyr's thoughtful words about the intricacies of economic history and the difficulties of historical explanation, as also with his warning about 'crackpots in love with their own tautologies or focusing too much on one particular aspect to the exclusion of others to qualify [one's theory] as a comprehensive "theory of economic history" ' (Mokyr, 2005: 196). As he argues, 'economic history is bigger than economic theory – vastly bigger' (ibid.). Yet, it so happens that all assertions are disproved, sooner or later, and at the same time, intellectual slumbers breed a bleak outlook and prompt caustic statements such as those by Keynes or Friedman. So, received views and methodological conventions must be challenged, as well as the sombre, stilted and boring academic writing style which, all too often, conceals lack of substance. Presentational formalism must succumb to the primacy of substance.

Insight gained from other theories must not be discarded. The neoclassical attempt to disguise aggressive individualism into a merely methodological one makes it all the more obvious, as when one blushes when telling a lie. Day by day, the intensifying, sophisticated rivalry of modern reality makes this more transparent. But treating every statement made on such matters as a logical proposition and trying to prove it in a rigorous manner, as is fond to mainstream economists, risks abolishing its content. So, Aristotle's advice must be heeded concerning the degree of certitude and exactness that is applicable, shedding the neoclassical obsession with rigour, which imposed a crippling grammar that reduced economic theorizing to exercises in logic.

So, we draw here from many. For example, our approach to consumer innovations shares much with Schumpeter's producer innovations, as well as with Keynes's investor performance. As for Marx, he expected workers to abolish the terms of their own exploitation and of exploitation in general. This speaks of self-awareness, which guides our footsteps. We discern in consumers' yearning for capital the result of long years of human alienation and cultural corrosion that enslaved them to their existential anxiety, so we owe a basic debt to Kierkegaard. But we also part with those we draw from. We reject any theory of conspiracy by any few against the many. Nothing of social validity can derive from anything else but from society itself. If masses are vulgar or noble, wise, ignorant, or whatever, it is the masses that have chosen to be such, in their way about life. And we part with the Veblenian explanation of consumerism as just ludicrous demonstration of cheap taste, and as concerning only a leisure class or the nouveau riche, aiming at prestige or distinction. We discern in it a pervasive belligerence for time-space, as frightening as the struggle for power that literally takes lives. We adopt Freud's premise that the further explanation is rolled back the further forward it can reach, so we push it all the way down to its psychological foundations. As Lawson (op. cit.: 217) put it: 'When an explanation of an explanation is successfully achieved, ... we are likely to have greater confidence in each part of the overall explanation of the original phenomena.' Or, more elaborately,

> In the social realm ... if structures and mechanisms endure over stretches of time-space it can only be by way of human action. If then we wish to explain some *relatively enduring* contrastive demi-reg, a full understanding of the situation requires that the mode of reproduction of the identified causal mechanism be itself investigated. In other words, it is necessary that the conditions governing the reproduction (and perhaps 'initial' emergence) of any identified causal mechanisms be accounted for, that the explanation be explained.
>
> (Ibid., original emphasis)

Economists shirk from pursuing their arguments to their psychological origins and avoid difficulties associated with uncertainty induced by knowledge. Looking squarely into these makes arguments abstruse, but this is in the nature of the issues examined. Our existential argument is abstruse because it touches upon what is repressed and surfaces only contingently. As Hume (2000: 293) noted: 'There is an inconvenience which attends all abstruse reasoning that it may silence, without convincing an antagonist, and requires the same intense study to make us sensible of its force, that was at first requisite for its invention.' But our argument is not submitted as a tentative one, as a working hypothesis, as analytically expedient or just as a fact. It is submitted as *the fact of life*. Not of any objective life, but of life *as it is understood: backwards*; which, as we will argue later, along with Kierkegaard, is never properly understandable. In such an 'imperfect understand-ability' sense, it is a truth of general validity whose malevolence protrudes under aeons of civilized pasting. And although it is not *the only* fact of life, it is the one that underlies all others, obliging them to its cause. It is as much of a fact as it is our 'privilege' to be so appallingly cruel against the members of our own species, a priv-ilege that should shock anyone who insists on being in his or her right mind. Economic systems, after all, are the long mechanical arms with which society reaches farther into the world surrounding it, so as to control and experience more of it through control over the power of humans. This is how we behave and what we aim at, regardless of whether we are aware of it or not.

Are we aware of it? Not exactly, but we also do not sense the pull of gravity, we still enjoy sun-*rises* and sun-*sets*, and ignorance is even less surprising when one *refuses* to know. Can we prove or disprove it? Certainly not, in any strict sense, in Popperian fashion, in some axiomatically based way, or in the way neo-classicists provide 'proofs'. There is no outside observer to whom these could shine through. Still, it may be that we do know about it, as when we talk about *vital* space, or when we say that money is *power*. And we have carved it on our myths: on the myth of Prometheus, who stole the secret of fire from the gods and was brutally punished; on the myth of Adam and Eve, who ate from the tree of knowledge, which was the tree of life, and were expelled from Eden for this; on the myth of Cain and Abel, the first fruits of that knowledge about life: Cain *took the life* of Abel out of envy, because Cain's offerings to God were *calculated*, while Abel's were not. Actually, taking Abel's life was the calculation itself, for which Cain was punished to do what we argue we keep doing ever since: taking lives. And God is testing us (while Aristotle and Nietzsche questioned as) whether we will ever be able to get past this. There is indication outside myth as well: In the news and in our conscience, the life of a single Westerner counts more than the lives of hundreds of starving African or Asian children, the children of a lesser God. The reason is simple: In our calculations, it is appropriated time-space that really determines one's social proportions. Anything else is of Sunday sermons and of wishfully thinking critics. But other than that, we go into the battle against each other with reduced awareness, since too much awareness does not help in war.

Now, few would subscribe to any connection between myth and science, but here is what Gell-Mann (1995: xiii) had to say about science-making:

> Nietzsche introduced the distinction between 'Apollonians,' who favor logic, the analytical approach, and a dispassionate weighing of evidence, and 'Dionysians,' who lean more toward intuition, synthesis and passion.... But some of us seem to belong to another category: the 'Odysseans,' who com-bine the two predilections in their quest for connections among ideas. Such people often feel lonely...

Given how poor the yield of economic Cartesianism has been, little harm could be done if theory became a little Odyssean, drawing from the rich deposits of incisive cynical philosophy. Odysseus could not wait for the compass to be discovered before leaving Troy and economists should not wait until philosophers of science decide whether verifiability, Popperian falsifiability or some other criterion of cognitive significance is proper for deciding what is science and what is not. It seems prudent to discard the notion of any absolute truth and to reason on the basis of relative degrees of confirmation and confidence in which we, as observers, cannot but be personally involved. That invokes our ontology, especially as this is expressed through paroxysmic consumption. Explaining capitalism upon anything other than a realistic consumer ontology does not make sense. It also helps to consider that other sciences advanced by leaps and bounds using unconventional methods for breaking out of an occasional impasse, when standard methods failed. In theoretical physics, playful perseverance led to breakthroughs such as Gell-Mann's quarks, and no physicist would laugh today at those who, intrigued by the relative weakness of gravity, investigate a theory about a geometric space of more than three dimensions. Finally, it is interesting to observe that however convenient dichotomies may have been in the physical sciences, these tend to be abandoned. For example, the classical separation between solids and liquids was abandoned in order to explain the swelling, rising or falling of the Himalayas.

So, given the playfulness of the reality that economic theory is called upon to explain, a certain degree of venturesomeness must be allowed. Economists must take issue with what has been uncritically adopted as truth. They must spell all implications out and follow arguments through to their consequences. Their object is singular. It is to follow Hermann Hesse's steppe wolf as he comes in society in order to soothe his existential anxiety by drawing from society, trying to reconcile the primeval animal with the rational human he hides inside. Such contradictions stir controversy in science, but life is in contradiction: a fear of death and an impulse to fight it, in full knowledge that fighting it is hopeless; a fear of the unknown and a desire to conquer it. Psychoanalysis teaches that once this is grasped, answers often emerge as next to obvious. For example, much as lack of self-assurance often shows outwardly as assertive power, so does niggardly acquisitiveness appear as profligate wastefulness.

Myrdal (1978: 5) maintained that 'Valuations are always with us. Disinterested research there never has been and can never be. Prior to answers there must be questions. There can be no view except from a viewpoint. In the questions raised, and the viewpoints chosen, valuations are implied.' It is honest, therefore, of an author to make his viewpoint clear, rather than dress it up with pretentious neutrality. Only then can arguments be judged fairly. Here, we explain capitalism as a summit of the rock side of a life lost in the clouds of consuming psychedelia, where no fountain quenches thirst, the sweetest fruit is juiceless *and the assailant is his own victim.*

An investigation into underlying causes is bound to touch upon too wide a range of topics, full treatment of which is impossible. So, we aim only at giving a general, initial outline of the basic idea, placing less weight on exactness or presentational formalism. In this chapter we have laid out this outline, taking a hawk-eye view of the human condition. In Chapter 3 we elaborate on our ontological theme, after taking a critical overview of other theories in Chapter 2. Then, in Chapters 4 and 5, we supply a more technical presentation of the main ideas, closing with Chapter 6 which addresses a number of related issues.

All theory is idealization, retaining of reality what it considers essential, abstracting from non-essential detail. Interpreting economics as *process* in every sphere of which value-creating activity takes place is fraught with difficulties. The theory presented embraces one aspect of behaviour that tends to become dominant. Selfishness and greed are seen not as aiming at pleasure, but as accommodating an urge to extend life. In the end, nothing is really material. All is ideal; an illusion. Methodologically, consumption is restored on an equal footing and innovative footstep with production, abandoning their usual dichotomous treatment. Capitalism is not just a technological affair, but a waltz dance of production with consumption, its pace being determined by income distribution. When any of these trips, capitalism flounders. When the slaves fail to synchronize the oars, the ship jerks with no speed or direction.

Our argument implies that the kind of reasoning implicit to statements such as that 'Poverty has not been defeated!' is false; because it hides that we never meant to defeat it. Highly publicized 'Make Poverty History' type of campaigns by politicians and celebrities are self-serving monuments of hypocrisy. Poverty is intrinsic to the choices we have made. Our choices produce squatters and starving populations. These do not mean that social differences can be uncritically edged off or wiped out, at a time when capitalism is heavy-handedly borne down upon many. Losing in the zero-sum contest has dire consequences. Many cannot even make ends meet, well into the twenty-first century. Losers have no say, winners pull strings, and there is awe-inspiring concentration of wealth and power in the hands of a few. But winners and losers are worlds apart, without having moved an inch from where they all started. They all belong to the same mortal species, they all demonstrate the same urge for control, as they are all guided by existential insecurity, and they all knuckle under the consequences of their choices. Extreme affluence, as extreme poverty, is strange deprivation. To one's social standing should be ascribed no more than befits. What matters is what each tries to accomplish, what each dreams of.

Dreams matter! And capitalism thrives on dreams. Grotesque or infuriating as it may sound, it matters, both in a narrowly economic sense and more broadly, if a Chinese miner dreams of a made-in-China Grand Cherokee Jeep while risking his life in the galleries of an antiquated coalmine, or aspires to something loftier for himself, for his children and for society. It matters if he determines himself, through his consuming behaviour, the surplus that will be expropriated of him and the extent to which he will trade his social awareness for commodities. It matters if, along with their gains, winners bear the consequences of winning by becoming depressed and getting on mood-elevating drugs, since the penalty for being rich is to live with the rich and compare with the rich, making any fortuitous advantage evaporate. It matters if social awareness is raised in the process of losing, as socialist thinking goes, or if, as we argue here, masses envy but admire those who win and sneer at those who fail.

Finally, Smith's (1937: 164) advice must be heeded: 'The desire of food is limited in every man by the narrow capacity of the human stomach; but the desire of the conveniences and ornaments of building, dress, equipage and household furniture, seems to have no limit or certain boundary.' But such desire must be explained. And to this end, theory must engage the entire population in its explanation, abandoning the absurdity of economics as a producers' affair. There are second- and third-class citizens, but there is also second- and third-class glitz, an all-permeating sham for which all compete, elbowing each other out in dubious battle for a place at a finish line that is moved further as it is approached, staying always out of reach. It is this that keeps capitalism moving. More than ever, compositions decide who gets what portion of produced value. Earned income sets only the scale. Capitalism feeds on and inflames existential anxiety, displacing dispositions such as sharing. People would be surprised today if one said that only what we give is really ours; not what we take. What is mine cannot be yours under such fear, and what is yours cannot be mine. My time-space may expand only at the expense of yours, and conversely. So, I put all my powers into this zero-sum conflict, letting emerge a serpent-like society from my primitive fear for vital space. An honest theory of capitalism must fathom this psychology of antagonism, instead of fancying with utility-seeking agents.

2   Critical overview

The discussion in this chapter is not meant as a rigorously documented critique. It is meant to underscore the urgency for a conceptual and methodological shift in the treatment of consumption, in a way that helps present our argument. And we do not aspire to contribute to the debate concerning what 'neoclassical' means. (See, for example, Arnsperger and Varoufakis, 2006.) Little in our theory hinges on this. So, somewhat abusively, we use this conventional term almost interchangeably with mainstream or dominant economics, referring in general to the equilibrium-oriented approach that fills the pages of almost all textbooks which is taught in most universities and reproduces itself as economic ideology.

General observations

A science is supposed to study impartially and in the broadest possible context some relevant universe that pre-exists its initiation and is separate from it. Modern economics, however, was born to the Industrial Revolution and never cut its umbilical cord with it. It unfolded not as an impartial discourse into the economic condition of mankind in broad, historical perspective, but as a series of ideological skirmishes over one particular arrangement, namely, capitalism. Neoclassicism covered up the dark sides of capitalism, picturing it as a stainless accomplishment. Marxism focused on its distributional injustices, internal contradictions and alienating powers, downplaying motivational aspects that might implicate an entire society. Neoclassicists wrote off all vices of capitalism with a single utilitarian stroke, hiding its blatant belligerence. Marxists saw vice only in the profit-seeking greed of capitalists, as if by some defect in their double helix that the exploited masses were miraculously spared of. Neither school projected its being a global pillage by Western society. Even economic historians made little reference to systems outside capitalism.

These disputed the indisputable continuity of human history, reduced the discipline's scope and trapped it under a limited perception of its basic concepts: those of scarcity and self-interest, stripping down the agents who make happen what theory is called upon to explain. Scarcity was interpreted as shortage of resources and commodities. There was indeed shortage of the necessities for life when modern economics was born. Self-interest was delineated by the need to overcome this kind of external scarcity, with hardly any thought given to the possibility that scarcity might be inward, psychological, self-generated. Economics became a discourse about *needs*, and it remained such when conditions changed with the Industrial and meta-Industrial Revolutions. The knowledge base expanded quickly and sciences took advantage. Physics went past Newton. Relativity theories, Heisenberg's uncertainty principle and quanta-like uncertainty took over, meshing physics with philosophy. Visiting social issues required new perspectives and interpretations, as a politically active population adopted the capitalistic perspective towards life and placed their stakes in it. Finer division of physical and mental labour accelerated productivity increases, making the old type of scarcity obsolete. Poverty as incapacity to produce enough was overcome. It became a matter of distribution whether all would have plenty, or not. Deprivation became psychological. Self-interest became mostly about desires, or *wants*.

Amidst such great changes, economic theory discovered near the end of the nineteenth century a Newtonian, laws-of-motion type of social determinism, as envisaged by Helvetius in the middle of the eighteenth century. The overbearing certitude of marginalism, based comfortably on exogeneity of tastes, was hailed as revolution by economists. But tastes as natural compulsion are same as needs. Set against the physicist's modesty (no event can be predicted with certainty, except with certain probability), an economist's deterministic certitude seems pompous, obstructing appreciation of the knowledge process that induces changes from within the system, to the end of gaining personal advantage. Thus, today one must struggle in order to show the obvious, namely, the energetic, creative participation of the entire population in the forging of capitalism, through consumption.

Scarcity was never treated as a worrisome psychological arousal and the negative sensation intrinsic to all deprivation was ignored by fancying with all kinds of utility concepts carrying positive connotations. Failure of such explanations was confessed through the neoclassical shedding of all connotations, by reference to preference orderings void of all psychological nuances. That such fundamental agnosticism may be claimed to found a science is a wonder unique to economics. Yet, it was through this that was made possible to sell to the general audience economic growth as an unqualifiedly desirable goal and attainment, at the same time as Western society staggered under the woes of post-scarcity and the world staggered under the consequences of its plunder. Development, progress and advance became synonymous with growth in the wordings of the economist and in the minds of the layman. Brute economism was hailed as victory over the hostile forces of nature. Progressive intellectuals and socialists saw their utopias as possible to accommodate within capitalism, as it reached a productive climax. Many saw in material affluence the possibility for freedom and human emancipation. For some, the material basis of socialism itself was in this forward capitalist motion. For most, *Small-is-Beautiful* type economies, or any other non-aggressive arrangement would constitute a despicable anachronism, against the interests of labour.

But we are just beginning to learn that if we all get what we want, and if we all get to want everything, then the Earth may knuckle under the weight of our greed, which is not a very progressive prospect. Actually, it may have already become regressive. But the truth is even uglier: As George Orwell noted in his *Raffles and Miss Blandish*, what fascinates the revolutionist in siding with the weak is a sense of just power, in their name and on their behalf; a power that should come down on the unjust, in a never-ending fight for dominance.

Interpreting life as pursuit of pleasurable physical states misses the obvious, namely, that life is a desperate compulsion to experience *more of itself*, since there is nothing else that (the successive moments of) life can be filled with. Most self-respecting economists (who refuse to be informed even by economic crime) will laugh at the idea that there may be something to learn from the fact that children dislike going to sleep, before finally resigning to drowsiness, or that myths like those cited above may be informative. So, when material scarcity was overcome for the few in the West, through aggression against everyone else on the globe, economics remained only with benefits deriving from growth and with a transcendental notion of utility that was never really explained. Utilitarianism (or Aristippeanism) underwrote theory, charming even those who were later quick to trade their adolescent utopias for a brute neo-liberalism of their adulthood. That such common good may be a nightmare has not occurred to formal theorizing, which turns a blind eye to the contradiction between pervasive individual aggressiveness and salubrious growth, implicitly suggesting that personal vices can work to social benefit or merit. No additivity requirement is demanded of theory. Agency is separated from structure, and we can all be depressed as our GDP grows, while a national economy may be aggressive and vulturous while its citizens are free, fair and gracious.

One may suppose that we have a right to interpret as we like the social reality that we ourselves create, and that we may even hide ourselves from it. Or, we may just hide from its ugliest aspects, so as to survive. And this may be what we actually do, as Feuerbach and Fromm maintained. But it belongs to science to straighten things out, and especially to the human sciences, among which is supposed to be economics. However, economics has drawn other prospects for itself. Unlike other sciences, which treasure their questions, economics assumes the most challenging ones out. While sciences seek to expand their method, scope and findings, economics discourages venturesome initiatives through its academic rewards system, turns the same stones around, strains at the gnat, twists its basic concepts, seeks status in technical jargon and tries to take a free ride on the glory of mathematics. It refuses to abandon the idea of non-conflictive utility. While human sciences keep a distance from their subjects, economics flirts with them, adulates and appeases them, precisely as it obliterates them into *homines oeconomici*. Exogenous tastes pronounce useless the inclusion of ethics in markets, letting individuals loose to go after animalish pleasure, presumably dictated by nature, but not in any kind of zero-sumness, thus concealing the fundamentally antagonistic nature of capitalist culture.

Language is precious because it is scarce, in the sense that it cannot fully express the wealth of our thoughts and emotions. Words are ideas. Antisthenes[1] argued that visiting words is the beginning of knowledge. For Nietzsche, language was ideology, and mainstream economics proves this to be right. It twists language in such ways as to promote a particular ideology. *Competition* is confused with *antagonism*, as if they were equivalent. But *con* means 'with' and *petition* touches upon 'community', as opposed to *anti*, which means *against*, and *agonism* (from the Greek ἀγών), which means *fight*. Capitalism is about antagonism. All try to snatch from the common pool as much as they can, in all possible ways: evading taxes, through rivalry in income distribution, crime, war, as well as through production and consumption innovations in search for comparative advantage. And since the only subjectively precious thing that goes into the pool through social production is knowledge, as personal time-space, it is such time-space, or human life, that all go after. It may help embellish this harsh truth to talk about 'goods', instead of about commodities, but only magic can explain how public good may obtain from mutual envy and only economists can see bliss in the faces of Western consuming maniacs, by twisting the meaning of welfare.

The way things stand in today's capitalistic societies, one better visit a competent psychiatrist if one sees greater contentment in the faces of affluent consumers than in the faces of less prosperous peoples. And it strikes as odd that one can clearly see struggle *for life* in the struggle between animal predator and animal prey, or between two animals fighting for the same prey, while thinking that the rivers of blood and immeasurable pain which humans inflict upon each other is only about oil as oil, fertile land as such, seaway passages, democratic values (as cynically claimed lately), etc. These are just pretexts. It all comes down to Life, basically.

Exogenous tastes wipe out motivation. As Hodgson (1993: 33) put it, 'confident in the Newtonian metaphor of the indivisible "individual" particle, mainstream economics traditionally proscribes discussion of the psychological or social foundations of individual purposes and preferences as being beyond the bounds of the subject'. But in spite of such brave concessions, economics earned little esteem among positive scientists. Here is a blow from a topmost physicist: 'Trying to fit human behavior, and especially problems of society, into the Procrustean bed of some necessarily limited mathematical framework has already brought much grief to the world. For instance, the science of economics has often been used in that way with unfortunate consequences' (Gell-Mann, 1995: 366). Similarly, Kalman (1980) argued: 'Most analytical economics today is done by trying to isolate some part of the problem from the whole and then hoping that exceptional brilliance (or oversimplification) can yield more insight than was had before.... I do not believe that it can work in system-determined problems.' And referring to the economists' obsession with optimization: 'it would be extremely naïve to jump to the conclusion that these [maximization principles] are the only interesting systems. Actually, most of the interesting systems (probably even in economics) do not arise from maximization considerations and at present their organizing principles are known incompletely or not at all' (ibid.). Things have come to such a head, that there are even those who protest that the Nobel Memorial Prize in Economics is just a money award by the Bank of Sweden (see the debate through the pages of the Swedish *Dagens Nyheter*, in December 2004), and there are scientists in other fields who claim that this reflects negatively on the status of their science and on their work.

Holub *et al.* (1992) claim that it is hard to find something worth reading in today's economic journals. And yet, economists enjoy a privileged relationship with power, which gives them effective immunity and establishes conditions favourable for the fulfilment of their prophecies. Their performance is not evaluated impartially and there has been agreed upon no dependable benchmarks, consistent performance criteria or measures of reference. When facts do not contradict their theories, economists demand praise. When reality refutes them, they claim that things would be worse, had their advice not been heeded. And when their advice is not heeded, they can argue that things would have been better if it had. They abuse concepts and language. They count hirings but not firings. They often even count firings as job openings. They can speak about free markets and free competition in the midst of huge conglomeration. (Considering stockholding structures, there are fewer car or camera makers or milk-producing companies today than there were before full-blown neo-liberalism, and there are not really many more telephone companies either.) None checks them for declaring now an economy to be overheated, while finding it to be sluggish in the very next conversation. For their services in diverting attention from its odious aspects, they are rewarded by the system. According to Di Ruzza and Halevi (2004: 141), 'the discourse of economists is not more informed than that of the lay person who bothers to read quality newspapers...The only element that can give the economist an advantage is the possible role of a priest in the corridors of power...The advantage comes from having insider's information.'

Fullbrook (2005) names eight acclaimed American academic institutions intimately connected with the American military and political establishment, and three 'top journals', which publish mostly articles written by economists affiliated in one way or another with the 'Big Eight'. Through such bootstrapping, 'The "best" departments are those who publish in their own journals, which are "best" since they publish the "best" departments. As they comment, this academic incest would be considered genetically unsound if it involved biological reproduction' (Canterbery and Burkhardt, 1983: 28). This works like an Ivy Leaf over a shameful gazing gap between theory and reality.

The gap is widening. Keynes (1936: 33) noted that 'professional economists... were apparently unmoved by the lack of correspondence between the results of their theory and the facts of observation; – a discrepancy which did not escape people's notice, with the result of a growing unwillingness to accord to economists that measure of respect which he gives to other groups of scientists.' This is no less true for today's mainstream economists who 'teach that all is for the best in the best of all possible worlds provided that we will let well alone' (ibid.), so: 'It may well be that the classical theory represents the way in which we should like our Economy to behave. But to assume that it actually does so is to assume our difficulties away' (ibid.: 34).

One may find even harsher self-criticism, as in Eichner (1983). Hodgson (1999: xvii) argues that 'the conceptual apparatus of much of mainstream economic theory is ill-suited to the task of both understanding our present condition and of envisioning a viable future. In particular, mainstream economics has become increasingly narrow and formalistic, unable even to grasp the institutional and cultural essentials of the market system that many of its exponents propound'. Blaug (1997: 3) protests:

> Modern economics is sick. Economics has increasingly become an intellectual game played for its own sake and not for its practical consequences for understanding the economic world. Economists have converted the subject into a sort of social mathematics in which analytical rigour is everything and practical relevance is nothing. To pick up a copy of *The American Economic Review* or *The Economic Journal* these days is to wonder whether one has landed on a strange planet in which tedium is the deliberate objective of professional publication. Economics was once condemned as 'the dismal science' but the dismal science of yesterday was a lot less dismal than the soporific scholasticism of today.

It may be more near the truth to say that modern economics was stillborn to the Industrial Revolution. However involved and detailed an analysis of production or supply-side issues may be, exogenous tastes and commodity-based utility annihilate its value by sidestepping active consumer participation, a vital component of a single, integrated process. Any theory that fails to explain tastes ignores the history and intentions of agents, their groping generation of knowledge in pursuit of some goal, in a word, their ontology. It ignores an obvious fact: In society, every choice made by one affects all others. Yet, consumers are treated by theory as supporting cast in a play where only producers take initiatives. Consumers do not contribute anything of import, and they are not accountable for their preferences. Lacking a uniform motive or connecting law, markets are assigned the opposite role from that which they really perform: They are supposed to reconcile confusion, when what they actually do is to help generate variety by inducing consumers to keep changing their tastes, cognitively and interdependently, precisely as producers compete against each other for profits. They help them invent wants, pushing the system away from every equilibrium or market-clearing state under which consumer tastes would be conclusively reconciled with the producers' desire for profits.

A theory of capitalism in which consumers apply no discretion is aimless. If all discretion were on the supply side, capitalism would be finished with the coals of Newcastle and the manufacturing plants of Manchester. A theory that does not accommodate an active role for consumers in generating economically relevant knowledge has a counterfeit relationship with time. As Hume (2000: 262–3) argued, the liberty to pursue some intent is always conditioned upon some causal necessity:

> We feel that our actions are subject to our will on most occasions, and imagine that the will itself is subject to nothing; ... But ... we can never free ourselves from the bonds of necessity. We may imagine we feel a liberty within

ourselves; but a spectator can commonly infer our actions from our motives and character; and even where he cannot, he concludes in general, that he might, were he perfectly acquainted with every circumstance of our situation and temper, and the most secret springs of our complexion and disposition. Now this is the very essence of necessity.

But the proper way to interpret such necessity is at the backdrop of its fountain and sink: All human necessity and intent are conditioned upon staying alive. Reason attends to this passion but, as Hume (op. cit.: 280) explained, what we construe as reason is actually passions that 'operate more calmly, and cause no disorder in the temper: Which tranquillity leads into a mistake concerning them, and causes us to regard them as conclusions only of our intellectual faculties.'

So, it is the passion for life that drives economic calculation, but the exogenous-tastes coup d'état did away with this and with its unpredictable endogenous disruptions, making room for an Arrow-Debreu, digital-logic kind of world, in which prices are able to shuffle things around until they come to rest at some state. But no agent is ever content with any *perpetuum immobile* state, however optimal this may be. They all want to do better, pulling away from every such state, towards gaining comparative advantage by exploiting knowledge that is not available to others, in a quest for what we may call 'exclusive non-ignorance'. Innovative advantages are constantly pursued, gained and annihilated. Attractors are made to recede through endogenously generated change. Targets are always moved forwards by action of producers and consumers alike, which unison, if ignored, makes theorizing like trying to decipher an ongoing encrypted conversation, after having deleted a random one half of the code.

These are not unknown to economists. Schmookler (1966) argued that the interesting part of economic change is not due to external causes, but to forces which develop within the system itself, and he provided historical data documenting that inventiveness is activated by demand-side forces. One may appreciate little the inventiveness that relates to needs, which are largely dictated by nature, although we will examine how these, too, become involved in the novelty-generation process. But wants have reached a crescendo in present-day capitalism that bears little relation to the conditions of the past. Consumer discretionary participation overtook Marxic analysis and limited, with its volatile dynamics, the relevance of the equilibrium paradigm.

Clearly, theory must abstract the vital features of reality and use simplifying devices. But as some of the details pruned off may become important with time, it must also be flexible enough to accommodate changes. Discretionary consumption has become too important to ignore. Dichotomous reasoning about demand and supply is not anymore capable of attending to changes, so it must be replaced by one that treats them in unison and acknowledges what they share. Distinguishing between capital goods and consumables obscures that they are both man-made and embody human time-space. It also leads to a capitalist-versus-worker division, obscuring the universality of agent motives and goals.

Separating production and consumption has provided facile answers to complex questions by assuming their crux out. Ignoring intersubjectivity of preferences, for example, allowed assuming them to be complete, consistent and transitive, which then allowed hypothesizing aggregate demand relations. A system was thus entertained that was self-contained and complete, whereas the real one was dauntingly under-determined, inexorably open to knowledge. Completeness implies that all competing alternatives are known. Then, since agents are rational and self-interested, as is the reasonable operational assumption, their selections among options must be optimal, under some criterion. In self-organizing systems, a selection criterion invokes a goal. In complete and closed ones, the notion of goal as activity is basically meaningless. Reality can never be optimal, except if one ignores the relation between real time and knowledge. Optimality is only of systems which are closed on knowledge, as are designed systems or mechanisms. In contrast, economic agents change with their own choices the sets of alternatives from which they are called upon to choose. Consumption-related knowledge in particular opens new possibilities, that is, buying opportunities, and places agents in volatile choice situations. At issue then is the mechanism and internal logic of this opportunities-generating process.

One cannot turn to neoclassicism for finding such answers. Radically different approaches are needed, which will tackle head on the issue of consumer participation in the process whereby appropriative knowledge is produced, complementing knowledge on the production side and augmenting output value. We know a lot about capitalists, as all emphasis in all theories has been placed upon them. They may sell a 'new' CD by a long-deceased singer. They can sell decorative cockroaches, or junk food as healthy. They can sell at very high prices rigged football games and Bermuda triangles. And we think we know why they do this, but we really don't, unless we discern the power element that underlies their visible profit-seeking and a similar motive that lures consumers into behaving *accordingly*. We need to explain why consumers do buy junk food or cockroaches, help elect neo-liberal governments that assist capitalists in making huge profits, and support a system that supports profit taking, in spite of their filing some occasional complaints. Actually, their complaining is about not having enough to spend in order to support the system even more effectively. We do know that people grumble when they are called upon to pay the high costs of their own choices. But we do not know why they make such choices.

No convincing answers can be found unless functional antagonism is acknowledged at all levels and unless the license of the lay person to collude is revoked, and he is held accountable. Unless, outside theory, a supersized consumer can sue a fast-food chain and win, but one can also sue parents for stuffing their children with junk food. This revoking campaign never took off, because anyone who might attempt it would face the wrath of the masses that always punish those who put to risk their short-sighted interests, or expose their insidious power that stems from ignorance and from their large numbers. The ordinary person is infected with a positive disposition towards growth, because he is convinced that he can reap benefits from it; that he can loot more from the commons (and from nature) if the gross output is bigger. To this end, he evades taxes and does everything a capitalist would do, for the same purpose. In what sense may ordinary people benefit, what such belief is based on and how it actually promotes growth, these must be explained in detail, as also why consumers become disappointed, once in a while, as in the recent protracted slow-down, which cannot be attributed to technological sluggishness, expensive capital, some adverse externality or explained through the usual income distribution arguments understood as relating simply to the volume of consumption. It needs to be explained how the system may stall due to *structural* inefficiencies caused by innovative sluggishness or dissonance on the consumption side, causing the two innovation processes to go out of tune with each other. But that presupposes that we acknowledge that a knowledge process does take place in the consumption sphere.

Grumbling about capitalist exploitation while refusing to look into such consumer-related facts impedes also social awareness. Siding with the underdog is soothing, but we must ask the millions of starving Africans who *they* think is an underdog in the West. Capitalism has not been imposed on anyone and, as Schumpeter has argued, it will wither only if people cease to be well disposed towards it. Or, our theory adds, if capitalists, swept by greed, become arrogant enough to regress to past inequitable states, stifling consumer innovative sentiment. Social homeostasis (defined as self-preservation within a variable environment) may be destroyed then, raising people's awareness beyond short-sighted materialism. (Cf. Wiener, 1948: 160–2; Hirsch, 1977: 95 ff., chs 10 and 11.) Critics of capitalism are quick to condemn those who succeed in getting what all want: to grab power through control and ownership of the product of the labour of others. But they neglect that people are happy if they think they are, so *he* may win who can make them think that way. People hate to think that they are not smart or capable enough. (Socrates argued that a fool is a fool because he thinks that he knows more than he really does.) So, they may choose to participate in a game of wits, even though there may be little or no chance of winning.

In view of such evidence, an honest theory of consumer behaviour and choice must explain rivalry in consumption, the genesis and development of tastes, that is, how demand is actually shaped. It must explain the ubiquitous cynicism of capitalistic rationalization. Barring this, the following hilarious passage may pass as a rough but fair description: A capitalist is one who owns capital and draws profits from its employment and from exploiting workers, according to competitive prices, given consumer preferences. A worker is a victim of capitalists. He works under conditions set by the market for factors and for commodities, upon which he has little or no say. Consumers are both workers and capitalists, but they enter as a separate species, helping the system to determine prices by revealing their preferences. They parachute equipped with set tastes, in markets complete with commodities, over which they have no say. As their tastes change in mysterious ways, prices adjust so as to make for capitalists the most profit out of capital (or surplus out of workers). As reward for helping capitalists to make such profits, an allocation is magically found whereby consumers maximize utility, which is something they like. The only task remaining for theory is to spell out the maximizing calculus, without having to explain the origin of anything or to decipher behaviour. Chaos that could result from uncontrolled volatility of tastes is avoided and the system is co-ordinated to make selfishness work to everyone's benefit through some nebulous mechanism intervening through markets and other institutions. This way, exogenous motivational diversity is smoothed out by some equally exotic *deus ex machina*.

These place theory at a distance from facts, providing material for tale or fiction. Surely, the concept of *transition* has challenged philosophers, but if emergence is missing from a description there can be no explanation. Emergence may be visited inductively. For example, one could draw from phenomena such as the huge-scale, unprecedented, one-shot privatization of public wealth after the collapse of the Soviet Block. Even before the emergence of a competent capitalist class, one may see the intriguing and telling emergence of large, rapacious consumer populations and of organized crime. Such enquiries could inform theory and disturb ideological complacency, but economists prefer to retain old views and methods dressed up in new modelling clothes, raising more questions than they answer. Little can be new in a new model. Real newness is in method and in theory. One such enquiry is: In what frame of reference is there a meaningful measure of individual accomplishment? What is in pecuniary gains beyond what appears to the eye? Without spelling economic motivation out and ascribing *specific* content to the notions of self-interest and scarcity, only makeshift answers can be provided. Explanation based on static concepts is bound to be overtaken by facts, since social dynamics entails primarily a development of human capacities. And explanation is *pro tem* if it pertains to one kind of economic arrangement only, without supplying a frame for explaining all stages of development. Motivation must embrace all previous and future stages, and this is Weberian. As Polanyi (1944: 45–6) pointed out:

> Max Weber was the first among modern economic historians to protest against the brushing aside of primitive economics as irrelevant to the question of the motives and mechanisms of civilized societies. The subsequent work of social anthropology proved him emphatically right. For, if one conclusion stands out more clearly than another from the recent study of early societies it is the changelessness of man as a social being. His natural endowments reappear with a remarkable constancy in societies of all times and places; and the necessary preconditions of the survival of human society appear to be immutably the same.

Ostentatious rigorousness

In economics, useful observables are contingent, diverse, seemingly disparate and conflated. What is regular or invariant is obscured by a mist of appearances. One cannot expect theories of behaviour to be provable in a strict sense, as is possible for propositions in logic, or to be refutable in Popperian fashion. As Aristotle (1934: X. i. 3) argued: 'In matters of emotion and of action, words are less convincing than deeds; when therefore our theories are at variance with palpable facts, they provoke contempt, and involve the truth in their own discredit.' But palpable facts are themselves mind-perceptions, to be constantly reassessed, and economic conduct is not haphazard. The turbulent surface may not conceal an all-permeating underlying regularity that is nebulously called self-interest. Once this nebulousness is cleared, it must be possible to construct robust theories grounded firmly upon sound principles, capable of explaining parsimoniously what derives from this fundamental regularity, and this includes almost everything that economic theory should be concerned with.

Such a theory must necessarily be a theory of knowledge. Knowledge processes do not lend themselves to the kind of description appreciated in mainstream theorizing, but experience with such theorizing has shown that from unwarranted rigorousness imposed artificially on a field that does not, by its nature, yield to it, only theological narratives can obtain. The initiating assumptions of neoclassical theory are indeed theological. Shackle (1972: 342) maintained that 'Proof, as the mathematician understands it, is very seldom attained in the kind of reasonings with which economists (rightly) content themselves. A rigorous proof is necessarily about abstractions. Proof exists in thought, and can be composed only of thought-entities designed for its purpose.' Therefore, discovering and explaining behavioural regularities is more important than providing correct proofs of unreal propositions, and theories should be judged on the basis of their logical coherence, plausibility and explanatory power.

We can draw more from Aristotle (op. cit.: I. vii. 18): 'we must not look for equal exactness in all departments of study, but only such as belongs to the subject matter of each, and in such a degree as is appropriate to the particular line of enquiry'. And 'discussions about our emotions and actions only admit of such degree of definiteness as belongs to the matters with which they deal' (ibid.: IX. ii. 6). Since economics is open to human initiation, it is impossible to construct exact theories of choice. Choice is non-exact, by nature. In a context that is closed on knowledge there can be exact *selection* among known alternatives, but that hardly constitutes *choice*. The substance of choice lies in its being made under uncertainty about the alternatives one is called upon to choose from, about yields and future outcomes, and it makes sense for an agent to engage in choice making only if he or she is guided by some particular goal. Moreover, choice entails risk: not being able to tell, even in retrospect, what choice would have been best (or better), because alternatives and measures of preferability are updated by the very process of making choices. The choices one agent makes, especially as concerns the way of expending (or saving) his or her income, alter the domain over which other agents are called upon to make choices and apply discretion, affecting interest rates, prices, fashions, etc. Discretion is context dependent. So, an exact theory of behaviour is bound to be too rigid to keep up with endogenously generated newness, flimsy and unreliable. In this field, exact is not robust.

Such is bound to be any theory that is initiated from industrial *Homo economicus*, who is void of passions and intellect that produce knowledge and is alien to time and to society. He may be omniscient about information but in the real world his calculations collapse, since the goal recedes as others, too, try to reach it. As others succeed, one loses ground and is spurred on to look for new knowledge that can help him catch up, not fall farther behind, or take over those who have taken over him. No closed theory can explain how such knowledge is produced, or predict what knowledge will be produced, because these belong with the future. Predicting knowledge is predicting the future, which is of astrology.

So, closure abolishes knowledge and choice. Under closure, consumers can simply reveal reactively their preferences over given commodities at set prices, which must always react to exogenously generated preference changes so as to pull the system towards a market-clearing level. The only relevant dynamics are gravitational, as the system lapses passively to some Pareto optimal equilibrium. Every attempt at gaining comparative advantage is foiled. Consumers observe commodities and prices but not their neighbours' purchases. The truth, however, is that all watch their neighbours, optimality is in comparative advantage, everyone hates market clearing, and there is nothing that pushes towards equilibrium other than a natural tendency of all systems towards least action, *if left undisturbed*. But, instead of leaving the system undisturbed, agents try to beat the market and subvert its clearing by taking advantage of private knowledge so as to improve their ranking, forcing others to do the same. Even simple bargaining is exploiting one's personal knowledge to one's own advantage.

There is ideology in market-clearing prices, which picture transactions as exchanges of equivalents, hence fair, to the presumed benefit of both parties. Such prior belief cannot be reconciled with the positional antagonism that characterizes capitalism, and the fault in such reasoning is in the implicit assumption about contemporaneousness. In real time, no two things can be contemporaneous, since the present is a non-dimensional moment, while every real process has duration and an own time profile, no two such profiles being same. Costs are not simultaneous with proceeds, utility drawing (whatever that might mean) is not simultaneous with purchasing, and so on. Thus, forces never really balance as they develop in time, upon ever fresh knowledge. Economic systems are knowledge systems, borne of the sublime agent whose performance determines their development path, within limits set by an environment. Therefore, they exist and are worth studying only to the extent that, and in the sense that, they are open to flows generated by this agent.

The impossibility of evading this knowledge-based reality is plain to the fact that even neoclassical reasoning is forced to admit it. By ignoring the sublime qualities of labour, 'old' theories of growth got stuck with the false idea of non-accumulatable labour, which implied diminishing marginal productivity of capital and the dismal conclusion that growth cannot be sustained, in the long run. Thus, all economics was Malthusean, in final analysis. *New* growth theories à la Romer or Lucas were hailed as great achievement for admitting the obvious: human-capital inputs do accumulate, in the form of a knowledge stock whose increments are partly embodied in capital items and partly in processes, institutions, skills, dexterities or other improvements to labour, so that diminishing returns could be overcome. Only, in typical neoclassical fashion, they assumed a production-function black box for knowledge, superposing it on the usual production function for commodities and making it shift by increasing factor productivities. Now, that is too inventive to be true: You travel faster than thought, catch newness in a bottle, and then sit and watch it work foreseeable miracles for you. So, where is newness?

Such defects prevent theory from tackling structure dynamics even of a purely technical nature.[2] The problem is already with definitions. A frequently cited definition of economics is that given by Robbins (1935: 16): 'Economics is the science which studies human behaviour as a relationship between ends and scarce means which have alternative uses.' And: 'Economics is entirely neutral between ends; ... in so far as the achievement of *any* end is dependent on scarce means, it is germane to the preoccupations of the economist' (ibid.: 24, original emphasis). Also: 'scarcity of goods ... is the subject matter of our science' (ibid.: 78).

Definitions must be sufficiently wide to be meaningful, but not too vague or general, lest they become useless. The above definition starts promisingly by invoking human behaviour, but (a) makes this void, by assuming neutrality between ends and (b) is vague by not defining scarcity. If scarcity is construed as emerging exogenously (say, as some natural shortage of labour, material inputs, etc.), then causes become out of the question. But affluence cannot be man-made, if scarcity is a plague. Scarcity has to be man-made as well, since the two are correlative. If there is anything that is scarce, this can only be in our minds, with which we value things and come up (or not) with a perception of affluence. If we could make up our minds about how much of each thing we need or want, we might be able to make all of them in sufficient quantities, allocating appropriately the needed resources, whence ... scarcity would be scarce. But we are in no position to make up our minds. We constantly *need to be generating scarcity*, because what we feel deprived of is what we ourselves put into commodities, obeying an impulse. And that is the time-space (or the energy, as is commonly understood) of those who make them. So, it is life that is ultimately scarce, as we experience it through the knowledge we ineluctably procure. Our yearning for artefacts is actually a desire for power over humans through command over their labour, which we experience as an extension of our personal and *own-ed* time-space.

Historical conditions bear on reality and on theory. While the basic needs of people were not met, it was reasonable for Smith to argue that some good should obtain from social activity in pursuit of self-interest, from butcher and baker *and consumer* alike, as there was little else that could drive people to engage in generating urgently needed value. But it is unreasonable to maintain the same today, when the issue is about unlimited wants. The logical gap between oppositional scrambling at the individual level and the notion of a common good reflected, say, in GDP growth has become gazing. GDP is too dubiously connected with welfare, as has been tenaciously argued by Hirsch, Scitovsky, Tobin, Nordhaus, Layard and others. But such a connection has been exploited ideologically, in order to hide the fundamentally distressful nature of capitalism. As Keynes (op. cit.: 129) noted: 'Pyramid-building, earthquakes, even wars may serve to increase wealth, if the education of our statesmen on the principles of the classical economics stands in the way of anything better.' Car accidents, natural disasters or other calamities may contribute to GDP growth. Crime generates demand for security services. These are, as Hirsch named them, 'regrettable necessities'. A worker who gets sick and uses capital-intensive, high-productivity medical services may add more to GDP by getting sick, than by his own lower-productivity industry. GDP would grow if illegal trade such as drugs, arms or prostitution were included in the social accounts. Should we make people sick, pray for disasters, mug each other, take drugs or seek sex in the flesh market? Would we thus promote welfare?

If such GDP growth advances welfare, then society has gone bankrupt. And if theory says that it does, then theory has gone bankrupt. The argument mainstream theory puts forward in defence of its obsession with GDP is that, if one feels insecure, then buying a gun increases his utility. But why not if for similar reasons one buys heroin? These ignore *unpleasant, worrisome arousals*, which are contingent upon choices made socially, focusing only on what calms or exorcizes such arousals and ignoring their causes. Discovering utility in every transaction that increases money velocity is absurd, and these illustrate the impossibility of addressing causes, if agents are assumed to be complete.

Completeness makes impossible a truthful analysis of dynamical issues. What is usually called 'economic dynamics' is the dynamics of mechanisms, or of designed systems. Such dynamics, whose pinnacle is optimal-control models, are better fit for centrally planned and controlled economies than for capitalist ones. Actually, they negate capitalism by finding something 'optimal', which means unprofitable to change, thus revealing through their exaggerated assertiveness that optimization is a façade for hiding the fact that power is the real capitalistic motive for all agents, in all their activities. Entrapped in such inordinate perception of dynamics, whenever real dynamical issues are forced upon theory, a dead-end situation arises.

Labour displacement by technological innovations provides such an example. Briefly stated, the question is: Do producers promote innovations that reduce dependence on labour because labour demands push its price higher, or does any change that lowers unit cost is equally welcome? In other words, is there a labour-induced bias of innovation, or is there not? Outside a knowledge context, it is virtually impossible to determine what causes relative factor prices to change, because it is impossible to explore the possibility of causality running in the other direction, so that factor prices, employment and productivities could be decisively changed by innovation. Similarly, it is impossible to distinguish what forces transmit through the system a cost-reducing innovation or a novel consumption pattern, or what determines (the movements of) price elasticities, which in turn determine diffusion of benefits to consumers.

Insatiability provides another example of a debate conducted upon wobbly conceptual foundations. For the optimizing calculus of consuming automata to apply, the utility hypersurface for any bundle of commodities must have, in the region of interest, positive first (and negative second) partial derivatives. For any particular commodity, demand is in this sense insatiable for rational agents, that is, more of the said commodity is better than less (at a decreasing rate). Some argue that demand for commodities is satiable. Ackerman (2002: 58) claims that 'consumer desires are satiable. That is to say, it is possible to have enough of many things. People typically stop eating before the refrigerator is empty.' So, it is right to say with Ackerman that the insatiability assumption is silly, if it refers to particular commodities. In fact, more may even be worse than less, meaningless or impossible. (One can choke to death by eating many steaks.) But, historically, the rate at which money is spent to keep the refrigerator from becoming empty keeps increasing, which speaks more of the provider than of the provisions, and so Ackerman is correct again in observing the irrelevance of a utility notion based on commodities, or on commodity-based properties. Demand for money, the general commodity or operational standard, is by all indications insatiable. Wants are endlessly expanded, because our angst always remains, and (which is another expression of the asymmetry between past and future time) the *experience* of buying a particular commodity does not coincide with the *expectations* before buying it. As soon as we buy it, its utility starts fading because of its positional nature. So, we turn our attention to the next purchase. In other words, the fixed-utility hypersurface in a fixed state space assumption of mainstream theory is irrelevant. Insatiability applies to a continuously upgraded state space, as new commodities appear that replace old ones, and to a continuously changing utility hypersurface. More money is better than less, because new wants emerge along with new knowledge about new commodities, and about old commodities which thus become in effect new.

These support Marshall's observation that each want may be limited, but wants are of an endless variety. What needs to be explained then is what makes wants emerge, in the first place. But what gives rise to demand for some item, that is, what the ultimate source of scarcity is, can be decided only by spelling intentions out. Such intentions cannot be drawn from the analysis itself, since that would be circular. Some initiating idea or universal abstraction must be found that drives the process in a cohesive way, and that cannot be utility. Theory must be informed about what humans try to accomplish by coming into society and through economic activity. Without spelling out the intent of agent conduct, scarcity, self-interest and efficiency are empty. Nothing is scarce unless there is demand for it that obliges society to decide how to allocate limited resources to it, instead of to some other use. But what causes demand to appear, rise or fall needs to be explained, *limited* must not be confused with *scarce*, and any presumed *telos* must not imply some stable attractor, induce determinism or prescribe particular outcomes. It must rather be construed as a stable and uniform *pursuit*. If this were not so, one could legitimately expect any fixed telos to have been reached long ago. So, with a little twisting of the language, we can speak in terms of some 'unreachable telos' or some 'dome attractor'.

Cohesion

The search for an underlying regularity that motivates actors and provides cohesion abides by what may be called 'First Principle of Science', stated thus by Friedman (1953: 33): 'A fundamental hypothesis of science is that appearances are deceptive and that there is a way of looking at or interpreting or organizing the evidence that will reveal superficially disconnected and diverse phenomena to be manifestations of a more fundamental and relatively simple structure.' Lawson (2004: 25) argues that 'the primary objects of science are the underlying mechanisms that govern the directly perceivable events and states of affairs of the world'. These mechanisms 'may operate inside and outside the experimental set-up alike. Thus the gravitational mechanism operates on autumn leaves…even as they fly over roofs and chimneys' (ibid.). Dopfer (2001: 173) insists that 'the essential question…is: is there any general sequential pattern that can be detected in long-run development, and what specifically accounts for the universality of such a pattern in time and space?' Shackle (op. cit.: 177) made a plea 'to find fixed relations amongst the wisps and eddies of a flowing mist'. Aristotle (1934: X. ix. 17) claimed: 'Science deals with the universal.'

In science, it is celebrated to resolve a complex riddle with a simple idea. Science is parsimonious. It purports to explain any observed diversity from a small set of principles, underlying causes or mechanisms, and it structures knowledge, instead of lining it up either randomly or taxonomically. The desire to discern order behind apparent chaos, to find harmony in variety and simplicity in the complex is a prime intellectual propensity. To be fair, there is also the metamodern idea of a 'flat' reality, with no depth, no underlying causes that need to be fathomed, and where all there is to events is equally visible (or equally not), in spite of what multifarious forces may be at work. The past does not enter the construction of the future. The future is created along the way, and nothing gets finished before time gets finished. These are two contrasting perspectives to openness, and there are others (e.g. the 'linguistic' perspective, as discussed briefly by Kaye-Blake, 2006).

We do not subscribe to a metamodern perspective, although its openness may tempt one to formulate aspects of our theory (e.g. the value-creation part of it to be discussed later) in such light. Instead, we seek to find a motivation-based theoretical structure upon which to explain the phenomenon of capitalistic cohesion, which has put conventional theories under strain. How does the system function in a more or less co-ordinated way, while atomistic conduct as understood neoclassically could, at least in principle, produce disruption or chaos? Our dissenting perception of the market apart, Metcalfe (1998: 6) gives a concise statement of the riddle:

> Modern capitalism presents us with a paradox. The individual acts of creativity on which its mechanisms of change depend are remarkable for their lack of co-ordination. Yet the consequences of this immense micro creativity depend deeply upon the strong co-ordination of the fruits of that creativity by market processes. The joining together of the uncoordinated striving for innovation with the subsequent market co-ordination of the resulting activities is for me the distinctive feature of the capitalist mode of change.

More generally, the issue is about uncontrollably flickering tastes in innovative pursuit of self-interest not causing havoc, but being reconciled, in some sense that needs to be explicated. Marshall and Ricardo attributed the system's self-adjusting capacity to fluidity of money wages. Keynes argued that interdependencies of real magnitudes are such that this explanation carries little value. The effects of money-wage changes may be varied, and there is little that ensures that they will not even be destabilizing. So, in chapter 18 of his *General Theory* he attributed any stability of economies to four psychological properties: the magnitude of the marginal propensity to consume, the propensity to invest in relation to the prospective yield of capital or the rate of interest, the relation between changes in employment and in money wages and, to a lesser extent, the rate-of-investment reaction to changes in the marginal efficiency of capital. But these are behavioural upshots, needing to be explained themselves, rather than performing as explaining agents.

No degree of exogenous diversity of tastes poses a problem of reconciling, *as long as they are treated as data*. The real question is: How are tastes produced endogenously and their *evolving* diversity reconciled, in view of the indisputable fact that they are interdependent and intersubjective? Mainstream theory has evaded this fundamental question, but volatility, which it could not deny, kept it alive. Aside from magic (invisible hands, auctioneers or demons), more matter-of-fact explanations were based on average modes of conduct in response to policy instruments. It was not explained, however, what makes such instruments to be both restrictive enough as to provide cohesion, and wide and flexible enough to provide room for the overwhelming capitalistic effervescence. From yet another angle, if society knew that it needed to impose constraints on itself so as to not go wild, then why want to go wild anyway? Implicit to such explanations is the assumption about some arbitrary power outside society, which judges on society's behalf about the appropriate degree of containment of (naturally?) generated variety.

Not far removed from these, institutionalist and evolutionary approaches also attribute cohesion to some kind of containment of behaviour through rules, laws, ethics and institutions around some hypothetical mean. Metcalfe (op. cit.: 130–1) notes: 'The evolutionary method does not conduct dynamic analysis around hypothetical long-period positions, but in terms of the prevailing distribution of behaviours in the relevant population. This is the method embodied in the replicator dynamic with its emphasis on the currently existing "distance from average behaviour".' Rules, ethics, etc. are seen as conventions or habits of thought that induce behavioural regularity through more or less voluntary subjugation, limiting freedom of will and keeping the informational load within manageable limits. Hodgson (1988, 1993) argues that without such structural rigidities agent behaviour could be chaotic. He also contends that institutions can be used as units of selection in an evolutionary model of the economy. Within such rigidities, imitation is also ascribed a role in avoiding chaos.

But how do averages about which things cluster come about? Or, which virtually amounts to the same, what contains behaviour around such averages? An evolutionary logic accommodates change through endogenous generation of knowledge, but this is seen basically as happening in adaptive response to changes in the environment. Systems are seen as evolving through adaptive selection among random variety. Selection is based on some criterion of fitness to a changing environment, and a common such criterion is that of reduced cost. Firms, the selection units, are better fit if they are more profitable. The boundary between system and environment is not made clear and the population over which 'average', 'least cost' and relevant measures are taken is set arbitrarily. In every case, changes are instigated by the environment. The system itself lacks any original and creative *intent*.

Evolution has always been a catchword concept. The concepts of variety generation, selection and fitness are wanting in accuracy. Almost anything changing seems possible to fit into an evolutionary description, to the point where this may become tautological: What materializes is (*ex post*) fit. What fails is unfit. The biological metaphor lets creep into social theorizing units of analysis possessing no motives, intention, ideology or meaningful ontology. Social variety is motivated and intended, and evolutionary approaches in general fail this. The belaboured way in which such explanations are put forward betrays that there is more left to be explained than is actually explained. The absence of *cause* is evident, but since causes reside *in the human ontology of agents*, if this ontology is ignored no causes can be found.

In principle, individualism and co-ordination are conflicting as notions. So, since it cannot be disputed that agents are self-interested, the only way the two can be reconciled is if there is some kind of intrinsic co-ordination to behaviour due to some underlying uniformity. In such case, the market becomes not a co-ordinating *mechanism*, but a *domain*, over which both conflict and co-ordination take place.

Note that just posing the question of cohesion disputes equilibrium, by admitting that the intentional conduct of agents is not such as to pull the system to rest, but disturbs its natural tendency towards least action. It is admitted, that is, that capitalism is restless, otherwise there would arise no issue of co-ordination or cohesion. The problem is not just that equilibrium cannot prevail if everyone tries to defeat it for personal gain, but also its informational content is almost nil, since it abolishes time. One way to be misled into thinking in equilibrium terms is by paying undue attention to followers. But when people emulate behaviour they are consciously and deliberately expanding their personal knowledge base through observation, and by acting upon such observation, trying to catch up or not fall behind, driven by the same urge that makes them innovate, at the same time. As a matter of fact, we may not even speak of consciousness without acknowledging some uniform motivation. Therefore, self-interest must be explained in a logical frame that, in itself, reconciles diversity.

Economics has adopted a different perspective. In chapter 2 of *The General Theory*, Keynes held it to be fallacious to suppose that 'there is a nexus which unites decisions to abstain from present consumption with decisions to provide for future consumption; . . . the motives which determine the latter are not linked in any simple way with the motives which determine the former' (op. cit.: 21). Even though this statement was made as part of the argument about non-coincidence of saving with investment (on which Keynes based his explanation about the logical possibility of involuntary unemployment due to a distinction between present and future, with respect to the latter decisions being of an expectational nature), such multiple-motive logic permeates all economic reasoning. But if I spend part of my income now and save the rest, I am not thus chasing two different goals, and neither is a producer chasing any third goal by deciding how much to invest. We both execute time-profiled strategies aiming at a single, time-dimensioned, which means *real*, goal. Such time-realism of economic choices makes necessary a money-medium for providing buffering and headroom for non-simultaneity. Uniqueness of this time-dimensioned goal then must supply the nexus that eluded Keynes, with *time* being *knowledge*.

A uniform motivational mechanism is not just an instrument. It is *sine qua non* for intrinsically coherent dynamics, and economic dynamics cannot but be intrinsically coherent. Without such mechanism, only piecemeal explanations of economic change can be provided, which is bound to leave major issues unresolved. For example, apportioning productivity growth from technological change to its sources proved to be extremely difficult. Even the lesser issue of aggregate output growth has not been resolved to general agreement. Antonelli (2003: 34) comments thus:

> The basic puzzle remains a problematic core for this interdisciplinary area of specialization. How innovations come to the market place, how novelty takes place in our understanding of the economic and technological interplay, how and why total factor productivity grows, how firms and economic agents at large generate and react to the introduction of novelty – these are still open questions.

In trying to resolve these, much common knowledge has been ignored. It is known, for example, that there can be no sustained development unless both producers and consumers reap benefits. To this end, consumers modify their demand patterns, which determine the composition of the market demand vector and, in turn, the composition of output. For fast structural growth, these vectors must be resonant with the eigenstructure of the technological matrix, as we shall see in Part II. However, the constructive role played by consumers was almost obliterated by reduction to utility hunting. Even when demand was given some thought, this was almost always through scale: as aggregate demand. Composition (structure), wherein lies all dynamic substance, was basically ignored. The notions of average or representative consumer employed, or the household, as unit of analysis, smoothe or wipe out consumer-knowledge dynamics. But as Polanyi (1958/62) hammered, *knowledge is personal*.

The decisive contributions by consumers would be impossible to overlook if it were not for the fact that, unlike producer innovations, they come in little pieces, dispersed, conflated with other variables and impossible to account for separately. Thus, no systematic effort was put into accounting for the effects of consumers' market decisions, except through artificial (for sidestepping intersubjectivity) market demand relations. But these individually negligible inputs are infinitely many and, after Leibniz, we know that the sum of infinitely many infinitesimals is not necessarily zero or negligible. It may even be infinite. Consumer intervention is inconspicuous, but while each contribution is impossible to account for separately, when amassed they make great difference. This is precisely the same fallacy as in the broader social context where it is erroneously thought that history is made by great leaders (or big crooks), that individuals do not count for making good or for making bad, so they are neither accountable, nor can one expect from (each one of) them any improvements.

Language matters. Fallacies inform language and language helps establish them as 'received views'. The above fallacy, which we may call *imperceptibility fallacy*, after having approached it as *misplaced innocence*, distils into saying, for example, that cars 'come equipped with alarms', implying tacitly that what goes into cars is in the car-makers' discretionary jurisdiction. As misplaced innocence, the same fallacy asserts itself in speaking about 'car accidents', or in suing fast-food chains and cigarette makers, but not parents. Employing false language carries its own weight. One is led to believe that all the observed ascription of value to mountains of garbage is no consumers' fault, but a feat or a ploy by greedy capitalists, to the end of reaping profits. One is then misled into seeing the use of such garbage as meeting some real need, or as innocent caprice. By imperceptible extension, consumers are thus also cleared of blame for alarms taking off in the middle of the night, or for the nutrition (and not only) crimes they commit against their own children. Actually, consumers are completely cleared of blame. They are...simply consumers! Thus, one would consider it outrageous if someone claimed (as I do) that these are all about life-taking, even though in less than full awareness and in indirect ways, and one would be even more enraged if people were held responsible also for any lack of awareness through habitualization.

One comes across this imperceptibility fallacy in various contexts. Take books, for example. Nothing could be farther from the truth than that a book is finished with its writing; that it is only a writer's feat. This may be true of books that were not worth writing anyway, but the true value of a book is behind the lines, in what the readers can make out, on their own, even by rejection after scrutiny. A book contributes its audience. If it arouses them to further(ing) thoughts, it is laudable. If it spells clearly all the details out, it is at best of very limited value. As a different example, if you tell someone that he pollutes by leaving appliances in stand-by mode, he will probably laugh at you, as he stands aloof to infinitesimals. But the stand-by mode of appliances has become an issue in environmental fora.

Why should economists who know about integral calculus need to be alerted to these? Because, if consumers' innovative contributions were accounted for, then they would have to be accepted into the picture complete with passions and brains, that is, with a human ontology, which would prohibit closing the system, speaking with certitude, concealing the malevolence that is intrinsic to their economic conduct and providing ideological cover for capitalism.

So, mainstream economics is content with consumers eating junk food simply because they like it. It actually *starts* from this, assuming with equal liberty that they maximize utility. The system becomes a mechanism then, and its response becomes in principle known: Whatever any agent may do is by force of some maximum principle. Such systems generate no variety. All variety comes from outside, is taken as datum, and there is no *purpose* or *choice*, which means no real *action*; only passive obedience to the principle. The relation between stimulus and response does not change with time, and it is definitely not changed by volition of the subjects themselves. If it changes for some outside reason, then the system is studied anew in a similar manner. Such response can always be placed in an optimization context (brachistochrone, least action, etc.), for which situation in economics Kalman expressed little appreciation.

Intent or Will is not invoked in the kind of self-organizing system typically envisaged in evolutionary theories. There, it is basically the environment that selects among generated diversity. However, treating a thoroughly purposive economic system either as a mechanism or as such a self-organizing one frustrates much of what is worth investigating about it. Grant it that economic systems self-organize, this must be construed as meaning that *they purposefully choose among options they themselves generate, inside an environment upon which they act, so as to improve some measure of performance that they themselves have selected.* The environment plays only a possibilities-delimiting role. Social systems *act* on their environment. Optimization makes no sense within such an endogenously generative flux of alternatives. Social systems change themselves and their environment from within, by action of their agents in consistent pursuit of some goal. Whether that is done in full awareness or not is beside the point. In fact, the more deeply rooted the motive, the less consciously and more mechanically it is likely to be followed, so as to conserve mental energy. (Cf. Polanyi, 1966/83.)

To conclude: What is conventionally understood as an impressive capacity of capitalism to revolutionize the means of production and at the same time to proceed in cohesive fashion owes much to the structural dynamics of demand, through imperceptible consumer contributions to the stock of relevant knowledge, in pace with production capabilities expanded by technological and other supply-side innovations. This twin knowledge process makes it possible to produce and consume new products and services through continuous reassessment of their time-space content, promptly abandoning old consuming habits. Technological innovations affect directly an economy's physical input–output matrix. Consumption innovations affect directly the system of prices. The two combine to determine the value put out. Cohesion results from an underlying motivational uniformity.

One-sidedness – evading passions

Economic development goes along with cultural change. This means that all of society is involved in it, on a round-the-clock basis, not just one part of it, such as producers, or the entire population but only during work hours. It also means, conversely, that a particular type of economic development can be rejected on non-economic grounds, if it fails to become intertwined with the general culture of the relevant population. Economic development goes beyond growth and permeates all social life. Society brings about changes and learns to live with those, in complete cultural adaptation. However, as Rosenberg (1982: 141, original emphasis) notes: 'Economists have had much more success in dealing with the *consequences* of technological change than with its determinants.' Actually, not with all consequences but mainly with the lesser one of mere (scalar) GDP growth.

Ascribing all initiatives one-sidedly to producers in their quest for profits places the cart in front of the horses, given that we produce (and distribute income, etc.) in order to consume; not the other way around. Desires do not emerge *because* there are commodities. Rather, commodities emerge because there are desires. Logically, then, if motivational precedence were to be given to one side, it would be more reasonable that that should be consumption, to which should be traced also the basic determinants of technological change and productivity growth.

But the truth is that either kind of one-sidedness is unreal. Mowery and Rosenberg (Rosenberg, op. cit., ch. 10) discuss critically research that adopts a consumption-side bias and argue cogently against either a demand–pull or a supply–push priority. The existence of a market demand and of a technological opportunity are both necessary but not sufficient conditions for innovation to materialize, and there is no *a priori* reason why either one should take precedence in motivating innovative activity. They argue that 'any careful study of the history of an innovation is likely to reveal a characteristically iterative process in which *both* demand and supply forces are responded to' (ibid.: 232, original emphasis) and stress 'the pervasiveness of uncertainty in the innovation process' (ibid.: 234). One of their statements is particularly pertinent: 'Both the underlying, evolving knowledge base of science and technology, as well as the *structure* of market demand, play central roles in innovation *in an interactive fashion*, and neglect of either is bound to lead to faulty conclusions and policies' (ibid.: 195, emphases added).

Even when acknowledging an interplay between production and consumption, economists still do not view consumption as involving any significant amount or type of knowledge generation. In their calculations, the pragmatic essence of consumption as the initiator and final purpose of economic activity succumbs to a conceptual primacy of production, which is seen as being differently motivated. This causes a rift in the three basic activities, with income distribution also receiving little treatment. Thus, the road to a uniform motive that can explain cohesively what goes on in all markets is blocked. The economic process is compartmentalized and only one of its parts is examined in any useful detail. As Loasby (1999: 11) marks: 'Economists often rely on separation theorems to legitimise independent frameworks for the analysis of production and consumption, of resource allocation and the choice of transaction mode, of labour and financial markets, or of the real and the monetary economy.'

A production-oriented mentality is so prevalent, that even those who most dealt with consumption could not escape it. Thus, Scitovsky (1976: 5, emphases added) writes,

> The market transmits information among competitors and between buyers and sellers, thereby harmonizing their action.... the market...puts pressure to conform on buyers and sellers alike, and most of the conforming is done

by those whose behavior is the most flexible.... *producers have the greater power and influence.* [They] spen[d] billion[s] in advertising...– ample indication of their willingness to use that power. Harmony, therefore, between consumer preferences and the pattern of production may simply indicate *the adaptation of man's tastes to the rigid requirements of the production system...*

Evolutionary work has instigated interest in visiting consumption as a knowledge process whereby diversity is produced and selection is made, and has revived interest in psychological motivators of underlying regularities, which may be cognitive and emotional (Schlicht, 2000). But bias in favour of production still creeps in and supply-side considerations overwhelm economic thinking, as if casting some spell. Nelson (2001) claims that 'technology and institutions should be understood as coevolving, and... this coevolutionary process should be seen as the principal driving force behind economic growth'. Similarly, in his Prologue to *Evolutionary Economics and Creative Destruction*, Metcalfe (1998: 5) informs the reader that 'the overriding concern of these lectures is with the microeconomics of change arising from competition between different business activities'. Uncannily then, as it invokes personal knowledge in the midst of temporal asymmetry, one reads on: 'it is the distinguishing feature of modern capitalism that what it capitalizes upon is this infinite scope for the distributed and disaggregated generation of variety. Two individuals faced with the same market information may claim to know differently precisely because their different past experiences or different expectations lead them to interpret that information differently' (ibid.: 36). Also, in the Introduction to the collective volume titled *The Evolutionary Foundations of Economics*, Dopfer (2005: 3) informs that the contributors 'address one of the core issues of evolutionary economics: the change of economic knowledge as it applies to technology and production'. Adaptation, variety and selection are typically seen as applying to firms, methods, processes, institutions or some unit on this side. Finally, Pelikan (2001: 142) claims that, for sustainable development: 'The only hope is that people can learn in time to adapt their demands on their society to the constraints upon what the society can possibly deliver', arguing further that what he calls 'flexible organizing information' is supplied 'from a relatively few key roles, usually referred to as entrepreneurs or organizers, than from others'. Moreover: 'To be precise, there may also be other key roles, such as investors, consultants or public policy makers, which may potentially contribute helpful information' (ibid.: 144). How about consumers?

One can find in the literature declarations of intent which promise to treat consumption as a knowledge process, but most of them fall right through. Most kin to our perspective is Shackle's account of 'kaleidic economics', where consumption is indeed sketched as a value-creating activity. But in spite of its admirable elaborations, *Epistemics and Economics* still has an enterpriser flavour and a measure of reference is missing from its account of consumption.

In close proximity with Shackle's earlier work (Shackle, 1958), Lachmann (1959) noted about a dynamic market theory, as contrasts with Robinson type solitary dynamics and with perfect forward markets: 'The central problem of such a theory... concerns the distribution and transmission of knowledge in a market economy. Men make use of one another's resources and satisfy one another's wants. How, in a changing world, do they acquire the requisite knowledge about these changing wants and resources?'

Such work raised high hopes for a 'Scheme of Things Entire', to use Shackle's words, and for a realistic theory that does not annihilate any part of economic activity. The next step in Lachmann's syllogism would be to address *what* knowledge is requisite, *how* it is generated and *to what end*. Lachmann himself insisted that economics should address questions of purpose and of cause in ways that differ from the determinist methodology of the natural sciences. He argued: 'economics needs a methodology *sui generis*, at least in so far as it has to deal with creative acts of the mind, with the setting of objectives and the interpretation of experience, which have no counterpart in nature' (ibid.). And 'causal genesis is a legitimate concern of the social sciences... It warrants the employment of genetic-causal schemes of interpretation which give rise to methodological problems *sui generis*' (ibid.).

Decades later, though, along similar lines, Loasby (op. cit.: 6, emphasis added) still was obliged to insist:

> the purpose of many decisions is not to respond to events but to introduce change. It is a characteristic of modern societies that people wish the future to be in some ways different from the past: we therefore require knowledge not only to understand and adapt to what exists, and to the changes in what exists, *but in order to create change which will be acceptable to others*.

Loasby is concerned here with the role of knowledge in economic evolution. He argues that economics is about purposeful knowledge accumulation in all spheres of activity, *based on expectations about the behaviour of others*: 'Economics... needs a theory of choice; but it is important to pay attention to the ways in which these agents set about making their selections, and the influences upon them; and that requires a much richer conception of decision processes, and of the learning processes which underlie them, than is found in conventional choice theory...' (ibid.: 29). Moreover, 'it should not be forgotten that markets can also provide frameworks within which new ideas may emerge, from consumers as well as producers' (ibid.: 30). And in arguing that markets facilitate the employment of what he calls *consumer capital* into fruitful activities, he claims: 'If we do not need to think about how to transact, we can think more carefully about what to transact, and what uses to make of what we buy. We thus develop both indirect and direct capabilities which are complementary to the direct and indirect capabilities of producers' (ibid.: 125). Further,

> Economic evolution is shaped by consumer capabilities as well as by capabilities in production. This is not only because market selection depends on consumers' interpretations of what is being offered; we should not forget that

> consumers are also generators of variety, through their abilities to make use of the characteristics of products and services to solve their own problems, perhaps in combinations that no producer has ever imagined.
>
> (Ibid.: 126)

Finally: 'The evolution of demand is at once a major influence on the working of market processes and channelled by market institutions, and its analysis requires something more than conventional consumer theory' (ibid.: 127).

With these, Loasby touches upon all real substance. Through his Mengerian 'assumption of increasing knowledge' (ibid.: 113), his assessment of Coase's theses on transaction costs and many other passages like the above, Loasby raises a serious consumer issue for theory. And yet, his attention is again drawn to the firm and to the supply side, on account of the fact that 'Since many of these decisions are taken within firms, the study of these processes requires particular attention to the capabilities of firms' (ibid.: 29). Not that one can disagree with this, but a balanced, joint treatment of production with consumption is still wanting. Approaching production as a purposeful activity may seem natural, due to the fact that there is in it a tangible *incentive* for generating change, namely, profits. But profits need cognitive consumer contributions in order to be reaped, and such contributions make consumption a purposeful activity. In every case, one must explain the *motive* for seeking profits, if the notions of motive and incentive are not to be confused.

Unlike profit, which is adequate reason for putting in the effort to please consumer desires, entertaining consumers realistically in analysis makes it difficult to dodge the fact that economic conduct is by definition intersubjective, conflictive and essentially malevolent. So, it was found convenient to treat value as being created only by producers and innovations as being only of a make kind. Also, due to its hardly perceptible nature, consuming novelty is difficult to grasp or explain. And yet, Mokyr (2005) notes that, after much hesitation and forced by events, economic theory abandons the cosiness of efficient equilibrium in order to investigate the explanatory potential of cognitive processes, which induce increasing returns, multiple solutions (that may not be Pareto optimal or even desirable) and other complications that tend to make theory more realistic but less neat and exact. He cites particularly North's 'reaching to cognitive science in order to understand institutions' (ibid.: 201) and his pointing out that 'institutions set up the incentive structure of society but... people make choices on the basis of pay-offs. The way they perceive these pay-offs is a function of the way their minds interpret the information they receive' (ibid.). 'Hence the focus of our attention must be on human learning... and on the incremental process by which beliefs and preferences change over time' (North, 1990: 6).

Still, there has been shown little resolution to pursue incremental cognitive processes through which beliefs and preferences are formed. Economists settle for the lesser task of letting rational agents interpret and exploit information. The difference, of course, is that *knowledge* refers to newness produced incessantly along the way and changing contours, while *information* concerns existing knowledge and the brain processes whereby this is intercepted, stored and processed. (For a discussion of issues relating to knowledge versus information, see Potts, 2001.) How new pieces of knowledge are generated and to what end is far more important than is the handling of information. Real-time choice making by agents on the basis of pay-offs is circular, because choices made affect pay-offs. Choice would cease to be real or meaningful, if decisions and pay-offs orbited around a fixed knowledge base, where pay-offs would affect choices, one way only. Such closure would soon lead to a stable Paretean state of affairs, whose only relation with reality would be that it would provide a sense of intellectual comfort precisely because of lack of any uncertainty about the future, as there would be no reason to disturb the attained optimal state. (No fear of unknown.)

But science is Promethean, and the gods did not allow Prometheus to find a moment's quiet. His body was always reborn *in order to* be torn to pieces again, the myth implying that man himself is made of knowledge, which dissolves itself as it is born. Complications arising from such knowledge openness are known to cognitivists, who have travelled a long way towards unravelling knowledge processes. Varela *et al.* (1991: 139) point out that, cognitive sciences move away from the idea of the world as independent, extrinsic and representable through input and output relationships, to the idea of a world as inseparable from the structure of self-modifying knowledge processes. They cite the following passage from Minsky (1986: 288):

> Why are processes so hard to classify? In earlier times, we could usually judge machines and processes by how they transformed raw materials into finished products. But it makes no sense to speak of brains as though they manufacture thoughts the way factories make cars. The difference is that brains use processes that change themselves – and this means we cannot separate such processes from the products they produce. In particular, brains make memories, which change the ways we'll subsequently think. Because the whole idea of self-modifying processes is new to our experience, we cannot yet trust our commonsense judgement about such matters.

Compare our disagreement with the treatment of new knowledge by the so-called *new growth theories*. Minsky's comments explain why it is difficult to incorporate knowledge in the study of economic systems, but at the same time highlight the lack of realism of informational closure, a handicap of which economists have been aware. Thus, in discussing insecurity of prognoses and the lack of precise calculations on the part of investors about the marginal efficiency of an investment during its life cycle in relation to the prevailing rates of interest, Keynes (op. cit.: 150) noted: 'If human nature felt no temptation to take a chance, no satisfaction (profit apart) in constructing a factory, a railway, a mine or a farm, there might not be much investment merely as a result of cold calculation.' Similarly, Adam Smith acknowledged in his moral philosophy and in his economic writings that people never part with passions and sentiments and with the unexpected results of such non-rational guidance.

Schumpeter acknowledged passion and intellect to the service of profit seeking, but the clarity of his one-sided explication of capitalist change through disequilibrating, creative producer initiatives helped push consumption to the background. Economics was perceived even more than before as an entrepreneurs' chronicle. Thus, today economists need to be reminded that consumers contribute knowledge to the economic process, while those who are in the medical profession know well that patients contribute to the development of medicine and general health services, and that little can be done without the patients' active involvement. Similarly, no grammarian or linguist would consider explaining language as the feat of a few language makers who impose their linguistic constructs on society. Instead, they explain it as a social accomplishment, in which an entire society makes ongoing contributions in reasoned, lively, passionate and emotional animation. Suffice it to consider the interplay between slang and formal language.

Thus, we see two different kinds of rationality, and two kinds of motive, in a field where it seems much more plausible that an agent's entire personality, passion, physical and mental effort are trained at a single target. Personal identity builds up with time, within an evolving social context. Passions may have reason for emerging, but they are not rational. It is rationality, rather, that obliges to passions. Even if seen as based on *complete* knowledge, rationality is still not devoid of passion, because information is intercepted actively, picked up selectively and interpreted subjectively, by looking into the future, which means into the realm of expectations according to previous personal experiences as these relate to the expected future behaviour of others in one's environment. Even if agents maximized utility rationally within information, the kind of information they would harvest and the kind of use they would make of it would still bear the stamp of their distinct personalities. Any expectation of satisfaction to be drawn from commodities depends on subjective past experiences with consumption, in relation to others. Experiencing is a live, open process that does not allow passions or knowledge to settle. It is a stirring of emotions by the waiving of ignorance. Rationality and ignorance do not mix, except if one *defines a priori* as rational whatever a sane person might do, in meaningless tautological fashion. Real agents are, at best, *rationally speculative.*

Basing economic theorizing on pure reason makes it impossible to examine newness against the background of its intrinsic uncertainty and its underlying causes, since newness defies reason. Based on reason alone, it is neither possible to explain the violent emergence of capitalism nor what supplies it with vitality and thrust to break through barriers, melting age-old traditions and ways of life into all-homogenizing consumerism. So, explanation needs isolating some common human trait that crosses the same barriers.

To sum up, a serial chain of causalities that starts from exogenous tastes and proceeds upon pure reason through production and income distribution to final consumption is technical fiction. It obliterates endogeneity and ubiquitous cyclical causalities. It just saves analytical trouble and serves a certain ideology. Mainstream theory reports on how agents would react under given circumstances, failing to account for the fact that they proactively change those circumstances. So, it is honest up to information, but dishonest about knowledge. It is faithful in space, but completely outside time. It is of a world where time and space are separated and time is ignored. Thus, it is unreal in time-space and hence, by Einstein's legacy, it is of an unreal world. Methodological individualism is ideologically instrumental but dis-functional. Even so, it does admit an extreme other-disregarding selfishness, except that it does not see it as envious, conflictive and zero-sum. And it does not admit that what is privatized and possessed is human life.

Marx, Marxism and consumption

In Marx's time, infant capitalism distributed income in ways that forced labourers to be concerned about needs, in hand-to-mouth conditions of uncertain survival. As Fromm (2004: 92, original emphases) marked, Marx was explicit about this:

> The needs of the worker are thus reduced to the need to maintain him *during work*, so that the race of workers does not die out. Consequently, wages have exactly the same significance as the *maintenance* of any other productive instrument, and as the *consumption of capital* in general so that it can reproduce itself with interest. It is like the oil which is applied to a wheel to keep it running. Wages thus form part of the necessary *costs* of capital and of the capitalist, and they must not exceed this necessary amount. Thus it was quite logical for the English factory lords, before the Amendment Bill of 1834, to deduct from wages the public alms which workers received from the poor law taxes, and to treat them as an integral part of their wages.

It should be understandable then why Marx expounded on the exploitative nature of that particular productive arrangement, focusing on income distribution and injustices therein as outcomes of a historical process of choices that led to modes of production which dehumanized workers by alienating them from the activity of labour and from its product. In these, he argued, lied the internal contradictions of capitalism that undermined its own existence. The working class was by far the most populous, the preoccupation of a few lords or early capitalists with luxuries provided no ground for building a theory of consumption upon, and there was no consumer inventiveness worth speaking of that could advance the cause of capitalism and keep its contradictions within safe limits. The great masses indulged in little discretionary consumption and Marx reprimanded as 'vulgar' the subjective approaches of his time. As a result, and as Fromm (ibid.: 45) notes:

> There is only one correction which history has made in Marx's concept of alienation; Marx believed that the working class was the most alienated class, hence that the emancipation from alienation would necessarily start with the liberation of the working class. Marx did not foresee the extent to which alienation was to become the fate of the vast majority of people...But as far as consumption is concerned, there is no difference between manual workers and the members of the bureaucracy. They all crave for things, new things, to have and to use.

Marx's tracing of the causes of alienation in the industrial mode of production was a hypothesis which was not far from the truth, at the time. But his historicism was not construed by his followers as developing, and as requiring constant updating. His own neglect of psychological foundations of behaviour contributed to this, as he subsumed individual motivation under the mantra of social relations explained as outcomes of productive relations and forces. These, under the meta-industrial mode of production, remained effectively same. What has changed and needs to be appended to Marx's theory is what may be called *capitalistic mode of consumption*, which has activated dormant psychological drivers. A better developed picture of humans has emerged that provides ample ground for theoretical revisions. But Marxists would consider any revision to Marx's theory as...revisionist, having taken his words as articles of faith.

Hodgson (1999: 130) notes: '[An] acute problem in Marx's perspective is that human motivations are not explained in any detail: they are assumed to spring in broad and mysterious terms from the relations and forces of the system.' And: 'In general, he saw individuals as "simply embodiments and personifications" of social relations.... What is missing is an explanation of the historical origin of such calculative behaviour and the mode of its cultural transmission' (ibid.: 131).

Marx's method was inductive, but he came across no shopping maniacs going after anything that glitters. Today, one may not fail to draw from widespread consumption of garbage, from the absolute lack of a modicum of good taste in a good part of consumption or from the desperate angst carved on people's faces. After overcoming hunger, people started looking greedily at life through the glass of possessions. Therefore, obsession with exploited workers risks making one accomplice to their greed, to social indifference and to perpetuation of confusion. One should also not miss that capitalists, too, have descended from fishermen, farmers or textile workers. Failing to take into account such information helps pass greed as virtue, and any dose of it less than maximum as social vice, in misplaced Marxist materialism. A painting with mean capitalists and humble workers is passé nowadays, *however uneven the distribution of income or wealth may be.*

Production relations in Marx's time were marked by the same crisp class separation in all spheres, prolonging the opposition between a developing historical context and the stagnant relations of property, which capitalism was just beginning to overcome. Today, this opposition has been obliterated. Social relations, institutions, ways of thinking and modes of conduct are all new, as are the conditions of trade, which constitute an important parameter in the process of historical change. As knowledge in general is impossible to contain and as consuming knowledge comes part and parcel with knowledge about how to produce, from the old asymmetric trade conditions, which were colonial or otherwise autocratic, there emerged competitors on all fronts. On the foreign front solutions ran out for the colonists. On the home front, time was needed for smoothing out the dissonance between a quickly evolving technology and the slowness of a native consumer force which, having not been trained in how to consume, could not match the economy's productive performance and absorb output. Also, the requisite institutions and methods of income distribution took time to come about, so as to make discretionary expenditures an occupation of large parts of the population.

Marx knew that theory should keep up with society's capacity for change and foresaw the increased relevance of demand. Thus, he wrote: 'this mode of production [of the modern industrial system] acquires an elasticity, a capacity for sudden extension by leaps and bounds that finds no hindrance except in the supply of raw material and the disposition of the produce' (Marx, 1906, Vol. 3: 79). He thus sensed that consumption would become pivotal, having to keep up with production dynamics in order to absorb an exploding output that changed commodities, and even the structure of society and the quality of life in it. As a classical economist, he did not place undue emphasis on scale, knowing that relatively little should hinge on the sheer volume of demand. He saw the importance of structural dynamics for the full deployment of capitalism, and of the entire society's contributing its energetic participation. He sensed that if capitalism ever failed to reproduce the conditions of its own existence, this would be due to consumers' incompetence in matching the innovative potential of science put to the service of production. So, there is good reason to believe that Marx had anticipated the need for a conceptual unification of production and consumption.

There is no leap of faith in these, since Marx understood technology as a *social* achievement, where broad social forces, not just a few energetic individuals, restated the problems that required solutions and shifted focus from one set of problems to another. In Rosenberg's (1982: 49) words, he saw that 'what is really involved [in technology] is a process of a cumulative accretion of useful knowledge, to which many people make essential contributions'. Surely, this cannot but involve also the discretionary expending of incomes. Yet, these did not register as genuinely Marxic ideas because Marx was generally guarded about goals, about how income should be expended if distributed fairly, and about the type of welfare to pursue and the measure of individual success that should apply. His main concern was with distribution, seen as determined by the proportion of labour power expropriated by producers, depending on the size of the reserve army of labour and other parameters but not on the workers' consumption behaviour, since there was little such to speak of. Thus, he remained vague about what relationship he envisaged between a non-exploitative distribution and the material base of a life in affluence.

For this reason, arguments have been put forward to the effect that: 'Marx's historical materialism... is... fundamentally, a version of utilitarian individualism' (Parsons, 1937: 110), or that: 'Marx's view of class consciousness is... as utilitarian and rationalist as anything out of Jeremy Bentham' (Mills, 1963: 113). However, all that can be deduced about Marx's view of post-affluence is to be scoured in his *Economic and Philosophical Manuscripts*, from which Erich Fromm drew in order to refute such opinions. But the *Manuscripts* drew much less attention than *Capital*, which left room for errors of interpretation. Growth did not become repulsive to the materialist Marxist ideal, the impression being that increased output should benefit all, provided that exploitation was abolished. Thus, the basis of Marx's dialectics was interpreted as endorsing base-grade materialism. But if the goal is growth, there is little in Marxism that could dissuade one from believing that incentives based on income inequities are most effective in promoting it, as Keynes suggested in chapter 24 of his *General Theory*.

And if capital accumulation as embodied human time-space is the goal, then there is little that can dissuade workers from pursuing it, even if only through consumption.

Capitalists soon learned about the sophisticated interplay between income distribution and consumption behaviour and about the necessity for fast growth and sustained profits of a native population that took part in positional consumption, spurred by endless procreation of wants. Collective bargaining, social security and other institutions were set up to support this. Masses quickly learned how to consume competitively, adding qualities to commodities cranked out by the capitalist machine and speculating over the value of their labour content, in a contest for relative ranking. Exploding productive capacity made necessary that not just willing consumers, but devouring maniacs should be created out of humans, with all their capacities trained single-mindedly at consuming. This required nothing less than that humans should be made to believe that their *being* coincided with their *having*, in resigned ignorance and in the faith that all there is to life is consumption of any kind of junk that the system may crank out. It required that people should find pleasure in not having to go through the torment of thinking about serious matters, in not *being concerned*, in exhausting all their mind activity on a unidimensional quest for material gain. To this end, from early age, at home, at school and in the marketplace, people were trained in the skills required for the make and use of parts of the expropriative contest.

In contrast, Marxists were slow to see the alienating power of consumption and the aggressive, towards people and towards nature, kind of rationalization which corroded human culture. They backed the materialistic aspirations of the masses, fighting for a 'fair' income distribution and giving little thought to motives, goals and what should be done with such distribution. But what is fair depends on the system of values adopted by society and being in effect, which decides what market conduct is rational, thus letting labourers themselves decide what economic value is produced by their labour, the degree of their exploitation and level of 'fairness'. Barring concern with *what* is to be done with earned income, the only standard for measuring distributional fairness is according to the gross time-space-expropriating outcome of the various alternatives, that is, through GDP: The greater GDP is, the more *fair* the distribution, however absurd this may sound, and this is what is involved in the universal obsession with GDP growth. There is then no other benchmark. So, unless motives, goals and agent ontology are fathomed, Marxists and critics in general will keep pounding the saddle instead of the mule, condemning capitalism, accusing capitalists and failing to apportion any blame on the workers for creating their own predicament. And that is not very Marxic.

To be fair, from a general heterodox perspective the power of consumption to corrode the workers' conscience has not entirely escaped notice. Wolff (2004) notes that

> workers focus on rising consumption as the point and purpose of their work....
> At a minimum, workers accept exploitation and its social consequences

because they are compensated by consumption. Better still, for capitalism's survival, workers may come to believe that exploitation does not (or no longer) exist, so that consumption can be viewed as the compensation simply for labor activity itself.

Now, if this is combined (as is done by Wolff) with Galbraith's and Hargreaves Heap's psychological explanation that 'Because their personal identities are now fluid and hence insecure, people turn to consumption as the means to define and refine individual identities' (ibid.), only one vital step is left to recruit consumption activity to the cause of life through aggressive expropriation of time-space.

Let us visit Marx from another angle. His life project was heeding Lao Tzu's advice that there is no greater disaster than not knowing one's opponent. So, he set out to investigate capitalism. But if the opponent changes, one must be prepared to adjust his tactics and strategies accordingly, which is also of Lao Tzu. Capitalism has evolved into a global culture of acquisitive rationalism that masses made into their own cause and way of life, to the enfeeblement of their intellectual faculties. As Schumacher (1973: 31) put it: 'If human vices such as greed and envy are systematically cultivated, the inevitable result is nothing less than a collapse of intelligence. A man driven by greed or envy loses the power of seeing things as they really are, of seeing things in their roundness and wholeness, and his very successes become failures.' Or, as C. Wright Mills wrote in his Introduction to the Mentor Edition of Thorstein Veblen's *Theory of the Leisure Class*: 'The [capitalist] rational apparatus itself has expropriated the rationality of the individual to the point where we must often assume that those in charge of the big institutions are normally quite stupid.' But since those in charge always reflect the ways of society, we may infer from this that people have been stupefied into chasing fantasies, mixing frenzied lifestyles with intellectual slumbers. Today, the layman dreams he can benefit from growth. And he does, as long as he thinks so, because dreams matter.

As Veblen (1912: 25–6) himself noted: 'The habit of distinguishing and classifying the various processes and directions of activity prevails of necessity always and everywhere; for it is indispensable in reaching a working theory or scheme of life.' But 'what are recognized as the salient and decisive features of a class of activities or of a social class at one stage of culture will not retain the same relative importance for the purposes of classification at any subsequent stage'. Such a salient feature of the capitalist stage of history is that capital has developed into a dialectical notion, with a capacity to be continuously regenerated through concentration and dispersion: through accumulation in the hands of a few in productive form, and dissolution in the wishful thinking of the many, as embodied in non-productive form in consumer commodities. In the absence of either side, it lacks content. It is reduced to a value-less, time-less *stock*, since time is made real only through an endless *flow* of additions to knowledge, as such knowledge finds shape in capital.

Therefore, an up-to-date picture of capitalism must be removed from that drawn by its advocates as noble, socially beneficial competition among entrepreneurs aimed at pleasing consumers' tastes, but it must also be more articulate and up to date than that drawn by Marx, who cast economics in the light of a fight between capitalists and an exploited non-capitalist, if not outright anti-capitalist working class. This casts modern reality in a distorting light diffracted through the lens of the past, drawing an incomplete picture of it. A good guy-versus-bad guy Manichaeism provides no firm ground for basing social theory on. We are all same in our desires, share aspirations, but pursue our goals in personal ways. And we differ in the degrees of our success.

Social phenomena cannot be explained by reference to supernatural or natural forces, heroism or the exceptional capabilities of a few individuals. Explanation must be based on the capacities of ordinary people, which let develop forces and relations of which economic arrangements are outcomes. Marx underscored our urge to dominate, to exercise control over the natural environment and over humans. But although he was aware that capitalism could assimilate the masses and erode their consciousness by means of artificially multiplied wants, he did not ground his theory on those. His social dynamics were delineated by a view of a proletariat that was not actively involved in capitalist dynamics outside the field of production, to which it was dragged *by necessity*. He anticipated workers to become aware of their predicament, throw off their yoke and create a new world. He expected capitalism to collapse under the weight of its own contradictions, uniting the working classes in co-ordinated action against it, after exhausting its progressive dynamism.

In historical time terms, 200 years is not much, but capitalism proved to be more resilient than most had expected. This should make one suspect that what sustains it must be something so deeply rooted and sturdily grounded in human psychology, that it remains active and intact after basic needs have been satisfied. Marx's idea about the exhaustion of capitalism's dynamism is opaque, because it can be construed only as an *ex post* argument. After its demise, it will be easy to claim that capitalism had exhausted its dynamism, but one needs to explain what that means *before* it happens. Marxists have made the prognosis time and again that the collapse of capitalism is eminent. After the collapse of Statist socialism and the advent of globalization, opaque interpretations reappeared. Desai (2002) argues that Marx would have been happy to see capitalism not collapsing or retreating yet, but spreading out, because he would want it to be fully deployed before it withered or was overthrown, lest it might resurge stronger. Well, with so many precautions, it is impossible to err.

Marx knew that the true development of human power and freedom begins beyond the realm of necessity, since needs are determined by nature. But this development can flourish only upon the material realm of necessity as its basis. A good part of such freedom is in the way people interpret and make use of it, in the way they choose to interpret their relation with life and with nature, as this is reflected through their relationship with the product of their own toil. Marx argued that man is what man produces socially. As his time was not beyond the realm of necessity, we can only make conjectures about what his thoughts would be today. He expected workers to abolish capitalism and emancipate themselves and the rest of society. The opposite seems to be happening. The old proletariat has been sociologically (if not genetically) modified into a mass of consuming maniacs, conservative dreamers of profligacy within full-blown managerial and stockholder capitalism. So, it is reasonable to assume that, had Marx lived to see the present situation, he would have been led by his historical materialist perspective to modify his views. We are at a stage where, while taking time by the forelock, a sagacious capitalist may nourish fewer illusions about capitalism and be less loyal to it than a deprived, uninformed proletarian who fears he might lose his illusions of sharing in the feast through consumption. It is highly probable that, today, Marx would not have drawn Marxist conclusions.

History can be explained only on the basis of choices made by society, as has been the emergence of a new breed of capitalists and a voracious consumer culture in formerly non-capitalist societies through surrendering of their wealth to the most rapacious and shrewd (basically, to an under-world) in one night, or the adoption by workers in the West of the terms and conditions of increased labour productivity in antagonism with cheap 'third world' labour and with capital. Instead of ignoring such firm statements of intent by the masses, it would be wiser to put under scrutiny their perception of self-interest all the way down to its psychological underpinnings and to its consequences.

To summarize our position on Marxism and Marx: In order to maintain its vigour and explain emergent phenomena, Marx's method needed updating. Instead, it was preserved and religiously defended by Marxists who missed that Marx was not *for* or *against* any particular class. He did not lash out at capitalists for exploiting workers, placing the labouring masses steadfastly on the just side of his social accounts. Instead, he insisted about the obligation of the masses to emancipate themselves and society, 'assigning' a great historical task to them. Actually, his was not a theory of social justice, but a theory about material man and his capacity to write history, which is the most assertive way of stating that *all* are accountable for their choices. At the base of his argument he placed an analysis of alienation, as subordination of the worker to the product of his own labour, thus implicating consumption.

Great thinkers do not need to be with or against anyone. They *are*, with their own thoughts and ideas. And where those take them, it is there that they stand. Ordinary people need to be *with* someone. Marxists needed to be with the crowds. So, when capitalism seduced the crowds, Marxists went along with them, failing to heed that only by pursuing the truth may one serve society. Thus, having not resolved the question of motives and goals, having reduced their scope to distributional arguments, having left for the psychoanalyst to delve into *Marx's Concept of Man* and having misunderstood the meaning of man's actual materialism, Marxists gave capitalism most effective support by opposing it. They pursued technicalities while the crowds rushed into making the most out of it. Through the kind of calculation that we are about to discuss, the crowds are able to sense where to look for time-space, and capitalism proved smart enough to put much time-space up for grabs. Workers know that they have reaped benefits from capitalism, as they compare their situation with that of others whom capitalist economies have exploited, usurping their resources. Thus, Western workers have become exploiters of 'less fortunate' peoples and of each other, so that many of today's Marxists would hardly feel at home with Marx's general philosophy, having interpreted dialectical materialism as a promise for a consuming extravaganza for all. And they may feel more at home, without publicly admitting it of course, with present day capitalism which has already made this dream technically possible, while all other attempts failed. In view of these, it is safe to say that, had he lived, Marx would proclaim again today: 'Tout ce que je sais, c' est que moi, je ne suis pas marxiste.' (The only thing I know is that *I* am not a Marxist.)

Heterodox thinking

For the purposes of this discussion, we can consider as heterodox those approaches which challenge the mainstream equilibrium-oriented perspective and attempt to reconstruct economics as a social discipline. From the viewpoint we have adopted in this report, the main contribution of such approaches has been the insight they have provided on the all too important distinction between real and extensive time and the non-equilibrium processes that take place in the context of the former. Shackle revived an age-old tradition of grappling with the concepts of time and knowledge, detailing out their connection with economics. More recent specimens of such work have been provided by Witt (2001), Potts (2000 and 2001), Metcalfe (1998 and 2002) and others. An open-system approach is generally favoured in such research and a perspective to structural changes through variation generated amidst fundamentally uncertain accumulation of knowledge.

The cognitive nature of the process whereby tastes are formed and preferences are decided is recognized. As Witt (op. cit.) argues, 'innovativeness on the part of consumers is no less important than innovativeness on the part of producers'. Then, Witt investigates the mechanism of building up wants and circumventing satiation through novelty, asking: 'why should an increasing purchasing power not lead eventually to the satiation of all wants and, thus, slow down the growth of per capita consumption until it finally comes to a halt?' And: 'How do consumers arrive at the preferences they have (are they innate or learnt, i.e. culturally acquired)? Do the preferences change and, if so, how? What are the objects of the consumers' preferences, i.e. what is it that people demand and consume, and why? What role is played by consumption knowledge and all the factors that influence it?' (ibid.).

Such questions highlight vital issues and diagnose theoretical lacunas. Declaring that consumers are active only brings coals to Newcastle. One must say what they are active about. What we claim here is that there is nothing to be *active* about other than *life*, since only in life is there activity. But for all the hopes raised, in the heterodox literature one finds the usual reluctance to abandon the supply-side bias and to reach radical conclusions. Something always seems to be missing from heterodox arguments, a lack made all the more striking by the clarity of diagnoses. For example, the non-levelling-off of per capita consumption in affluent societies has been tackled with allusions to some passion as underlying our gargantuan consuming appetite. Tibor Scitovsky's *Joyless Economy* and Fred Hirsch's *Social Limits to Growth*, proceeding along lines similar to those of Veblen and Duesenberry, provided a wealth of insight about the consumers' relativist behaviour. But neither pursued such arguments all the way through. Hirsch subsumed rational malevolence under 'positional competition', which he defined thus: 'By positional competition is meant competition that is fundamentally for a higher place within some explicit or implicit hierarchy and that thereby yields gains for some only by dint of losses for others' (Hirsch, 1977: 52). This speaks of zero-sum antagonism, diagnosed thus by Hirsch: 'getting ahead of the crowd is an effective and feasible means of improving one's welfare, a means available to any one individual. It yields a benefit, in this sense, and the measure of the benefit is what individuals pay to secure it. The individual benefit from the isolated action is clear-cut. The sum of benefits of all the actions taken together is nonetheless zero' (ibid.: 7).

Still, Hirsch's analysis of socially induced scarcity remained with what Michael Polanyi termed 'proximal terms', which had already been enunciated by David Hume long before capitalism was in full swing. Actually, Hume had gone into 'distal terms' as well, diagnosing rivalry, envy and the pursuit of power in people's conduct.[3] So, speaking generally, one should conclude that, for all its gallantry, heterodoxy has dispatched its forces down a confined track, not crossing any Rubicons and not providing what Shackle called a Scheme of Things Entire, without which a theoretical edifice lacks identity. Fear of the masses holds questions at bay, fudges answers and wastes energy on critique, internal debates and protest. Highly advertised pluralism may even distract from hard-pressing issues, while redundant dichotomies such as that based on gender may misdirect thought and misinform social queries. As Georgescu-Roegen (1971: 343) argued, 'for a science of man to exclude altogether man from the picture is a patent incongruity. Nevertheless, standard economics takes special pride in operating with a man-less picture.' But by not addressing human ontology, it may turn out with time that heterodox thinking poured water in the neoclassical mill.

In science, there is no such thing as theoretical void. As Duesenberry (1967: 15) admonished: 'Most people would rather have a bad theory than no theory at all.' Indeed, theories seldom crumble under the weight of criticism, however well grounded this may be. As a matter of fact, criticism may even galvanize a theory's advocates into strengthening their positions and raising stauncher support. Theories simply give way to superior ones, and neoclassicism will reign as long as there is no better alternative theory. For the moment, heterodoxy lacks the nerve to provoke or displease the masses. So, it is a praiseworthy but unconsummated intellectual experiment that is starting to produce a new sociology, sitting apart from the mainstream one, but not as clearly apart from its ideology.

The usual reluctance to take the next explanatory step into what is approached as a twilight zone of consumer ontology is encountered even in avant-garde research. Steam always runs out before explanation gets to the root of conflictive selfishness. Thus, in Bianchi (1998), the new idea is that novelty should be added *as a source of pleasure*, when purchasing commodities. Consumers draw pleasure from discovering new uses, new qualities and new combinations of goods. They enjoy ice-creams, plus they enjoy discovering new ice-creams, or combinations of ice-creams with other commodities, and so on. These are animating, but differ little from the interpretation of economic activity as aiming at some kind of positive reward, or from the idea that humans are born to be pleasure hunters. They fail to discern decadence ideology in such Aristippeanism: that as people become addicted to the ideology of consumption, as they become slave to their desires, whether natural or of their own making, they discredit higher pursuits, they nourish no higher ambitions, and it becomes easier to condition their reflexes in Pavlovian fashion, to stupefy, control and subdue them.

Mayhew (2002: 54) concludes thus: 'All consumption is visible and made visible to mark the consumers as members of their group, to mark the status of each, and to inform outsiders that each is a member, not an outsider.' Of course, the spirit of the wolf pack is always in group identity, seeking power in unity. People follow banners, get thrilled with military parades, become football club fans, Harry-Potterites [*sic*!], etc. Hooligans are plain about all this: It is a desire for self-assurance by means of registering one's name in power structures, so that one may reach further through the group by identifying with others through shared interests or experiences, extending one's imperfect, incomplete self by intrusion into the time-space of others. Autonomy, on the other hand, is lack of such backing and requires enhanced self-assurance and psychical powers to withstand adversities.

Psychologists throughout the spectrum, beyond the Freudian cycle, have long been aware of the connection between social success as a pervasive status–class–prestige system, and power. Kardiner (1945: 445) who studied the psychology of Western man as he tries to overcome his anxieties through success and prosperity, in contrast to the salvation sought by people in the Middle Ages, concludes his long study in the following way, which is extremely close to our present argument:

> [I]n comparison with the individual who merely sought salvation, the psychological task for modern man is much more arduous. It is a responsibility, and failure brings with it less social censure and contempt than it does self-contempt, a feeling of inferiority and hopelessness. Success is a goal without satiation point, and the desire for it, instead of abating, increases with achievement. The use made of success is largely power over others, since the advantages in the form of luxurious types of subsistence, 'conspicuous waste,' are easily exhausted.

These internalize pressure, ascribing it to one's own angst for existence, even though the connection is not made explicit. Moreover, referring to the emotional values created by the Western socio-economic set-up, Kardiner marks: 'Social well-being is governed by the coercive power of the state, and the state defines aggression according to the rules made by those who control this coercive power' (ibid.: 452).

But what is the use of power over humans? For answering this, Pfouts (2002) endorses Lawson's call for paying attention to the ontology of the consumer. He acknowledges that ontology entails psychology but advices that: 'For psychology to be useful in economics it must be aimed at the problems of economics. When this is done, psychology is potentially of great use and importance' (ibid.: 77). He cites the work of Herbert Simon, Daniel Kahneman and Amos Tversky as examples, but warns against making 'the vulgar or Veblenian error', as would be the basing of explanation on 'the anal retentive stage of the psycho-sexual genesis' (ibid.), deriding gender-type absurdities in economic theorizing. Then, he makes a call for an ongoing search for 'additional explanatory variables in economic theory' and argues that 'we cannot rely on Occam to excuse us from further searching for explanatory variables, or indeed any facts that may be relevant to the theory' (ibid.: 76).

There is much to agree with Pfouts. We have vowed for avoiding dichotomies and made a negative allusion to gender-based theorizing. But, reading through Pfouts's essay, one finds a lapsing back to the usual argument: 'Economic motivation is almost always simple and straightforward. Economic actors are seeking gain in some form: Satisfaction and pleasure, in the case of consumers, benefits for members in the case of unions and perhaps political power to be used in obtaining further gains. Profits, perhaps market share and market power and continued existence and growth in the case of firms and so on for other economic actors' (Pfouts, 2002: 77). Also: 'Consumers seek the set of goods, among those known to them, that they believe will provide the greatest satisfaction without exceeding their budget' (ibid.). Finally, 'the conclusion being argued is that the functioning of the consumer is simple in theory because it is actually simple' (ibid.: 78).

What consumer ontology then, beyond the ghost of Aristippus? Why so many distinct pursuits for just one campaign? What could those 'additional explanatory variables' be? Pfouts wonders whether 'purely economic considerations offer promise in developing an ontology of the consumer' and examines the wealth effect and income distribution. But 'purely economic' is well within the conventional confines and Pfouts correctly finds little promise in these, whence he correctly concludes: 'There is little point in speculating about ontological matters; they should be settled by careful observation. But speculation about new borders for the universe of discourse is a necessary preliminary for establishing or rejecting them' (ibid.: 79).

To make a long story short, preoccupation with a theory's faulty conclusions or method may draw attention away from the malignancy of the actual system run by real agents. Theoretical relevance brings up the intricacy of the relationship between social theory and social practice, and the identity problem which haunts heterodoxy. A theory is thought to be irrelevant if it fails to describe what happens in some real domain, seen as external to it. But in the social domain, theory can never be external or neutral. There is two-way interaction between society and theory. Theory then may serve practice and practice or policy may be made to abide by a theory. As Theodore Roszak put it in his Introduction to Schumacher's *Small is Beautiful*, theory may be *made* to work by forcing it down 'upon a confused and recalcitrant human material which none dare ever consult except by way of the phony plebiscite of the marketplace, which always turns out as predicted because it is rigged up by cynics, voted by demoralized masses, and tabulated by opportunists'.

The plebiscite turns out as predicted because those asked are the same who make up the market. So, we disagree that the market plebiscite is rigged and phoney, and with the implied divisions (e.g. into opportunists and non-opportunists). But society can indeed create the conditions under which a theoretical prescription becomes fulfilled. This is a characteristically Weberian proposition that touches upon the intricate relationship between structure and agency. Yet, since the obviousness of the direction of causalities is questioned here, let us for the argument's sake define relevance in this unorthodox way: A theory is irrelevant *if it does not serve its purpose*, which might include defending some ideology, promoting the interests of some class, or even concealment. From such angle, neoclassical theory is perfectly relevant, the dialogue is misplaced, misleading, and serves neoclassicism rather than its critics. From the angle the latter visit the issue of relevance, nothing can make neoclassicism relevant, which explains why it has been twisted so much as to allow neoclassicists to claim that the term *neo-classical* is empty. However, the more people are seduced to indulge in maniac consumption, the less irrelevant will seem to be the utility-maximizing fiction on which the capitalist ideology and its theory rest.

To put it bluntly, critics must decide whether their dissatisfaction is with neoclassical theory for providing inadequate explanation of economic reality, or with the social reality itself. In the first case, they can wait until social practice abides by the theory; until people behave as neoclassical logical circuits, as *homines oeconomici*, which is not too remote a possibility. With so much besides stock markets responding to the self-serving prophecies and control by few, and with so many economists produced to a neoclassical genome and let loose in the market for ideas, the spectre of moulding society into modes of conduct that yield to a laws-of-motion, social-physics type of analysis appropriate for automata-citizens and cybernated societies may be near. In the second case, instead of quibbling, they must focus on substance. Like every ideology, capitalism comes with its theoretical weaponry. Falsely taking it as naïve, irrelevant or deductivist, only works to increase its effectiveness.

So, challenging can only be done upon contrasting ideological, epistemological and methodological premises that need to be staunchly defended, since these cannot be expected to be faultless at inception, or appear equally reasonable, concrete or elegant as those which have long been worked on by generations of economists. Dissenters cannot aspire only to describe capitalism better than its advocates, or to grumble about its breeding greed in humans (e.g. Edney, 2005). They should aim at finding the root of its success and at studying its consequences, to the end of effecting better social arrangements. The greatest hurdle to be cleared in this quest is the layman's cultivated interpretation of personal advantage and well-being. Without clear ideology, social theory is treading water, getting nowhere.

There has already been produced extensive, spirited and eloquent criticism, so that little of significance can be added. We know so much about the limitations of equilibrium, exogenous tastes and other such orthodox concepts, that only a disequilibrated person may have faith in equilibrium. What is needed is honesty, and a theory's relevance hinges on the truthfulness of the ontology of the agents it acknowledges. For the time being, while neoclassicism is *intentionally* irrelevant, no other theory can seriously claim to be adequately relevant.

Choice and language

Economics is not in technical relations but in interpersonal ones, reflected in the way we appraise ourselves in relation to others through the glass of general and economic values and activities, economic ones being the most social. Clothes others wear, cars they drive, houses they live in or toothpastes they use affect how we appraise man-made items through the time-space that went into making them and, hence, those who possess them, *privately*. This is how we appraise each other and how we allocate our energy and income between various options. Optimization is meaningless under such conditions. The decision landscape is reshaped through purposeful action aimed at expanding one's social displacement, or presence. Every choice made affects future choices. Stepping on the decision landscape here makes it swell there in unpredictable ways that redraw its contours and level curves. Allen (2001: 346) contends:

> The real issue, therefore, is the acceptance of 'irreversibility', of the real passage of time and the reality of change... It is that of making models which accept that the systems we are interested in may be always 'on their way' to something, but never arrive, because their external environment and their internal components adapt and change as history unfolds. Instead of a fixed landscape of attractors, and of a system operating in one of them, we have a changing system, moving in a changing landscape of potential attractors. Creativity and noise (supposing that they are different) provide a constant exploration of 'other' possibilities. Some of these mark the system and alter the dimensions of its attributes, leading to new attractors, and new behaviours, towards which the system may begin to move, but at which it may never arrive, as new changes may occur 'on the way'. The real revolution is not therefore about neoclassical economics as opposed to non-linear dynamics having cyclic and chaotic attractors, but about the representation of the world either as having arrived at a stationary attractor, or as a non-stationary situation of permanent adaptation and change.

According to Simon (1969: 187): 'The idea of final goals is inconsistent with our limited ability to foretell or determine the future. The real result of our actions is to establish initial conditions for the next succeeding stage of action.' And Fullbrook (2005) argues: 'An economics that has nothing to say about the formation of tastes and preferences is silly and irresponsible, especially in an age of consumer societies'. Moreover,

> neoclassical economics is by its own axioms incapable of offering a coherent conceptualisation of the *individual* or *economic agent*. It cannot explain where the preferences that supposedly dictate the individual's choice come from. The preferences cannot be explained through interpersonal relations, because if individual demands were interdependent they would not be additive, and thus the market demand function – neoclassicalism's key analytical tool – would be undefined. And they cannot come from society, because neoclassicalism's Newtonian atomism translates as methodological individualism, meaning that society is to be explained in terms of individuals and never the other way around.
>
> (Ibid., original emphases)

The type of society established depends on the goal pursued through social activities, and consumption is a most decisive one. A capitalistic society is in pervasive conflict through consumption, which is completely erroneous to see simply as an activity for satisfying personal needs in social isolation. Actually, this conflict tends to degenerate into a Hobbesian war of all against all, where every one is for himself and only about God there may be disagreement.[4] What one draws from consumption may be named anything, but is actually an inner distress given vent in supposedly harmless ways. More generally, through its economic activities society tries to increase its assurance. Therefore, apprehension sits at its base. Economic society is formed in order to soothe such apprehension, but capitalistic affluence raises it anew, as chasing wants introduces self-apprehension through the back door.

Unallayed fear generates the need for constantly making new uncertain choices. As Fullbrook (op. cit.) put it: 'Without indeterminacy there can be no choice. Without determinacy, there is no neoclassical model.' According to Loasby (op. cit.: 23), 'ongoing selection is incompatible with perfect competition, which not only excludes variety but cannot exist outside equilibrium, and can therefore at best be a consequence of selection, but never a context for it. Selection processes cannot operate in perfectly competitive markets.' Thus, 'perfect competition can never be legitimately invoked to explain movement towards equilibrium' (ibid.). About systems in general, there is adequate knowledge that makes an equilibrium logic in economics inexcusable. As Prigogine advises, 'social systems are trivially *non-linear* and also trivially (as all living systems) *far from equilibrium*. Each action leads to negative or positive feedback.... Each decision implies the remembrance of the past and an anticipation of the future' (Prigogine, 2005: 68–9, original emphases).

In order to support that 'purposeful behaviour is entirely consistent with trial and error, as long as people have no way of knowing that their actions will achieve their purposes' (Loasby, op. cit.: 24), Loasby cites Marshall's (1920: 5) thesis that the fundamental characteristics of modern industrial life are 'self-reliance, independence, deliberate choice and forethought' rather than competition, and Mises's (1949) view that a distinctively human aspect of economic activity is 'purposeful behaviour, both in response to events and in the origination of new products, new methods, and new forms of organization'. Success in the terms of flora- and fauna-type evolution – where successful mutations are not decided purposefully by the evolving species itself, but obtain instead as *ex post* outcomes of what our ignorance interprets as matching fit of the species with the environment – does injustice to economic systems, which develop through self-interested choice making. In economics, 'selection' is a misnomer for genuine choice, the substance of which lies in that some other choice could have been made – and, indeed, it could have been made to succeed – on account of the fact that everything depends on conscious knowledge gathering, which partakes of the future, whereas rational logic does not. As Loasby again notes:

> Non-logical processes are even more important when . . . the purpose of many decisions is not to respond to events but to introduce change. It is characteristic of modern societies that people wish the future to be in some ways different from the past: we therefore require knowledge not only to understand and adapt to what exists, and to the changes in what exists, but in order to create change *which will be acceptable to others.*
>
> (Loasby, 1999: 6, emphasis added)

Real economics makes no sense outside an ever-expanding knowledge context, in which consumers, like investors in Keynes's theory, make choices by forecasting the behaviour of others. This affects every economic magnitude, including efficiency. In an open to knowledge context, efficiency cannot be understood as the attaining of some optimal value which is better than others that are also feasible and known, but as a process of constant improvements to any efficiency already attained. That is, it is efficiency improvements and rates thereof that matter, not any attained efficiency as such. In his dialogue with Oscar Lange, Hayek was right that it is no stationary feasibility that matters (in which central planning could excel), but the capacity of a system to generate newness through some appropriate incentives mechanism.

Mainstream theory has promoted a complacent intellectual tradition that evades these most challenging issues, seeking refuge behind a mathematical façade. For all their other qualities, mathematical models cannot impute relevance, if the theory that backs them lacks such. Regrettably, less stylized but potentially more fruitful approaches were demoted and alternative theories could not find their way into textbooks. Serious misgivings about this have been voiced, of which Hodgson (1993) gives an account. Therefore, socially relevant theories must be put forward that will explain how desires emerge, what goal is pursued by agents, what methods they employ and how that reflects at every higher-level up, all the way to the national and the global economy, in their relation to humanity and to the environment. Such theories must be concerned with processes and relations whereby inputs are transformed and exchanged in such ways as to achieve well understood individual objectives. And they must entertain collective outcomes that are not at variance with individual motivation.

To produce such theories, all distinctions must be carefully made and language must not be twisted. Language acts on the mind in various ways, even by repetition or by omission. By avoiding ideologically charged terms, neoclassicism built for itself an image of impartiality. But as Coddington (1972, original emphasis) noted:

> The language of economic theory, like any language provides a framework for thought: but at the same time it constrains thought to remain within that framework. It focuses our attention; determines the way we conceive of things; and even determines what *sort* of things can be said. . . . A language, or conceptual framework is, therefore, at one and the same time both an opportunity and a threat. Its positive side is that (one hopes) it facilitates thought within the language or framework. But its negative side arises from the fact that thought must be within the framework.

Moreover, as Strassmann (1994) observed: 'Economic conversations, like all scientific interactions, are conducted in language – in oral and textual forms – and participants must adhere to conventional disciplinary forms if they wish to be heard.' And since 'economists of current vintage expect theory to be expressed in formal, mathematically delineated models' but 'the valorization of mathematical language constrains what counts as theory', it follows that 'critique of the rhetorical code in economics is a necessary first step to changing theory in ways not possible under current rhetorical constraints' (ibid.).

However, it is imperative that social critique produces constructive ideas and theories. For judging their merits, Kincaid (1996) set forth certain standards, grouped in three broad categories: evidential, explanatory and formal: The theory should not be refuted by evidence, it should display explanatory power, and it should meet certain formal criteria such as elegance, concreteness, parsimony, internal consistency and tractability. Orthodox theory is lacking on the first two counts, committing what Alfred North Whitehead has named 'fallacy of misplaced concreteness'. It is also lacking in terms of elegance, since Kincaid's is not simply decorative, and certainly not about writing styles or forms, which, if elegant, may even mask lack of substance.

Finally, as Prigogine (op. cit.: 69) warned: 'It goes far beyond the competence of a physicist to describe the origin and variety of human values. . . . To describe nature, including our position in nature, we are looking for a narrow path – somewhere between the deterministic description which leads to alienation and a random world in which there would be no place for human rationality.' But the rationality we must look for in economics research is that of the thick masses of real, active citizens, not that of orthodox automata, since the Great Masses are the General Motor of today's capitalism. If the motor misfires, the system is in trouble. A body of passively optimizing consumers is of a *res*-like economy, which capitalism certainly isn't. And this is another way of saying also that consumers are accountable.

3 The life project

Solo el misterio nos hace vivir. Solo el misterio.

'Only the mystery makes us live. Only the mystery', scribbled Lorca under the sketch of a face that he drew in 1934. A little earlier, in 1905 and in 1916, Einstein (who is quoted as saying that 'The most beautiful experience we can have is the mysterious... the fundamental emotion which stands at the cradle of true art and true science') submitted his Special and General Theory of Relativity, which introduced a radical reinterpretation of the concepts of time and space. Simultaneity in space depends on velocity. Space and time are connected by motion. Relativity of space and length is waived in the context of a four-dimensional time-space. In his General Theory, Einstein showed that a gravitational field is a natural consequence of such four-dimensional geometry. In our perception of the world, time and space are inconceivable in isolation from each other, and there can be no absolute definition of time or space. There is only a combined time-space.

What joins Lorca's *unknown* and Einstein's conception of time-space is *Experience*: our pulling in time our veil of ignorance about the future, living our lives forward. Our life experience is in registering impressions while being in sensory contact with our environment, in constructing relational ideas about its objects, and in acting upon such impressions. Our reality consists of thus experiencing time-space, each present moment being the snapshot that tells apart the past, which is known, from the future, which is unknown. The fact of our life is in building up of our consciousness of time-space by expanding our stock of knowledge about it. In this way we mark the passage of time, becoming aware of its duration, as we acquire a sense of the extent of cosmic time-space and of our infinitesimal but vital displacement within it. What remains unknown (the rest of cosmic time-space beyond our reach, or displacement) is a source of discomfort and disquiet. What remains unknowable is the source of an angst. Death is the utmost unknown and unknowable.

Long before Einstein, Hume (2000: 31) had exclaimed:

The parts, into which the ideas of space and time resolve themselves, become at last indivisible; and these indivisible parts, being nothing in themselves, are inconceivable when not fill'd with something real and existent. The ideas of space and time are therefore no separate or distinct ideas, but merely those of the manner or order, in which objects exist: Or, in other words, 'tis impossible to conceive either a vacuum and extension without matter, or a time, when there was no succession or change in any real existence.

It follows then that a hiatus in knowledge making would mean stoppage of time. No newness is non-existence. And the only 'real and existent' some-thing that can fill 'these indivisible parts' is our self, since every other 'object [which] exists' is of our own 'manner or order'. In this lies the distinction between real time, on one hand, and extensive or logical time, on the other. The latter is a derivative 'object', in the above-said manner. In extensive time, all relevant parameters can, in principle, be known, whence the operation of a system can be modelled and its path may be described, given a set of initial conditions. In extensive time there is no future. All is known, *at the present*, in which is exhausted the relevant time-space; it is in our complete knowledge; *we have control*. Such is the world of differential or difference equations. Here, all (pseudo-) dynamics is exhausted at the moment of selection of the initial conditions and transition mechanism. In reality, *transition* is a most incomprehensible concept. In logical time there is no newness, or unique events. There is only information, which may be asymmetrically distributed, or whatever, but it is extant.

Why are these distinct notions of time often confused so that, for example, many think that differential equations describe real dynamics? Because, while living in real time-space and making choices under uncertainty, we arrogantly think of our reconstructions of the past and of our projections into the future and into space (assuming for one last time their separation) as being fully informed and exact. However, *real events are not really reconstructible*. The opposite would defy (real) time and would be a contradiction in terms. And projections cannot accommodate novelty without banishing it. But our urge to control our situation makes us discount the subversive powers of time, achieving a false sense of security and an exaggerated estimate of our powers to be precise. We are thus led to believe in the faithfulness of our reconstructions and in the certainty of our predictions. Michael Polanyi criticized this exaggerated, pathological pursuit of exactitude and mechanistic interpretation at the expense and peril of a social science's bearing on its subject matter, and considered it to be 'a wider intellectual disorder: namely the menace of all cultural values, including those of science, by an acceptance of a conception of man derived from a Laplacean ideal of knowledge and by the conduct of human affairs in the light of such a conception' (Polanyi, 1958/62: 141). Nicholas Georgescu-Roegen referred to this as our 'mechanistic propensity' and thought more generally that

> The greatness of the human mind is that it wonders... The weakness of the human mind is the worshiping of the divine mind, with the inner hope that it may become almost as clairvoyant and, hence, extend its knowledge beyond what its own condition allows it to observe repeatedly.

It is understandable then why the phenomena that man can repeatedly observe exercise such an irresistible fascination for our minds while the idea of a unique event causes intellectual discomfort and is often assailed as wholly nonsensical. Understandable also is the peculiar attraction which, with 'the tenacity of original sin' (as Bridgman put it), the scientific mind has felt over the years for all strains of mechanistic dogmas.

(Georgescu-Roegen, 1971: 207)

Uncertainty is impossible to harness and uncertain choices and events are intrinsic to real time-space. As Louçã (1997) put it: 'If time is to be considered, not as a simple parameter, a space coordinate or yet another variable, but as real evolution, then a paradigmatic shift is fully justified.' But before we decide upon a meaningful paradigm, we must answer whether fundamental uncertainty is also *complete* uncertainty, that is, if new knowledge comes up in a random way, so that there is little that can be anticipated about it, or it is directed, so that there is something that can be said about the kinds of knowledge that are more likely to obtain. This speaks of intent. The question is: Do we get actively involved in how we experience the duration of time and the extension of space? And if so, driven how and aiming at what?

In answering these questions, we must note first the incompatibility between time and logic that was pointed out by Shackle, who warned that rigour must be relaxed if a compromise is to be reached between these incompatibles, and if the intractable implications of time in an analysis appealing to logic are to be accommodated.

Time is a denial of the omnipotence of reason. Time divides the entirety of things into that part about which we can reason, and that part about which we cannot. Yet the part about which we cannot reason has a bearing on the meaning of the part that is amenable to reason. The analyst is obliged to practise, in effect, a denial of the nature of time. For he can reason only about what is *in effect* complete; and in a world where there is time, nothing is ever complete.

(Shackle, 1972: 27, original emphasis)

Kierkegaard visited the temporal/existential issue in the following impressive way: 'Philosophy is perfectly right in saying that life must be understood backwards. But then one forgets the other clause – that it must be lived forwards. The more one thinks through this clause, the more one concludes that life in temporality never becomes properly understandable, simply because never at any time does one get perfect repose to take a stance: backwards' (Hong and Hong, 1967, entry 1030). Therefore, if there is anything that *living* life and *understanding* life share, which we must take as certain, this must be what fills the space where *we* cannot get *repose*, between past and future, in the present moment. But nothing can fill a durationless moment except its own intent: *the intent of its own succession*, that is, its own *extension*, pointing 'forwards', *by understanding itself*, that is, by constructing ever new knowledge by drawing from the past: knowledge which is therefore useful for the practical conduct of Life. This *transition* between moments defies all our efforts to explain. If we did, we would know the future: we would be Gods, which is our ultimate ambition. But we may only reasonably *assume* that such knowledge is by its nature 'economic', in the sense that it vows to expand itself into the future, by exploiting the past, at the least possible expense of the present. From our human viewpoint, this speaks of our intent *to be there*, to experience (more of) life: the intent to live by understanding, by knowing. So, life may not be possible to understand 'in temporality', but it can be understood in and through its own intent; through its desire to extend itself from each present moment to the next, that is, to extend its own presence, in time-space.

This answers the questions posed in the affirmative, implying that human pursuits have been consistent through time, both in general and in their economic particulars, in spite of all apparent multifariousness. Following Kierkegaard, Prigogine and Stengers (1984: 293) contended that 'Whatever we call reality, it is revealed to us only through the active construction in which we participate'. Thus, at the base of any construction of reality sits (the intent of) our ontology, which is actively involved in the way we experience time-space and make things happen in it. No explanation can go past this ontology, which is imposed on us through no choice of ours, by birth, when we are called upon to face a most threatening regularity: the certainty of death. At birth and at death, these extreme situations, we are alone and we are powerless. Between these moments, we try with all our powers *to remain*: to be in control of our situation; to survive; to experience what intervenes between these extremes. This we call *Life*. Eating whets the appetite, so our capacity of constructing presumptuous projections into time and space is also a curse. If we can do this much, why not everything! Why not become immortal and expand through the entire universe?

So, we form bonds and join forces with others in order to augment our powers over nature, producing means through which we deceive ourselves into believing that we can thus gain control over our destiny. Thus, economics becomes our long, strong arm for reaching into the world that surrounds us. Polanyi (op. cit.: 142) argued that 'the objectives of power and wealth acquire a moral sanctity which, added to their supposed scientific necessity, enforces their acceptance as man's supreme and total destiny'. These constructs of the mind, in which we have almost absolute faith, help us overcome our 'objective' weakness against the awe-inspiring infiniteness of the universe. As Gell-Mann (1995: 276–7) notes:

> [W]e impose on the world around us, even on random facts and chance phenomena, artificial order based on false principles of causation. In that way, we comfort ourselves with the illusion of predictability and even of mastery. We fantasize that we can manipulate the world around us by appealing to the imaginary forces we have invented.... Numerous beliefs, including some of the most tenaciously held, serve to alleviate anxiety over death. When specific beliefs of that kind are widely shared in a culture, their soothing effect on the individual is multiplied.

Western capitalism takes us to a summit of such soothing illusions. It is a culture and mass faith to which are mustered our mental powers. But what appears to the eye through a capitalistic prism is what is artificially superposed on the meaning of life, about which we may seek guidance in Aristotle:

> As far as the name goes, we may almost say that the great majority of mankind are agreed about this; for both the multitude and persons of refinement speak of it as Happiness, and conceive 'the good life' or 'doing well' to be the same thing as 'being happy.' But what constitutes happiness is a matter of dispute; and the popular account of it is not the same as that given by the philosophers. Ordinary people identify it with some obvious and visible good, such as pleasure or wealth or honour – some say one thing and some another, indeed very often the same man says different things at different times: when he falls sick he thinks health is happiness, when he is poor, wealth. At other times, feeling conscious of their own ignorance, men admire those who propound something grand and above their heads; and it has been held by some thinkers that beside the many good things we have mentioned, there exists another Good, that is good in itself, and stands to all those goods as the cause of their being good.
>
> (Aristotle, 1934: I. iii. 8-iv)

Concerning the 'Good, that is good in itself', Aristotle (ibid.: I. i. 4-ii) had this to say:

> If...among the ends at which our actions aim there be one which we wish for its own sake, while we wish the others only for the sake of this, and if we do not choose everything for the sake of something else (which would obviously result in a process *ad infinitum*, so that all desire would be futile and vain), it is clear that this one ultimate End must be the Good, and indeed the Supreme Good. Will not then a knowledge of this Supreme Good be also of great practical importance for the conduct of life? Will it not better enable us to attain what is fitting, like archers having a target to aim at? If this be so, we ought to make an attempt to determine at all events in outline what exactly this Supreme Good is, and of which of the theoretical or practical sciences it is the object.

Following Aristotle, in an effort to unravel the details of human intentionality, we must take into account his provisos on the notion of 'the good of a nation or a state [which] is a nobler and more divine achievement' than 'the good of one person'. His first proviso is that 'uncertainty surrounds the conception of the Good, because it frequently occurs that good things have harmful consequences: people have before now been ruined by wealth' (ibid.: I. ii. 7-iii). Moreover, throughout his *Ethics*, especially in Books IX and X, he insisted, along with Plato, that pleasure is not the Good. The Good, he explains, is *life* in pleasure, or life for life's sake: 'And life is defined, in the case of animals, by the capacity for sensation; in the case of man, by the capacity for sensation *and thought*. But a capacity is referred to its *activity*, and in this its full reality consists. It appears therefore that life in the full sense is sensation or thought' (ibid.: IX. ix. 7, emphases added).

These make purposiveness, as foresight of a goal, an original Aristotelian concept that does not imply equifinality, in the sense that the same final state can be reached from different initial conditions. What it implies is: 'Directiveness based upon structure, meaning that an arrangement of structures leads the process in such way that a certain result is achieved' (Bertalanffy, 1969: 78), and 'the order of process in living systems is such as to maintain the system itself' (ibid.).

As we saw, Aristotle saw the goal as being *practical*. And as society is formed upon an original calculation of promoting life, it appreciates only what is practical in a life-promoting sense. In fact, Aristotle identified the Supreme Good in this urgency for life: in knowledge which is 'of great practical importance for the conduct of life'. This could be just in prolonging a life of animalish grade, or of a loftier one, as he hoped. Modern economics, along with ordinary people, naively perceives the Supreme Good to be in 'some obvious and visible good, such as pleasure or wealth or honour'. An economics based on such Aristippean premises is ideological sophism that prospers only because it substitutes a seemingly innocent or 'legitimate' goal for the real one, which is repulsive. Somehow, the Good must be too Bad for us to admit, so we fancy with naïve ideas, as is the idea about 'utility'. Although science aims at augmenting our knowledge of the world, it is often fearful to take the cost of reconciling humanity with its fears, especially with its fear of the unknown. And, as nothing can be more unknown than (what comes with, or after) death, what we fear most is death.

This inescapable and grave truth about ourselves evolves into a fear of ourselves and of all truth that relates with ourselves, obstructing self-awareness and nourishing delusion. But fear breeds aggression, which thus appears as defensive. We conceal our cruelty in order to make it more effective. (Every Sunday morning the wolf pack goes to church.) While we rush to explain how smart we are, compared with other species, and how superior, we hush that we are also more cruel to our own species than is any other animal. Rules of civilized conduct aim at taming or controlling such cruelty, but they fail to eradicate it. They try to channel its force in productive occupations. Social systems try to contain and put animal vigour to the task of promoting life *with* the species, not against it, but the more this animalishness is repressed and re-channelled the more savagely its aggressiveness spurts out given vent, becoming irrational. However, what is irrational in one system of logic may be rational in another, and we argue that such savageness is at the heart of what we call *capitalistic rationalization*, although it borders on the metaphysical: It is an expression of our yearning for life, by taking life, looking forward to an eternal life after death. And yet, fear continues, in the threat of an ever postponed Final Judgement. The wrath of all gods always came ferociously down upon those who tried to clear these delusions, and 'holy' wars were always unspeakably ferocious, because Absolute Good fights Absolute Evil, on either side. Cruelty climaxes when fingers point to the sky.

The self-interested part of social life (assuming that there is also another part) is based upon the calculation of one's own life-expanding interest against that of all others, but we must all pretend that we do not know what we all know we know. We also know how much cruelty has resulted and can still result from this conflictive calculation, but at every historical stage we thought that that set-up could provide a solution. It never did. In its greatest part, the 'solution' had been economic, establishing economics as diverted violence. Already from the Greek etymology of the word (oeco-nomics: οικος-νόμος = house law), the assignment of roles in the family and the containment of the resentment of women, slaves and children by submission to an arbitrary power, the power of the father, attests to these. So, Keynes (1936: 374) could argue that

> dangerous human proclivities can be canalised into comparatively harmless channels by the existence of opportunities for money-making and private wealth, which, if they cannot be satisfied in this way, may find their outlet in cruelty, the reckless pursuit of personal power and authority, and other forms of self-aggrandisement. It is better that a man should tyrannise over his bank balance than over his fellow-citizens; and whilst the former is sometimes denounced as being but a means to the latter, sometimes at least it is an alternative. But it is not necessary for the stimulation of these activities and the satisfaction of these proclivities that the game should be played for such high stakes as at present.

With these in mind, we can return to the 'Good, that is good in itself', but instead of saying with Aristotle that 'experience is the fruit of years' (ibid.: VI. viii. 6), we may say that *the years are in experience*, in the sense that experiences provide a sense of duration. Being conscious of our existence means that we are aware of our imminent non-existence. We know that life is a marginal state: an accidental walk on a razor's edge, with unpredictable start, certain end and very short duration, for all that matters to us. But we are obliged to deceive ourselves that it will last, clinging desperately on to it, until we are finally defeated, become resigned and succumb to our fate. Until then, we try to extend our experience of it by generating life-related knowledge. It is, however, in our discretion to decide what *kind* of knowledge we will pursue, with what moments we will fill the successive blanks between past and future, which means what *kind* of life we will lead. And we have chosen to pursue a life of control over nature, *through control over humans*. This is our main thesis here.

The connection between control over nature by joining forces *with* other people, and control *over* people, is direct. If a collective effort can increase control over nature, then whoever controls those who put in that effort gains increased power over nature and, presumably, over his or her own destiny. Capitalism inflames the desire for such control by fuelling existential anxiety, perpetuating the conditions of its own survival *as separate and distinct from necessity*: through ever renewed *wants*. Therefore, explaining capitalism without understanding wants is like engaging in economic astrology, or in pre-Copernican astronomy with pebbles.

All disrespect for the time-space of others is unrightful expansion of one's own vital space, at the expense of others: an expression of his power over others; a depriving of part of their lives. This includes usurpation of anything common, brutal behaviour within the family, parking a car at one's own convenience, littering on public places (much as animals mark their vital space by leaving their scent), driving recklessly or making noises.[1] As such aggressiveness is psychologically devastating, we avoid remaining in continuous awareness of it. We become accustomed to it, accepting it as a *fact of life*.

Being aware of some such connection between violence and economics, historians have tried to explain the European predilection of capitalism. The link with religion along life-and-death lines did not escape notice. The conduct most revered in the calvinist and puritan ethos is one of control and suppression of pleasure in its natural forms and its channelling into material progress. This is why the most puritan Western cultures did not practically stumble upon any excesses of conduct, however impious, inhumane, indecent or despicable, as long as they helped promote such materialism (mountains of Hollywood-style reproducible violence, a huge porno industry, etc.) but raised insurmountable barriers on other occasions. (If gay and lesbian marriages could increase money velocity, they would be applauded by the puritans.) So, material progress is counterfeit pleasure, not real: a futile effort to evade angst.

Western religion pictures God as expecting humans to conquer the Earth (White, 1963; Weber, 1978). Hirsch (1977, ch. 10 and *passim*) noted the secular scheme designed by religion, in which earthly pay-offs are to be drawn for sure if all comply, whereas next-world rewards are in the jurisdiction of God: 'A more effective inducement for cooperative action could hardly be devised deliberately' (ibid.: 142), since earthly controllers are limited in their capacity to handle relevant information, whereas an omniscient God is not. The only thing that is certain is that, in both worlds, there are sanctions for non-compliance and rewards for complying.

Landes (1969) noted the value placed by Christian Western civilization upon rational manipulation of the environment and upon an unreserved alignment of means with ends. At the same time, and in seeming contradiction, a clear connection has been made between the Industrial Revolution and the Enlightenment, whose *raison d'être* was the intellect's opposition to religious obscurantism that treated the fear of death with a hatred for earthly life, promising a better one, after death. The fact is that there is no contradiction. Western capitalism is a climax of the said cultural disposition, precisely for being a dialectical synthesis of obscurantism with the Enlightenment. The dawning of the seventeenth century raised high hopes about 'going beyond' (*plus ultra*), against theological metaphysics and its *ne plus ultra*, towards the feasible plans of mankind in exercising control over nature. Intellectuals in Europe shifted attention from the supernatural to the natural and from destiny to volition. Descartes proposed a quasi-mechanical conception of the universe and thought it possible for humans to exert total control over it, extending without limit their experiences.

Yet, existential fear underwrote both religious obscurantism and the Enlightenment's opposition to it. As a result, one century later, Hegel's idealist and Marx's materialist dialectics were juxtaposed. But, from experience gathered with the struggle to control nature through control over humans through the product of their toil, living by the false *Idea* of extended time-space through material possessions, this particular synthesis of *being* and *non-being* into *becoming* can bridge the two dialectics: There is a material underbase to life-extending knowledge, in that it comes with material humans, concerns humans, and is embodied in material artefacts. But this campaign to control human destiny is an infeasible *Plan*. *Plus Ultra* crossed Hercules' columns, into the Atlantic, to discover a New World and build ruthless capitalism, North American style. Intellect was put to the service of cruelty, which was given vent into massacring natives, usurping their land, importing slaves, expanding the conquerors' reach by means of railroads, gun powder and other *structures*. Spinoza's ideas about a trusting and peaceful life as outcome of trade proved to be unreal. The birth and childhood of capitalism were so bloody, that it would be a miracle if its adulthood were blessed. No intellect was wasted on lofty excursions. The masses became even more vicious, cruel and cunning in promoting their end. But according to Socrates, this made them unwise:

> [T]o fear death . . . is in fact nothing other than to seem to be wise, but not to be so. For it is to seem to know what one does not know: no one knows whether death does not even happen to be the greatest of all goods for the human being; but people fear it as though they knew well that it is the greatest of evils. And how is this not that reproachable ignorance of supposing that one knows what one does not know?
>
> (Plato's *Apology of Socrates*, West and West, 1984: 29b)

Existential angst kept haunting people, even worse than before. Materialism and metaphysics mix in coveting under fear of death the time-space of others, as this is shaped and formed into commodities by means of production. The instruments are material, the goal is ideal, and it is the contest that eventually matters, not its outcome. As a matter of fact, if things ever reached any final solution, that could only be death. The process of ascribing value to commodities is about an idea, as we will have more chance to explain. But, as fear breeds aggression, a theory which places fear at the engine must place aggression at the driver's seat, while a theory which aims at concealing these must be initiated by something foreign to fear, even if that has to be as absurd as utility. Marx acknowledged fear, seeing through his materialist perspective man to be insecure against nature's hostile forces. So, the social forces on which he based his theory were fighting ones. He acknowledged aggressiveness.

In a nutshell: People chose to submit to a metaphysical fear, which becomes the source of all other fears, especially the fear of each other, as each knows that others covet his *own* time-space. Fear breeds both submissiveness and aggression, the mix of which depends on the circumstances. Thus, people become 'submissively aggressive' (or 'aggressively subservient'). In every case, humans are neither pleasure-seeking machines nor ministering angels, but scared to death of death, trying to cling on to life for as long as they can, claiming this right from each other. If pleasure or regard for others may serve this on occasion, so much the better. But as this truth is repulsive, we refer to it plainly only when we refer to the *power* that accrues to wealth. Most of the time, we hide it from ourselves (or we hide ourselves from it) with a lie, as when we talk about status, recognition or pleasure. If there was much genuine pleasure in consuming commodities, many Westerners would have blown up from bliss. The truth is that, beyond natural pleasures of the senses, all other pleasure there is to consumption (and there is much such) is in that we know that others are deprived of what we possess. And if one insists on finding also some other pleasure in such monolithic pursuit of the mind, that must be in the bliss of a mind gone numb by surrendering its right to think elaborately, to be concerned, to pursue a fulfilling but tormenting involvement with serious matters.

Economics of angst

We can live each experience only once. The present has no duration. Time only goes *forward*, irreversibly, in the sense that what is known cannot become unknown and be discovered again. The experiencing of time with causality running only in one direction, from records of past events (memories) to resolution of the uncertainty that is intrinsically associated with the future, yields a psychological arrow of time. Every new impression or idea, every mystery solved, every new piece of knowledge marks this unidirectional passage of time and gives us a sense of its duration. Thus runs also our personal hourglass out, to our despair. We try to revive the past in counterfeit ways, through class reunions, trips of nostalgia, collections, recollections, etc. Memories, even unpleasant ones, are treasured because they are irreversibly past. Experiences tick our time, bringing us nearer to death. Thus crushed between an unchangeable past and an unknowable future, living only one moment at a time, we feel our lives to be zero-dimensional inside an infinitely dimensioned reality, as we construe it. So, we try to extend ourselves into it, to experience more of it. And since we can do nothing about the past, we try to extend ourselves into the future. This can be done in two contrasting ways: One, which we may call 'creatively destructive', gives a quick end to things, trying to pack as many experiences per unit of clock time as possible, in panicky escape forwards, and another, which we may call meditative or Buddhist, in which experiences are slowed down. In the first case, time seems to be running faster, much as water quickly escapes when one tries to grab it with force in his hands. In the second case, time seems to last. Water is let seep slowly through one's fingers. In the first case, people try to act on things and on nature, being in war with them and trying to exercise control and power over them through power over humans. The second is a state of contemplative, reconciled tranquility within nature.

For Kierkegaard, fear of the future is fear of ourselves: an own, irrepressible *angst* over our fragility and minuteness. We try to fight it with joviality: There is sadness in jovial faces. Against it we are alone, so we gather in crowds: There is loneliness in the crowds. We feel despondent as we realize that time takes a toll that we refuse to shell out, wearing our bodies out, taking away our most beloved ones and otherwise. The narrower our intellectual horizons become and the more they are reduced to economic materialism, the more we tend to seek solace in spiritual absurdities. Apprehension and despondence turn into aggression, after they first become hatred for ourselves for not being as important, powerful and lasting as we want, for being impotent against time-space. We are taken by awe when we compare our mortal nothingness with the infiniteness and permanence of the cosmos. Every change to the world that surrounds us reminds us that some part of our lives is irreversibly gone. These slowly turn into enviousness, as we falsely think that others are spared and are happier. So, we see their happiness as being, at least in part, legitimately ours. And this is actually so, to the extent that division of labour depersonalizes (the output of) human toil.

Historically, humans have always tried to snatch life from each other indirectly, by usurping (the product of others') labour. Slavery, in various forms, has been a most common method, the most pervasive of all being 'slavery' within the family. Civilization tries to channel this into ever more productive outlets, in less animalish, more civilized or, one might say, more concealed ways. Today more than ever, we attempt to expropriate life in organized ways, within institutions and rules of property and economic conduct. But no matter what we do, the cosmos remains infinite in our perception and our minuteness is inescapable. So, nothing can allay our fear, our desires become insatiable and our thirst for life is unquenchable. In *Politics*, Aristotle argued that because people's desire for life is not limited, their desire for goods is not satiable or delimited either. This is the main line of causality. Failure to win life and soothe our angst feeds positively back to intensify our fear, making us more addicted to man-made commodities that stand as tokens for life through the human time-space that went into making them. Or, as Schumacher (1973: 33) put it: 'Every increase of needs tends to increase one's dependence on outside forces over which one cannot have control, and therefore increases existential fear.'

So, time-space is scarce for us, as this is registered through knowledge. But as the perception of time-space is a construct of the mind based on life experiences, which are always social experiences, the time-space worth wanting is social time-space, that is, time-space as accumulated social knowledge that is useful in our fight against death or, to quote Aristotle again, knowledge which is 'of great practical importance for the conduct of life'. And what knowledge is of such importance depends on what kind of life is pursued, according to culture. Noble life goes with lofty knowledge, cattle life with base. Depending on culture and knowledge, we can share in greatness in various ways. We can admire the Sistine or the Parthenon or rejoice with the Ninth. But if culture is vulgar, it entices us to usurp greatness and make it *own*; to *privatize* it, which means to deprive it from others. (*Private* comes from the Latin *privare*, which means *deprive*.) But upon more serious inspection, one can see that it is the possessor who is actually deprived, as revealed by the ludicrous behaviour of the nouveau riche, which found its nemesis in Thorstein Veblen's pen. Then, we break and seize the marbles of the Parthenon, and we are able to 'share' in Renoir only by privately possessing his paintings. Hume (2000: 202, original emphasis) contended that 'property may be defin'd, *such a relation betwixt a person and an object as permits him, but forbids any other, the free use and possession of it*'. This is why, in capitalism, the only knowledge that is valued is that which can be embodied in commodities: Because only such knowledge can be had property of.

Through such deprivation private ownership entails conflict. Enmity is added by one's also deriving pleasure from making others aware of such deprivation, demonstrating what they are deprived of. So, this kind of pleasure is not any self-contained, harmless motive. Most of what passes under the guise of utility is a reflection of the others' relative deprivation and, in this sense, it is for the bearer a spiteful giving vent to an inner distress; a vengeance for what we consider is the others' undeserved advantage. In the same sense, all privatization of commonly produced artefacts or of common resources is in considerable measure other-disregarding.

Private consumption above basics and economics in general seen as life-taking or, more precisely, as time-space expropriation, may appear as provoking exaggeration, reminding of Proudhon's, who argued in *Qu'est-ce que la Propriete?*:

> If I were asked to answer the following question: 'What is slavery?' and I should answer in one word, 'Murder!' my meaning would be understood at once. No further argument would be required to show that the power to take from a man his thought, his will, his personality, is a power of life and death, and that to enslave a man is to kill him. Why, then, to this other question: 'What is property?' may I not likewise answer 'Theft'?

So, lest there be any confusion, apart from instances such as the trade of human organs from living persons, which are literally life-taking, but one can reject them as not constituting serious argument, 'life-taking' is used here upon an interpretation of life as being in experienced social time-space, which is what is contributed to production by those who engage in it. To give an example, the high-cost and presumably high-quality medical services hired by those who can afford them are knowledge and skills acquired by doctors or other medical personnel through practicing upon those who could not afford to pay, although none would argue that the latter were deprived of their lives in this way. In every case, the life-depriving interpretation simply pushes to its logical consequence what has been long known, but lacking shape. Veblen, whose leitmotif was presumably only about ludicrous, fashionable consumption as a means for gaining status, did trace the source of such desire to demonstrate power in the taking away of life (of beast and enemy) and to the owning of life (of women or slaves). Moreover, in industrial society: 'the concept of ownership extends itself to include the products of their industry, and so there arises the ownership of things as well as of persons' (Veblen, 1912: 34). We take for granted then that these would not have been so, if ownership of persons were not appreciated by society at large, through respect for whoever manages to attain it. In this lies our argument about responsibility, collusion and accountability, which are often passive, as in the male-chauvinism example.

So, we expend effort in seeking self-assurance through what others appreciate in us. In most cultures, time is money and one *is* what one *has*. But, by coveting what others have or have made, and to the extent that we manage to obtain these, we live a life that is not ours; we live a commodified life. Seen from a creativity angle, reducing the substance of creative work and enjoyment (of *work in enjoyment*) to a strife for control over work put into commodities amounts to fossilizing life, to eventual hatred for life and loss of its true content. Because commodities are fossilized life, they provide a false sense of security: By being owned, they stay put: they *belong*. But when one's *being* is made to coincide with the objects one owns, one feels insecure that what is had may be lost and thus he or she will cease to *be*, for having little else to draw self-assurance from. This contradiction between real life and life as found in artefacts, and their dialectical merging into one's *becoming* through possessions, is what characterizes modern capitalistic life. And as money is general equivalent, we acquire what Mitchell (1937: 306) called the 'habit of mind begotten by the use of money' in a culture where 'the money economy...stamps its pattern upon wayward human nature, makes us all react in standard ways to the standard stimuli it offers, and affects our very ideals of what is good, beautiful and true' (ibid.: 371). This 'habit of mind begotten', Aristotle would call 'cattle life'.

Because our angst is difficult to tame or confront, we superpose a consuming and possessing psychosis on it in order to distract our attention, much as a toy distracts a kid and makes it stop crying. With age, our angst grows deeper, until we resign. Before that, we make sure that we pass it on to our children, *our nearest passage to eternity*, by teaching them to appreciate commodified lifestyles: to buy trinkets and frills they would not care about, had we inculcated other values in them. Thus, before they come across any fear of death, even before they come to think about death, life is made to coincide in their minds with consumption and with the particular kind of knowledge which relates to it. Soon, this is all the knowledge they value, until the relationship between consumption and (the fear of) death is obscured in their minds, appearing to them as a relation between consumption and (good) life; between commodities and enjoyment, from which neoclassical theory picks up, surreptitiously.

As Fromm (2004: 157–8) argued:

> [I]t is consciousness of nature, which first appears to men as a completely alien, all-powerful and unassailable force, with which men's relations are purely animal and by which they are overawed like beasts; it is thus a purely animal consciousness of nature (natural religion).
>
> ...this natural religion or animal behavior towards nature is determined by the form of society and *vice versa*. Here, as everywhere, the identity of nature and man appears in such a way that the restricted relation of men to nature determines their restricted relation to one another, and their restricted relation to one another determines men's restricted relation to nature, just because nature is as yet hardly modified historically; and, on the other hand, man's consciousness of the necessity of associating with the individuals around him is the beginning of the consciousness that he is living in society at all....
>
> This sheep-like or tribal consciousness receives its further development and extension through increased productivity, the increase of needs, and, what is fundamental to both of these, the increase in population. With these

there develops the division of labor, which...only becomes truly such from the moment when a division of material and mental labor appears.

Life comes first, and upon this is built everything else. We grab on to life by marshalling all our faculties, especially our mental ones. *We live only in mental tonality.* Some of the means we employ are selfish; others are other-regarding, or even self-disregarding sometimes. But they are all aimed, in one way or another, at resisting the second law, both in its physical and in its psychological ramifications. We try to resist a law that implements nature's predilection for homogeneity at low potential, undermining life by wearing physical and mental structure out. Life being strife, it eventually wears our tonality out and we finally resign. This makes death more bearable than if we did not relent, if we remained in full consciousness of our abating tonality, or if life were about pleasure, as is falsely assumed.

In order to promote this life-goal more effectively, many species form permanent or temporary bonds, gaining better control over their biological niche by joining forces and saving energy. Wolves prey in packs. Birds migrate in flocks, taking advantage of natural laws, as when flying in V's. They develop social structures, use division of labour and assign tasks, in order to promote also species survival as a condition for attaining their personal life-expanding goal. As individuals exploit social structure to personal gain, underlying individualism is concealed. The private gets meshed with the social. Humans always reconfigure this entwining of private with social, adjusting their conception of private gain from the joint effort. 'Social' implies give and take. Culture strikes a balance by acting on the participants' intent. Therefore, the presence of a natural underbase for acquisitiveness does not imply any 'selfish gene' type of asocial (and apolitical) argument, clearing individuals of responsibility and the system (the structure) of blemish. As Fromm maintained, the line is drawn at the instant of division of physical and mental labour, *at the instant of making choices.* Certain choices decide the culture through setting norms, upon which subsequent choices are judged. Thus, we have both concurred that taking life is heinous, *and* we have chosen to do so indirectly: by usurping others' time-space, as this becomes with advance of socially accumulated knowledge more effectively embodied in commodities.

Our history is one of choices made presumably towards civilized ways of conducting this life battle, from brute ways to symbolic ones: from cannibalism, brute force and slavery, to civil society obeying norms of conduct. This has been our strategic answer to the entropy law, which gnaws at our presence. We try to compensate for our physical impotence by flexing our intellectual muscles, employing mental faculties to generate life-related knowledge, with which we (in-)form dynamically changing social structures and arrangements. While we are individually defeated and our bodies wear out, our collective knowledge base and our social structures expand irreversibly, defeating the entropy law on the intellectual front. We might call this *collective tonality.* In this knowledge-related sense, society's arrow of time goes counter to the physical disintegrating law, pointing towards higher order social structures.

Language is one such structure, designed to help us communicate and advance knowledge. Economic knowledge is communicated by means of commodity prices. As Hargreaves Heap (2004) argues, 'consumer goods have more clearly come to form a language system.... We use consumer goods to say things about ourselves and as our identity has become less fixed through traditional bonds of one kind or another, we have had increasing recourse to the world of goods to do it for us.' Stated differently, we embed knowledge practical for the conduct of life in commodities, generating economic semantics that we call values. These then are communicated through (relative) price *movements*. Innovative consuming conduct adds knowledge, updates values, and informs others about it through price changes. Thus, what is or potentially can be in commodities, that is, their value, is not determined exclusively or conclusively by technology, but by anything that adds, along the way, knowledge to the making or to the using of them. Value is in exclusive non-ignorance.

Commodities can be anything, even pebbles (diamonds *are* pebbles), since they only function as tokens, or as 'words' for the said language, not different in their essence from precious metals, horns or shells used by cultures past. Their function is to signify their owners' relative prowess at expropriating time-space from others, not in any objective or measurable sense, but as socially appraised *through the very process of its expropriation*. This is why decorative cockroaches on haute couture dresses can sell for thousands of dollars, and the picture of a Hollywood star picking his nose may sell for as much. To the extent that people acquiesce to such symbolism, commodities do have such power, irrespective of any other properties they may or may not have, which may be normatively judged as absurd, disgusting or detestable. Nostrum or quackery was no less effective than modern medicine, *in final analysis*. And this is true also about entire systems, such as capitalism, which 'work' only to the extent that people think they do.

The increasing importance of such symbolism is manifest in the increasing impact of financial markets on real economies and on people's lives. It is implicit to Keynes's apostrophe about pyramid building, earthquakes, war or hole digging. Capitalist society is a display society: a *societe du spectacle*, in Guy Debord's celebrated terms; an exhibition of shrewdness. People *seek* to be impressed. And when they find none else to be impressed by, they impress themselves. They fool themselves. This does not necessarily mean that they are fools. It just speaks about how they choose to go about life. And the bigger the money that is involved, the less is left to mere chance in this surrealistic impressionism. Thus, only a small, calculated dose of it is allowed in the Oscars, the Eurovision or the World Cup. (The only trouble with the World Cup is that it is difficult to rehearse all the details, so something often goes wrong.) And if there is anything left to strike as odd, this is that economic theorizing has not been based on such presumptions, considering the fact that, beyond basics (food, clothing, shelter and medicine), the greatest part of a modern economy's GDP is in one way or another associated with spectacles or with 'defence', which speaks plainly of power.

Capitalistic reality, therefore, is a show, where all value is reduced to a capacity of artefacts to substitute for life, acting as instruments for life-taking. Wealth thus decides the power over each other's life, in debauchery of Aristotle's vision of Life as Supreme Good, as a noble intellectual activity in which 'its full reality consists' as 'sensation and thought'. Modern life is in *predatory* sensation and thought, where *homo [est] homini lupus* (although this might offend the wolves, who are not as cruel to their own as we are to ours).

Aristotle's vision of the Supreme Good was in the spiritual realm, in virtue and nobleness. His position was summed up in the final Book of his *Nichomachean Ethics*: 'that which is best and most pleasant for each creature is that which is proper to the nature of each; accordingly the life of the intellect is the best and the pleasantest life for man, inasmuch as the intellect more than anything else is man; therefore this life will be the happiest' (Aristotle, 1934: X. vii. 9). And 'the activity of God, which is transcendent in blessedness, is the activity of contemplation; and therefore among human activities that which is most akin to the divine activity of contemplation will be the greatest source of happiness' (ibid.: X. viii. 7).

For Aristotle, pure *Thought* (*Theoria*) as disinterested contemplation about the truth was the highest form of activity and source of happiness. He saw happiness itself as secondary; neither as a cause, nor as an End. However, he thought of 'the generality of mankind' as preferring a cattle life. Therefore, an intellect gone sour with the materialist twist history took should not have taken him by surprise, since he knew that 'worldly goods may almost be said to be a hindrance to contemplation' (ibid.: X. viii. 6) and that 'theories...are powerless to stimulate the mass of mankind to moral mobility. For it is the nature of the many to be amenable to fear...since, living as they do by passion, they pursue the pleasures akin to their nature, and the things that will procure those pleasures, and avoid the opposite pains, but have not even a notion of what is noble and truly pleasant, having never tasted true pleasure' (ibid.: X. viii. 13-ix. 3–4). Many centuries later, Schumacher (op. cit.: 116) commented: 'Nature...abhors a vacuum, and when the available "spiritual space" is not filled by some higher motivation, then it will necessarily be filled by something lower – by the small, mean, calculating attitude to life which is rationalized in the economic calculus.'

An intellectual state being tonal, it is prone to an alarming kind of positive feedback: As one lets his intellect fall in disuse, it becomes enfeebled. And the more enfeebled it becomes the more difficult it is to shift it back into gear. One then sinks into pliant individualism, not caring to develop a faculty that doesn't pay off. Meritoriousness in a humdrum life goes only as far as market pay-offs, and a zero-sum contest for life makes one cunning or smart, but not wise. In this, one may then excel, while being globally ignorant. These, along with fear, can make one gullible, giving to an observer the impression of a non-creative puppet. According to Aristotle (op. cit.: VI. Xii. 9-xiii): 'There is a certain faculty called Cleverness, which is the capacity for doing the things...that conduce to the aim we propose, and so attaining that aim. If the aim is noble, this is a praiseworthy faculty: if base, it is mere knavery; this is how we come to speak of both prudent men and knaves as clever.'

So, the impression that consumers are puppets is false and misleading. As Shackle (1972: 5) noted, economic motives are 'concerned with acquisition and with the sharing, or the tearing into portions, of the product of man's collaborative effort.' This involves conflict, so rules are set to contain it. In capitalism, such rules are also designed to inflame angst, hence more conflict and more governance, in a spin of value production. Everything is subordinated to a ritual of expropriative shrewdness. But when animal spirits are ignited towards mundane pursuits, they will intimidate all restraints. As people know that life is violent strife in one or another way, they refuse to abandon an established regime, however bleak their life and future in it may be, not just because of fear of the suffering that revolt entails, but also because of fear of the unknown forms of violence that will replace the ones they have become familiar with.

One original, many derived scarcities

Because mortality is insurmountable, our fear of death cannot be allayed and the felt life-scarcity is unappeasable. This is the only real scarcity, in final analysis. All other scarcity stems from this. What appears as desire for goods is a desire for life, seen as embodied in those. We want more man-made artefacts because of the human time-space that went into making, valuing and using them, beyond any other quality they may have, which could be nil, beyond some agreed upon level of decent survival. And we value such time-space subjectively as experienced or perceived time-space; not in any Euclidean sense. This capacity for experiencing time-space, our capacity to live, is the only resource that we try to save on and augment, because this is our only *own resource*. It is time-space that we *want*, literally, to experience more of, to expand our presence in it, to make our *own*.

As part, of the universe, we are incomplete and imperfect. And as Leonardo da Vinci maintained, the part is always inclined to unite with the Whole to which it belongs, in order to escape its being *wanting in extension*. To quench our unquenchable thirst for life, we must first stay alive, which means we must satisfy our basic physical *needs*. These are satiable and constitute the material underbase of life. Everything else is in the realm of ideas. Actually, when one feels that the content of one's life, that is, its extensiveness is lost and he gets resigned, all scarcity disappears. Therefore, there is no intrinsic scarcity to anything bought or sold *as such*, other than its capacity to make us feel that we can extend ourselves through its possession. And as the time-space we value in commodities is socially contributed and appraised, especially under industrial production, its merit depends on the behaviour of the rest of society. In Polanyi's (1944: 46, added emphases) words:

> The outstanding discovery of recent historical and anthropological research is that man's economy, as a rule, is submerged in his social relationships. He does not act so as to safeguard his individual interest in the possession of material goods; he acts so as to safeguard his social standing, his social claims, his social assets. He values material goods only in so far as they serve this end. Neither the process of production nor that of distribution is linked to specific economic interests attached to the possession of goods;... *the economic system will be run on noneconomic motives.*

But where is consumption? Or isn't it among the social relationships? So, once again, in the sphere of production and entrepreneurship, these have not escaped notice, and certainly not that of Schumpeter's. In his *Theory of Economic Development*, referring to the motives of entrepreneurs, he first did away with any idea of equating effort or disutility with pecuniary gains on the margin: 'Effort... does not seem to weigh at all in the sense of being felt as a reason to stop' (Schumpeter, 1934: 92). Second, he did away with hedonism: 'Hedonistically, therefore, the conduct which we usually observe in individuals of our type would be irrational' (ibid.). So: 'This... points to another psychology of non-hedonist character', which he found to be

> the dream and the will to found a private kingdom, usually, though not necessarily, also a dynasty. The modern world really does not know any such positions, but what may be attained by industrial or commercial success is still the nearest approach to medieval lordship possible to modern man. Its fascination is specially strong for people who have no other chance of achieving social distinction. The sensation of power and independence loses nothing by the fact that both are largely illusions.... Then there is the will to conquer: the impulse to fight, to prove oneself superior to others, to succeed for the sake, not of the fruits of success, but of success itself.... The financial result is a secondary consideration, or, at all events, mainly valued as an index of success and as a symptom of victory...
>
> (Ibid.: 93)

If one reads this and other passages of Schumpeter's with consumption in mind, one may not help wonder how it escaped him that similar motives may drive consumption, also. It is indeed difficult to believe that agents are so schizophrenic as to pursue aggressively power in one field, while passively seeking something else in another, or to think that there are two different kinds of agents who pursue different objectives.

Max Weber maintained that significance does not reside in things, but is constructed by the individual under social influences. Such social influences must hold sway of all agents, in all spheres of activity, allowing any odd commodity to perform as symbol of dominance. Indeed, there have been used to this end all kinds of objects in various cultures, the valuing of which could hardly be explained in any other way, and certainly not as objects of any other kind of utility. (Actually, some even inflicted physical pain as, for example, those that had to be pierced through the wearer's body.) Significant is also their mercuriality, or value-volatility. Since we can only usurp others' time-space by anticipating more successfully their appraisals than they anticipate ours, it is necessary that we turn continuously to new wants, abandoning particular commodities promptly, seeking uniqueness in newness and in exclusive non-ignorance, given that value is not in commodities but in that to which they serve as instruments. Incidentally, while it is often received that labour mobility is the most basic complement to capital mobility for increased production of value at low cost through high productivity, our theory finds equally important for the unobstructed performance of capitalism to be the spirited mobility of consumers between commodities (which actually *induces* the said mobility of capital and labour), and this requires adequate expendable incomes and galloping consuming spirits.

Success in the contest for time-space depends on how much expropriating knowledge one produces per time unit relative to others, so we may see that *knowledge* is the ultimate scarce resource on which depends the extension of one's life experience, and this is just a different expression of the same unique, original scarcity. Given adequate supplies of this resource, nothing else can be scarce. Does oil run out or pollute? We find alternative energy sources, *in time*. Our civilization is Promethean: By inventing the wheel and taming the fire, we got one half of it. The other half is in the way we appreciate their value, in what we do with them, which is also an intellectual task and a matter of discretion. These two halves of a single knowledge process speak of production *and* of consumption, and in both of them muscle is subordinate to intellect. Animals and machines undertake a good part of menial tasks. Humans undertake the rest, that which is not yet functionally embodied in capital as reusable labour, until, through the same knowledge process, this too is assigned to capital of newer vintages and amplified, becoming roundabout as we will explain. 'Labour', there-fore, should be construed in such mind-guided sense.

A time-space contest marks everyday life. In thinly populated arid lands and in densely populated cities, conflict for vital space is commonplace. *Vital* means that it is about life. According to Hobbes (1991: 87), 'if any two men desire the same thing, which nevertheless they cannot both enjoy, they become enemies; and in the way to their End (which is principally their owne conservation, and sometimes their delectation only,) endeavour to destroy, or subdue one an other'. One comes across this in crowded cities, where one might logically expect people to avoid reducing vital space below some minimal threshold, where aggressive behaviour sets in. One might expect those who can afford it to abandon or not cram into the cities when violence becomes unbearable and privacy and other conditions are greatly compromised. Also, one might expect aggressiveness to subside with increasing space. This is what other animals tend to do, anyway. Yet, what one observes is precisely those conditions that help intensify the time-space conflict. People pack themselves up in the cities, claiming space from each other even when there seems to be none, peeping into each other's life, fighting for a job place where there are not enough, and so on. Rats would commit mass suicide under such living conditions, but humans do not; not for this reason, anyway. Why? Looking for jobs where there is capital concentration and other such explanations address not causes, but effects. The point is that the only thing humans feel an urge to lay claim on beyond basics is *social* time-space. No time-space has any pragmatic value, unless it belongs to, or is coveted by others. Only such time-space does it make economic sense to *want*.

In areas with low-population density there is less variegation in friction, as people try to intrude each other's literal space laying claims of control over it, regardless of how much they happen to possess. They miss no chance at misappropriating irrigation water or pastureland, and these are life-claiming, as are the guns they carry. Land in the countryside is not scarce, except in its capacity to perform as token for life under a value system based on socially contrived scarcity, where one wins what another loses. Even when there seems to be no overriding factor and people can make composed choices, they act in the same way. Middle-class families, for example, can judge more composedly than those pressed by necessity whether to live in a city, or the usefulness of a car, given its cost and general driving conditions. In many cities, room is exhausted. Driving and parking is a chore. Economic calculus of commodity-based utility should predict that, as the utility drawn from a car goes down and associated costs go up, people should buy fewer and smaller cars. But the number of cars per family keeps rising, as does their size and wastefulness. Large engine-displacement huge SUVs carrying only their drivers – in apogee of individualism reflected in the *auto* (Greek: ἑαυτόν, for *self*) mode of transportation – clog the streets of the cities, wasting the planet. On weekends, things are changed somewhat: SUVs also house the family, as they get jammed on highways instead, trying to get out of the cities. Then, they make a U-turn and get back to be parked on sidewalks.

But whether jammed or parked, they perform. Hume (2000: 191) held that: 'We … judge of objects more from comparison than from their real and intrinsic merit' and 'the custom of estimating every thing [is] by comparison more than by its intrinsic worth and value' (ibid.: 197). Therefore, the more scarce time-space *is made to be*, the greater its symbolic value and the more urgently people will try to claim control over it, intensifying further the sense of its scarcity. Capitalistic rationalization is founded upon such felt, man-made, life-taking scarcity. Whether driven or not, SUVs assert their owners' displacement in a milieu where parking- and driving-space scarcity is actively produced as time-space is expropriated, and it is irrelevant whether one judges this to be stupid, or not. Even the fascist-like design and aggressive driving of these monsters reveal an irrational, life-taking urge, suffice it to consider that their driver will tell you straight in your face that the more massive his vehicle is, the safer *he* will be, in case of an 'accident'. But how about 'others'? And such vehicles' other-claiming potency is also plainly monetary: They are financed in part by others, whose insurance premiums go up with increased costs of damages, for whom gasoline prices go up with increased demand, and otherwise.

To reiterate, there is a single source of scarcity and of our need to be social in a give-in-order-to-take way. The desire for commodities, which makes them appear as scarce, is due to their performing as instruments for tempering this basic scarcity. The standard conception about individual scarcities (of commodities, factors, etc.) is impossible to explain without first explaining tastes. How do people come to realize that they missed something they never thought of, suffice that it only appears in the market? How and why do they switch preferences in what appears to be fashion, fad or some such? Well, they neither missed commodities, nor do they realize that they did. It is just that commodities sit in as mercurial tokens for a time-space contest, which would not be possible without such mercuriality.

The idea that there exists some commodity-based scarcity or commodity-based utility upon which tastes take effect may be simplifying, but it is a hindrance. Such proximal scarcity is but a means to some non-observable, distal end, which is far deeper and more stirring than any lack of material things. Consumption beyond a certain minimum for decent survival that may be socially determined is discretionary. So, economic conduct must be explained only in the light of a clearly specified intent. Any differences in behaviour between individuals, groups or entire populations and any changes across time must be explained upon such *scarcity by intent*, while fallacies such as that of the stable-through-time requirement of the so-called Axiom of Revealed Preferences must be shed. This requires that if bundle A is revealed through purchasing to be preferred to bundle B that costs no more than A at some set of prices, then for bundle B to be purchased *ever*, prices must change so that B costs strictly less than A. With tastes formed and values decided as discussed here, such axioms are pointless. They assume a timeless frame, as is the orthodox one, saying nothing about how prices change.

To illustrate some of the points made, let us consider the saving behaviour of various groups, say, of country and city families. The former are known to have a higher propensity to save, typically attributed to insecurity caused by fluctuations in their income due to dependence of crop yield on natural conditions. But with income of city families being also precarious due to unemployment and flexible labour markets, this cannot provide more than rudimentary or partial explanation. Only some general difference in attitude between the two groups can have a lasting such effect.

The difference is simple. Because the time-space contest depends on socially framed appreciation, it is keener in the cities where its outcome is continuously put to close-up public view by proximity, much like increased competition in sports advances records more quickly. It is not easy to live in a city with monastic lifestyles or consuming patterns, whereas in the countryside one can mend his boots or patch his trousers. This is basically Duesenberry's (1967: 27) 'demonstration effect', which states that consumer preferences are influenced not so much by knowledge about the existence of some commodity, as by frequent contact with it, by seeing others possess it. Proximity and niche play a significant role. Thus, saving or hoarding, versus consuming, implement different strategies in the people's socially contextualized bout with time, as there are differences in the way various people go about consumption. Actually, one can find many such differences depending, say, on national or cultural parameters, history, climatic conditions, etc. Specifically as concerns saving, due to our insecurity about the future, we save money in order to be able to buy time-space in the future. The degree to which this future can be postponed and the way such time-space is valued (the discount rate) depend on how others in our niche appraise things, granted everyone else's chance to compete for time-space in the present, making gains at our expense. In the cities, such chances abound and changes are fast. Income counts more than wealth, due to time asymmetry. One who hoards in the city falls more conspicuously and quickly behind than in the countryside. Thus, country people can afford, in this sense, to allocate part of their income on saving, whereas city people are in the same sense under greater pressure to stretch their expenditures beyond what their income allows, even borrowing at onerous terms.

To sum up: People need to make man-made things scarce so as to be able to ascribe value to them and then claim it from others, because they view life as a bout for human time-space, on which they capitalize by possessing commodities. And since human time-space or, rather, the knowledge accumulated within it, is the only thing that people originally possess and can trade, it is only this that they can claim from each other. In modern capitalistic societies and in previous ones, social standing has always been proportional to one's relative performance in life-snatching, although the ways in which this was pursued and demonstrated were different. As long as conditions for survival could not be met with previous modes of production, one could speak of natural scarcity, based on limits set by nature on exploitable resources. But even under conditions of such base scarcity, population size, which affected the degree of its compulsion, was still under human discretion. Anyway, once survival is guaranteed, all other wants are of human making and choices made concerning those decide what resources become scarce. This then decides relative values. People do not produce means of living well under *external* constraints, measures or tastes. They themselves create the scarcity terms upon which living well is defined.

We take part in the time-space contest without much conscious thought or attention to details, thus saving energy. As Smith (1980: 41) observed, those things which we believe have been resolved 'float through the mind of their own accord, without obliging it to exert itself or to make any effort in order to pass from one of them to another'. But once one sees the mechanism, much falls easily in place. When one buys human organs for transplanting, there is no arguing that one seeks to extend his or her own time-space. When we travel, communicate by phone or watch television, we feel that we reach out to people and places; that we extend ourselves. We may have little such idea when we buy bread, but we do when we search for 'qualities of bread', or when we buy a Rembrandt: By buying it, we deprive others of what they value and want most, reducing their reach to what is socially valued and increasing ours. A good part of our felt *utility* is precisely in this.

The idea of an intriguing relation between economics and knowledge and between knowledge and time-space can be traced back to the classical economists, in their explanation of economic development as aiming towards increasing power and control over nature and over humans. This was made more explicit in the 1930s with Pigou and Keynes, and it was given further impetus and content with the work of Shackle (1958), which prompted Lachmann (1959) to comment: 'Time and knowledge belong together... the impossibility of prediction in economics follows from the fact that economic change is linked to change in knowledge, and future knowledge cannot be gained before its time. As soon as we permit time to elapse we must permit knowledge to change, and knowledge cannot be regarded as a function of anything else.' Further insight on the intrinsic unforeseeability of future knowledge, through which is registered the passage of time, was supplied by Kornai (1971), Caldwell (1982), Addleson (1995), Loasby (1999) and others. Mokyr (2005: 201) notes: 'as economic historians have long understood, technology is knowledge: something that exists in people's minds.... It is the outcome of a game against nature. The rest is commentary.' And: 'Formal, deductive economics does not help us a lot with theories of knowledge, which are quite distinct from information theory' (ibid.). Also: 'What counts for the economic historian interested in the impact of new technology on growth and living standards is how new knowledge came into being, how it spread, how it came to be believed and how it persuaded households and firms to alter their behaviour' (ibid.: 201–2).

We need to add to Mokyr's first quotation that it is a game played against nature by its being against humans, and this is not just commentary. And we need to add further that consumption, too, is part of the said knowledge activity, although little has been done to pursue this. Still, some suspicion that consumption is about gaining some kind of control is not altogether missing, although status and rank have monopolized interest. Thus, Layard (1980) comments that 'since the institutions of the world are mainly devised by those who have succeeded in the competitive struggle, one cannot assume that the social cost of competition (to the loser) has been fully taken into account'. And, as Witt (2001) notes, 'the trivial purpose of consumption, i.e., the corresponding expenditure, is to gain command over the consumption item. But why people want this command is usually left open. Their motives are considered a matter of subjective preferences which are not explained.'

For such insightful queries to produce concrete results, a particularization of the knowledge-procurement idea is needed, which will explain acquisitiveness as a rational act in some well-specified sense of the term 'rational', which may not fail to consider the ontology of consumers, and hence their goals and motives. This entails openness of the knowledge process whereby value is created, that is, uncertainty, in a world of many admissible solutions among which agents in their desperate pleading for more life are called upon to choose.

Irreversibility

The second thermodynamic law holds for closed physical systems, that is, systems that do not exchange mass or energy with their environment, inducing a physical time's arrow: a direction in the movement of time. For such systems, the law decrees that *entropy*, a magnitude providing a measure of the system's structural homogeneity, or of our ignorance about its component states, can only be increased, irreversibly. With time, such systems leak structure. Their energy is changed from *available* (capable of providing work) into *non-available*, or degraded forms that cannot produce any more work. Potentials tend to diminish. Available energy (negative entropy) may be increased only if the system is open to outside energy flows and the rates of inflow exceed their second-law deterioration. The law still holds then, since the entropy of some higher-level system from which the flow is drawn loses structure. So, time works on physical systems in a deconstructive way. This supplies a time's arrow from past (low entropy, high structure or informational content) to future (high entropy, etc.).

Closed (isolated) systems are hard to find. The systems we can observe are open to various flows. Economic systems are open to flows of knowledge originating naturally from the sublime agent, which prises them open also to selected flows of mass and energy from material inputs and physical labour. Through knowledge, these other flows are transformed and made into tokens of their producers' time-space, and on the basis of this they are valued. Generation and acquisition of economically relevant knowledge is supported by institutions and mechanisms which are agreed upon, according to some particular rationalization or purpose. Movement in the direction of this goal is recorded through the building up of a particular type of knowledge structure and through improvement of a particular type of efficiency that we will discuss in the sequel.

In a way, this arrow of time is opposite and superior to the thermodynamic one, as it anticipates monotonic *increasing* of the system's informational content or structure. Although any amassing of knowledge would do as a means for documenting the passage of time, a time's arrow for economic systems must accommodate some rational intent, since otherwise economic conduct would be aimless, haphazard and meaningless, in which case there would probably have been observed a slow, unco-ordinated, directionless movement, dissimilar to the one which has developed into today's capitalism. So, before theorizing, we must agree in principle upon a well-defined concept of purpose to all economic activity, anything promoting it being rational, *in this particular sense*.

There is another difference between the second thermodynamic law and the above concept of social irreversibility. Whereas a physical system can increase its structure only at the entropic expense of some other, higher-level system inside which it is embedded, no such thing is *necessary* for economic systems. Increased value deriving from increased structural roundaboutness does not necessarily imply higher physical entropy, and the use of physical resources is not related in any simple way to it. Given a certain structure, growth does increase the use of all physical inputs by the same proportion, but the sublime agent always changes the system's structure, improving its efficiency. Since the final desideratum is symbolic value, not physical commodities, increased use of physical resources does not necessarily accompany growth. The sublime agent that is responsible for generating value is supplied generously by nature, cannot quit functioning and makes everything that relates to the system, and in particular tastes, endogenous.

Assuming this agent out, no value would be possible to produce, however abundant all other inputs, including raw physical labour. In Laborit's (1996) words: 'When a human being hewed a stone, he passed information on to matter.' The first club or dart *made* by a human was a brain-child, not a muscle-child, *and same with its use*. Knowledge and the skills of the muscles, not their raw power, allow us to produce and use anything from a primitive tool to today's high-tech gadgets. Therefore, if we could measure the contributions of this agent, that is, the new pieces of knowledge as they came, we would have found ourselves some minimal ground to base an ultimate theory of value on, where transactions would be seen not as exchanges of value-equivalent, distinct physical items, but as exchanges of different instances of a single mental resource, namely, of these contributions as valued subjectively according to the cognitive capacity of each transacting party, no two such capacities being same.[2] Equivalently, the valued resource could be seen as social time-space expended to the production of these disequilibrating innovations. However, the sublime agent is not tangible, its yield is uncertain, wards off closure and rules out completeness. It frustrates exactness and certitude of closed-form modelling, and it makes a mockery of the type of concrete statements mainstream economists like. And yet, no realistic account of economic phenomena is possible by ignoring it. Openness to it allows the system to increase its structure and the value it produces per time unit, which is an impressive characteristic of advanced capitalism.

Irreversibility implies asymmetry. As time is irreversible, life is in the conquest of the next moment, of the next piece of knowledge, not of knowledge already annexed. As psychologists and neurobiologists know, we are more sensitive to changes in sensory stimuli, than to absolute stimulation levels. Changes of perception alert us more than constant levels of awareness. A stock of wealth differs from a flow of current income in our perception of our relationship with time, and this is more keenly felt in the modern, accelerated lifestyles. The same asymmetry explains the difference between consumption commodities, which have a low investment–goods ratio and to which many have access, and capital goods which are owned only by few. Only the latter can reach into the future, by retaining further productive potential. Finally, due to this same asymmetry, looking forward to pleasant experiences revives us more than does their memory, which may even cause melancholy.

Shifting emphasis from information and equilibrium to disequilibrating knowledge casts most issues in new light. Stated picturesquely, it all starts from the idea that consumers do not 'shop till they drop', as the saying goes, while seeking utility, but they shop *because* they drop, hoping that they can thus stay afloat. This reversed causality capsizes much of the usual economic reasoning and reaches beyond economics proper. As resources and power accrue to those who excel in acquisitive banality and are withdrawn from others, banality prevails in everyday conduct.

This relates to values and concepts in general. Among others, it requires revisiting the issue of poverty. The usual way of looking at this issue is in terms of income. If this is below some specified level, then one is said to be poor. But if we abstract from survival and focus on time-space, the view is different. The perception of poverty becomes subjective and the poor (or 'poor') emerge as losers in a game of wits in which not all can win, a game in which everyone tries to outsmart others in usurping, attaining different degrees of (self-) esteem according to his or her relative success. Thus, a new set of ethical issues is raised and exploitation is cast in new light, emerging not as a result of malice of a few against the many, but as an agreed upon arrangement and as personal success in all-out rivalry by anticipating the moves of others and capitalizing on such foresight. With all being eager to reap private benefits from the commons, it becomes then hard to side with those who have failed, or with those who have squandered the fruits of former success. Emphasis is shifted from persons, states and outcomes not to classes of persons, as chosen by Marx, but to intentions and motives, which he largely sidestepped.

Further, both capital and consumption items are (embodiments of) knowledge, so either kind does for expropriating time-space. This smoothes the distinction between capital as *restraint* on enjoyment through deferment of consumption, and as a *means* towards increased enjoyment in the future. Since consumer and producer knowledge are not synchronized, they need to be buffered by capital to reduce obstructions, shortages or bottlenecks. The degree of buffering depends on the degree of non-contemporaneousness between these parallel knowledge processes, as well as on system velocity. Advanced capitalist economies need more such buffering than backward ones, and this feeds back to intensify the capital accumulation process.

Besides ideological issues, consumption-related knowledge raises methodological and analytical ones. Ackerman (2002) notes the havoc played with uniqueness and stability of equilibrium due to the fact that consumption of many commodities and a commodity-based notion of utility induces too many dimensions of possible variation. As Saari (1995) has shown, when the dynamics of the price system is collapsed onto fewer dimensions, by aggregation, all possibilities become open. So, Ackerman claims that 'this framework...is unproductive. Useful mathematical analysis of consumer behavior requires a more compact and manageable structure. In particular, it requires a low-dimensional representation, which cannot be defined in terms of individual commodities' (op. cit.: 63). And: 'A better model of consumption, therefore, is an essential step toward better economic theory in general' (ibid.: 64).

Our answer to these is the single-underlying-scarcity, uniform-motive hypothesis. We propose, that is, a representation over a single psychological dimension, that of perceived time-space, although this is hardly any one-dimensional space in physical terms that yields easily to misleading mathematical quantification. And we endorse Ackerman's concluding comments, which provide an apposite discussion about the nature of a meaningful theory of consumer behaviour along such lines. He argues: 'Rejection of...commodity-based utility, would call for a different kind of rethinking of economic theory....Consumer behavior needs to be reconceptualized in terms of other fundamental variables' (ibid.: 67–8). Then, he cites three attempts that 'came to the brink of a breakthrough' in the 1960s and explains why they were not completed. Finally, he advises that to get through the stalemate 'it will be necessary to impose some structure and limits on the list of desired characteristics or experiences...perhaps departing even farther...from the established patterns of neoclassical theory', claiming that 'many contemporary economists would conclude that such a theory was not really economics. Yet, the alternative theory would be more secure than the wobbly and unwieldly neoclassical edifice, for it would have repaired the flaws in the foundation, deep in the theory of consumer behaviour' (ibid.: 68). Our campaign in this investigation is precisely according to these lines, by submitting as a candidate for 'other fundamental variables' the notion of experienced time-space.

An all-encompassing theory?

All-most. Social theories are condensed descriptions of some complex reality, typically needing lots of particularization in order to provide a full account, which would be useless. In economics, what we observe is contingent and could always have been otherwise. Subjective appraising of situations and of commodities gives rise to apparent contradictions. So, let us try to anticipate some objections or queries from two general sources: (a) isolated behaviour that goes against one's own interest and (b) other-regarding behaviour.

In a literal sense, expanding personal time-space means living longer and reaching farther. But the theory should not be interpreted in such narrow sense, or out of context. It refers to a conception of time-space that is social and experienced and subjectively appreciated, in a certain social environment. Under such circumstances, to improve their standing people may smoke, drive dangerously, travel by airplane and do other things that do not seem to be conducive to expanding literal time-space (they may even entail risks to it), or to promoting one's self-interest as this is commonly understood. And, of course, wars are waged, in which people get massively killed, which is a rather macabre way to expand time-space. But we have made clear that what we mean is that acquisition of artefacts is acquisition of human time-space in the form of socially gathered knowledge that goes into making those. Such acquisition may take various forms and expressions, many of which may seem quite bizarre. This is how 'we form a notion of different ranks of men, suitable to the power or riches they are possest of; and this notion we change not upon account of any peculiarities of the health or temper of the persons, which may deprive them of all enjoyment in their possessions' (Hume, op. cit.: 192).

One may feel like reaching out into time-space by talking over the phone, travelling faster and farther, making new acquaintances, sending SMS messages to TV shows, or even by smoking. Smokers will tell you that smoking is not just about pleasure. Often, it is even a great displeasure. But no matter what doctors may say about addiction to nicotine or what psychotherapists may say about relaxing, a smoker feels like reaching out by lighting up. (I speak from experience, fortunately past.) There is no arguing that this is a suicidal way of extending life, but the life-campaign as driven by angst is suicidal in some important sense anyway, and filled with contradictions, the greatest of all being war, which keeps making historically manifest that life is (in) taking life. And it must also not escape that even what we might arguably call literal time-space expansion, in the sense of lengthening the duration of one's life or of expanding one's living space, is subject to the man-made conventions of clock time and Euclidean space.

Patterned behaviour, as is smoking or eating junk food, queries about imitation versus innovation. These mesh with each other and merge dialectically. Banality may be prevalent, from cliché, commonplace expressions of language to passing fads of all kinds. Upon reflection, though, it becomes clear that people are different in their sameness, like different bricks in a Pink Floyd wall. Newness is what everyone goes after, even while imitating, so one should look into whatever newness there is even in aping manners, be it a new sport, hairstyle, brand of cigarettes or smoking style. Imitation void of newness can explain nothing, because such behaviour is of genuine fools: Those who start dancing after the music has stopped playing, paying for the gains of others (through price differentials, as we will explain) and getting nothing in return. Birth and diffusion of patterns is an intricate and intriguing matter, entailing what Stigler and Becker (1977) called 'the demonstration of alert leadership, or at least not lethargy, in recognizing and adopting that which will in due time be widely approved', which is 'social rivalry, and it is, like all rivalry, both an incentive to individuality and a source of conformity'.

So, imitation, too, is forward looking. It looks into generating knowledge by first picking up information that can help one anticipate correctly the behaviour of others. People use any means of collecting such information, but they all involve being with others rather than staying apart. Those who have fallen behind engage in mimicking those who have done better; never those who have fallen even further behind. While thus trying to catch up, imitators also try to break new ground. Only against the backdrop of leaders may one get the false impression that mimicking is passive. As Alchian (1950) argued, while imitators copy others, they may also 'innovate by wittingly acquiring some unexpected or unsought unique attributes'.

In cases such as buying health services, real estate, etc., time-space expansion is as literal as it can be, but it is also symbolic. As anything beyond basics is vanity and as the logic that guides vanity is un-refutable, everyone knows that others will not stop coveting the time-space he or she put into socially divided production. So, one cannot afford to slow down or walk out. It is a catch-22 situation. Cigarettes may serve this, as do health services or bread. If the two of us worked to make bread and cigarettes, only, and if I usurped all of it (except what was necessary for you to survive and keep contributing work to my benefit), then I would have usurped all the *relevant* time-space *for as long as it would matter*, that is, for as long as I would live, even though I might be killing myself by smoking all those cigarettes. Now, that does not dispute that I would also prefer to live longer, but killing myself does not refute the above claim either. This helps explain a lifestyle in which 'a growing number of Americans – perhaps a majority – would live longer and healthier lives if they had less constant access to processed foods and beverages, motorized transportation, energy-saving "conveniences" ', as Ackerman (op. cit.: 67) noted. Social displacement goes beyond just living longer or healthier lives.

We do prefer pleasant experiences to unpleasant ones, but some enjoy what others hate, and we prefer more experiences per time unit to less. Simple pleasure does not avail as motive or goal, and our perception of what is worthwhile to pursue in life is not exhausted in its duration, or in gathering pleasures. Emotions of which humans are capable of can generate different experiences that can qualify as extenders of *felt* presence in a social environment. For example, we yearn to live with our children and those whom we love, to revive past moments and shared experiences. We would like to be able to turn the clock back. Yet, career hunting and hectic lifestyles – which go in the opposite direction, rupture such bonds and entail particular health risks – also work to the same expansionary effect, albeit in different ways. The life project is about striking a balance, by discretion.

Let us turn to the other source of possible refutations. Frustrated with *Homo economicus*, but also inhibited about the real situation, many thinkers turn to other-regarding instances of behaviour. (Solidarity, reciprocity, generosity, fairness, etc.) From the perspective adopted in this investigation, whether aimed at challenging the neoclassical world view or at pointing to alternative possibilities for a more humane society, these theoretical excursions into goodwill-economics impede self-awareness. Humans are capable of noble conduct, as they possess both good and bad traits. So, they could forge and mould all kinds of bonds in society, which they have actually done, upon various historical occasions. The question, therefore, is: Which traits prevail culturally and become dominant, how, and why? In the chosen acquisitive path culminating with capitalism, people need schooling in order to be virtuous and other-regarding. But, as such schooling is part of the culture that led them to be in need of it, all they are likely to learn from it is how to conceal their wickedness. Indeed, there are many ways in which the selfish can be made to appear as unselfish. Therefore, basing economic theory on those who return to their owner significant amounts of money they found in the street or leave tips is stretching arguments too far and is counterproductive.

To accommodate other-regarding behaviour and aggressive individualism in the same frame, the dialectical association between individual and social must be taken into account. We do not get very far within society by disregarding it. Strange and twisted as it may sound, the only way to go about surviving is against society, at the expense of society, usurping each other's time-space, which means *within* society, but not *with* it. (Cf. the Hobbesian complesance.) The very constitution of society is a result of calculation. It is pointless to make theory from the fact that people leave tips to waitresses they will not see again. They may just like them, if I may resort for once to a neoclassical argument, since even the blind, asexual *Homo economicus* might not be able to resist in certain occasions (and neoclassicists would not be offended by this). Similarly, moguls are happy to contribute huge, by normal standards, sums of money to charity. Such charity has always been very fashionable, and very highly advertised, which is quite telling. (Two recent cases are those of Warren Buffett and Bill Gates.) But more telling, according to our theory, is that even the beneficiaries would laugh at anyone who gave away his wealth, without any calculation. So, self-interest is most effective when it is successfully concealed. Occasional calculated regard for those to whose suffering we have contributed is a most effective way of soothing our scruples, deceiving others and promoting further our own interest.

Picking selectively among human traits in order to come up with an argument does not make for a robust theory and provides no explanation. What would make sense (and this is what we undertake here) would be to accommodate seemingly diverse traits in a coherent and comprehensive framework upon some unequivocal ontology. Only the initiating idea may be left unexplained, taken for granted or considered as natural. In our theory, this is the fear of death that joins us, driven by which the individual becomes meshed with the social, and self-regard with other-regard. Of course, nothing prohibits other-regarding to be genuine at times. But altruistic behaviour is by far the exception rather than the rule. Capitalism is not founded upon altruism, and altruism does not avail for explaining it. Simply, as all is about life and as none knows what lies beyond, why not take precautions and be nice, from time to time, in small, calculated doses?

Speculative consumption, value and prices

Knight (1923) maintained that 'life is an exploration in the field of values' and that wants are cultural and provisional. A good part of this exploration is in the sphere of consumption, which has exploded into a phantasmagoria of such wants, perceived as needs by consumers. In a certain way, they are needs of an impelling kind that reaches into the existential realm, where paradox reigns. In order to escape from the grip of their angst, people create an artificial realm of wants and symbolic consumption, surrendering to a psychosis which deepens their angst. Oscar Wilde's advice works in reverse here: The worst way to get rid of this angst is by yielding to it.

Exploration into value means creation and appropriation of value. But as Shackle (1972: 8) explained, 'valuation is an act of the mind', and 'though valuation is in origin the personal and private act of the individual mind, yet it becomes through the device of the market a public and objective fact upon which every individual, at least in regard to goods for immediate consumption, agrees' (ibid.: 9). Further, 'knowledge is a "raw material" of value' (ibid.: 208). And as time and knowledge belong together, the raw material of value is time-related knowledge, that is, knowledge which is of 'practical importance for the conduct of life'. But Aristotle's 'practical' needs to be made specific, and our theory does that – the practical nature of this knowledge is in that it discovers the relative efficacy of the various commodities for appraising and individually claiming back the time-space that was contributed to the joint effort of making them; an effort whose output is not otherwise allocatable, except through the very same knowledge process that employs such time-space to produce it, under a single motivation that keeps in-forming commodities even after their production stage.

This efficacy hinges on prices. As Shackle (1972: 83, original emphasis) put it: 'the question what it is now worth . . . while to pay, in exchange for some specific good, depends also . . . on what the *price* of that good is going to be in the future'. And (op. cit.: 231): 'We do not know how much to value this thing in terms of that, because we expect to find out on future days more and more, perpetually, about what these things can do'. And as it is obvious that what things can do is what humans can make them do, it follows that Shackle should be understood as alluding to the consumption stage and to consumption behaviour in general. So, consumption is a speculative activity based on fusion of knowledge with ignorance, that is, of the past with the future, at the present, at the moment a (decision about) purchase is made, and every purchase must be construed in terms of a time profile; not as a snapshot. Through transacting, we experience a sense of control over the yield of our collaborative effort and thus over others; a sense of our capacity to cope with our social and, through this, with our natural environment. As what *will* become known is unknown, this entails dynamic uncertainty within which, and in coping with which, choices must be made that aim at some goal. This provides direction in the particular teleological sense of Aristotle, where some property or quality is identified at higher levels, condensing a meaningful description of coherence at every lower level, all the way down to the individual.

There are theoretical pursuits which are prompted by pure intellectual curiosity, and impulsive pursuits, guided by what may be seen as animalishness. But economics is a practical and deliberate occupation or campaign. Pleasure (utility, or whatever) is not *the object* towards which the conduct of life is aimed. It may *derive* from success in such conduct, but it is at best an arousal: a smell that tells us where to look in order to find that which we are after, which is not the smell itself, much like what hunting dogs go after is not the smell of the prey, but the prey itself. The difference between economics and dogs is that the former is not just about animal instincts, or 'naturals', but has a strong discretionary, culturally fabricated component. Under such prism, pleasure and hardship need not be logically juxtaposed, equated on the margin and played pointless technical games with. They are both naturals (smells) that do not provide ground for self-interested calculation. Economic value, as all social value, needs its own system of reference to acquire semantic content, besides a vocabulary, a syntax and a grammar; in order to form a language of economic communication. The needed ingredient is human time-space contributed, appraised and appropriated *socially*. The strong emphasis being on the social dimension, pleasure or utility in social isolation, as is their common perception and use in mainstream economics, have none of the qualities needed for such semantics.

A production innovation aims at supplying a given commodity at the lowest possible cost of production, yielding a price and profit differential to the innovator. Given a certain state of affairs (for initiating the argument, one may assume a steady-state), an innovator sells at a certain market price a commodity which he produces at lower cost than his competitors, or one that promises to give consumers something better, at a comparable price. But these hinge on how consumers will appraise the situation. Consumers do not just try to exploit any service-providing potential of commodities that is fixed upon them by construction. Instead, they add value to them by inventing uses, *in social proximity*, so that their expenditures on any given basket will render the human input that went into its making more valuable and underpriced. 'Uses', then, should not be understood in the usual sense that collapses everything down to needs. The modern situation is replete with vain wants. It must be interpreted in an efficacy-related sense. In other words, consumers employ the same innovative agency as producers do in constructing expropriative potentials. This may be easier to see in cases where consumer items can be put to further productive use, as is the case with cameras, computer software, etc., but all consumption is actually such, and combining services of commodities provides ample room for consumer innovativeness beyond anything that their producers had in mind, amounting effectively to production of new commodities. (Cf. Bianchi, 1998.)

Given his or her budget constraint, each consumer tries to appropriate more socially contributed time-space by purchasing now those commodities which he or she believes will meet increased demand in the near future, driving their prices up. That is, while not discarding any commonly available information, consumers also try to innovate: to create and seize new opportunities by starting a trend, appraising commodities in novel ways and anticipating others to follow suit. This then becomes new knowledge, possessed privately for a while and making the said consumer a provisional monopsonist who enjoys a price differential.

The budget-constraint clause implicates income distribution and involves a decision about a way of life, or way *to* life, given one's exploration equipment. Given the state of production technology and *any* definition of necessities, hence, also of 'necessary labour' for making those, anything beyond that constitutes surplus. The question then is: To what end does society devote such extra effort? Pleasure-seeking assumes an unreal prior: a cost-benefit kind of decision that cannot be resolved in any coherent way because, even if we assume that the hardship part is known and computable in advance, the pleasure that needs to be equated with excess hardship on the margin is not to become known before all value has been decided, which is never actually decided conclusively in a dynamically evolving social context. It is always on the making, according to the way others behave temporally with respect to commodities. Therefore, the decision must be based upon some real, ontological prior. And the only kind that avails for this is a uniform, stressful emotion seeking relief. In other words, it must be toil versus something that is also to be averted, and of which we are aware of in advance, at the time the decision is made. That is allaying our angst.

Consumer innovations look forward to their demise. An innovator wishes that others follow her lead and that she does not stay a monopsonist for long. And as others catch up, she is forced to move on to new innovations, which explains what appears as general or money insatiability, not associated with any particular commodities. New commodities must always emerge, with cockroach-type excesses being unavoidable. Innovation and imitation perform like blades of a scissors. If others do not pick up a novelty, this may even incur losses to the innovator, in the form of an opportunity cost, as it will turn out that the basket she bought found diminishing acceptance in the market and its price went down, instead of up, and she will have misallocated her income. It may even confer ridicule, making the innovator a jerk for driving a 'lemon car', wearing an eccentric dress, eyeglasses or hairstyle. Latecomers provide an edge to the innovator by raising the bids for the commodity she bought, financing her gains with their losses. Because they are late, they claim back less time-space-value with their expenditures than that which they contribute to the process. And they are also derided for wearing old-fashioned or imitation clothes, picking up habits with delay, in a word, for being backward. (This is the revenge the nouveau riche take on the 'bus class' for not always following their lead promptly.) The price hike their demand induces reflects the value of the innovator's contributed knowledge, and this is her reward. So, all gain is due to knowledge, somehow. None is windfall. And, which matters most in terms of traditional theories, the degree of exploitation in society in general, not only of workers, keeps being determined through the consumption stage.

These face up to monetary considerations, but there are others as well, which are more tenuous and indistinct. Put in psychological terms, the requirement to be unique while being followed means that for something to give us pride it must be 'peculiar to ourselves, or at least common to us with a few persons' (Hume, op. cit.: 191). But 'the pleasant... [must] be very discernible and obvious, and that not only to ourselves, but to others also.... We fancy ourselves more happy, as well as more virtuous or beautiful, when we appear so to others' (ibid.). If none covets what we already have, we cease to appreciate it ourselves, which may make us not appreciate *ourselves*, which brings us back to where it all started as a psychotic acquisitive urge fuelled by lack of assurance. And if many covet it they will soon follow suit, it will cease to be 'peculiar to ourselves', and we must move on to new ways of distinctiveness.

Nuances of consumption behaviour flicker and surface with varying degrees of opaqueness. An example may help explain the symbolic and intersubjective nature of value and the process whereby needs blossom into wants, often preposterously. If any objective measure of it could ever provide proper ground for appraising whatever real value there is to commodities, we should be able to discern it with some degree of clarity and confidence in certain simple cases. Take soap made from olive oil, for example. This is a pure, natural product with many good properties, having proved itself for millennia. It lasts longer, where olive trees grow it is much cheaper than cosmetic soaps, shampoos and antiseptics, even though its production is small scale and labour intensive. It is thus less polluting. It is great for the hair, dermatologists and gynaecologists will insist that their patients use this in the most difficult situations, rather than pharmaceutical antiseptics, etc. So, by all known standards, it appears as a fine option for satisfying *the 'needs' part* of cleanliness, beauty and hygiene. Yet, demand for it is low and declining. Actually, if you tell anyone today that you wash with such soap, chances are that they will laugh at you. These mean that all the 'objectively' desirable properties that associate mainly with needs have become (have been made to be) socially laughable. The reason is that *the incremental knowledge content* of this kind of soap has long been exhausted. Thus, the social appraising of the human time-space going into its production, not the clock time or the energy in calories (which has to be replaced so as to maintain workers, etc.) is little valued. And this in turn implies that the need-meeting attributes of soaps have been replaced by their want-satisfying ones, as we will discuss further in Chapter 5.

The conventional ways of explaining such behaviour are well known, supposedly pragmatic and perfectly incomprehensible. Of course, with value and demand in general, little is concrete, but that does not mean that a theory of value cannot be convincing. To be convincing, however, it must explain odd and obvious cases upon the same conceptual basis. Economic value has little to do with what is intrinsic to, or steadfast about things. Economically relevant knowledge has the peculiar property that each new piece of it helps dissipate the worthiness of every previous one, in every sphere of activity. Schumpeter explained this in production. Soap illuminates the same in the sphere of consumption, by showing how basic needs are transfigured into wants served by commodities that are manufactured through more capital-intensive techniques, allowing more human time-space to be roundaboutedly put into their making and then to be put up for grabs, through a sustained process of small, gradual changes that keep the name of a commodity but change its substance. Thus, 'soap' is not just...soap. If consumers stayed with steadfast commodity attributes that met their *needs*, capitalism would now be a memory. What they actually (and actively) do is to ascribe secondary significance to basic qualities of commodities as is cleanliness or hygiene in the case of soap, upgrading the role of socially appraisable attributes. Such appraisal is ultimately about life itself, which is made marketable through such knowledge increments. So, it is neither off the mark nor beside the point that there is a pungent odour to cosmetics and aromatic soaps in that they have taken precious whale life for only this little reason, in precisely the same attitude of ours towards all life in general, whether it be of the mink for its fur, or of our fellow humans.

These help bridge two views: The one (supported by Smith and Keynes among others) that people produce in order to consume, and the view of Frank Knight that this assumption is faulty. The two processes are actually inseparable, so that people do produce for consuming what they produce, but they consume in such ways as to help produce more output, so as to raise the stakes in the time-space expropriation contest which they interpret as constituting life. This is how they discovered that electricity is needed for drying dishes! And the soap example also shows how popular this has become, showing the layman as abetting through his consuming behaviour this process, which is presented, from a Marxic point of view, as a process of his own exploitation. The way in which he spends his income is at his discretion, and he does that in the same life-taking, capital-seeking way as every capitalist: He shops beauty soaps. So he, too, is a capitalist at heart, *pace* Marx.

In Hume's terms, ''Tis a quality observable in human nature...that every thing, which is often presented, and to which we have been long accustom'd, loses its value in our eyes, and is in a little time despis'd and neglected....and where we cannot by some contrast enhance their value, we are apt to overlook even what is essentially good in them....and 'tis remarkable, that goods, which are common to all mankind, and have become familiar to us by custom, give us little satisfaction; tho' perhaps of a more excellent kind, than those on which, for their singularity, we set a much higher value' (ibid.). This is as if Hume spoke about soaps, but the point is that he speaks about all goods, and so do we. Such singularity can make collectors value antiques or works of art into the millions, and it may sell a ball with which a known soccer player missed a penalty shot for about as much. The point, again, is that what is familiar for a long time is hard to attach new knowledge to, unless its singularity is renewed. This explains how and why needs are changed into wants.

From Polanyi's (1966/83) tacit knowledge point of view, the human time-space one commands through commodities is the distal term in our tacit knowing about value, and this is what we really go after. But our knowledge has phenomenal structure so, we can learn about distals only from proximal terms, which are the commodities, as they *become*, through their being socially appraised. There is no other way of knowing how much is worth paying, say, for a car, returning to the question posed by Shackle. In this consists the social nature of economic conduct. Being social, we must collect such knowledge and act *according* to it, *and upon it*. We must differ, as we walk in line. We buy the same, cheap, unsafe tin cans (to save money?) and then add alloy wheels, spoilers, stickers or sound systems to make them *look different to others* and 'special', on the road. *That* is what we value in ludicrousness.

Translating the above in more familiar terms, we can say that consumers try to stretch the purchasing power of their income, not just seeking to buy any given bundle at the lowest possible price, but also discovering bundles, or qualities in bundles, before others do and their price rises. Thus: 'Value is mutable and even inherently self-changing, compelled to disillusion one or other of the bodies of opinion which determine it and so to destroy its immediate basis' (Shackle, 1972: 46). These go along with Marshall's (1920: 368) view that

> In the world in which we live, every economic force is constantly changing its action under the influence of other forces which are acting around it. ... In this world therefore every plain and simple doctrine as to the relations between cost of production, demand and value is necessarily false: and the greater the appearance of lucidity which is given to it by a skillful expositor, the more mischievous it is. A man is likely to be a better economist if he trusts to his common sense, and particular instincts, than if he professes to study the theory of value and is resolved to find it easy.

The kind of reasoning involved in the process of value creation is what Lawson (1997: 177 and *passim*) calls 'reflexive monitoring of conduct', meaning that agents steer their way through a social flow by monitoring the actions of others, which decide the return of their own previous choices. This is how we grope our way through the mist of economic life, and in this we are uniform. All visible differences stem from the personal element which is inherent to gaining an edge over others, to local, historical or other such differences. The knowledge involved is fuzzy, conjectural and speculative. The search is by necessity local, limited by our mental capacities, especially the capacity of quick-access memory on which such decisions are largely based. These remind of Herbert Simon's (1969, ch. 3) ant that gropes its way back to its home, on a wind-and-wave-moulded beach. It zigzags, makes detours around obstacles, and so on, none of which will bring it back home unless there is a sense of direction; a sense of what it is looking for; *a purpose* to its groping.

In this process, there is continuous fluxity and disruption. With diffusion of each innovation, or even with its rejection, the landscape is changed. It swells here and sinks there with every transaction that involves even the slightest of new knowledge, as everyone monitors all others. An innovator tries to anticipate where others will step, so as to step there first before the landscape swells under his feet, lifting the value of his expenditures. He will thus enjoy holding a highly valued basket that he bought at a low price, stretching the time-space expropriating power of his income. Much like producer-investors, he invests on consumption bundles whose yield is to be determined in real time, by the similarly speculative conduct of others. In Shackle's terms, which remind of our exclusive non-ignorance: 'The most powerful resource available to a real-life contestant may be to exploit the ignorance of both, or all, contestants concerning the ultimate conditions of the contest. . . . Contest is . . . an endless drawing on the unknown. The most dramatic and spectacular secret of success is novelty, and novelty is that which an infallible algorithm must, by definition, exclude' (Shackle, 1972: 426).

The last thing the above are kin to is neoclassical consumers. Real consumers do not respond to price changes like rats respond to differently tasting cheese thrown to them. In trying to outsmart others, consumers reassess the time-space content of commodities upon the same canvas that producers assess what conventionally lets pass as 'cost'. This content is the ultimate capital that everyone goes after, and so it determines the life cycle of commodities according to the moves made by agents in the commodities world, that is, in markets. As Loasby (op. cit.: 28) contends, 'contrary to the Schumpeterian image of the innovator who drives the original conception to success, most imaginative conceptions which succeed are substantially changed along the way'. Such changes add good or bad taste, style, exaggeration and so on. Barring consumer initiatives, eccentric ('seductive') designer's underwear would not have found any considerable market and bodily healthy drivers would not have been convinced that they need electrically assisted hydraulic steering wheels, at least not before they were developed enough to allow the driver to have a 'feel' of the road. It is precisely these consumer initiatives motivated as discussed earlier that make everything become outmoded as its edge is exhausted by diffusion, and also give everything novel, however eccentric, bizarre or grotesque, a chance to find a place in the market. Nothing that may keep this process going is rejected out of hand, and this is the only criterion for judging its economic merits, whence also its social merits. (Recall the puritan ethic and gay marriages.) This includes mixing of old with new, imitation with novelty, etc., as is plain to widespread commercial exploitation of retro, from motorcycle styling to music and mobile phone ring tones. In capitalism, one can roll a stone over many times, suffice it that one can sell its moss as new.

These highlight that it would be impossible for consumers to be passive even if they tried, because they cannot avoid ticking their life's time away by generating knowledge. From their position, purchasing knowledge and use-knowledge are the only kinds of economically relevant knowledge they can produce, about the other qualities of which all normative judgement is beside the point. Missing this half of the generative activity does not miss only one part of economic dynamics, but all of it, as the failure of one-sided theories of growth has notoriously shown.

Spurious riddles arise then that can be 'explained' only by means of twisted arguments, untenable hypotheses, arbitrary categorization, or high-handedly by dubious 'laws' that assume equilibrium in one way or another, but which cannot stand up to the test of reality and are eventually jettisoned. (Say's law provides example.)

The explanatory potential of one-sided theories is impaired by unsound first principles and basic propositions. As Aristotle (1934: I. viii) maintained, 'if a proposition is true, all the facts harmonize with it, but if it is false, it is soon found to be discordant with them'. The claims made by an equilibrium-bound theory are put under strain in real time, where what is normal appears as anomalous. Then, Giffen goods, normal, inferior and other categories of those, made-to-fit combinations of substitution and income effects and a host of other such contrivances are recruited for explaining 'pathologies'. These can be dispensed with in an open context, where it is easy to explain why demand for a certain commodity, in a certain market, for a certain period of time may rise with its price, or why consumers may turn away from some item if its price is not high enough, and keep distancing themselves from it even more while its price is falling. If, due to any reason, a rising price of gold or diamonds makes prospective buyers think that others will rush to buy such items, then they may haste to do the same first, in an effort to secure speculative gains. That will increase aggregate demand. In the case of a price decrease, if consumers expect that others will turn their back to some item, whereby its price will fall further, they may be inclined to do so first, in order to avert losses. Positive feedback mechanisms are set in motion with awkward effects, as in all speculative situations. This is due to the anticipative, social, symbolic nature of a game of successful deviation, which proceeds independently of what 'objective' qualities the commodities themselves may have.

Such positive feedback phenomena are not exclusive to financial markets. There is intersubjective speculation in the way people make choices such as buying a car or kitchenware, beyond any *need* they may have of those. Consumption expenditures are speculative to the extent that they are not determined by precise, sure calculation on the basis of reason in its enduring sense, as forced by necessity. What matters about such consumption is not any sensible, intrinsic or enduring quality of things, but their capacity to act as time-space tokens. This can explain nauseously bad taste and exaggerations of all kinds. As Shackle (1972: 12) explained:

> The exploitation of ignorance is called speculation. It becomes possible when one man is willing to trust his own guesswork in preference to that of majority opinion in the market, or to adopt a new opinion earlier than that majority, and this is only possible if he can assume the market to be at least not perfectly informed. It is of course the future of which the market is not and cannot be informed. The value of any thing which has any prospect of durability depends largely on what value people think it may have at future dates, because by acquiring it now and preserving it, they can hope to secure that expected price. But that 'expected' price is merely a conjecture, and

there can be as many conjectures as there are persons in the market, even if they only make one 'best guess' each.

As the system becomes more roundabout and a certain type of efficiency that we will discuss grows, an increasing proportion of consumption expenditures become speculative. In a world of speculation, he who has power can use coercion and make self-fulfilling prophecies. Moreover, those who freely take part in such games tend to overestimate their power in determining values, rates of exchange, discount rates and final outcomes. They ridicule laws of demand, exogenous tastes, independent preferences and all fiction that purports to tie them to exchanges of equivalents. They try to *beat* equivalences, to gain or to loss. Final commodities markets share much with futures and stock markets, in which there are no substitution and income effects, diminishing marginal rates or such rigid concepts. None expects one stock market to go down if others go up, or marginal investor utility to diminish. Speculation generates its own dynamics. To their bad luck, however, real markets were abducted by the orthodox postulate that, *ceteris paribus*, marginal utility must diminish. But what can remain *paribus* when consumer behaviour is intersubjectively anticipative?

From this angle, massive consumption of industrial junk food and beverages (a home-delivered Coca-Cola culture) is seen to be a rational exercise in vanity, which may seem foolish by other standards of reason, such as from a doctor's point of view. People who consume in such ways are informed, and seek ways to be kept informed. They do not stop at a rest area along the highway just because they are hungry, or because they need to go to the restroom. They flock there in order to mingle with others, picking up information about how others behave and appraise things, precisely as when they browse through lifestyle magazines. This is why they look around, leaning a bit forward as they take a bite on 'juicy hamburgers'. They make comparisons. They take bites at each other. They *browse on* each other.[3] This is how they discovered all kinds of 'exotic' cuisine of doubtful authenticity and quality. In such food they purchase more time-space than can be got with home cooking. And the same holds about winter sports, fashion clothes and so on *ad infinitum*. The usual explanation in terms of fads, imitation, identity, etc., is beset by the obvious question: What do these aim at?

All this commotion that distils into value assessed through prices is not a sure-footed walk in any firm direction, but a fumbling, speculative, uncertain expedition of foretelling the intentions of others. In the end, the conduct of the many decides what is economically relevant; not the attributes of commodities, which would make producers the sole arbitrators. Value is in the knowledge of making and using commodities, as this evolves through joint, incremental, mutually supporting steps. About what knowledge will be produced little can be known, since this partakes in the future. There is no way of knowing how we know, because finding out entails an infinite regress. Only general principles can be laid out, not any exact account of the process whereby economic value is generated, precisely as there is no way of telling how social values develop in general. This is why, to achieve exactness and certitude, mainstream theory is obliged to pick up from a point well past the production of new knowledge, *after* a shock, *given* tastes, so that it may then consider transactions as being between equivalents and, through equimarginality, follow the system as it *naturally* lapses to a new rest (steady) state where rational agents maximize utility. In capitalistically rational agents' action and calculation, however, nothing is natural, except maybe their said fear.

Relative prices act as indexes of the scarcity-allaying (and fear-allaying) capacity of commodities, that is, of the relative amounts of incremental human time-space in the form of knowledge that went into their making and using, while attained efficiency depends on the degree to which market prices reflect correctly agent behaviour at the margin, that is, the true appreciation of these increments of knowledge. However, this is all *before* the next shock takes place, about which nothing is known, as if there could be ample time between two successive knowledge moments for prices to find rest and for the theorist to study the situation. But there can be no such time, since any interval void of knowledge-induced disturbances lacks duration. This prevents prices from being correct reflections of the knowledge content of the various commodities. Prices are always on the making. Transactions are always between *different* appreciations, not both of which can be 'true'. Actually, neither one is. If this were possible, time would lack durée, and all of it would be at the disposal of the theorist. And it is, to a neoclassical theorist. Yet, even avoiding treacherous waters, neither uniqueness nor stability of neoclassical equilibrium is guaranteed, as shown through the 'SMD theorem'. (See Ackerman, 2002.) The keyword is Uncertainty.

Before setting out 'to suggest how useful economic theory can indeed be built on this [incomplete knowledge] foundation', Loasby (op. cit.: 1) caustically summarized the pointlessness of reasoning under full certainty, in the opening statement of his book:

> Robert Lucas...once declared that 'in cases of uncertainty, economic reasoning will be of no value' (Lucas 1981: 224). It is true that in Lucas's model economies there is no way of handling uncertainty, in the sense of uncompletable lists of contingencies, causes, and even options; but it is no less true that only in cases of real-world uncertainty does economic analysis have any potential value. If uncertainty is absent, then every problem situation can be fully specified...and choice is reduced to a logical operation. This is indeed the world of rational choice models. But then the process of choosing, and the ways in which the process of choosing is organized, are empty topics.... If all optima can be calculated...well-motivated economic agents (and to economists like Lucas no other kind is conceivable) will have calculated them already; and economists will be the last to know. In such a world economists can demonstrate only that what has already happened in practice can also happen in theory. Thus not only are there no hundred-dollar bills lying on the street, there are no hundred-dollar bills on offer for economic advice. Economic analysis is of potential value only if people do not already know what to do: the foundation of useful economic theory must be incomplete knowledge, or partial ignorance.

Or, as Shackle (1972: 280) put it: 'Choice is always amongst thoughts, for it is always too late to choose among facts. Then the problem we are engaged with is pushed back one stage, and the question becomes: What determines the thoughts?' Concerning which, Shackle maintained that uniqueness of the future is not implicit in the uniqueness of the past, as yet another expression of asymmetry in real time.

Acknowledging the impossibility of long-run drawings of the economic situation due to non-coincidence of savings with investment and to the uncertain consequences of deferred consumption, Keynes (1936: 149) also argued that 'The outstanding fact is the extreme precariousness of the basis of knowledge on which our estimates of prospective yield have to be made. Our knowledge of the factors which will govern the yield of an investment some years hence is usually very slight and often negligible.' These hold about every transaction which involves money, since parting with money now relinquishes all the many time profiles that it could make possible, opting for one of them. This is necessarily speculative, because those infinitely many other profiles will never become known. In every transaction, the unknown future is weighed against a known present: something uncertain, against something certain.

In the same way we can approach decisions concerning work versus pay, and such a perspective subverts any steadfastness attached traditionally to the notion of real wages, immersing it into extreme precariousness. Income holders determine through their money-expending behaviour the actual value of their income. On the side, it may be noted that 'leisure' and 'leisure time' take on a new semiotic. They become an activity and the time devoted to it, respectively, for demonstrating one's possessions and thus establishing one's social power, constituting an ineluctable and integral part of other economic activities.

Let us return to prices. Market-clearing prices present transactions as fair exchanges of equivalents to the presumed benefit of both parties, allowing no surpluses. Thus, they clear capitalism of all unfairness or conflict. Aggressive antagonism turns out to be to everyone's contentment. But why does it show on their faces as stress? Or, is it boredom, depression or despair? Carrying such absurdities to the markets for factors of production also does away with exploitation, picturing capitalism as a fair system in all spheres: production, consumption and income distribution. Besides in the fantasies of its critics, unfairness may exist only in monopoly situations, which are treated by theory as anomalies anyway, leading to and caused by lower than optimally static efficiency. All such informational asymmetries due to transaction costs are presumably smoothed out with time, assuming that no new information is produced.

However, these do violence to reality. In an open dynamic context there is generative asymmetry in every transaction, through which asymmetry value is born. Therefore, we may speak about discretion, accountability, false calculations, winners and losers, but fairness is meaningless. Each party tries to foresee the future conditions in the market for the transacted item in relation to all other items, so as to gain advantage over the other party (and over others in general) by selling it now at the highest possible price or buying it at the lowest. If demand for this item rises, the buyer's anticipative, speculative ideas prove to be right and the seller's wrong. The foresight of the former becomes market-knowledge, adding to the existing stock. His ideas find a market and sell in it, to the benefit of the innovator. *The price change* then must provide a measure of the value of this knowledge increment and it is a reward to the innovator, with the new price reflecting the new appraisal by the market of the time-space content of the said item or, since time is knowledge, the cumulative knowledge gone into it, from its inception all the way up to this last transaction. The same price change in its negative (price at which the transaction was made minus new price) is a loss to the other transacting party, which was outsmarted, according to the thus evolving social judgement.

As Shackle (1972: 268, original emphases) argued, 'prices are *convention*. They depend upon expectation, which is *originative*.' And: 'The speculator holds particular assets because he *disagrees* with the market's valuation of them. His valuation of them is private, for if it were publicly agreed his hopes of gain would be gone' (ibid.: 111). Equivalence makes little sense in a dynamic context not only because 'the preference systems in existence at one moment are the consequence of actual purchases in the past' (Duesenberry, 1967: 14), but because they are also based on speculative anticipation of the future. Only by discounting at an arbitrarily set rate can past and future time, that is, real time, be collapsed down to a moment, upon which, and only upon which equivalence can acquire content. Thus, in reference to enterprisers' profits, Shackle (1972: Preface) noted: 'The picture *ex ante* can fail to be vindicated by the picture *ex post*. There can be an unexpected surplus over the revenue just sufficient to pay their factors and reward themselves with a return just satisfying them for their scale of production.... It can, of course, prove to be negative, a loss.' And he went on to interrogate: 'What is the source, in money terms, of such a windfall profit or loss?' (ibid.). The answer is: Knowledge. And there is nothing windfall.

Such value has none of the Euclidean properties that individual demand and supply relations must have in order to add into aggregate market relations. Basically, it all hinges on the fact that knowledge is not homogeneous, measurable or comparable, and it expands, but not additively. New pieces of knowledge take effect through combining with others and modifying their characteristics, or replacing them and rendering them obsolete. The value of each such piece of knowledge is not set in advance, but takes shape along the way, according to the market's response to it in time. Every new stock of knowledge is qualitatively different from every previous one, not just this or that much 'bigger'. These subvert basing macroeconomics on micro-foundations and: 'It captures also the fact that, despite all the concrete individuality that goes into exchange-value's making, the exchange-value of every unit of every commodity is irreducibly and fundamentally a SOCIAL relation that extends as far as the economy in which the exchange of the unit takes place' (Fullbrook, 2002: 295, original emphasis). In fact, it would be strange if things were otherwise, since economic value would then have to be different from all other kinds of social value.

The last part of Fullbrook's statement is worth noting also, namely, that the effects of value-creating relations reach into the entire economy. Any conduct is inspective of the entire picture, cross-sectionally and time-wise. So, it cannot but take into account and affect all the time profiles of the money that a consumer considers expending on any one transaction, as well as the profiles of other consumers and producers. No conduct is void of repercussions through the market, however minute or indirect these may be.

A fine specimen of playful perseverance

The basic idea in this report is so obvious, that one can either run away from it to avoid its repugnance, or stumble upon it by turning a blind eye to it. So, it was two mainstream economists who came nearest to its disclosure. In a thinly disguised way, under the veil of utility maximization, Stigler and Becker (op. cit.) tinkered surreptitiously with orthodox premises, picturing consumers as impulsively creative for gain. The stated purpose of Stigler and Becker (S&B, for short, with all quotations being from their paper) was to protest against the economists' coping out of their obligation to search for economic explanation, urging 'not to abandon opaque and complicated problems with the easy suggestion that the further explanation will perhaps someday be produced by one of our sister behavioural sciences'. They protested against exogenous tastes for being unreal, bereft of content and counterproductive. So, they used the following paradox: They challenged that 'Tastes are the unchallengeable axioms of a man's behavior', to be treated as data, and 'translated "unstable tastes" into variables in the household production functions for commodities', showing that much more can be explained by applying 'standard economic logic as extensively as possible' on pure economic variables such as prices and incomes.

Provocatively, they assumed tastes to be uniform across agents and stable across time (the 'self-same hypothesis') and portrayed consumers as trying, under income constraints, to 'maximize a utility function of objects of choice, called commodities, that they produce with market goods, their own time, their skills, training and other human capital, and other inputs'. Thus, they saw consumers as actively engaged in a purposeful knowledge process, investing what they called 'consumer capital', which amounts to an inherent capacity to seek an edge by generating novelty, and which capacity would remain active even if consumers were made artificially to begin from the same uniform and stable preferences. In other words, they acknowledged perfect consumer discretion and generativeness. Any edge or advantage, any diversity or change, were seen as obtaining from this generative capacity that we call *sublime agency*. In Part II, we will provide a specific form for S&B's 'household production function', which they left unspecified, explaining also some missing details.

It is important to note that time enters the S&B argument not as a capital endowment that consumers can invest or waste, and not only with an uncertain-yield attribute that acknowledges asymmetry of past and future, but also in its existential/ontological sense since, while investing in the production of commodities, consumers also take into account the time horizon ahead of them, according to their age. Remaining-life time enters as argument in the commodities production function. Through such plainly ontological, cognitive strife, consumers expend their income in discretionary ways. Therefore, S&B's saying that this is all about utility is more guise than gist.

There is more that is common to S&B's work and ours, and it is worth even to repeat some quotations. This is how they describe the speculative and antici-pative nature of consumer innovations in their discussion of fashions and fads: 'The commodity apparently produced by fashion goods is social distinction: the demonstration of alert leadership, or at least not lethargy, in recognizing and adopting that which will in due time be widely approved. This commodity... sounds somewhat circular, because new things appear to be chosen simply because they are new.' And style, or social distinction, which is according to S&B the commodity produced by fashion goods, 'is social rivalry, and it is, like all rivalry, both an incentive to individuality and a source of conformity'. And they find the same in advertising expenditures.

So, S&B are undaunted by the usual masquerading of rivalry into gentle competition. Also, under the self-same hypothesis, a cohesion issue (reconciling diversity) not only does not arise but, on the contrary, what needs to be explained then is real diversity that brings about change. In S&B, as in our theory, this obtains from the inherently personal and individualistic nature of the generative knowledge process, within markets. Markets thus emerge as domains where generation and dissemination of information takes place, not as co-ordinating mechanisms. There is no reason to get bogged down with invisible hands, obscure market mechanisms, auctioneers, etc. Thus, S&B, too, attribute the capitalist fecundity largely to consumers in their sublime capacity to produce knowledge purposively. Then, they argue:

> The real income of a household does not simply equal its money income deflated by an index of the prices of market goods, but equals its full income (which includes the value of 'time' to the household) deflated by an index of the prices... of the produced commodities. Since full income and commodity prices depend on a variety of factors, incomes also take subtle forms.

And they define full income as 'the maximum money income that a household could achieve by an appropriate allocation of its time and other resources'. Therefore, real income is self-determined, dynamically, by each household's (person's) sublime capacity to produce knowledge: It is atomistic. And leisure time becomes thus more work than idle time, which wreaks havoc with taxation theories à la Mirrlees, for example, which assume that households differ only in the levels of skill in employment, but not in how they exploit leisure time. Households emerge in S&B and in our theory as self-employed producers of value, on a round-the-clock basis. And last, but not least: 'The extension of the capital concept to investment in the capacity to consume more efficiently has numerous other potential applications.'

To sum it up, in place of our uniform and stable motive, S&B entertained uniform and stable tastes, but they endogenized the knowledge process whereby preferences are determined. They thus avoided speaking openly about ontology and its psychological ramifications that introduce malevolence and conflict in the capitalistic process, staying with utility seeking by an obvious stratagem not meant as real. Still, little of equilibrium-based theories would have remained standing in their sweep if S&B's approach had been pursued further, and no criticism has undermined mainstream premises more than S&B's 'defence'.

Part II

4   Production innovations

Making some concessions and using caution in our interpretations, we can illuminate the quantifiable parts of our argument in mathematical language. In this and in the following chapter we attempt an analytical presentation of our theory through a comparative statics scheme based on a Sraffian-flows model. We derive a selection criterion that orders steady-states by preference, where a steady-state is characterized by a technological component, a set of prices and a consuming pattern. Concessions and caution relate to the fact that newness and fundamental knowledge-dynamics uncertainty escape mathematical modelling, which submits to requirements of closure. Such analytics may mislead one into thinking that what agents do during transitions is to maximize time-space. But this is only of steady-states, where all knowledge is fully diffused and the response-hypersurface and state space are stable, which are of extensive time. Real systems are always in transition. So, what we aim at with the following discussion is not to describe the details of the novelty-generation process, but to outline its effects, derive simple measures of performance and describe the nature of the motion and of the changes to the general structure of economies, as these develop in a capitalist direction.

The simplified scheme employed ignores a number of issues which, if accommodated, could enrich the theory, especially as concerns its time-related aspects. One such is that of capital vintages: When we speak about exact capital replacement, we see productive capital *services* as being maintained, not necessarily by similar capital commodities, implying that one part of such replacement expenditures is for maintenance of existing capital items and another is for introduction of new ones, offsetting depreciation. Similarly, we ignore differences in qualities of labour other than those reflected through different wage rates, although this does not fit very well with our reasoning about expanding knowledge and skills as constituting the real essence of labour. Still, our analytical framework helps organize thought on issues relating to structural aspects of growth, in which is innovative knowledge solidified incrementally.

We take a holistic view. The system is born to a human component from which it draws its generative power, while raw materials are drawn from a physical environment that sets limits on their types and on the rates at which they may be exploited. Part of the said generativeness is aimed at evading these limits, so that the system does not simply adapt to conditions set by the environment, but also creates its own performance criteria and conditions by acting upon it. So, its ultimate limits are cognitive. Forming the initial social connectives is already an intellectual feat, after which every subsystem of the social system that obtains is itself a knowledge-based system. The economic subsystem is a most important one, as it self-organizes towards improving its appropriative performance through endogenously generated, structure-modifying, equilibrium-evading innovations. First, these aim at and provide individual advantage. Then, by diffusion and efficiency-enhancing, generalized application obtains a collective advantage for the economy as a whole, relative to competing economies. At the system level, a goal-seeking description is just a conceptual convenience towards an efficient specification, not implying any kind of collective volition. There is little point in arguing whether the system is pursuing this or that goal, or no goal at all. Volition is only of agents. Any consistent outcome of this may be seen, somewhat abusively, and only conventionally, as 'collective intention'.

Extensive supply-side theorizing has produced considerable knowledge which, even though one sided, can be fruitfully exploited in discussing consumption innovations, symmetrically. We devote the present chapter to production. An index is derived for time-ordering structures so that, by comparing any two values of it, one may tell which structure comes later in time, that is, it is more advanced and preferable, for being associated with increased produced value per unit of direct human input and, therefore, with increased economically relevant knowledge. The predilection of capitalism towards structural growth of this kind emerges as condensation at the system level of an all-out individualistic antagonism. Micro-foundations are laid that help reconstruct the process as combination of the producers' urge to increase profits through Schumpeterian-type innovations, and through imitation so as to catch up or not fall behind, thus effecting diffusion. Aside from any consumer-side considerations and knowledge contributions, which will be addressed in Chapter 5, the system's development path is described as obtaining from co-action of a profitability and an efficiency criterion.

The terms 'advance', 'progress', or any other such that appear in the sequel are always meant non-normatively, to imply only a capitalistically preferred direction. What legitimizes the use of such terms is that technological advance is a largely unpredictable, fundamentally uncertain unfolding of knowledge generating *and choice making* by economic agents under a multitude of influences, whose richness cannot be subsumed under any single theory or model. Yet, both logically and from available evidence it may be deduced that it is not accidental or aimless. It is an intentional, endogenous response to the pull of demand and to the lure of profits, as a familiar expression goes, in a push–pull kind of forward motion forged by passions and playing a key role in the growth of output. It is natural then to seek a *measure* of economic advance, and we intend to supply one, explaining why the most frequently employed one, namely, GDP growth, is inadequate. A quick way to see this is that if GDP declines for any period of time, this does not mean that knowledge is not advanced, that no progress is taking place.

The received, although not sufficiently documented view among economists and more generally is that capitalism is subject to a growth imperative. Gordon and Rosenthal (2003) support that a capitalistic firm will go bankrupt with certainty in the long run, and with high probability in the short run, unless it attains a positive growth rate, preferably well above average, through monopoly power. They claim that 'growth is necessary for future survival for each capitalist and perhaps for the system as a whole', and they end with the question: 'But how is it achieved for an entire system?'

The lack of a satisfactory indicator of progress has also been recognized. Potts (2001) argues that given the relation between the structures of interactions that occur in markets, an appropriate performance criterion is lacking. So, if 'some sort of welfare principle for evolutionary economics [were found] in the form of a change in the connective structure of a rule that made the knowledge mechanism more open...evolutionary microeconomics might have the welfare theoretic implications requisite for evolutionary economic policy'. It might be better to moderate the normative connotations of the term 'welfare principle' and refer instead to a *preferred attribute* or *symbolic attractor*, in view of the contentious nature of the conventional notion of welfare. For systems which evolve by intentional, endogenously generated change, searching for receding attractors is a methodological imperative, because evolution is guided, but also never complete. This is then the only relevant kind of attractor, unlike equilibrium points in a fixed state space or fixed point attractors, which are relevant to complete, self-sufficient systems subject to exogenous shocks. And this kind of receding attractor implies a teleology that is different from the usual one, which envisages or alludes to some goal that can be reached from various initial conditions, at least in principle, given proper employment of means to it. Ours invokes a *process* of incessant purposeful changes rather, than any finite goal.

System and analytics

We employ the following definitions and concepts: A *system* is a collection of parts connected with functional relationships. The one under study is:

Complex: It has more relevant detail than an observer or model can cope with, explicitly.

Uncertain: It has elements whose behaviour is at least partially unpredictable.

Integral: Its elements act in some important sense as a unity.

Open: It admits flows to and from an environment that includes the physical world and other economies, affecting those and being affected by them. Most importantly, it is open to generative mental flows from its own participants.

Goal seeking and cognitively adaptive: It evolves, changing its structure by generating and exploiting knowledge to the effect of improving its relationship with the environment, where improvement is meant in terms of value-generating performance.

Self-organizing: Patterns, at the level of the system, and in particular structural changes, emerge from interactions among its lower-level components. Such interactions may be spurred or otherwise affected by external influences, but are internal to the system.

Evolution: It is the historical outcome of the system's adaptive self-organization.

Our concern being with the underlying causal simplicity of structural change, we employ a fixed *n*-sector-disaggregation scheme as in Sraffian-type analyses, before breaking up demand into two component parts, in the next chapter. Such fixity has certain drawbacks, but it can still illuminate the ideas discussed. We search for a time-ordered property that characterizes the development of technological matrix *A* and of the composition of the final demand vector in an economy's linear input–output representation

$$(I - A)\, x = y \tag{4.1}$$

written also as $x = A\, x + y$. Here, *A* is a $n \times n$ technical coefficients matrix, *y* is a *n*-vector of final demand and *x* is a *n*-vector of total output. This describes a fictitious stationary operation, that is, steady-state with zero growth, in which all disturbances are assumed out so that the system has retired at static equilibrium, with prices at market-clearing levels. (Natural, or cost-of-production prices, uniform profit rate on capital invested, etc. We will be referring to such state in the sequel as steady-state, since structurally, which only concerns us, everything stays fixed.) There are no innovations, no technique changes or changes to the structure of the final demand vector, and agents are price-takers. There are no scarcity constraints. Net investment is zero. So, final demand consists conceivably of consumption, government expenditures and net exports, which remain same from one period to the next. Productive stocks are precisely replenished so as to maintain a fixed productive capacity from one period to the next. Under such circumstances, the operation of the system must be linear, while transitions between any two such states (the development path) are strongly non-linear, inherently unpredictable and impossible to model realistically.

Analytical description of transitions is impossible, and indeed not even meaningful, due to the said fundamental uncertainty. Here, we are concerned with their overall structural outcome, an issue that standard growth theories have essentially evaded. In 'old' growth theories, the marginal productivity of capital was taken to be diminishing, as labour could not accumulate along with it. This supposedly induced diminishing returns and a ceiling to growth, which, however, was contradicted by reality, over long periods. Capitalist economies kept growing and productivity gains did not seem to taper off. This led 'new' growth theories to include knowledge as a factor. A critical component of labour was treated separately, as 'human capital', which could accumulate in the form of a stock of production-related knowledge. But, due to the usual obsession with exact modelling, which needs closure and fails in the face of newness, the analogy with tangible, material capital was taken too far. Knowledge was submitted to a production-function black box logic, where investment of conventional inputs was related to production of innovations through a mathematical-function type of relation, with innovative output in turn fed into the usual production-function black box along with other inputs, as one more factor of production aimed at explaining observed increases in productivity and output. Under such prism, there was no possibility of change or improvement without net investment in this new factor, or any such improvements had to be treated as a residual. In other words, knowledge generation was not seen as intrinsic to social humans by their *being* and functioning in real time. But one production black box is as good as any number of them, so the net yield of such intellectual investment was simply one more incomplete chapter in the history of economic thought: the chapter on *new* theories of growth.

Here, we consider changes induced by new knowledge to be qualitative and of uncertain productive proportions, since advance that comes with knowledge belongs with the future. In other words, we admit that we cannot explain transitions or describe their time-paths with any degree of specificity and exactness. In the dynamics induced by knowledge, capital stock-flows are more important than any purely stock characteristics. Capital accumulation that takes place must be appreciated in its continuous reaffirmation, rather than as a state, and this continuous reaffirmation process needs to be reckoned with. After all, capital (or wealth) by itself confers no power. Power and control is established through the flows of capital services, which assert the present means to a future flow of such benefits. It is flows and changes thereof that provide the material for analyzing dynamics. Exact replacement flows guarantee that productive capacity is maintained, while capital stocks remain constant in steady-state. Steady-state assumes also the stock of available *knowledge* to be fixed. In reality, as time goes by, the knowledge stock base is ineluctably expanded even without any investment to this end, and even without any additions to the stock of material capital. Any direct investment to such an end may only accelerate things. So, we concentrate on finding a relation between two distinct steady-states that allows ordering them by preference, which means ordering them in time. Two such states may place different requirements on the volume, composition and quality of the capital base, but these may be ignored, along with the transition between them. After all, a fixed-sector scheme can accommodate only quantitative changes, not qualitative ones. Besides, it would be too conceited to believe that we can resolve an issue (transition) which has defied all efforts by the greatest philosophers, for centuries.

We can decompose the magnitudes that appear in relation (4.1) further and exploit an alternative decomposition of vector x, according to inputs. First, we make the following notational conventions: A lower case letter will denote a column vector. The same upper case letter will denote the diagonal matrix with the said vector on its diagonal. Upper T denotes transposition of a vector or matrix. By $\|v\|_2 = \sqrt{\sum_{i=1}^{n} v_i^2}$ will be denoted the L_2 norm of vector v, by $\|v\|_1 = \sum_{i=1}^{n} v_i$ the L_1 norm of non-negative vectors, and by $\|v\|$ either of the two norms, for convenience, when there is no confusion, or does not matter for our argument.

Let L be a $m \times n$ matrix of physical labour coefficients l_{ij}, $i = 1,2,\ldots,m$, $j = 1,2,\ldots,n$, representing the quantity of labour type i required per unit of sector j output. This acknowledges m types of labour, which is not typical of standard analyses of income distribution and of the price system.

Let R be a $n \times n$ matrix of physical technical coefficients r_{ij}, measuring the physical quantity of the i-th commodity per unit of sector j output. We take R to be from an array of available production techniques defining technology $\mathfrak{R}$, which is expandable through new techniques that obtain by diffusion of innovations made in pursuit of monopoly profits. Then, (R,L) represents the technological situation with the economy operating as in (4.1). If d is the vector of physical final demand and q is the vector of physical output, relation $(I - R)\,q = d$ holds. Then, weighing by prices p obtains

$$P\,(I - R)\,q = P\,d \quad \Leftrightarrow \quad (I-PRP^{-1})\,P\,q = P\,d \qquad (4.1')$$

which is a detailed out form of relation (4.1), with $A = P\,R\,P^{-1}$, $x = P\,q$ and $y = P\,d$. This relation shows that all relevant magnitudes, that is, x, y and A, depend critically on prices, and since these are determined conclusively only at the stage where consumers reveal their preferences in the commodities market, system dynamics are volatile and open to knowledge produced continuously up to that final stage. Any change to R, d or p will have repercussions throughout the system, affecting its performance. Moreover, resonance of d and p with the eigenstructure of R is seen through $(4.1')$ to be critical.[1] Different ways of expending the same income in an economy with a given technological structure may have quite different global outcomes, in terms of total value x produced and in terms of GDP, or $\|x\|_1$. (We will supply a simple numerical example of this later.)

From an income distribution point of view, we may decompose x column-wise by input (cost) component, in order to find

$$x = K + VA \qquad (4.2)$$

where $VA = Q\,(I - R^T)\,p = X\,(I-A^T)\,\mathbf{1}$ is value added, $K = Q\,R^T p$ is the cost of the means of production (material input costs) and $\mathbf{1} = [1, 1,\ldots, 1]^T$. In the Austrian tradition, this distinguishes between 'produced means of production' and 'original means of production', which comprise all non-produced inputs to the production of x and, in particular, human inputs and services. Decomposing VA into wages, W, proportional to the quantities of various types of labour as determined by the rows of matrix L, with m associated wage rates $\vec{w} = [w_1, w_2,\ldots, w_m]^T$, and into profits, Π, proportional to the value of the means of production K, obtains $VA = \Pi + W = Q\,R^T p\,\pi + Q\,L^T \vec{w}$, where π is a uniform profit rate. Vector W thus obtains as a resultant of m components, $W_i = w_i\,(q_1\,l_{i1}, q_2\,l_{i2}, \ldots, q_n\,l_{in})^T$, $i = 1,2,\ldots, m$.

Note that $\Pi = \pi\,K$ does not imply that any bundle of capital items must yield profits at rate π, but only bundles composed as K, in steady-state. And, as we will discuss also in relation to consumption innovations, by venturing away from such collinearity and investing in novel mixes of productive capital (and labour), monopoly profits are made possible, subverting equilibrium and keeping the system in constant self-organizing, goal-seeking development.

The price system associated with these models is

$$p = R^T p\,(1+\pi) + L^T \vec{w} \tag{4.3}$$

of n equations in $n + m + 1$ unknowns. A uniform profit rate is a concession to the steady-state idealization, justified by the fact that, due to capital mobility and competition between sectors, profit rate differentials should tend to be wiped out, with due allowance made for differential risk, although risk should be negligible or nil in steady-state, since there is no net investment to new lines of activity. Logically, then, Π becomes collinear with K. But even so, degrees of freedom do remain, as long as even only two different types of income are acknowledged, namely, profits and wages, which is minimally necessary if issues related to income distribution are to be addressed. These degrees of freedom are as many as there are wage rates.

Since only relative prices matter, one price can be set arbitrarily as numeraire in (4.3), adding one more equation, say, $p_1 = 1$, leaving m degrees of uncertainty that cannot be waived. A sensible thing to do then would be to face squarely this fact and examine how choices are made in practice among the infinitely many alternatives, that is, among the solutions to (4.3), presumably in such a way as would serve some particular goal set by some pragmatic motivation of agents. Resolving these should also supply a meaningful measure of performance which is meaningful both at the individual and at the economy levels.

Unfortunately, such options were not investigated with any degree of persistence by standard theories, so as to produce, hopefully, with time some worthwhile, robust results. Instead, it was attempted to close the model by brute force according to some theory of income distribution, but this had to be realistic, meaningful and convincing, since the issue was about the actual workings of an economy and the ways in which it distributed the fruits of its operation. And since this should be easier if the assumed degrees of freedom were as few as possible, a single average wage rate w was also hypothesized (even though the usual steady-state and mobility arguments should not apply for wages), so that $m = 1$, thus receiving

$$p = R^T p\,(1 + \pi) + l^T w \tag{4.4}$$

a system of n equations in $n + 2$ unknowns, plus the numeraire equation. As setting one more price from outside the system would be meaningless, one of the two distributive parameters should be decided, whence the remaining unknowns would be determined uniquely by the above relation.

Note that if this task were to be successfully accomplished, it would imply a tight bonding of distributive with allocative variables, which is not realistic. As it turned out, after an often heated debate over various options [determining the wage rate on the basis of biological requirements, connecting the profit rate with some interest rate or rate of growth (e.g. the Cambridge Growth Equation), etc.] no consensus was reached. Proposed solutions were arbitrary, mechanical and unconvincing. So, looking back at the situation, it would seem much more reasonable to address the allocation and distribution issues jointly, that is, in logical unity, but not simultaneously, in the sense that they are determined over a uniform behavioural domain that embraces prices, demand behaviour and social relations, which also determine the path of development for technology. In some way that needs to be specified, it must be acknowledged that agents actively determine the above by making choices in pursuit of some goal more cohesive (and coherent) than the utility-seeking one, while at the same time agents are themselves shaped by these choices. Hodgson (1999: 76, original emphasis) put these thus: 'socio-economic systems do not simply create new products and perceptions. *They also create and re-create individuals.* In a learning economy, the individual not only changes their purposes and preferences, but also revises their skills and their perceptions of their needs. Both in terms of capacities and beliefs, the individual is changed in the process'.

We can draw a pictorial diagram of flows within the economic system (ES) as in Figure 4.1(a), consisting integrally of the production subsystem (PS) and the human subsystem (HS), connected through reciprocal transformations y and VA, whose L_1 norms are equal, in steady-state. (L_1-norm equality is indicated by a dashed line with slope -1, in part (b) of the same figure.) Through ES, subsystem HS expands its reach into and control over the environment, drawing needed resources from it. Alternatively, through the agency of HS, whose current input is remunerated as VA, ES exchanges mass and energy with the environment, transforming them in such ways as to increase value throughput measured by money velocity x, in order to increase control of HS over this environment. In different words, system ES tries to increase its metabolic efficiency. This shifts emphasis from final demand as an end in itself, to the way cognitive action works to improve efficiency towards increasing output value x. Since the project is launched from a personal perspective and system properties obtain from individual agency, they must be consistent with the postulated individual motivation as discussed on the basis of existential anxiety in Chapter 3. Because of the intrinsic generativeness of HS, PS remains open to new possibilities that expand the set of feasible routines, rules, institutions, materials and commodities, improving some performance criterion. Inclusion of HS to ES renders such changes endogenous, obtaining from self-interested action.

Figure 4.1(b) draws a vectorial picture of the situation. Figure 4.1(c) adds a box representation, with all three parts illuminating a peculiar asymmetry: Whereas value added is split into profits and wages, nothing analogous is foreseen in standard theory about final demand. This asymmetry will be removed in Chapter 5.

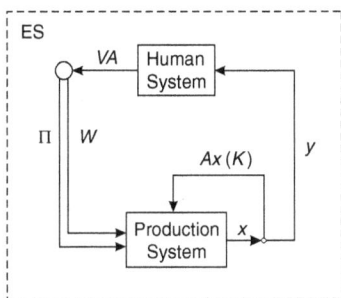

(a) Value flows

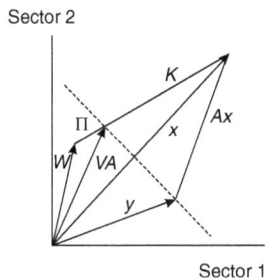

(b) Vector representation

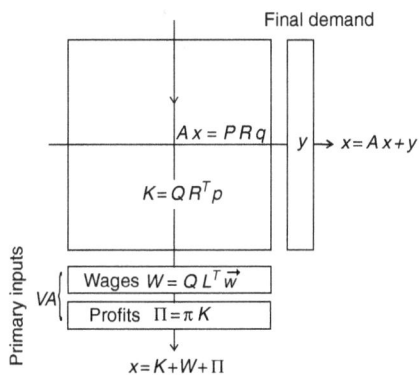

(c) Row and column decompositions

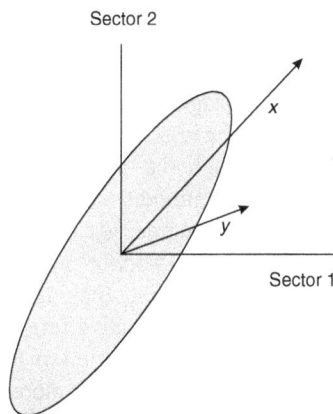

(d) Eigenstructure ellipsoids

Figure 4.1 The economic system: a Sraffian representation with asymmetry in the treatment of consumption.

Before we examine these in detail, two observations are in order. First, by profit, under steady-state and no net investment, is meant income accruing to capital owners as reward for the employment of capital, to the quantity of which it is assumed proportional, at uniform rate π. Such income (say, as a capitalist's take-out) may be seen as reward for their services, not as compensation for entre-preneurship or for taking risks, and is expended on consumption: Whence, $\|VA\|_1 = \|y\|_1$. Second, the standard interpretation of Figure 4.1, especially of part (b) of it is as follows: Money income VA is distributed to participants in some agreed upon way (collective bargaining, etc.) for their contribution to producing output x. With this, they buy commodities constituting y. Part K of x is fed back as maintenance expenditures due to physical deterioration, wearing out or otherwise lost productive capacity, so as to maintain total productive capacity precisely, from one period to the next. Seemingly, this is internal to the production process and does not reach final commodities. Normally, it is deducted before arriving at any net measures of national income. But from our point of view, it is 'embodied' in final commodities and constitutes a great but neglected part of their time-space appropriating content.

Thus, we ascribe great importance to the Sraffian roundabout flows of intermediate inputs. As Rosenberg (1982: 72) observed referring to the structural interdependencies within the economic system, by 'jump[ing] directly...from primary inputs at the beginning of the productive process to final outputs at the end of the process, an enormous amount of interesting information is completely lost from view'. From our perspective, the transition must go through and take into account these intermediate flows, which are habitually ignored as...mere replacement. The cycle goes like this: Agents trade their direct labour (personal time-space as economically relevant knowledge) for wages and profits distributed according to VA, producing through social division a certain amount of physical output, which is not identifiable with any individual producers, and whose value x is not to become known before the process unfolds and is completed at the consumption stage. Output consists of the net product, to be consumed, and of replacement for intermediate inputs, the whole of it being placed in a common pool from which the participants will draw by expending income $\|VA\|_1$ on consumption commodities. The whole of x is what is actually claimed back by expending this income, not just the commodities composing y, as is commonly thought. In the commodities purchased as y is embodied directly or indirectly all time-space that went into making the gross output, including internally circulating part Ax (or, in its productive form, K). Things could not be otherwise, since y is just a different decomposition of VA. So, if VA produces the whole of x, then it is the same x that y can buy, no more, no less, and no other.

One more point needs to be amended. It appears as if agents receive income $\|VA\|_1$ for contributing their time-space (knowledge, skills, etc.) only to production. But the gross value x that will materialize will also include the value of use-type knowledge to be contributed during the consumption stage and relating to how the above income is going to be allocated to the n available commodities. Everything is determined conclusively at the consumption stage, at which is completed the cycle of drawing from nature raw inputs, transforming and ascribing economic value to them, and finally returning them back as waste, from the consumption end of the system. This is the metabolic cycle of ES, with the rate of metabolism being determined mainly by the roundabout flow K (Ax) that reflects the 'capitalistic efficiency' of the system, as this will be defined later, that is, the degree of its technological advance, the degree of resonance of consumption to this technology and the efficiency of its price mechanism.

And there is more to all these. For example, it is by their conduct through the whole cycle that consumers determine the real wage, any surplus usurped and all other economic magnitudes. Nothing is set, given or fixed without their cognitive contribution. Their market conduct does not determine only the prices of consumables, but also the value of capital, the yield of investment, macroeconomic indicators such as the level of employment, etc.

The time-space content of commodities is never enough for consumers, because their yearning for life, that is, for power over (the time-space of) others is insatiable, due to the inescapability of their angst, and because that part of *x* which accrues to one of them is loss to others. Now, if we also consider that capitalists have the power to usurp part of the collectively produced income just for owning capital, beyond anything that could be seen as comparable and fair reward for their personal input to production, it follows that for the rest of the contestants the game is actually negative-sum, not just zero-sum, from the start. Therefore, demand (for time-space) always exceeds supply, and rather than saying with Jean Baptiste Say that supply generates its own demand, it is more appropriate to say that consumers put the pressure on supply to find ways of producing more tokens for their life-taking contest, themselves vowing to behave in technologically resonant ways so as to increase the overall stakes. A demand slump then is not so much refraining from expending income volume-wise, but rather unwillingness or incapacity of consumers to resonate innovatively, due usually to depressed sentiment.

Normally, innovations are continuously inspired and mutually supported on either side, with price changes reflecting the value of the resulting knowledge increments. These push *x* up at rates which depend on the rates of the production- and consumption-innovation processes and on the degree of their resonance. Distribution of income *VA* thus becomes intimately involved, since different distributions do not promote such rates and such resonance equally effectively, stimulating or depressing consumer sentiment differently. Returning to the issue of the real wage, it obtains from the above that the more resonant an agent's personal consumption behaviour is in relation to the overall innovations process, that is, to the conduct of the totality of agents, the greater the portion of *x* the agent will manage to claim back from the pool, with any given money income, so the greater his or her real wage. In other words, 'real wage' is personal. We turn now to the kind of performance these imply.

System performance

Mesarovic (1972) proposed a method of preference-ordering technologies based on input–output (stimulus–response) and goal-seeking specifications. An input–output specification is a relation $S \subseteq \mathbf{X} \times \mathbf{Y}$ where $\mathbf{Y}$ is the set of inputs (here, demand vectors) and $\mathbf{X}$ is the set of outputs (output vectors). For a goal-seeking specification, a decision object D and a value object V are added, as also two functions: An outcome function, $F : \mathbf{Y} \times D \rightarrow \mathbf{X}$ and a performance function, $G : D \times \mathbf{X} \rightarrow V$, where $D = \mathfrak{R}$ in our case and F is a Leontief relation. Set V with a preference ordering on its elements is to be decided so that the elements of $\mathbf{S}$ are determined according to the following optimization: $(x, y) \in \mathbf{X} \times \mathbf{Y}$ is also in $\mathbf{S}$, if and only if there exists a $d_y \in D$ such that $x = F(y, d_y)$ and $G(d_y, F(y, d_y)) \geq G(d, F(y, d))$ for all $d \in D$. If a meaningful G can be found with ordering, then the same criterion must govern the expansion of D, making elements $(\mathbf{Y}, \mathbf{X})$ of $\mathbf{S}$ into time-labelled input and output alphabets $(\mathbf{Y}_t, \mathbf{X}_t)$. These would supply an evolutionary law, defined by Georgescu-Roegen (1966) as a proposition that describes an ordinal attribute E to serve as evolutionary index, so that if $E_1 < E_2$, then E_2 follows E_1 in the ordinal pattern, that is, observation of E_2 is later in time than E_1.

According to these, to define a principle that underlies technological advance means to determine G from the HS–PS relationship, which is twice circular as seen in Figure 4.1(a): Part y of total output flows from PS to HS, net of current account requirements Ax, while HS returns an equal value in the form of VA to PS. [As both VA and y project on the same axes, only sectoral composition differences show through analytics, not their all too important qualitative differences. This brings up our main point: As VA is (reward for) the sublime agency currently contributed to PS, it is also the human-knowledge attributes in y that should be considered in any analysis that acknowledges agent ontology and respects openness.] The remaining part, Ax, which consists of intermediate inputs plus maintenance of fixed capital, is positively fed back into PS, encouraging y by replacing embodied system-produced inputs, so that productive stocks do not get diminished and productive capacity is maintained. Thus, final demand value y may be seen as encompassing both the primary inputs (original means of production) remunerated as VA, and intermediate inputs K, which is the productive decomposition of employed capital. One may also see the productive capacity of VA as being augmented by leverage from K, towards an overall effect x. The primary goal is to increase this leverage through innovation, producing commodities by means of more and more commodities, that is, through more roundabout methods, so that x can be increased. In fluid-mechanics terms around Figure 4.1(a), sucked-back flow K is increased through innovation, so that total flow x is speeded up, for any given final outgoing flow y.

But these magnitudes are vectors, not scalars, as in the physical metaphor, therefore, even though the analytical scheme compromises qualitative aspects, a decent analysis may not fail to acknowledge that a structural, that is, a composition issue is critically involved, which makes necessary that the structure of y be innovatively decided in such ways as to increase its alignment with the leaking-back flow. Otherwise the latter's leverage will not be put to good effect, that is, total flow x will fail to be increased to the extent that is maximally possible and part of the production knowledge accumulated and reflected through the technological matrix R will be wasted. That will make for a technologically advanced economy of backward consumers that is huffing and puffing to find its way towards growth. These provide a general technical description of the orientation of capitalistic advance and a notion of goal for the system as Whole, deduced from motivation at the individual level and promoted through behavioural resonance.

From a mathematical point of view, structure and resonance refer to the eigen-structure of the technological matrix and to the relation of the demand vector to it. From this angle, we may get some basic intuition about the situation through a geometric picture and a physical analogue. But there is no intent to carry mechanically anything from the physical to the social realm, so the next should be read with caution. The response of a mechanical system to shocks follows some extremum principle, such as least action or maximum velocity. Economic systems, in contrast, develop or respond according to human intent. Whether such development can be made to fit some mechanical frame is a spurious matter. In every case, we mean it here only as a tool for facilitating the communication of a crude part of the submitted ideas.

In two dimensions, assuming for ease that A is symmetric (realistically it is not, and this makes its eigenvectors to be slanted, that is, non-orthogonal), the geometry and mechanics of (4.1) appear as follows: Loci of points **x** equidistant from the origin (i.e. **x**, such that $\|(I-A)\mathbf{x}\|_2 = c$, constant) form ellipses (ellipsoids, in greater dimensions) with axes along the eigenvectors of $I-A$, which coincide with those of A. A typical one is shaded in Figure 4.1(d). Lengths of half axes are proportional to $1/(1-\lambda_i)$, with λ_1 being the Frobenius (maximum) eigenvalue of A, so that ellipsoids are elongated along the associated eigenvector, v_F^A. A body of such shape subject to a uniform force field y would tend to rotate until its first principal axis aligns with the field, so that remaining potential is minimum. Then, if the medium inside which the motion of the body took place applied resisting forces proportional to the area exposed in the direction of motion, the body would attain a maximum constant velocity such that resistance would precisely cancel y. Velocity x, force y and the principal axis would then be aligned.[2] In every other position, forces should exist that account for any remaining potential, a situation which is not favoured by nature, due to the second law. Finally, if the system could change its shape as would best serve such motion, those changes should in principle be favoured which would further decrease potential, elongating its shape and increasing velocity x for any given y by increasing the ratio of the two eigenvalues.

In the physical analogue, $\|x\|_2 / \|y\|_2$ should be increased. However, $\lambda = \|x\|_1 / \|y\|_1$ is economically more meaningful. (Below, we employ notation $\|\cdot\|$, indiscriminately.) So, the two knowledge processes combine to effect structural changes and demand resonance, mediated and supported by appropriate price dynamics that aim to increase the system's roundaboutness and efficiency.

Since $\lambda = (\|Ax\| + \|y\|)/\|y\| = (\|K\| + \|VA\|)/\|VA\| = \mu + 1$, increasing λ through innovation implies increasing μ, which means that more capital (past, embodied human inputs or reusable knowledge) and fewer current human inputs are employed per unit of gross output x, by accelerating the flow K that is fed back into PS. Each unit of the current human input remunerated through VA (expended as y) combines with more indirect, previously accumulated human input embodied in capital K (or Ax), augmenting its multiplier effect. Each unit of currently added value results in greater output, so that more value is put up for grabs in the final commodities market. That is, more output is produced with less expense of present human effort or sacrifice, valued as VA. In view of the purpose of life as discussed along Kierkegaardian lines, these amount to expanding economically relevant knowledge (or knowledge x which is practically useful for the conduct of life) into the future, by exploiting knowledge past (reusable knowledge, or capital) at the least possible expense of the present. This also conforms with the Austrian approach, which explicitly defines the object of production to be in economizing on the original means of production. Relatedly, according to Metcalfe (1998: 27): 'Under the capitalist rules of the game, transformation processes are activated for a purpose, to make the value of the output exceed the value of the input.'

Overall, λ provides a measure of the system's structural complexity. It is also an index of total factor productivity that summarizes system performance characteristics in a way that meets some of the requirements set by Cantner and Hanusch (2001). Structural complexity is the outcome of the workings of selection (by markets) upon chance (innovation), through which unpredictably discovered bits of knowledge are sorted out according to their potential for increasing the value put out (desired output) by the human effort put in (valuable inputs). In communication-theoretic terms, the set $\Re$ is expanded with new codings that recognize more regularities in any given message string x, so that its content can be codified into a more compressed description y. Capital is the medium on which is recorded the accumulated social knowledge that raises system complexity. Index λ is independent of scale and of the level of prices, but depends on the sector-disaggregation scheme.[3] It may grow while GDP slows down or even contracts, and it may contract only due to dissonance between p, d and the eigenvectors of R, allowance being made for noise and interference from various sources. One such source might be from maladjusted capital accumulation patterns implemented during transitions, another may be due to changes in the rates of capital utilization, policy interferences that induce maladjustment of prices, etc. With dissonance may be associated irregular phenomena, such as stagflation.

These go along with empirical findings that innovation is associated effectively with greater complexity and structure (e.g. Hage, 1998). Gell-Mann (1995: 371, emphasis added) gives a comprehensive account that relates to systems, in general:

> As time goes on, more and more frozen accidents, operating in conjunction with the fundamental laws, have produced regularities. Hence, complex systems of higher and higher complexity tend to emerge with the passage of time through self-organization, even in the case of nonadaptive systems like galaxies, stars, and planets. Not everything keeps increasing in complexity, however. *Rather, the highest complexity to be found has a tendency to increase.* In the case of complex adaptive systems, that tendency may be significantly strengthened by selection pressures that favor complexity.

Further, as Loasby (1999: 113) explains:

> Menger's assumption of increasing knowledge implies that people will find increasingly indirect means of meeting their needs; and the principle of increasing roundaboutness is used to structure his logical sequence, which is not to be taken as a historical hypothesis. Starting with direct consumption of what lies to hand, this sequence continues with the use of what lies to hand to produce consumption goods, then to produce goods with which to make

consumption goods, and so on into more complex production sequences which depend on structures of complementary capital goods...

Our theory explains the meaning and cause of roundabout dependence on the structures of complementary capital goods in a way that goes beyond the usual understanding of capital accumulation. After all, λ is about flows of capital services, rather than about stocks, and increased such flows are seen to be in the producers' interest, as follows: Fixing everything on the consumption side, that is, assuming fixed p and d, given two physical technologies, R_1 and R_2 with associated ratios λ_1 and λ_2, respectively, such that $\lambda_1 > \lambda_2$, one should naturally expect producers to prefer and employ R_1, so that no production opportunities will be lost, and so that they can reap a greater Π with a smaller π, as vectors in Figure 4.1(b) are likely to become more stretched out. From the cited physical analogue's point of view, the ellipsoidal body will move at higher velocity x, given force y, and equilibrium $P(I-R_1)q = Pd$ would be more stable than $P(I-R_2)q = Pd$, if things were given time to settle down. Given that these should hold on the part of producers, our theory adds that it is natural to expect consumer competition for human time-space to push in the same direction, so that, as we will further discuss in Chapter 5, greater value of contributed time-space may be claimed back, both individually and collectively. This makes coincide individual interest with apparent system 'intent', and it also avoids all schizophrenic inconsistency in what agents pursue in their two complementary capacities as consumers and as producers, as fits a holistic, organic view that does not rely on artificial separating dichotomies.

The foremost purpose of a self-organizing system is to maintain and enhance its structure and to keep functioning in a metabolically more efficient way. So, it tends to increase its structure, given all relevant constraints, the level of its structure relating positively to its capacity to process flows with minimal exertion, economizing on its own resources. In different contexts, this takes on various forms that can be logged in different ways. In our context, λ provides a measure of such processing capacity.

Ulanowicz (1996: 228) proposed an accounting scheme for these, in terms of conditional probabilities. Besides aggregate amount of system activity T, measured by total system throughput, he explored by estimating probabilities in terms of measured flows the propensity of system autocatalysis to 'streamline the topology of interconnections (processes) in a way that abets those transfers that more effectively engage in autocatalysis at the expense of those showing little or no participation. In effect, as autocatalysis progresses, the network will tend to become dominated by a few intense flows.' He came up with an 'average mutual information' measure, I, for the 'degree to which autocatalysis (and possibly other agencies) have organized the flow structure' (ibid.), which is 'an intensive and dimensionless quantity i.e., it depends on the system topology, not on its physical extent' (ibid.: 229). Thus he derived 'a network property called the system ascendency', so that 'autocatalysis is hypothesized as a formal agency that imparts a *preferred direction* to evolving systems. That is, in the absence of major perturbations, *autonomous systems tend to evolve in a direction of increasing network ascendency*' (ibid., original emphases). Ulanowicz argued further that increasing ascendency portrays development in economic systems, it is an index of system performance and: 'The ascendency and its related variables give the economist tools that are more powerful than the gross community product for judging the vitality of an economic system' (ibid.: 231), but warned that 'With increasing ascendency may come greater vulnerability to external perturbations' (ibid.: 229).

In our context, increasing λ imparts a preferred direction in the system's evolutionary advance towards increasing network ascendency, as reflected through intersectoral flow properties that determine the connective structure of technological matrix A, in the particular quantitative sense that its multiplier effect, namely, $(I - A)^{-1} = I + A + A^2 + \cdots$, tends to be increased with time. Knowledge-wise, the successive terms in this expansion account for the productive-knowledge contributions in all successive periods, from time immemorial up to the present, as these have been inscribed partly on capital and partly as consumption-related knowledge, the latter entering through current consumer behaviour that affects prices p, which in turn enter the calculation of A, and via the structure (composition) of d in relation to R.

The usefulness of a welfare principle in the form of a change in the system's connective structure was underscored also by Potts (2001). Again, in mechanical terms, advanced economies exhibit a density of connections determined by A, placing the fulcrum in such way that a small force y produces a great overall effect x: A small demand makes the economy spin faster, increasing money velocity. The urgency of capitalist economies to speed up value flows, both from perishable necessities and from 'the services of machines and buildings in general' has been noted thus by Shackle (1972: 157): 'There are urgency and pressure to use it [time], and in the highly specialized economy, use of time means exchange of goods and of services for goods and of means of production for products. There must be exchange continually if life is to continue and if it is to continue in the richest flood it can achieve.'

Vulnerability is then increased, as warned by Ulanowicz, since a small drop in y may result in lots of idle productive capacity and big output loss, as seen from the differentials relation $d(\|x\|) = \lambda \, d\,(\|y\|)$, which shows that demand perturbations have greater impact on x, the greater is λ. Similarly, in clock-time terms, since $d(\|x\|)/dt = \lambda \, d\,(\|y\|)/dt$, maximal growth rates along growth turnpikes of short-run, fixed-technology dynamics (McKenzie, 1963; Tsukui, 1966) are thus extended through increasing λ into the domain of technical advance, which is shown to be a process of developing higher-speed turnpikes. With open economies, these raise depression concerns as elaborated on by Krugman (2000), even though he, too, reasoned only on the basis of the aggregate size of demand: 'the question of how to keep demand adequate to make use of the economy's capacity has become crucial' (ibid.: 154) and 'free markets...are unlikely to survive in a world where insufficient demand is a continual threat' (ibid.: 157).

As noted, λ depends on the norm of $(I - A)^{-1}$ and on the relation of its eigenstructure to y. By scale invariance, over all y such that $\|y\| = c$, constant, volume E of the convex hull of maximal $\|x\|$'s, possibly weighed by some probability distribution over y, could serve not just as ordinal, but indeed as cardinal attribute in Georgescu-Roegen's frame, waiving the dependence of λ on y. Then, a new R will stand for advance (it will expand D in the Mesarovic frame) if λ, hence E, is increased for at least some y. But uncertainty that surrounds all behaviourally determined magnitudes, especially those that concern the relation between p and d, makes knowing the hull E not practically possible, so there can be no certainty about the degree of an economy's maximal aptness. Finally, from a control system point of view, λ may be seen as an efficiency index in controlling output x, through choice variables D, in a most economical manner, that is, so as to minimize cost function y.

So, in increasing λ are indissolubly confounded three effects: A technical, a demand composition and a price effect, as will be discussed. Moreover, testing the validity of relevant statements should hinge on difficulties associated with the construction of reliable input–output matrices and vectors, and on the fact that these are typically estimated on economies which are not in steady-state.

Structure and profit-seeking innovations

Setting aside for a moment existential considerations and assuming that producers seek profits for their own sake, we can start from physical system $(I - R)q = d$ where, as said, given d and any two techniques, producers should prefer the one that maximizes $\|q\|/\|d\|$ so that no physical production and profit is foregone. Translating into values, it is reasonable to expect that, unless dis-functional, prices must not oppose this preference, given that money profits should by and large be proportional to employed physical capital, which in turn must be directly related to gross output. Thus, λ, which is a measure of such amplification, translates in value terms the common conception of technical advance as moving in the direction of increased output from any combination of inputs, prescribing a welfare principle or preferred direction in the system's development path.

From (4.1′) is seen that increasing λ involves technique improvements, adaptive consumption preferences and accordingly adjusted prices, so as to produce demand structures that resonate with technology-eigenvector constellations. These extend Pasinetti's (1993: 46) argument that 'The price system is determined by the structural evolution of technology' and go along with Schumpeter's view that relative prices are in constant flux, pursuing an equilibrium which is always disturbed by the same market conditions that lead to progressive structural changes and which, in the neoclassical theory, are mistakenly thought to establish competitive equilibrium.

Schumpeter's illuminations concerned particularly his argument that the substance of growth lies in innovation resulting from the impulse of capital's earning power, as entrepreneurs try to capture monopoly profits by venturing away from competitive equilibrium market regimes and internalizing market-creating monopolistic externalities. As Abramovitz (1989: 10) argued, 'these prizes were transient, being diluted and eventually eliminated by the imitative inroads and further innovations of rival entrepreneurs'. So, 'monopoly power, therefore, was...constantly limited, but also constantly renewed' (ibid.). And: 'In a less...competitive atmosphere, established firms may well prefer to extend the market life of existing commitments to products, tools, methods and distribution channels...But the threat posed by the possible advance of rivals prods firms generally to increase their efforts and to accept the costs and risks of keeping up and moving ahead' (ibid.: 38). These view the process in autocatalytic terms. Pressure by other firms that grow and command more resources imposes a growth imperative on each one of them. The primary effort of innovators is to increase the capital they command and employ, that is, their shares of K, by means of which increased shares of VA can be appropriated. From an inputs point of view, these amount to increasing the productivity and lowering the cost of human inputs rewarded as VA. To this end, and to stay in business, producers must expend effort on growth by securing monopoly profits to invest.

Relative profitability of production routines under prevalent demand structures judges which ones will be diffused and will proliferate. Routines that might have been more profitable under different condition sets may not be well received and may not be applied.[4] This distinguishes general knowledge, which concerns what is technically feasible, from economic relevance and application, which concerns what pays off. An evolutionary economic theory must explain how interactions between the various components affect the changing requirements for profitability, and how routinized firm behaviour channels organizational change on an economy-wide scale, blending regular behavioural patterns with the system's evolutionary trajectory.

A good place to start discussing the innovations process that makes possible the changes above is from a historical controversy. Unit profit of a price-taking entrepreneur operating in sector j is $p_j - \left(\sum_{i=1}^{n} p_i r_{ij} + \sum_{k=1}^{m} w_k l_{kj}\right)$. Prompted by the persistently greater increases in the aggregate productivity of labour, as compared with those of capital, a debate was launched upon two opposite ideas: One, supported by Hicks (1932) and economic historians, who argued that a fall in the price of capital relative to the price of labour (say, due to labour scarcity, labour demands or resource abundance) would induce inventions of a labour-saving type, and a challenging one by Salter (1960), supported also by Fellner, Samuelson and other theorists, who argued that entrepreneurs have no reason to be biased and that they should opt indiscriminately for any changes in r_{ij} and l_{kj} that promise to reduce unit cost, increase profits and improve their position in a crowded competitive environment. To explain differences in factor productivity trends, Salter suggested that emphasis should be placed on the substitution induced by cheaper capital goods. As neither productivity trends could be disputed nor Salter's basic argument, or even the observed relative constancy of distributive shares, and yet the systematic cheapening of capital could not be explained in the traditional closed frames of reference, Rosenberg (1982: 15) concluded that 'this disagreement between the theorists and the economic historians remains unresolved.'

The element induced by openness is that with price changes determined endogenously, through incremental knowledge, causality must be reversed. Price changes which are not explained endogenously cannot explain progress in any specific direction, with any degree of consistency. Entrepreneurship is not in *responding* to changes, but in *creating* changes. It is innovations that make one or the other factor relatively cheap, increase its employment and decrease its productivity. We try here to explain these in a formal way, but one must be aware of a few complications. The demand-side knowledge component is deferred, although it is confluent with the production part because, paradoxically, only through such separate initial treatment can their inseparability be exposed. Further, qualitative aspects that are inherent to innovative changes and on which consumption innovations take effect are suppressed. If there were no such changes to commodities, there would be little for consumers to innovate about, and cost reductions would simply let higher profits accrue to innovative producers, changing distributive shares consistently in their favour. But it is not possible to address such qualitative aspects sincerely, since any kind of quantitative analytics based on a fixed-sector scheme must rigidly associate commodities with sectors and express everything in all-homogenizing, monetary magnitudes. That is, no qualitative heterogeneity can be accommodated beyond that which is permanently fixed with the disaggregation scheme employed. Even new commodities (which associate all too often with innovation – for example, changing from film to digital photography, new soap fragrances, etc.) must be accommodated in the same old sectors, along with older commodities.

Since these hold also for capital items, producer innovations can only be presented from an analytic perspective as input substitutions, missing the qualitative novelty which associates with new types (vintages) of capital. So, in the following discussion of the various types of innovations, newness should be somehow envisaged as being present in what is treated as substitution.

The prevailing (average) unit cost in sector j being $r_j^T p + l_j^T \vec{w}$, with r_j and l_j the j-th columns of R and L respectively, under the above circumstances a producer should try to reduce cost and increase profits by reshuffling inputs r_j and l_j, or to discover new uses of them (which also entails novelty) so as to increase their yield, exploiting better their productive potential in a way that renders the prevailing prices suboptimal. Equally frequently, he exploits new pieces of knowledge in the use he makes of material inputs, to the same effect; knowledge possessed only by him, for some time. Then, as such new routines get diffused and prices adjust to the new situation, price and profit differentials and monopoly advantage evaporate, while system efficiency is improved as the new ideas are exploited by the system as a whole. Such endogenously generated change provides consistent orientation to the system's path of development towards improving its structural relationship with the environment and towards increasing its metabolic efficiency.

Focusing on the two extreme situations associated with each innovation in isolation, namely, its initial emergence and the prevailing monopoly condition, on one hand, and the state after its full diffusion and establishment of competitive equilibrium, on the other, neglects the importance of intermediate stages that overlap for various concurrent innovations. For new routines to get diffused, so that there may be efficiency improvements, profitability thresholds at all intermediate structures of prices must be surmounted. In other words, routines must be economically relevant *with respect to evolving market conditions* as these develop in response to a multiplicity of new options that are made available by each individual innovation, through cognitive consumer involvement. Thus develops a hierarchical causation through different macrolevels that form layered networks. In the end, since competitive equilibrium is basically about average modes, innovations are not, as a rule, adopted by all producers. Instead, they stop spreading when some profitability threshold cannot be exceeded due to consumer response, and they are gradually abandoned, within the same innovations-overlapping process that stimulated them.

We turn now to the characteristics of innovations which may meet such requirements. Reshuffling labour inputs without tampering with the r_{ij}'s is non-proprietary, easily and quickly imitable, hardly qualifying as new knowledge. With differential wage rates effecting efficient allocation of the l_{kj}'s, adaptation of $\vec{w}$ in (4.3) could quickly contain impacts, adjusting prices optimally to the 'novelty', wiping out all possibility for monopoly profits.

Substituting some l_{kj} for some r_{ij} is reversing to a more labour-intensive technique, it is easily imitable again, and it gets quickly diffused, allowing little or no extra profits. In terms of economic relevance, as this was defined earlier, it would promptly reduce λ, which means it may hardly qualify as a profitable technique. To see this, we write $\lambda = \|P\,(I - R)^{-1}\,d\| / \|P\,d\|$, with R satisfying the Hawkins-Simon conditions.[5] By Frobenius theorem $(I - R)^{-1} \geq 0$. Column sums being less than one, $(I - R)^{-1} = \sum_{k=0}^{\infty} R^k$ is decreased by such innovation, and so is λ.

Moreover, if such an innovation got diffused, W would be raised due to rising w_k through rising demand for l_k, Π would be lowered for fixed π, counteracting diffusion forces and inhibiting the willingness of producers to proceed with its application. In short, such 'innovations' fail early on to exceed profitability thresholds.

So, there remain two possibilities for an innovator seeking monopoly profits, given p, $\vec{w}$ and his share of q_j. These are: (a) Substituting one r_{ij} for another and (b) substituting r_{ij} for l_{kj} in such ways as to reduce unit cost $\sum_{i=1}^{n} p_i r_{ij} + \sum_{k=1}^{m} w_k l_{kj}$.

In case (a), the $\sum_{i=1}^{n} p_i r_{ij}$ component is reduced. As such firm routine gets diffused into an economy-wide technique, the j-th components $K_j = q_j \sum_{i=1}^{n} p_i r_{ij}$ of K and of $\Pi = \pi K$ are reduced, under previous prices and quantities. Therefore, the routine will proliferate to any considerable extent only if Π is increased for the same π, after competitive adjustment of p and d to the new R. Otherwise, it may be stored as a temporarily inactive but readily recoverable routine that may be profitably employed under future demand conditions. (See note 4.)

Innovation type (b) increases $\sum_{i=1}^{n} p_i r_{ij}$ and can be organizational or operational, as when reorganizing a warehouse or switching from a manual record system to computer filing changes capital flows and labour requirements. The difference between r_{ij} and l_{kj} is that the former objectifies previously discovered knowledge and is proprietary, while the latter is not (assuming out direct slavery). So, each producer tries to increase his income-generating capital, by means of which he can also command greater current labour inputs, indirectly. Type (b) innovations are not only monopolistically profitable, but also when diffused, even at old prices, which are now rendered suboptimal. The innovating firm's structure is increased, providing advantage in the competition for resources and raising its market share and value, a property which becomes more important as the weight of the market-value criterion is increased with management-run businesses that appear with size. Thus, the firm's chances are increased relative to other firms that are less expropriative due to their lack of command over the new piece of knowledge. During diffusion and adjustment of market conditions to the new technological regime, all profitability thresholds may be surpassed due to increased employment of capital. At full diffusion, where competitive conditions are established, K is increased and hence also Π, for fixed π. The system annexes more resources, enhancing its fitness relative to competing economies. Alternatively, innovations may be seen as equivalent to the discovery or creation of resources.

A general conclusion is that changes of type (b) are the most favoured ones, considering also that in complex systems the human component is taken to be the least reliable, prone to error and failure. The impression up to this point is that such innovations reduce known labour tasks and make it easier to further homogenize and trivialize those remaining, reducing labour's market power and the capitalists' dependence on an unreliable factor by innovatively embodying knowledge in capital commodities, which substitute for current expending of productive capacity effected through L and compensated as W. Thus, with all the supporting, user-friendly software and graphics user interfacing, a kid with some training may be able to install and set up a computer network or software, sending computer science graduates to compete for low-paid jobs.

This impression needs amending. Schumpeterian-type innovations as above help increase the flow of services from system-produced inputs *per unit of currently employed labour*, and per unit of gross output. But gross output is increased by at least an amount equal to the value of the new capital commodities which are called upon to supply these services, and such increased and upgraded flow is produced by labour assigned to new tasks, skills and dexterities, which are highly paid before they become trivialized and only few experts can supply them (e.g. computer science graduates). So, newly created tasks for labour, which are initially compensated at high wage rates, attach on to new types of capital or processes, are usually more centralized, isolated from trivialized labour, and relatively easily controlled, beginning immediately their own cycle of becoming trivialized and obsolete, and these cycles become shorter and shorter. In all, by saving on labour per unit of output, type (b) innovations allow greater output x for any given current labour input (VA) by means of increasing the flow of services K, in this sense saving on VA or, which is more correct, increasing its productivity. Factor replacement is expedited further by non-uniformity of labour accounted for in system (4.3), as opposed to (4.4). So, increasing functional division of labour is imperative to the capitalist mode of growth.[6]

Due to familiarization, the above seem adequate by themselves for rescheduling processes and restructuring the system, but they are not. In fact, they do not even make sense, unless matched by a similar innovations process on the consumption side, as we will discuss in the next chapter. Moreover, other innovations also take place, normally induced by relative factor price changes due to a variety of reasons. Shares of aggregate wage and salary income earned by low-paid, trivial jobs are known to be declining with advance, relative to those of higher-level occupations. This suggests that changes to the composition of the l_{ij}'s do take place. (It makes more sense to replace a technological commodity than repair it, and a toner cartridge costs more than a printer of newer vintage, designed and produced by such 'higher-level labour'.) Actually, a column c_j in the technological matrix A averages a number of different techniques employed by the firms in sector j. When any firm in it implements a type (b) innovation, this by itself changes the a_{ij}'s, which change further as other firms pick up the new scheme, and as firms in other sectors adapt to the new requirements set by sector j. Classical production functions, if one likes to think in such terms, are shifted outwards.

To repeat: Everything depends critically on the capacity of those who receive VA to absorb as consumers the thus increased productive capacity, not only volume-wise, but also in its novelty attributes. And as this requires resonant consuming innovativeness, everything hinges on *consumer sentiment*. To the extent that such sentiment needs dream-igniting income to be drummed up, distribution becomes critical. Distribution is critical only in this sense, since any volume of output, however large, could in principle be absorbed by any small number of wealthy consumers, except that they would not be able to supply the variety that is needed for matching the novelty that comes at a rapid pace from producers, whence the system would be slowed down. Actually, this was the greatest obstacle that capitalism was called upon to overcome immediately after its first stages, and its overcoming was its greatest success, which still keeps it going. Among few, there is less than needed incentive to compete fiercely for newness, as proved to be the case with Veblen's leisure class, or during the Victorian period.

Relatedly, it may also be noted that for income distribution shares to be such as to sustain capitalism's forward motion, since K is expanded mainly through type (b) innovations, these must be accompanied by a general falling trend in π and in the profit to output ratio, a hypothesis that has been put forward by Marx and has been empirically verified. So, capital is actively made cheaper relative to labour as technology advances, in reversed Hicksian causality. An innovator's demand curve is shifted upwards so that, at going market prices, he gains a price and profit differential. Innovators are proactive. The system is reactive but not reactionary. Unlike equilibrium-seeking, mechanistic response to external stimuli, human creativity perceives market conditions as a challenge to overcome, always revising plans from optimal allocation, equilibrium positions. Except for nature's general predilection for least action and low-potential states, neither the rationality or self-interest of agents nor the system's evolutionary mechanism promote equilibrium. Capitalistically rational conduct on the part of agents is their existentially driven effort to break away from market regimes, in the hope that others will follow.

Exclusively homeostatic, stimulus–response, mechanistic theories of behaviour fit only with a mechanistic intellectual tradition and with the principle of least action in behaviouristic psychology, that is, with a tendency of organisms to rid of tensions, stresses and drives and to retire at some low-potential equilibrium. But these are strongly disputed in behavioural sciences today, as they are extended by the 'beyond homeostasis principle' into the realm of creative activities which are their own reward, such as play, exploration and self-realization. Autonomous activity is considered the most primitive form of behaviour identified with human culture. According to von Bertalanffy (1969: 108): 'Just what we consider to be specific human achievements can hardly be brought under the utilitarian, home-ostasis, stimulus–response scheme.' Thus, a degree of tension is designed into modern management systems as a means for generating change.

Innovations are marketable pieces of information about possibilities formerly unknown. They provide a surplus at current prices, which are thus made suboptimal, *including the price of the mental resource which produces such cost-saving novelty*. Investing a portion of such surplus feeds positively back into the process, inducing more innovations that render previous ones obsolete. Advance thus appears as a retreat forward, *employing new types of labour for producing inno-vations that reduce the requirement for existing types of labour*. However, since labour reductions are per unit of produced output, as long as output is increased, labour requirements for any one type of labour, or in total, may be non-decreasing. Of course, as explained, when a highly advanced economy contracts, the problem of labour is more acute and the economy is more vulnerable to a depression of wage incomes. Normally, though, labour is shifted to new employments, some of which tender to new technologies and are expert and in short supply for a period of time, hence highly paid, while others become more trivial, with their former tasks being taken up by tools, machines and other capital items. So, there is no reason why distributive shares should move consistently in any particular direction, and it has indeed been confirmed (e.g. Hirsch, 1977) that these have remained relatively stable. But, again, it serves the interests of capitalism to pay those who know how to spend their income innovatively and resonantly, and learning how to spend innovatively takes large numbers who can provide requisite competition and innovative variety.

Traditionally, standard theory views this structure-increasing forward motion as a profit-driven one towards aggregate growth that presumably benefits everyone, placing relatively little emphasis on its structural and qualitative aspects. But even before considering consumers, one may see that the real motive of producers in trying to snatch a greater portion of Π is not just monetary. (If it were, the question about what they want profits for would still request an answer.) What is thus snatched is a greater portion of x, through snatching a larger portion of VA, that is, live, currently contributed human time-space, by means of previously contributed knowledge embodied in K. As K and x are stretched out in Figure 4.1(b), Π tends *grosso modo* to align better with *VA*, so that a greater part of the latter can be allocated to profits before the first wage rate becomes negative. (For a comprehensive relevant discussion, see Pasinetti, 1977, ch. V.) This relaxes the constraints on income distribution. Whoever controls K has greater flexibility to fiddle with π and appropriate more of the net income, suffice it that its final overall distribution is such as to help absorb an increasing capacity for new types of output, by keeping consumer spirit and innovativeness high. If this is not achieved, the system will slow down, overall Π will be reduced, and the profit-seeking purpose of producers will be defeated. This is an Achilles' heel for advanced capitalism, as is lately felt rather painfully. Thus, growth appears to be a forced outcome, that is, an imperative; a struggle, where any real benefit accrues to those who can snatch more value than that which they themselves contribute to production. It is a consequence of the strife for relief from some inner distress, having little to do with genuine welfare.

From the above follows that only 'pattern prediction' or 'explanation in principle', to use Hayek's terms, and a general Wittgensteinian understanding may be expected, not any exact prediction of actual paths of development. A successful innovative mutation is one of many that could have occurred, leading to growth through almost any path, given the symbolic nature of value-carrying commodities, which makes any such avail for appropriating time-space. However, it is reasonable to expect that options examined will follow a probability distribution whose mass is near already utilized routines. So, the search must be local and advance must be path dependent, but little can be said beyond that. Idea-generation processes are fundamentally uncertain. Ideas may have small or great impact that may spread quickly or not. The phenomenon may appear macroscopically either as gradual, or as a series of punctuated equilibria.

Profitability and efficiency

The *raison d' être* of innovation is to capture externalities and to weaken those forces which work to push prices down, towards competitive market equilibrium. Both sets of countervailing forces develop within markets, which provide a domain for their synthesis. But as innovative activity is intrinsic to humans and cannot be escaped, it is false to view markets as equilibrium-promoting mechanisms. On the supply side, as Fullbrook (2005) explains, 'competition is a process by which firms continually seek to re-establish the conditions of their own profitability. To compete in a market requires firms to seek out and exploit differences between them in production, technology, distribution, access to information and awareness of trends in consumption. These differences are the essential dimensions in which competition takes place.' More generally, by including consumption also as an innovative activity, innovation socializes all sides of the economic process, dividing labour more deeply and creating psychological distinctions among goods which may be otherwise identical, or nearly so. Make-knowledge is embodied in products or processes on which property rights can be claimed and profits collected, followed by use-knowledge, which means by consumers' congruent innovative encouragement, appraisal and exploitation of such distinctions, in exhibition of an organic social capability to procure advance and abide by it. Exploitation by consumers implies a similar motive as works on a typical capitalist's mind. Things could not have been otherwise, and any claim to the contrary, such as that producers care for profits whereas consumers go after utility, is schizophrenic, since all are producers and consumers, simultaneously.

As competition diffuses knowledge, its capitalization is diluted and renewed *ad infinitum*, producing ever-increasing flows of information. To survive, rivals must catch each other up. As they do, comparative advantage evaporates, prompting further innovations, with the self-regulating mechanism autocatalytically fuelling the self-augmenting one, in typical positive feedback. If this process is not renewed, there may be entrapment into once optimal positions and eventual falling back (lock-in). The essence of marketable knowledge is in its continual re-creation, dissemination and destruction. It is a flow, not a stock that can be stored without perishing. Its value is diminished as it is taken over by new knowledge, in time. This is a structure-augmenting instance of the second law, showing proprietary knowledge to be wasteful: An innovator's price differential buys him products of higher value than their sellers are aware of giving away, so extra value is privately confiscated and socially wasted.

At the firm level, a profitability criterion is thus in effect, given prices and market share, as an outward, economic expression of an ontological urge. Innovators search for new ways of exploiting inputs to increase their profits. With diffusion, the innovating sector's profit-earning capacity is increased first, and then of the economy as a whole. With profit rate equalization, the price of the innovating sector's product should drop; demand and output should rise, for a positive general relationship between sectoral rates of productivity and output growth, considering only isolated effects and forces, ignoring overlapping effects deriving from other concurrent innovations. Indeed, industrial sector analyses have shown that the rates of growth and profits in sectors with high innovation rates are considerably higher than the average in an economy. (See, for example, Losman and Shu-Jan Liang, 1987.)

Being part of a common goal based on coincidence of motives, an innovator's pursuit is harnessed by competition that diffuses benefits and adjusts structure towards greater efficiency. The combined effect of the two criteria is a complicated order in the system's evolutionary trajectory, and the interaction of the related activities forms the connecting, dynamical law through which the social can be reconstructed from the individual. Separating *states* resulting from this law from the law itself leads to mechanistic, stimulus–response type of interpretations. Again: At the economy level, through diffusion of innovations, vectors K and x are lengthened, so that the same portion Π of VA may be captured with a smaller π, or a larger Π with the same as previously π, the latter case being more assertive of rights of ownership. Thus, a given profit income is actively made to provide control over more labour-embodying capital resources. But as the capitalist experiment rests on the social capability to invent and abide by invention, the first of the two choices above has been made *grosso modo* historically, as attested to by the empirically documented facts of falling trends in the profit rate and relative constancy of distributive shares. Disrupting this balance may have deleterious effects on capitalism.

According to Ashby's (1954) Law of Requisite Variety, organized complexity is variety controlling variety. That is, for a system to function stably, its control mechanism must possess a degree of variety-handling commensurate with that of its perturbators. In our context, this requires that innovational variety be matched and controlled by imitator variety, by each firm being also a potential imitator, and analogously for consumers. Pioneering agents blaze new trails in new directions. At the same time, they also adapt by pilfering on the innovations of others. Each agent's and the system's goal is promoted only to the extent that both forces are at work. Such duality of forces has been diagnosed in many instances. Franke (2000) provides a discussion in a Schumpeterian context. On one hand, what inhibits innovation inhibits growth. On the other, what restricts controller variety inhibits competitive diffusion and organized efficiency. The control mechanism tends to reduce technique panspermy by selecting among those that are profitable for the individual those which are also fit for the system in its relation with the environment, increasing the frequency of their appearance. This is selective fitness. To cope with environmental changes, relative fitness provided by diversity is also required. By organizing diversity according to such active, rival but coexisting principles, nature favours systems that can survive a variety of perturbations. Change that results in this way is not planned or designed. Although always within context, it emerges spontaneously and evolves by organizing its own diversity.

In one extreme, marketing socially accumulated technical knowledge and allowing uninhibited action of the profitability criterion may lead to overpricing, underproduction and system inefficiency, increasing the power of innovative firms and reducing variety. In the other extreme, lack of monopolistic advantage (uninhibited plagiarism) reduces incentives and inhibits advance. So, positive laws that guard the innovator's market power must also guard against its excesses, as monopolists or colluding oligopolists raising entry barriers may cease fearing that others might catch up or forge ahead and may become placid price makers and power keepers, stifling innovation and slowing down efficiency improvements. Schumpeter made the distinction between innovative activity, which creates the system's development path in non-equilibrium, and adjusting activity by agents taking notice of price and profitability differentials, sharing in those and pulling the system towards equilibrium. Thus, disruptive, goal-seeking component activity is reconciled with system stability. This is an instance of Ilya Prigogine's stability formed away from equilibrium 'by way of co-action of ensembles of quanta of information ... cooperatively engaged within a controlling context' (Pribram, 1996). It is an instance of an autocatalytic, open-system category that can be traced back to holistic epistemology that focuses on the system's *kinetic form*, as rivalry fosters cross-fertilization.

Through this co-action – or strange coalition – the type of efficiency promoted is a result of community choice. Basing profits on the value of the means of production sets K (Ax) as desired output, in a dominance-tainted sense. Thus, primary inputs have declined historically relative to intermediate inputs. (See, for example, Carter, 1970.) But since income derives from primary inputs which are known to have grown historically, or at least they have not declined, intermediate inputs must have grown even faster. Growth thus entails increased roundaboutness, along with accumulation during transitions through a large investment component in demand. But this component depends critically on consumption's being resonant. When consumption lags or becomes dissonant and prospects for the yield of investment are poor, growth is impeded. Moreover, as we saw, this may be more pronounced for structurally advanced economies. This seemingly contradictory 'innovative conformism' trait of growth is what pacts or endangers social cohesion, not some vague common interest.

These suggest what the relevant concept of efficiency should be. In physical terms, first-law efficiency accounting for limits imposed by the conservation law is a ratio of desired outputs over valuable inputs: $\varepsilon = W_{out}/Q_{in} = (Q_{in} - Q_{out})/Q_{in}$, where W_{out} is output work, Q_{in} is input heat, Q_{out} is heat waste. But once we go beyond the sheer physical domain and start engaging society, what is desired and valuable ceases to be so clear. As Fullbrook (2005) notes: 'No efficiency claim is ever based on an identification of all the consequences, and quantitative guessti- mates of the future inevitably have a crystal-ball dimension. In the final analysis, "efficient", like "beautiful", is little more than a way of expressing a positive opinion.'

In a profit-driven system, first-law efficiency is $\varepsilon = (\|x\| - \|y\|)/\|x\| = 1 - (1/\lambda)$, which shows λ and ε to be monotonically increasing functions of each other. This saves on y relative to x and relies on transforming available matter and energy through the circular flow whose value is Ax into non-available forms, *without con- sidering them as waste*. In such capitalistic efficiency, present human contribution is reduced per unit of output. In Repetto's *et al.* (1989) words:

> Man-made assets...are valued as productive capital and are written off against the value of production as they depreciate. This practice recognizes that a consumption level maintained by drawing down the stock of capital exceeds the sustainable level of income. Natural resource assets are not so valued, and their loss entails no debit charge against current income that would account for the decrease in potential future production.

Thus, the more capitalistically advanced an economy is, the less value is delivered to final demand per unit of gross output, net of depreciated or worn out means of production, at the expense of entropic waste. Moreover, since Ax and y are normally not lined up, from the triangle (strict) inequality follows that $\|x\| < \|Ax\| + \|y\|$, whence $\varepsilon < \|Ax\|/\|x\|$. Equality would hold only if d were along v_F^R, but then output would not be maximum. Thus, λ-type efficiency is seen to obey Odum's (1983) 'maximum power principle', which states that open systems competing for available energy tend to operate at that efficiency which maximizes power (output) and entropy, but this efficiency is less than maximum.

From an information point of view, resources are given economically relevant form (they are in-formed), with information being reduction of uncertainty and potential for control. Critical in this being the distinction between primary and produced inputs, in a less antagonistic, not profit-driven environment, desired outputs and valuable inputs could be defined differently, leading to different types of efficiency and welfare principles becoming relevant. Assuming out capital ownership and profits would send us to the other extreme. It would count Ax as loss to the environment and by extension to society, which would recommend considering efficiency $\varepsilon' = (\|x\| - \|Ax\|)/\|x\|$, instead of ε.

From the triangle inequality follows also that $\varepsilon' \leq 1/\lambda = 1 - \varepsilon$. Increasing ε'-efficiency means favouring labour-intensive, Schumacherian, 'small-is-beautiful'-type techniques. In expended effort terms, it implies that an economy would crank out a smaller output x from a greater effort VA. But the currently unshakable popular paradigm of progress, which rests on competitive advantage, produces an ideology of mass production and consumption that proceeds upon increasing ε and decreasing ε', in accelerated operation of the entropy law. As Daly (1989) put it: 'Our growth-bound way of thinking makes it hard for us to admit the concept of throughput, because it brings with it the first and second laws of thermodynamics, which have implications that are unfriendly to the continuous growth ideology.' Thus, ε could go down only due to (temporary) dissonance between demand and technology, making the diamond-shaped quadrilaterals in Figures 4.1(b) and 5.2(b) wider.

Three indissoluble effects

From $\lambda = \|P(I - R)^{-1}d\|/\|Pd\|$ can be seen that a technical (R), a demand composition (d) and a price (p) effect are mixed indissolubly, forming closed circuits of causality that can be traced around the circuit and back, through whatever position is arbitrarily chosen as starting point for a description. Their confounded effect goes beyond the physical and price confounding that is acknowledged in work on making input-output structures comparable across time and across economies. (See, for example, Carter, 1970; Dietzenbacher, 1990; Seton, 1992.) Starting from prices, these affect A, given R, but also d through consumption preferences and, cyclically, the choice of R and p. So, 'repricing' input–output matrices, and also inter-country comparisons, are haunted by serious problems, especially those associated with different changes in price structures.

Seeing $\mathfrak{R}$ as a set of crisp blueprints and demand relations, call them F, as being determined exogenously, allows seeing price formation as a mechanism towards timeless equilibrium states, in which no productive potential remains unexploited, but neither is any newness introduced. That means solving the problem: $\max_p \lambda$ s.t. $d = F(p), R \in \mathfrak{R}$. In such state, prices are 'correctly calculated' towards realizing all technically feasible output for the said demand relations, modelling an engineered, non-evolving situation. Such optimal-allocation artefacts are self-contained systems of clearly designated parts and well-defined relations, that is, unique structures ascribable to the observable behaviour of some *external* order, computing the consequences of their own assumptions and rules built in, their internal consistency resting upon an objective-reality, unique-optimum hypothesis.

As Hayek has argued, such complete-knowledge contrivances assume the real problem away. They assume novelty out and fail to capture the richness of system interactions. They miss integration of PS with HS into ES, interpreting HS as 'observing' PS and ES. Thus, they proscribe endogenous change by ignoring motivated behaviourism from HS, which causes tensions and affinities that upset equilibria and fuel the search for more efficient (p–d–R) combinations. However, it is not the amount or dispersion of information that makes it impossible for any single agent or authority to handle, or to control the situation, as Hayek maintained. If such information were fixed, only a technical problem would arise, which would be easy to solve. The difficulty is with the *genesis* of new information that effects changes through two-way causal relations between all entering factors. Such indeterminateness, seen by orthodoxy as a degrees-of-freedom curse, is actually (and factually) a blessing for capitalism. It provides headroom needed for innovation.

Given dependence on how well and how promptly prices are able to reflect consumer behaviour through their changes, the process is a large-scale, full-information application of Thaler's (2000) 'guess the number' game in which contestants are asked to guess a number from 0 to 100, aiming at making their guess as close as possible to, say, two-thirds of the average guess. As Thaler explains, the correct answer depends on two kinds of heterogeneity in sophistication: (1) differing levels of processing capacity of agents and (2) heterogeneity in how much agents think about the sophistication of others. Thaler's criticism is that standard theory and modelling apply to a static environment that ignores both the limited capacity of agents to learn, and the few chances usually available for learning, due to non-repetitiveness and to the learning process being slower than the process through which new information is generated.

Figure 4.2 depicts such an indeterminately connected system. Increasing λ is the performance criterion relative to the structure-formation goal, p is the goal-seeking variable exerting influence on the essential physical relationship between d and q, their ternary relationship given by relation (4.1). GS is the goal-seeking element that modifies p after observing q (feedback action) and also determines p from d before observing q (feedforward, anticipatory action). Such systems exhibit anticipatory behaviour that resists algorithmic description. Prices provide signals for acquisition of new knowledge pertaining to partners and conditions of transactions (information about rivals' and consumers' reactions), catalyzing convolution of production capabilities with demand, connecting the payments and final sectors *via* technology. Such behaviouristic outcomes are not easy to model. According to Stock and Campbell (1996): 'Where prices are free to rise and fall in response to changing conditions, price adjustments ... are powerful interpreters of diverse information. ... [A price] integrates information about the cost of labour and material, trends in fashion, the competitive activity of other firms, and the general economic climate. ... The marketplace is integrating information and interpreting it continually. ... it is a processing system that is massively parallel.'

Prices reflect relative appraisals of parts within a Whole, forming a system linked through a dynamic relation that optimizes some performance criterion. They are connecting elements that provide systemhood properties to the disaggregated by

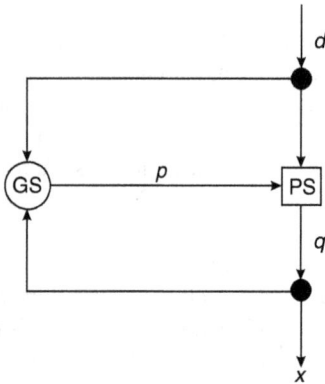

Figure 4.2 An indeterminately connected, anticipatory, goal-seeking system diagram.

sector production and consumption system. Ignoring dynamical relations misses important information about the system. Whatever the performance criterion is assumed to be, components must be dynamically connected through some appropriate goal-seeking specification. Increasing λ is such a criterion, providing a principle of price formation which, given R, allows setting K, x, VA, Ax and y up to a numeraire, establishing (4.3) as a distributive relation. The bond between market-effected allocation and socially effected distribution is thus relaxed. Distributive variables and prices are determined neither in strict mutual relationship nor simultaneously, as would be required by a state-oriented logic, in contrast to a process-oriented one. Changes in distributive variables do affect prices, albeit in ways that involve also consumption-versus-saving inroads, all of which are determined behaviourally. This upgrades the significance of wages, ascribing to them a role in assisting consumer innovativeness. Beyond providing for survival, they can be made into active policy instruments towards shaping the composition of y, so as to make it resonate with A to the end of increasing output.

Hayek (1945) considered prices as rates of equivalence that reflect relative resource scarcities, and he saw two kinds of relative scarcity changes: (a) elimination of a supply source and (b) change in the relative use of a resource. From our viewpoint, price changes reflect eventually the scarcity value of the sublime resource which generates economically relevant knowledge, meaning knowledge that translates into value, including the value of the items considered by Hayek. They are not marginal productivity prices, equilibrating demand with supply. They are instead information augmenting, and the thus implied uncertainty reduction is from both types of Hayekian scarcity. The first type relates to the uncertain and volatile relationship of ES with its environment and to the relative rates of resource use and replenishment. The second type relates to endogenously determined changes, whereby innovations change the uses of inputs. Scarce being the economically relevant output of the sublime agent, and with scarcity depending on prevailing demand patterns which are themselves a behavioural output of the same agent, price changes help effect efficient allocation of resources towards increased such output. So, they are 'natural' (gravitational) in that they work towards effecting vector configurations of low potential, countering the upsetting effect of the increments of information that are registered through them. They are functional, in the sense that they help effect efficiency improvements. And they are rational, in the sense that they expand the output x of human input VA, promoting structure expansion and expropriative fitness.

Technical aspects relate to the eigenvalues of R, to the topology of its eigenvectors and in their relation with d, all being affected by production and consumption innovations. The degree of tuning between demand and this techno-structure reflects consumer self-affirmation through socialization by participation (or indulging) in consumption patterns that are resonant with the prevailing technical conditions. This complements the other kind of socialization, that which is achieved by participation in socially organized production, with division and specialization of labour. Thus, not only demand drives innovation, but it is itself shaped by evolving production capabilities, which inspire a dominant ideology of progress through imitation, promoted standards, controlled quality and planned obsolescence. Preferences become perfectly endogenous through acculturation of skills, norms and tastes, by schooling or imitation of successful modes, towards accumulating wealth and social recognition, as the received view goes, or power through time-space-expropriation, as asserted by our theory. To be in the game means to behave in an economically resonant way, that is, to produce and consume resonantly. The cost of non-resonance is falling socially behind, or dropping out.

Endogenous dynamics obtain from producers' inventing ways to evade market determinacy and from consumers' inventing new wants and new ways to meet these wants, driven by an impelling desire for life as appropriatively understood. The degree to which these two searches resonate determines the system's expropriative performance and its ε-type efficiency. Thus is produced equilibria-upsetting variety, through which the system modifies its structure so as to be stable in its motion. (Le Chatelier's Principle supplies an analogue from physical chemistry.) Stability becomes focal, especially if intervals between disturbances are small relative to the system's relaxation time, and it rests upon degrees of freedom provided by flexible factor rates and commodity prices. These supply regulative or control capacity that serve the natural proclivity of the system to be stable. Uncontrolled oscillation and chaos is avoided if the variety of the control mechanism matches that of the perturbator. Freely moving prices amplify control information. Such metacontrols regulate information flows in viable systems, towards increased internal negentropy.

In view of the above, λ provides a metasystemic performance criterion. From agents trying to improve their lot, given the environment, obtains an opaque process of adjustments. The system cannot know at each point in time how much better it could do by such and such change in technique, prices or consumption behaviour. Only *ex post* can two states be compared, based on the response of demand and the resulting λ's or ε's. Survival provides no *measure* of successful adaptation, since what survives is not some single order, but an order flux. The system floats within a judgmental n-space, behaving as a learning machine with adaptive controllers. These preclude optimization.

A simple, two-sector example may provide basic intuition about resonance. We consider four 2×2 technological matrices, differing in the degree of connectedness between sectors and in the relative intra-sectoral flows, and we examine the effect on output of a change in y from its most resonant position, y_1, to one rotated by $45°$, y_2, keeping fixed the total consumption expenditure at one unit. That is, we keep $\|y_i\|_1 = y_{i1} + y_{i2} = 1$, $i = i$, 2. Rotating y while preserving A is unrealistic, since it assumes infinite price elasticities of demand, if R is assumed to be same. But for our purposes this is immaterial. Summary measures come out as follows:

$$Case\ 1:\ A = \begin{pmatrix} .6 & 0 \\ 0 & .3 \end{pmatrix},\ y_1 = \begin{pmatrix} 1 \\ 0 \end{pmatrix},\ y_2 = \begin{pmatrix} .5 \\ .5 \end{pmatrix},$$

$$GDP_1 = 2.5,\ GDP_2 = 1.96.$$

$$Case\ 2:\ A = \begin{pmatrix} .8 & 0 \\ 0 & .1 \end{pmatrix},\ y_1 = \begin{pmatrix} 1 \\ 0 \end{pmatrix},\ y_2 = \begin{pmatrix} .5 \\ .5 \end{pmatrix},$$

$$GDP_1 = 5,\ GDP_2 = 3.05.$$

$$Case\ 3:\ A = \begin{pmatrix} .8 & .2 \\ .2 & .1 \end{pmatrix},\ y_1 = \begin{pmatrix} .79 \\ .21 \end{pmatrix},\ y_2 = \begin{pmatrix} .37 \\ .63 \end{pmatrix},$$

$$GDP_1 = 6.81,\ GDP_2 = 4.69.$$

$$Case\ 4:\ A = \begin{pmatrix} .6 & .2 \\ .2 & .3 \end{pmatrix},\ y_1 = \begin{pmatrix} .\overline{6} \\ .\overline{3} \end{pmatrix},\ y_2 = \begin{pmatrix} .25 \\ .75 \end{pmatrix},$$

$$GDP_1 = 3.3,\ GDP_2 = 2.81.$$

GDP ratios and losses are summarized in Table 4.1.

Figure 4.3 gives a picture of the corresponding geometries. A quick look at statistics convinces about the complexity of the situation. The effect of demand-versus-structure changes depends both on the degree of streamlining in the structure of A and on the degree of sector connectedness, both of which become more complex as concepts with a large number of sectors. And what complicates matters even more is that the entire situation depends on what specific sectors are contemplated.

Table 4.1 Response of GDP to technological eigenstructure and demand changes

	Case 1	Case 2	Case 3	Case 4
GDP ratio	0.79	0.61	0.69	0.84
GDP loss	0.54	1.94	2.11	0.52

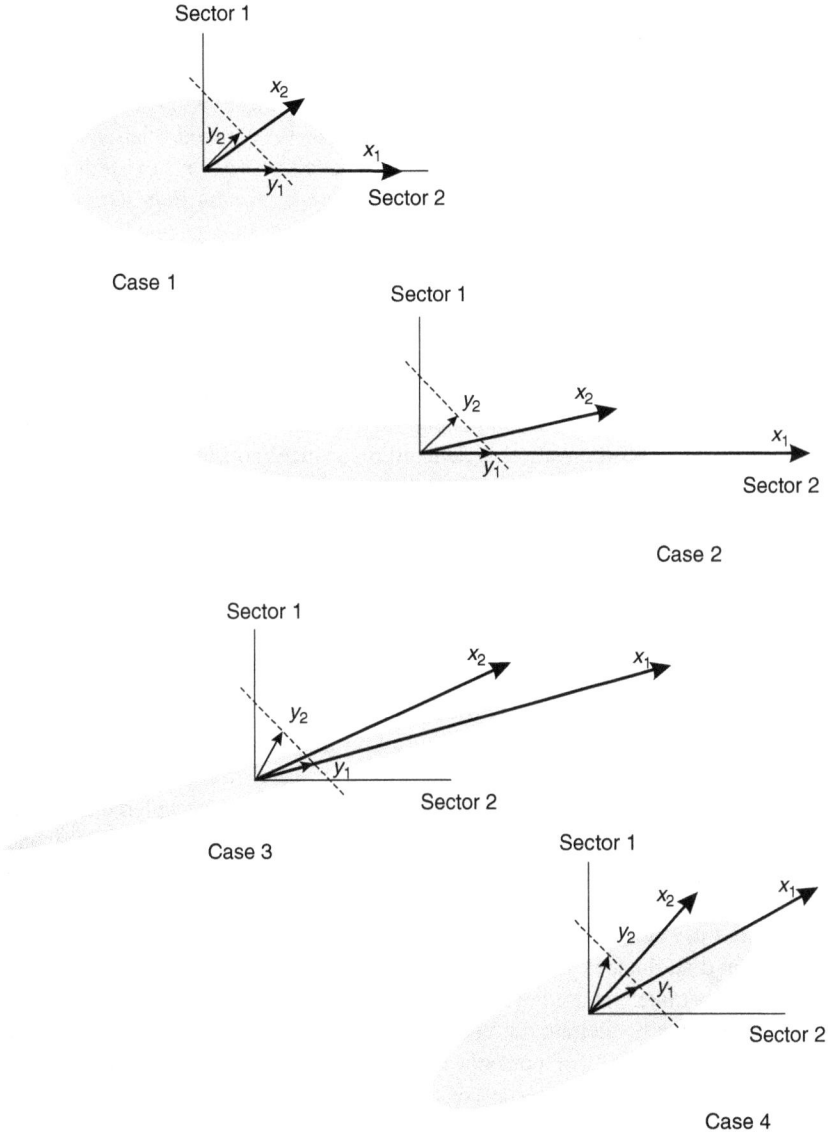

Figure 4.3 Connectedness, streamlining and resonance.

Some general observations

From the above is evident that the relationship between GDP and productivity growth with structure and its innovative streamlining in step with resonant demand is quite complex. Focusing, as conventional approaches do, on aggregate measures makes matters look much easier than they really are, evading the problem and obscuring the picture. These have failed to produce a body of affirmative knowledge that sheds adequate light on economic dynamics. Thus, in studies of the relative performance of advanced economies, only divergent empirical findings and explanations were drawn (see Pack, 1994). A time's arrow for competing economies relates to structure, not to scale, and to vectors and relations thereof. An economy may contract in size, but its knowledge base always expands and the rate and type of such expansion may be far more important than its mere size. Therefore, conclusions drawn from growth accounting, such as that technological advance is less important a source of growth than is capital accumulation, market expansion or population growth, confuse causes with effects and are a source of further confusion (e.g. Jorgenson, 1995; Young, 1995). An economy thrives and grows to the extent that it manages through structural advance and λ-type dissipative growth to conquer market space. R&D and investment on equipment or human capital affect the structural component of growth. Since λ contains technical advance (production innovations), demand resonance (consumption innovations) and price system performance (transmission of information), it all comes down to who wins in a knowledge race. *Ceteris paribus*, an economy's growth should accrue losses to other economies which lag behind in the resource-expropriation contest. So, the contest is zero-sum between systems also, as it is between individuals within the same economy.

Outside *ceteris paribus*, all relevant measures are mixed outcomes. Growth accounting provides evidence that growth performance in various countries is marked by Golden Ages and periods of slow-down, as *physical* investment exhibits diminishing returns. Productivity and output growth do relate to scale and to other scale-related phenomena. But what advances irreversibly, in 'forward' fashion, is the two innovation processes that run in concert, complementing each other, increasing the stock of relevant knowledge and effecting demand resonance to a technological eigenstructure that keeps advancing in the described way. Thus, although information transmitting by prices is subject to noise, any debate about growth that ignores the structural component is misplaced.

Random disturbances can produce unstable dynamics if there is maladjustment of prices, most likely caused by lack of resonance between production capabilities and consumption behaviour. As λ is increased, efficiency of the price mechanism becomes more critical. So, not only markets are *sine qua non* for capitalism, as Hayek insisted, but the efficiency of the market mechanism must keep up with advances in the innovative capacity of society, in terms of technology and in terms of absorbing its output. The state of an economy's advance is not a matter of technical knowledge only, but also of the skill to make quick relative value appraisals, registered through prices. Maladjustment of prices to changes in relative sector-efficiencies can lead to technical improvements not being properly or promptly reflected in valuations, to awkward phenomena (such as stagflation), thus hindering progress. Modelling this adjustability so that price changes are explained by the technical conditions of production in relation to demand behaviour requires degrees of freedom in the price system, as is allowed for in system (4.3), but hardly so with (4.4), which is the one employed almost always.

Sustainably adjusting demand into technologically resonant patterns eliminates forgone production, keeps tonality up and increases efficiency. As is typical of evolutionary processes, the capitalist one tends to maximize not present output necessarily, but prospective future streams of output over relevant time horizons. Controlling demand reduces variety that may match producer innovativeness and, conversely, it reduces behavioural diversity that producers are called upon to match, blunting their competitive (namely, innovative) tonality and slowing growth. Diversity generates more information than is possible by any design or plan. This information is relevant to *competitive fitness* in a limitationless environment, but there is also information that is relevant in terms of *sustainable adaptability* within a limitative one. The extended order that evolved historically into capitalism is a synthesis of spontaneity and control, based on a great variety of types of relevant information. Policy decisions induced by environmental, equity, or other considerations intervene with this process, leading to technology, demand and price dynamics that interfere with its path of development. Non-selfish modes of conduct also may slow innovation, extend commitments, or favour labour-intensive techniques. Publicly owned firms provide an example, exhibiting different factor-utilization profiles relative to privately owned ones in the same industry, typically employing more labour and less capital.

Depending on how an innovation expands K, compositions of VA and x can change in different ways, so that structural change entails differential productivity growth rates. Positive rates often associate with negative ones, so that negative industry-output growth may associate with productivity improvements. Macroeconomic indicators exhibit properties that depend on the dynamics of their composition. Structure is in interrelated components functioning as Wholes. Structural change is a process of inner organization, irreversibly advancing towards higher order forms. Irreversibility is implicit to the fact that systems which evolve smoothly into complex, specialized, interdependent structures are asymmetric in their parameters: In decline, they do not reverse smoothly to any previous position. Instead, they fragment or decay quickly. For Metcalfe (2002), who cites the work of Abramovitz, Burns and Kuznets in support, structural change is diversity in growth rates among sectors, with rates eventually declining, until they finally become negative and sectors retard. This means that balanced growth and aggregate measures are of little value, when it comes to endogenous dynamics.

Value added may be distributed into Π and the W_i's in infinitely many ways. In steady-state, what we called profits, denoted them by Π and set them proportional to a uniform rate π, is all consumed. So, it can be viewed as a wage component paid to firm owners for supplying one more type of labour and adding one more row (row $m + 1$) to matrix L, with wage rate π. Assuming no net investment, there can be no R&D expenditures. These would affect the *rate* of advance, but according to our reasoning there can be innovation even without any investment, as this is intrinsic to humans. So, although R&D investment may exhibit diminishing returns, the overall rate of innovative outcome is uncertain. Alternatively, profits could be allocated partly to inventive activity at a constant rate and treated as just one more sector in the Sraffian frame, as was actually the logic behind *new* growth theories. Profit rate π then should be such that, over relevant time horizons, some multiple-criteria objective would be promoted that should include measures of present and discounted future gains. Relevance of time horizons (discount rates, intergenerational equity) and efficiency/equity mixes must be resolved by society under uncertainty concerning the relationship between R&D investment and innovation.

Advance raises K relative to VA, increasing labour productivity defined either as value added or as total output in constant prices, per unit of labour. Stretching x out in Figure 4.1(b) tends to align K with VA, allowing both W and Π to range from $\vec{0}$ to VA. Thus, distributional options are increased, since the part of VA which can be apportioned to profits before any of the w_i's reaches zero is increased. But these are according to the conventional view, which sees income as being determined at the production stage, independently from consumption [with the two sides in Figure 4.1(b) logically and functionally separated, meeting only at market clearing in unreal and uninformative equilibrium] and distributed through institutional conventions such as collective bargaining. For us, only monetary income, which sets the scale, may be determined outside consumption, and even this is not in oblivion to the economy's λ-type performance. In any case, the actual distribution of *real* income is determined conclusively at the consumption stage, as a matter of expropriative shrewdness, through choices consumers make about structuring their expenditures. The most capitalistically appropriate distribution is that which rewards agents according to their contribution to the two innovation processes, that is, according to their aptness in producing and consuming 'techno-resonantly', in the sense of creating and appropriating K and Ax, respectively.[7]

Increasing λ is a receding target, a dome attractor or symbolic fixed point, which sets an evolutionary property or systemic trait, in a sort of expanding-universe type of situation rather than a gravitational one. It is a measure of the system's well-being, or, somewhat abusively, a 'welfare principle'. It is a way of formalizing the fact that, since capital goods are means of production embodying historically accumulated knowledge: 'The rate of growth of labour productivity is the proper measure of technical progress, as it should be when labour is the only primary factor of production', and also that 'technical progress means that a given rate of saving commands a greater effective labour force employed in the production of capital goods' (Metcalfe, 2002). But it is jejune to understand this in naively Darwinian survival terms. It must rather be seen as a system of systems: A holistic concern in which parts may compete, but to none's extinction (unless by mishap or by short-sighted, malignant avarice). Thus, although some parts (economies, sectors, individuals) may decline, others emerge and the system as Whole keeps going: The higher-level order is preserved. Capital makes better profit between connected, competing economies in mutual dependence, than in any isolated context, between connected, competing individuals, and so on.

According to Abramovitz (1989: 224), 'as followers' levels of per capita income converge on the leader's, so do their structures of consumption and prices'. So, the point is not exhausted in the *level* of incomes. The point is in that consumption behaviour and knowledge come part and parcel with those in production, and to these attends the price-adjustment mechanism. Thus, closest to our point, Georgescu-Roegen (op. cit.: 353) noted that 'If...an isolated country comes in full contact with an international market, there will be not only a change in its industrial structure, but also a change in its social patterns i.e., in the regulating principles of economic transactions...the contact with the more advanced countries will gradually disrupt the old forms and replace them by the economic patterns of the richer countries.' Globalization carries this further, towards unification of structures, but it may turn out that this is actually an impediment to advance in the long run, through reduction of the evolutionary diversity needed for enhanced adaptability to environmental disturbances.

These imply neither teleonomy nor equifinality. Only, economies sharing information (besides capital and labour inputs) may exhibit similitude of techno-logical, price and demand structures, overriding diverging factor effects and phasing out disturbances, false starts or overshoots. This is confirmed by the failure of foreign investment alone to help develop a number of underdeveloped economies, in the recent past. Equifinality (independence from initial conditions) is only in the sense that a property of increasing λ avails itself for an efficient specification of the system as goal seeking. This does not rule out the possibility of persistent and even widening differences in structures, and in levels and rates of growth. Actually, such divergence is implicit to dominance, as pressure on systems at a lower level of organization is increased, and these may become subdued and retard. On this, there is empirical evidence (see, e.g. Crafts, 1999).

As a conclusion, understanding motives, means, goals and the type of efficiency economic systems pursue is important for policy making and in relation to sustainability, equity and other considerations. The answer to the question of what a goal-oriented system is adaptive to depends on the perspective adopted. In reality, purposive systems usually pursue different goals and attain them to different degrees of success. Therefore, operationally meaningful ways of measuring per-formance are relative. Self-organizing systems respond to external stimuli, but their evolution is activated by what could be seen as 'errors', meaning deviations from statically optimal equilibrium states. These errors produce internal stresses, maintaining tonality. Such systems exhibit autonomy, changing their input–output relationship with their environment and promoting internal cohesion according to the way they perceive the latter. That is, they are observing and cognizing systems. Evolution is improvement of their structural coupling with the environment, so that new structures are produced that are better fit in its context.

5 Consumption innovations

It is hard to dispute that 'the demand side of the innovation process needs more attention than it has thus far received' (Metcalfe, 2002) and that 'we have ended with a perspective dominated by supply side considerations. However, there is a growing body of evidence...which gives the consumer/user a very active role in shaping innovation' (ibid.). Also, 'a knowledge-based theory of growth will emphasise the link between the micro diversity of behaviours and processes of creativity and the formulation of novelty by consumers as much as by firms. Indeed it is the continual generation of novelty on both sides of the market relationship that underpins the idea of restless capitalism and keeps capitalism "far from equilibrium"' (ibid.).

A lacuna in the treatment of consumer behaviour is so obvious, that hardly anyone would deny it. All agree that this is the Achilles' heel of economic theory that needs fixing, but it is only recently that mostly heterodox economists have dared address the issue, and as we commented in Chapter 2, even they have been inhibited to tackle it head on, delving into the dark sides of consumer ontology which must definitely be involved in such frantic commotion. As always, it is basically about poor little consumers trying to find ways to get some enjoyment out of consumption. Even Stigler and Becker, who came very close to a generative consumer ontology, refrained from being open about it. We have disputed all these, and we are about to provide a more analytical presentation of our disputing theory. But given how stubbornly standard fallacies have been defended on this score, the reader is asked to bear with a degree of repetitiveness, which we think is not only excused or justified, but mandated.

Behaviour invokes psychology, of which mainstream economics fastidiously steers clear, in quest of a positivist image that helps camouflage its ideological undertaking. Witt (2001, added emphasis) comments:

> One reason for the rather unproductive state of affairs seems to be the preoccupation of modern consumption theory with the decision making calculus and the logical explication of formal axioms...In order to go beyond such 'explanations' some more substantial conjectures must be introduced which can help to answer the really important questions: How do consumers arrive at the preferences they have (are they innate or learnt, i.e. culturally

acquired)? Do the preferences change and, if so, how? What are the objects of the consumers' preferences, i.e. *what is it that people demand and consume, and why?* What role is played by consumption knowledge and all the factors that influence it? Once consumer theory is able to answer questions like these it should much better come to grips with the significant changes taking place on the demand side of growing economies.

Pasinetti (1993: 113, original emphasis) commented about the structural dynamics of production and its lack of connection in theory with the evolving dynamics of demand:

> [T]he explanation of the sources of the structural dynamics of production must be sought in the *evolving structure of demand*. The lack of and insufficiencies in the development of a satisfactory theory of consumption demand, both at the level of the single individual and at the level of society as a whole, within a context of technical change and increasing incomes, must be considered as the major factor responsible for the underdevelopment of this whole area of economic theoretical research.

In previous chapters we argued for the necessity of finding a uniform psychological motive and a single goal that provides cohesive guidance to the action of individual agents and, by extension, to the system as Whole. We also argued for the necessity of a common methodological treatment of production and consumption. And we answered specifically the question posed by Witt, claiming that what matters most in everyone's economic aspirations, weighing calculations and interests is the value of embodied capital, whether it be of a productive kind or not, since it is in this that human ingenuity finds material substance and it is this which is, in final analysis, the only scarce resource, practically amounting to life. Even this separation into productive and unproductive capital may be eased to a certain extent, as consumers try to exploit consumer commodities for further production, in their quest for time-space.

There is no use for a theory that speaks about what speaks for itself. What we need theory for is to explain what is not obvious. That consumers want to consume, that they draw something – often pleasure – out of it is perfectly clear. If they didn't, they would not be consuming beyond bare survival. Obvious also should be that they would *like* to maximize that 'something' *if* they could; if that were possible. But most substance lies underneath these (the rest is commentary, as Mokyr would say), so the first thing that a theory should be called upon to explain is 'what is it that people demand and consume, and why?' (Witt, op. cit.). Then, it could proceed with questions such as how people go about attaining this goal, how successful they can be, why in spite of rising per capita incomes and consumption levels consumers do not seem to become happier, and a host of other related questions, in particular social ones.

In other words, if economics is in final analysis about consumption, as is generally agreed, economic theory should be based on a robust theory of consumer behaviour. In every case, it may not ignore or contradict what is manifestly going on in this sphere. The commodity-based utility concept and the exogeneity-of-tastes assumption eliminate all possibility of such foundation. It is an agnostic evasion and a submission of theory to ideology, under all known interpretations of utility. It relinquishes the right and fails the obligation of theory to search for and provide basic explanation by wiping out the substance of conduct, a good part of which is to be discovered in interdependencies that keep haunting us ever since we came out of isolated caves to live in society. It allows fictitious market demand relations to be contrived as adequately stable characteristics at the macrolevel, fancying a macrotheory that contradicts microreality.

Our method is at variance with these. In this chapter, using the familiar Schumpeterian frame of reference, we discuss how consumers go about attaining their capital-claiming-back goal. The analytical part of the description is based on simplifying conventions employed in the theories of production and income distribution. Qualitative features are pruned off and emergence and transitions are out of the question, as always. But enough substance is retained of our theory of consumer behaviour, which has formal qualities (internal consistency, elegance by symmetry, parsimony) and completes the picture drawn of the production and income distribution sides by Marxic, Sraffian and Schumpeterian theories. It is shown how the uniform-motive, time-space hypothesis integrates the three activities in a coherent way that does away with childish fiction such as of inter-secting demand and supply lines, etc., on which must rely a theory that falsely envisages producers as going after profits and consumers as going after utility. All other apparent or conceivable partial pursuits must oblige to this uniform and stable one.

General observations

After a *basics* component in consumption is agreed upon that is ineluctably imposed by nature as survival-*cum*-reproduction requirement (the *humanization* problem, as we are going to visit it in Chapter 6), theory must explain how the mix and texture of the remaining part is decided in ways that are obviously discretionary and antagonistically intersubjective, and yet not disturbing the cohesion and advance of the system as Whole (the *self-control* problem). Modern reality leaves no room for disputing that, far more forcefully than ever, consumers engage in an aggressive expropriating contest that is very kin to that between producers, sometimes even undertaking a good part of what used to be under an orthodox perspective in the producers' jurisdiction. For example, they enter mazes of banking, communications or other services, engaging in literally *creating* commodities according to their personal aptness, discretion and budget, valuing commodities through money-spending choices and inventing uses of (mixes of) them. They speculate on loan interest rates, on movements in the stock markets, on anything that is uncertain. (Horses, football games, the weather, ... anything.) Speculation is their most favourite game. Their entire life is nothing but a game of wits against the odds of nature and against each other; a game of improved guessing about the future, a game of staying alive. More to our point, consumers never buy what someone else sells them. They always buy what they themselves make out of it. Not just in songs, music or books, as we have already contended. The photography and film-making industry is becoming to an increasing extent a consumers' affair. Suffice it to compare the film-developing and printing tasks of the recent past with the corresponding ones with today's digital cameras, or to see how the Ipod or other such gadgets passes on to consumers part of the decision making traditionally belonging to record companies. Or even the often pervert use made of cell phone cameras and blue-tooth technology, where even little kids can set up (as recent news inform us) their small porno markets and businesses.

In every case, it is hard to see how one can be an aggressive, active and creative producer of goods and a fierce contender when claiming income, while being at the same time and in the same human capacity an unimaginative, passively reactive utility maximizer in social isolation, not taking initiatives and not exercising discretion or prerogative in expending thus earned income, or in deciding the use that he or she will make of purchased commodities. One should expect that a theory which sees humans in such schizophrenic light would expect neuroscientists to decode the biological determinants of behaviour, and this is actually what some of the advocates of mainstream theory hope for. But the obvious truth is that only after completely retiring from production *may* one behave passively also as consumer, simply making it through each single day, without looking into any future, speculatively. Even this is quite rare, and there is no doubt that capitalism does not thrive with resigned elderly people spending their retirement benefits. Incidentally, juxtaposing the behaviour of this group of people with that at the other end of the spectrum, that is, with young, hyperactive consuming maniacs, illuminates brightly the asymmetry of time: of prospects, expectations, or of lack thereof.

So, the only reasonable way about theorizing is to treat the consumer as a creative agent, precisely as he or she is creative in production, and to search for some uniform and stable object of such creativity. Profit is not of consumers and pleasure is not of producers, so there must be something else that is common to both these activities, and this is capital in a very broad and general sense: capital as employed in production (which is the usual undertone of the word) and capital as embodied in consumption commodities. In a word, whatever embodies human time-space, either historical or present. The accounting convention of entering depreciation on the debit side and the nuance of 'waste' attached to the capital that is worn out in the production of consumer commodities obscures that such capital resides in consumables and is worthwhile for consumers to pursue. Yet, this is what actually happens. Everyone is obsessed with capital. Not profits ($\Pi = \pi K$) for producers and utility for consumers (no formula here as yet, but we will provide one), but human time-space that resides in commodities.

We have cited three categories of standards set forth by Kincaid for judging theories, and we would like our consumer theory to meet all. The evidential and explanatory qualities of the theory proposed here are based on the same reasoning that informs the standard analysis of production and income distribution, and they must be as good (or as bad) as the Schumpeterian picture drawn in standard analyses of producers' affairs. In view of the long history of analyses on the production side, and in view of the passion-based nature of human behaviour in general and of consumption behaviour in particular, it would be unfair to ask of a theory of consumer behaviour to do better than that. Quite on the contrary, it should be required of theoretical improvements to proceed symmetrically and simultaneously over the two activity spheres, because they are really tandem. As far as formal aspects are concerned, our theory provides considerable elegance by easing the embarrassing asymmetry that is plain to the first three parts of Figure 4.1 and taints conventional theory: Whereas net income VA is divided into W and Π, which are essentially seen as reproduction and surplus, respectively, no similar distinction is made on the consumption side between 'basics' and 'luxuries', or between literal *consumption*, mandated by nature, and discretionary *spending*. Vector y is seen in one piece, its entire composition being determined according to tastes which are set exogenously.

Nothing in everyday life indicates that the psychological factor of rivalry that is proudly acknowledged as a driver for producers' action abandons anyone when the factory whistle blows and all tear past the gates, dashing to the market to purchase what they produced. The Hesseian wolf remains wolf. He neither becomes sheep, nor even bothers to put on a sheepskin. In the final commodities market also, he shows his teeth. Garbling about pleasure is ideology. Rivalry is a prime motive for choice making and general action by consumers. Markets provide the primary domain and the conditions for the administration of rivalry, helping advance the structural dynamics requested by Pasinetti. Markets do not *co-ordinate* the two processes, promoting competitive equilibrium. They facilitate antagonistic disequilibration through innovations aimed at monopolistic and monopsonistic advantage, however temporary this may be. And they accomplish this by bringing together those who possess some early knowledge or foresight, with those who still have ignorance of it. (We have termed this situation exclusive non-ignorance.) The only way that the accusation of heinousness may be toned down is through appeal to the fact that application of innovativeness is inescapable to humans as they go about experiencing life through non-stop generation of knowledge, and every other application of it known historically has been even more bestial. But rivalry is definitely there.

This individualistic appropriative impulse translates at the system level into annexation of resources from the greater environment. Notwithstanding the fact that economics is not narrowly about physical matter/energy appropriation but about value, this does serve nature's predilection for diminishing potentials and smoothing asymmetries through operation of some kind of second thermodynamic law. Expropriative, highly dissipative man-made systems do speed up the process. Such dissipativeness cannot be promoted by, or ascribed exclusively to any one-sided, production-bound considerations. It must have at its basis an unquenchable desire by large populations to absorb the produce of an ever faster metabolism of resources, and this is by now well documented, both experimentally and through the work of economic historians. It is also incontestably established and obvious that the structure of demand evolves along with the structure of technology.

Therefore, consumption, production and income-distribution decisions must be explained as integrated, so that all taken together and each one of them separately may make sense. It is through such joint process that the structure of demand is determined, rather than important aspects of it being ascribed to outside factors that induce the need for *a priori* assumptions. A production growth imperative without a similar consumption component is meaningless. So, a dynamic perspective must unify all sub-processes, explaining technical and demand structures and relations thereof on common theoretical grounds and minimizing reliance on assumptions made for convenience or ideology.

A basic precondition for this is that, in all their capacities, agents compete for a single scarce resource infused to commodities, because it is only in such way that these may become positional, providing agents with power within their niche. Such power depends not on gains or possessions as such, but on gains relative to those of others; and not just on the volume of expenditures, but also on their structure, subject to continuous updating. Through cognition, an individual's demand may be structured more effectively, so that a smaller total expenditure can be made to yield greater gains of power. Much as producers try to increase their share of value (which is) added by human labour by expanding their capital base, consumers also try to increase command over this same scarce resource through the commodities they purchase, manipulating, reshuffling and upgrading wants and needs in seeking ways to satisfy this desire with commodities carrying greater capital content. Thus, for example, they switch from 'basic' olive-oil soap to luxurious cosmetic soaps, from tap water to drinking bottled water with style, etc. *Style* is keyword here, marking the object of such behaviour, which is to be *de rigeur*: to be in, establishing publicly one's standing (or social displacement) and relative power. It is not only about consuming or about purchasing, but about purchasing and consuming conspicuously, and not just in an innocently ludicrous fashion, as Veblen's pen let be imagined, but in a ruthless, time-space claiming sense.

Further, much as a producer's comparative advantage evaporates by being inexorably diffused (the stock of everyone's knowledge can only be increased), so also a consumer's positional status needs to be constantly reaffirmed and reasserted. And as power is analogous not just to the commodities purchased, but to the means of production that are embodied in them, and as these means are continuously upgraded through technological innovations, such commodities must be constantly updated, in public view, even at the expense of good taste, prudence, thrift and other such considerations. That is, because of the incessant updating of the capital content of commodities as technology advances, a commodity which had great capital content and social impact in the past may be outdated and have nil, or even negative such in the present. As a matter of fact, due to the symbolic and intersubjective nature of appraisals, things can even go in the opposite direction, as with antiquities, antiques, folkloric items, etc. These induce constant restructuring of each agent's and of the market's demand through a process of innovative participation in socialized consumption that imposes a growth imperative also from (and on) the consumption side, complementing that on production.

As it stands, the scheme in the last chapter leans heavily on one side. Such bias is crippling. It makes it appear as if the bout for gain is conducted only in the production sphere, where the struggle over income distribution takes place. But when it comes to expending such income, a truce is silently called, whence each agent goes to the market neutrally disposed towards others, to buy whatever it is that commodities supposedly provide. No contest can take place and no rivalry can there be in consumption if tastes are set from outside and if there is nothing *in* commodities that is worth fighting for. Such a description should raise theoretical revolt, were it not for long ideological brainwashing.

We contend, therefore, that we must incorporate in the analysis of consumption the concerted continuation of whatever antagonistic process is acknowledged as taking place among producers. In the analytical frame we adopted, we let (R, L) stand for the physical technique employed in a n-sector economy, with steady-state specification described by (4.1). As said above, the analytical and conceptual asymmetry of traditional theory is in that VA is split into two different components, namely, profits and wages, each supposedly serving a distinguished end. Profits are set proportional to the capital K employed during current production, and are traditionally seen as possible to either consume or invest on capital expansion, research and development or otherwise, unlike wages which are typically seen as relating to necessities and possible to expend only on consumption, so that labour power can be reproduced, but no control over capital can be gained. Such wages are seen as relating to prescribed labour inputs, which may be either physical or mental, but not involving any generative (innovative) properties or talent.

Thus, $VA = \Pi + W = Q\,R^T p\,\pi + Q\,L^T \vec{w}$, and a capitalist economy advances in the direction of increasing λ, producing more value per unit of the human input that is compensated by such income. Through Schumpeterian innovations as discussed in the previous chapter, producers try to increase their share of Π by commanding more capital and increasing flow x by increasing the circular flow K. But why should nothing analogous be foreseen about y? Why is no innovation process accounted for on the part of consumers for satisfying wants by more capital-intense commodities, which could explain capitalism's predilection for capital intensity and accumulation in a truly organic way, in the sense that there is an integrated and complete social participation, through all spheres of activity? If such a process were accounted for, the conventional divide between production, consumption and income distribution would be abolished, tastes would be possible to explain endogenously, in a way coupled with the system, but then consumer psychological dispositions would be impossible to evade or ignore.

The orthodox asymmetry entails behavioural schizophrenia. Schumpeter argued that a producer's self-evaluation is relative. Entrepreneurs strive to gain room in a crowded niche by means of innovations that help them gain non-competitive price and profit differentials, shaping their techniques. However, in their capacity as consumers, no positional, antagonistic motive is foreseen that helps shape their preferences, and the same holds for everyone else, in their two complementary capacities as producers (workers) and consumers. The usual 'more is better than less' principle of utility draws an image of supposedly sovereign but isolated consumers whose tastes are '*states* of mind', not antagonistic *processes* attending to any socially ignited goal. Such sovereignty is empty. Each is oblivious to the states, tastes and market conduct of others. While as producer each one cares about what competitors do and what preferences consumers reveal in the market, nothing similar is seen in the way consumers allocate their incomes to *n* available commodities and, by extension, the way market demand is shaped. Therefore, consumption is not seen as co-evolving with the endogenous flux of technological advances.

Since *consumption* of any particular good or service cannot but be satiable, there must be something else to *demand* that makes it non-satiable under conditions of lasting growth of per capita income, and the emphases are meant to underscore a particular kind of distinction between consumption and demand. What consumers demand with their expenditures is not to consume the commodities purchased, but to serve some pressing desire that goes beyond literal consumption, something that attaches to *owning* commodities. Much like producers, so are consumers driven by some unappeasable psychological urge that sustains an endless 'catch up, forge ahead, or fall behind' kind of conduct, which is not eased by consuming. So, the same urge must explain two *apparently* different insatiabilities, those for profits and for consumption. As no producer is content with his profits, however large, so is no consumer content with his or her gains from consumption.

Whether assuming a limitative or a limitationless environment (the latter being an assumption that existentially overwhelmed humans may injudiciously make), it is important to agree first upon what is scarce and what is not. Economics, both in theory and in practice, can be conducted only upon such agreement, because scarcity, whether factual or perceived, determines what is economic and what is not, that is, what is *commonly* worth striving and fighting for, inducing antagonism in human relations. Schumacher (1967) said, 'Call a thing immoral or ugly, soul-destroying or a degradation of man, a peril to the peace of the world or to the well being of future generations; so long as you have not shown it to be "uneconomic" you have not really questioned its right to exist, grow and prosper.' Sir Geoffrey Vickers (1970) added, 'Never did a concept so limited and so factual attain a meaning so general, so normative and so saturated with unjustified connotations of value.' And soon as an honest search for a minimal base of functional scarcity is conducted, only the human resource in its creative, not its physical dimensions, emerges as scarce, determining the type of efficiency that is applicable by determining what the 'valuable inputs' are. Value added to the production of commodities is what is economized on, relative to total value put through, or put out, and this is accomplished by expanding the use of capital, which stores historical surpluses of this scarce resource. By producing and consuming appropriately so as to increase this roundabout value, agents pursue greater command over this resource. And the greater this value the greater are supposed to be the chances that all may grab an 'adequate' portion of it, as the usual argument in favour of growth goes. But, in this zero-sum race positions are relative, time-space is not really conquered, angst is inescapable and the finish line remains infinitely far and unreachable.

Capital goods may be seen as tools for satisfaction of production *wants*, whose reward seems to be profits above any fair reward of the capitalist for his personal labour, and which replace 'unreliable labour', etc. But it is false to assume that profits are the real goal for a capital owner, given among other things that they are largely invested back into more capital. If this were not so, we should all be sitting idle now after centuries of labour-displacing innovations that allowed increased profits momentarily and *ceteris paribus*, having depressed wages, having suppressed workers' dreams and having sent down the drain consumer sentiment, elation, creativity and a favourable disposition towards capitalism. For workers and capitalists alike the final reward is definitely something beyond profits, wages or utility, and that something must be in the realm of *wants*. And since wants are creations of the mind, not of the stomach or the palate, the reward must also be such. And there is only capital to fill that role, because capital is a brain-child. So, it is control over capital inputs for which they all fight, of this or the other kind, whatever kind each one may have access to. Through investment of profits, capitalists gain control over productive forms of capital, looking into the future. Through consumption, consumers claim unproductive forms of it, trying to claim back the unique scarce resource they put in, as this is accumulated (stored, embodied) in the products of their own workmanship.

This is the only way in which production can team up dynamically with consumption. Economics has become the bulkiest and most focal part of a feverish social life. So, economic theory is obliged to explain how all its components are organically integrated into the latter. In particular, it must explain how socially produced value is funnelled into consumption *in a social way*: Not in isolation, not in submission to transcendentally set tastes, but organically tied up to all social activity. In every case, socialized production is meaningless without socialized consumption. If the system is to behave as Whole, these two processes, as all other processes, must be co-ordinated dynamically, not just by crossing of static and meaningless market demand and supply relations. They must substantiate and invigorate each other.

Human behaviour and social development are complex, mixed outcomes, which are impossible to exhaust in any one theory or model. But when it comes to the allocation of a resource that is *made to be* or *perceived to be* scarce, only antagonistic facets of behaviour are relevant, however well antagonism may be concealed. And institutional set-ups are aimed at covering up, channelling and civilizing conflict. So, economics should be a discourse about civilized rivalry. The more scarce a resource is or is thought to be, the more antagonistic becomes its allocation among members of the same economy and among competing economies. Scarcity is not so much a property of the resource itself, or of actual human needs, as it is of our self-projection on a particular social proximity or environment. That is, scarcity is man-made, relativist, and contextualized within a generalized time-space. Thus, a resource seen as precious or scarce in one culture may be worthless in another, excluding survival requirements which are, by and large, common to all, although even these can be met in quite different ways. This is why affluent societies may very well be more *deprived* than less prosperous ones.

Economic relations and behaviour go with culture. The more greedy a society is, the greater its sense of deprivation of a greater number of resources. But although these appear to be many, they all come down to the perceptive capacity of the mind to generate the *idea* of scarcity upon the basis of the single, gravely felt scarcity of life. This uniqueness has evaded even those investigators who have been seriously concerned with the apparent insatiability of wants in modern societies. Witt (op. cit.), for example, underscores the 'huge associative capacity of the human brain' and adds: 'A particular and important category of acquired wants, which have a similar significance for many people, are those for universally usable reinforcers like money, power, public attention, etc.' True, there is a phenomenal panspermy of directly or proximally observable wants, which may trap one into thinking in terms of such multifariousness. This is why so little has been done in the way of reducing these down to a minimal base, even when considering universalities, as done by Witt.

The importance for such reduction is made all the more pronounced by considering the fact that whereas a single theory of capitalism (if not of economic systems in general) is what we are after, wants, scarcity, precious resources, and even 'universally usable reinforcers' vary with time, culture or geographical area, in various ways. Observable characteristics and outward manifestations of the acquisitive disposition that accompanies the sense of scarcity are context dependent and socially malleable. But one hardly comes across any culture in which wants do not reflect, in one or another way, the Will to Power, which ultimately reduces down to a mere *will to competitively survive*. Societies are formed by necessity, as cooperative structures that can face more effectively external threats to the life of the individual, to the existence of the species, and to the satisfaction of their needs. At the same time as these targets are gradually conquered through amplification of productive powers, wants are generated and multiplied that introduce conflict between individual and common interests. For group survival, this conflict must be sustained so as to maintain tonality, but at the same time, for society to not break apart, conflict must be controlled through competitive allocation of the benefits that obtain from the union. By co-action of these two principles, efficiency is further enhanced. Efficiency enhancement works to the effect of sustaining the hope that, with time, all can draw benefits, prompting participants to keep their interests vested in the union.

In other words, capitalistically rational conduct is individualistic, within a social context. Individualism (actually, the individual itself) is a social reflection and stance that cannot be captured by exclusively introvert or exclusively extrovert hypotheses, or by outward motivational assumptions about commodity-based utility and exogenous tastes. Avarice and antagonism generating conflict for the purpose of dominance prevail in life. Freud's penetrating analysis traced 'Gewalt' back into man's intestine impulses. Three and a half centuries ago, Hobbes had underscored the insatiable nature of the dominance underbase in economic behaviour:

> [T]he Felicity of this life, consisteth not in the repose of a mind satisfied. For there is no such *Finis ultimus*, (utmost ayme,) nor *Summum Bonum*, (greatest

> Good,) as is spoken of in the Books of the old Morall Philosophers. Nor can any man any more live, whose Desires are at an end, than he, whose Senses and Imaginations are at a stand. Felicity is a continual progresse of the desire, from one object to another; the attaining of the former, being still but the way to the latter.

(Hobbes, 1991: 70)

Felicity, which Hobbes signified more descriptively with the Greek word μακαρισμός, is the dynamic pursuit of an unspecified state of mind that is never pleased with what has been begotten. It animates

> a perpetuall and restlesse desire of Power after power, that ceaseth onely in Death. And the cause of this, is not alwayes that a man hopes for a more intensive delight, than he has already attained to; or that he cannot be content with a moderate power: but because he cannot assure the power and the means to live well, which he hath present, without the acquisition of more. And from hence it is, that Kings, whose power is greatest, turn their endeavours to the assuring it at home by Lawes, or abroad by Wars: and when that is done, there succeedeth a new desire;

(Ibid.)

Human behaviour occasionally dissents from sheer economism, but it can safely be assumed that, at least in capitalism, this is of limited impact and not as frequent as it appears. In Adam Smith's science, the driving sentiment of economic action was avarice. Avarice was seen as innate, cooperation as acquired, and used as needed to the same end of selfish appropriation. Apparent generosity, compassion, other-regard, etc., are often self-interest in disguise. To see this, one needs to focus on hidden motives and goals, rather than on means, and on aspects of social life that escape notice under the usual prism. If this is done, then a notion of utility will be seen to pertain that is relative not so much to different states of a given person in isolation from his or her social context, but in relation to the states of those he or she associates with.

This indicates that received views and habits of mind must be confronted with suspicion. There is nothing to spuriousness other than our own failure at classification. In the social realm, apparent spuriousness often provides the best clues for underlying regularities, much like outlying observations provide the statistician with information that 'well-behaving' observations fail to provide. In the social realm there are *facts*. But when these are treated as *data*, an unknown proportion of their substance is lost. Social theory cannot afford to dismiss with a layman's ease of conscience pieces of information that appear to be discrepant at first sight, or according to received views which are all too often received uncritically. It must consider it as an obligation to explain what appears to be irregular.

There are indisputable facts. For example, most of us drive cars and use air-conditioning appliances. It has become banal or old fashioned to walk, ride a bicycle or use cooling fans (having become too placid and dull even to perspire).

Yet, although we may feel sorry for the next door neighbour who died from cardiovascular or respiratory problems, or for those who get killed in car 'accidents', we will not feel any remorse for throwing our heat and bacteria out on neighbours, and we will not quit driving, often recklessly, even though it is brighter than daylight that many of us are absolutely incompetent as drivers. So, where is the point in these seemingly irrelevant observations? The point is that they may help the theorist *restore a connection* between what passes in cursory fashion as utility, self-interest, pleasure, regard for others, or even as self-disregard, and an all-out contest for life-expanding *through* life-taking, or at least *in spite of* life-taking, in legal and illegal ways. Then, to our utter but pretentious dismay, the distinction between 'normal' everyday conduct and damage to life becomes blurred. This is another way of saying what Keynes said about dangerous human proclivities being canalized into economic action.

Utility-based explanations of selfishness abound, but a single convincing explanation has been elusive. Utility is a mystic notion whose loose use and liberal abuse have conditioned the way economists look at things. There is something *in* the things bought that makes us want to buy them, but it is not the thing – any thing – itself. Yet, we are misled by the fact that it is easier to *see* the object of a transaction (the observable part) than *discern* what is in it that we go after, which is non-observable. For example, the *need* for communication when a conventional phone is not available is clear, but a good part of expenditures on mobile communication satisfies more than a need. It satisfies a desire 'to be in', to exploit modern technology. And this desire needs to be explained.

Such demand is acquired, and particular to a certain sociological context. Producers do respond to consumers' needs. Thus, if demand adjusts, say, to the techno-structure of a more advanced economy through imitation, the local techno-structure will tend to advance in the same direction, improving its capacity to tender to the new types of demand. But neither producers nor consumers are reactive. They are proactive producers of wants passed on to society, each member of which then thinks falsely that they are of his or her own inception. As noted by Georgescu-Roegen (1966: 66), 'we would be utterly mistaken to believe that technological innovations modify supply alone. The impact of a technological innovation upon the economic process consists of both an industrial rearrangement and a consumers' reorientation, often also of a structural change in society.' And this action is amphidromous. Scitovsky (1976: 5) explained: 'The market transmits information among competitors and between buyer and seller, thereby harmonizing their action. . . . the market . . . puts pressure to conform on buyers and sellers alike . . . Harmony, therefore, between consumer preferences and the pattern of production may simply indicate the adaptation of man's tastes to the rigid requirements of the production system.'

Being visited from a production-side perspective, these speak of the bulk of cases, but there is enough evidence to inform theory better. The trouble with an inductive approach is that it is often unclear what part of the data informs theory wisely and what is just spurious, temporary, local, and thus potentially misleading, especially when this comes from as broad a context as is that of consumption activity. And yet, however reserved one may be due to this, one cannot discard a general condition that is patent, simply because explanations of particular instances of it look strange. For example, there have been such harmful habits made legitimate and promoted for no sensible reason, that one may not fail to discern a blatant underlying economism. Tobacco, alcohol and guns are typical and addictive drugs wait in line. Little can stand in the way of uninhibited growth. Nothing is safe from the developers' violence, and certainly not nature, culture or ethics. This provides an auspicious angle from which to explain everyday reality, as concerns disrespect for what is common and for human life.

Of course, there are always excuses, and one may, if one wants, swallow any explanation, but there is little room for flagrant evasions. Take the following instance, for example. Table 5.1 shows traffic-police data in the wider Attica prefecture around Athens. These concern (a) motorcyclists fined for riding without wearing a safety helmet and (b) drivers of all categories of vehicles fined for using a mobile phone while driving. The reader is informed that motorcycle helmets, besides being very expensive anyway, during the period concerned they were taxed by the state as ... luxury items, with a 36 per cent value-added tax tagged on to them. The question is: Does the State care about skulls, or about growth? As far as trends are concerned, the reader is informed that motorcyclists not wearing a helmet have become (or have been made) scarce, while finding someone who drives without visibly handling a mobile phone is like searching for a needle in a haystack. As for fines, these are scheduled to change: €100 for mobile phones, €350 for helmets!

'Civilizing' harmful habits often comes in strange, but always more capital-intensive, λ-increasing ways. The trend is also to switch from 'natural' habits or ways to industrial ones, as by rediscovering and reviving salubrious but largely abandoned diets. (Compare the Mediterranean, Chinese and other formerly natural and healthy diets that are currently marketed in industrialized form around the globe.) In the thus increased money velocity and the time-space appropriation that that reflects, one must search for the mystic content of 'utility', both at an individual and at a general level. It is clear from Table 5.1 that the Greek society, through its institutions, finds such *utility* in ticketing drivers in the way of the Table (Table 5.1). Now how many lives are saved or lost is secondary, both for

Table 5.1 Saving skulls, or promoting growth? Traffic-police ticketing data in Attica, Greece

Period	Driving a motorcycle without wearing safety helmet (Fine: €83)	Driving while using mobile phone (all vehicle types) (Fine: €33)
1 Jul. 2003–31 Dec. 2003	39,975	5,343
All of 2004	60,281	8,599
All of 2005	56,630	13,662
1 Jan. 2006–30 Jun. 2006	31,370	11,395
Total	188,256	38,999

Source: Attica Prefecture Traffic Police. Personal communication, 10 August 2006.

society and for our theory, and we have hopefully made clear for the reader (through war, reckless driving, the smoking example, obesity and otherwise) that human time-space usurped is meant in such perceived and socially appraised sense, not necessarily and exclusively in a literal sense.

And, again, there is also multifariousness, which must not confuse us into mistaking event-irregularities for irreconcilable, non-uniform individuality or for negation of uniformity in motives and goals. For example, with all the sound and picture quality that may go into a CD or DVD, a ticket for a concert or for the opera buys high quality, direct and indirect human input, and it does so in public view, effecting comparisons that effect social power-sharing. So, 'the upper class' goes to concerts, and so does 'the bus class', somewhat sheepishly, often with little understanding of music, and not for the relatively innocuous reasons that fit a Veblenian narrative. They vie publicly for that highly valued human time-space put in by topmost conductors, musicians, opera house and music theatre makers, etc. A DVD, on the other hand, buys less of the same, at a lower price. But they must share this time-space control quality (or something meaningful else, if one finds our life-taking explanation as too gross) in order to be fully comparable and in order to allow genuine choice, *as alternative ways to the same effect*. What is absurd is to argue that they buy two different kinds of music-related utility, asso-ciated with two different kinds of purchased commodities, fit for two different kinds of social classes, etc. Utilities that are not comparable across agents and conceivably not even comparable for the same agent are just not convincing.

An excursion into two games

We have argued that economic theorizing should be truthful all the way down to the psychological underbase of human conduct and we have expressed little appreciation for rushing into modelling and for mistaking it for theory. Because time, knowledge and context are of paramount importance in economic practice, they must occupy a front seat in theory. In particular, the way individual agents actively structure their consumption expenditures must underlie all economic explanation. And as such complete context is missing from experimental situations, one must be sceptical about drawing quick and easy conclusions from them. Contrived games and social experiments provide such simplified, isolated contexts, somewhere between modelling and reality, but they often fail considerably to meet the above requirement in a satisfactory way. So, we do not mean to base any part of our argument on those. Yet, since they are generally employed as methodological instruments, we briefly discuss two such games, in order to get a rudimentary idea about how our theory fares in such contexts. Recall also that we have recognized the truthfulness of neoclassical theory up to information, in which context it admits extreme, albeit vacuous (for being other-ignoring) selfish-ness in agents.

A main object of experimental economics is to provide evidence about the way people make decisions in real contexts, by observing their behaviour in contrived situations. In such games, *Homo economicus* is often led under strict neoclassical assumptions to outcomes which are from a neoclassical viewpoint extremely suboptimal. Although neoclassical models capable of accommodating *separately* all imaginable types of situations (and thus supposedly answering all criticisms) abound, such reductionism cannot qualify as comprehensive, convincing theory. Gross discrepancies between theory, reality and game outcomes raise an issue of relevance, that is, of the degree to which assumptions miss crucial determinants of social interaction, or the degree to which *Homo economicus* can represent modern economic agents. One thing that emerges from such experiments is that utility is something more intense than what comes through either the standard interpretation of it within social vacuum, or through a mere 'keeping up with the Jones's' principle void of conflict, which has been reluctantly accommodated into the neoclassical method. But bridging such games with reality and translating their outcomes is tricky. Differences between artificial game environments and real contexts are substantial but largely imperceptible, and their influences are uncertain. There is framing. Instructions to players, communication between them or other factors may affect their behaviour. Most importantly, real-time knowledge generation (value creation) is absent. So, only nuggets of truth and basic insight may be gained through games, after careful inspection.

The centipede

In this game, there is a finite sum of money (say, ten euros) and rational players A and B take turns pinching either one or two each time. If one is pinched, the turn passes; if two, the game stops and any remaining euros are lost to the players. Under the usual rationality assumptions, backward induction dictates that, should the game ever reach state (4, 4), player A would be compelled to close with (6, 4), a prospect known to player B by full information. So, B must wrap up the game at (4, 5), and so on backwards, rendering (2, 0) the only rational outcome. The extensive form of the game's diagram is shown in Figure 5.1, where downstrokes mark a choice of two euros and an end to the game. The numbers in the first row of parentheses give total gains for A and B, respectively.

Real people are clearly less contained in the outcomes they can reach, and a number of authors (Pettit and Sugden, 1989; Hollis, 1991; Hollis and Sugden, 1993) have argued that no restatement of assumptions allows realistic outcomes,

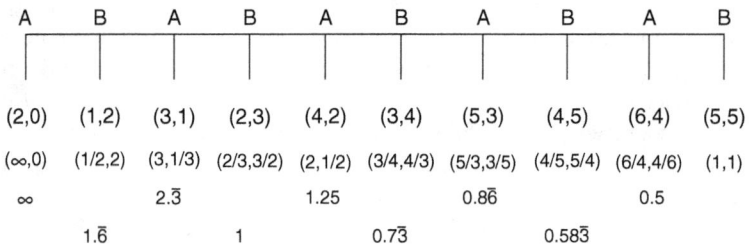

A	B	A	B	A	B	A	B	A	B
(2,0)	(1,2)	(3,1)	(2,3)	(4,2)	(3,4)	(5,3)	(4,5)	(6,4)	(5,5)
(∞,0)	(1/2,2)	(3,1/3)	(2/3,3/2)	(2,1/2)	(3/4,4/3)	(5/3,3/5)	(4/5,5/4)	(6/4,4/6)	(1,1)
∞		$2.\overline{3}$		1.25		$0.8\overline{6}$		0.5	
	$1.\overline{6}$		1		$0.7\overline{3}$		$0.58\overline{3}$		

Figure 5.1 The centipede game.

unless psychological factors are accounted for that leave room for cooperation and conflict. This, however, would violate basic neoclassical assumptions, which bar *Homo economicus* from indulging in passions, politics, altruism, cooperation or interpersonal comparisons. Thus, at each stage of backward induction, player A compares only his own absolute gains, in the simple knowledge that the other player will do the same, which is why the induction can be initiated. Conflict, defined generally as *intentional destruction or waste of resources for the purpose of obtaining relative advantage*, is barred. But if players are assumed to be taking the social context into account, a rich domain of choices opens up.

Unlike real humans, being by construction a perfect economizer *Homo economicus* finds at once the optimal spot within any given condition-set and body of knowledge. He does not generate associations or equilibrium-upsetting variety, because he does not produce new knowledge. So, he is outside both real time and real society. He does not engage in interpersonal comparisons or conflict, he feels no envy, shame, scruples, mistrust or other passions and sentiments. Therefore, if one wants to move away from such an irrelevant creature towards more realistic situations, one must know how sentiments enter people's calculations. Further, even in well-designed games or experiments, the time horizon players or participants face is very short and the social context extremely narrow. Therefore, their socially induced discount rates are forged. The sum to be split between them is usually given and no value is produced, in social interaction. Even in games where there are spending strategies and allocation of gains to various options, there is no real newness. Therefore, drawing conclusions is risky, and if there is anything to be drawn either from *normal* outcomes or from extreme, mutually defeating ones such as the (2, 0) in the centipede, these must be probed in cautious light.

Under such light, we can draw the following from the centipede in relation to our theory: Outcome (2, 0) is an extreme expression of dominance, and hence an extreme expression of capitalistic rationalization. In a once-and-for-all, none-watches-anyone type of situation, it maximizes the relative gain for the player who plays first, the two players seeing themselves as a group in perfect social isolation. This maximal dominance is measured by the ratio of gains, which is infinite under the said outcome and far greater than any other. So, to the extent that a player feels socially, mentally and psychologically confined to the narrow context of the game, to the extent that there is no hope of cooperatively increasing the value which is to be distributed (no production of value) and to the extent that consumption of gains within a greater social context is framed out (the dominance co-ordinate has no scope outside the game), each player is prompted to act in a domineering way that appears irrational when placed in any other frame, inside which it definitely incurs utility losses. But to the extent that players take into account any of these other factors or circumstances, they may allow for some passes, the number of which depends on how they perceive their opponent and themselves within the wider context. In all cases, though, it is basically dominance that players aim at, and to this they recruit their generative capacities. Other explanations are twisted and not firmly grounded, their possible verisimilitude being due to the fact that the relevant social context is always fuzzy. As soon as the game's relevant social context becomes so confined as to be clear to players with perfect clarity (perfect isolation), the zero-sum ferociousness of a (2, 0) outcome should be quite telling about the players' disposition towards each other. Their urge for control and dominance over others projects right through.

Beyond basic needs, gains are positional not just in the way of simple comparison, but also in the sense that one knows that what one gains is at the expense of others. It is in such enviously relativistic sense that position is rewarding, which explains the hysteric way in which people go after commodities and their general equivalent, namely, money. Non-envious, non-conflictive and non-mistrustful natural insatiability is fiction, not to be found in the animal kingdom. A lion could not care less about how much food other lions (or hyenas) have, once he has fed his hunger, maybe hiding also a few provisions for the next lunch or so. He gets *fed up*. If he has other means of demonstrating and asserting his power, he will rely on no possessions for that. Possessive insatiability is lack of self-assurance and envy due to awareness that what others have is not ours, and that their possessing it is at our expense. Any degree of these to be encountered in other animals is considered pathology, particular to the animal or to some group or species, arising investigative curiosity. Among humans such enviousness is considered normal, because humans seem to be more fully aware of their finiteness and filled with angst. People judge their well-being not in absolute terms or on the basis of own temporal comparisons, but by comparing their possessions with those of others in their social proximity. And they do so not just because of a natural tendency to want to be better off, but mainly because the standing of others on this relative scale gives them a measure of the degree to which they have succeeded or failed in expropriating more time-space from others than others have expropriated from them, perceiving this as a measure of the extent of their own existence; as a measure of their social *displacement*.

These do not constitute a big leap of faith, since the usual notion of utility already relates to possessing rather, than to literally consuming, and to the boosting of one's ego from commanding the goods bought. What may be considered new is an explicit admission that ownership of goods that are produced socially is proof, in the eyes of others, of command over the social labour that went into their making and, by extension, indirect command over humans. Therefore, when thinking about utility, the full value of social resources embodied in commodities must be taken into account, an increasing with technological advance part of which is indirect inputs.

In evolutionary psychology, the capacity of humans to recognize motives behind the behaviour of others and the fact that this influences their preferences are well established. An understanding that consumer behaviour reflects insecurity and fear of falling behind in some kind of vital race has been plain to the writings of many authors, although not directly connected with existence. Thus, van den Bergh and Gowdy (2003) note: 'consumption beyond the level of (basic) needs is characterized by the striving for "positional goods," ultimately (unconsciously) aimed at enlarging fitness'. But this prompts one to ask about what is fitness. There is also neurophysiological evidence that assigning values to options (goods, actions, etc.) reflects expected fitness-enhancing characteristics within one's social domain. Securing these is a prime function of the emotional system, which is the biological substrate of choice (Gifford, 2002). Although a cursory look may give a wrong impression, inhibition also controls behaviour to the same end. It 'facilitates higher cognition by ... reducing responses to ... things in the current environment ... enabling the animal to secure future rewards of higher [fitness-enhancing] value' (ibid.). This is a knowledge process in a most complete sense, as attested to by the fact that educated people are more productive at reducing the remoteness of future pleasures through lower discount rates (Becker and Mulligan, 1997). Thus, discount rates are cultural parameters and reflect real wealth-enhancing capabilities and prospects, which in turn determine fitness and, conversely, culture, in two-way interaction. Investment-versus-consumption behaviour is a prime expression of this, and a prime determinant of one's aptness in the race for expropriation.

Social values and emotions bind together virtually every type of information that the brain can encode, so all information is intrinsically social and, as is known with respect to consciousness in the cognitive sciences, all processes of cognition take place within an evolving hierarchy of biological, social and personal subjective values. To decipher the passion-driven knowledge-accumulation processes is so challenging, that neuroscientists are currently trying to understand this value-guided process by studying brain activity. Thus, Platt and Glimcher (1999) correlated firing rates (neuronal activation) in the lateral intra-parietal area of a subject's brain (the area involved in decision making) with expected gains and with probabilities of gains. Understanding of neural processes is also pursued about the way these representations change when subjects play against an opponent, when they reach a Nash equilibrium, etc.

With similar reservations as ours, Ortmann and Gigerenzer (2000) warn that designed experiments must avoid isolating subjects from factors that are major determinants of behaviour. This means that content and context must be taken into account. But at the same time, one would hope that such experiments could help us identify these very determinants, so the problem is to a certain extent circular. In the centipede, the main determinants neglected are the content of utility and the context within which this acquires its relative character. In view of our reducing all scarcity down to that of human time-space, the crudest way to bring centipede utility closer to such relativist context is to assume it proportional to ratios of monetary gains of the players, which is crudest because it ignores any wider environment. Then, if (without loss of generality) the proportionality constant is set equal to one, utilities are as given in the second row of parentheses in Figure 5.1, so that calculation can be made in forward fashion, independent of knowledge, fixity or finiteness of the total endowment, avoiding awkward, backward induction reasoning. Under all circumstances, each player knows forwardly, with certainty, and independently of the other's subsequent moves that, at every stage of the game, a 'grab-two' move is optimal for himself in the reduced social context of the game, *and also that a 'take-one' move is worst*.

Unlike the *more is better than less* interpretation of utility, under which a pass would incur for either player at all stages a fixed loss of one unit if his opponent stops the game in his next move, relative to his having pinched two himself, the relative gain criterion incurs the losses appearing in the last two rows of Figure 5.1 for players A and B respectively, measured in utility differences. Losses are different for the two players and for the same player at different stages, diminishing with every take-one move the incentive to stop, thus encouraging more realistic and collectively less suboptimal outcomes. Along with relatively smaller losses for B, this could affect a player's interpretation of a pass by the other and would allow for more outside considerations to creep in that would increase the richness of possible outcomes, given also that 'indeterminacy breeds indeterminacy not only in B's mind but also, through feedback, in the mind of A doing the original calculation' (Hollis, 1991). These may be crucial in other cases, where only the tail of a game is relevant (players come in after the game has started), as is in fact the case with the economic process, which is ongoing and unfolding through time. It is easy to imagine weighted combinations of the two criteria that could account for a multitude of outcomes, without recourse to any other particular sentiments.

Uncertainty adds realism and flexibility. This can be in not knowing, or in knowing only probabilistically the grab in the next move, in not knowing the initial endowment, or whether it is finite or not, fixed or varying and with what, in probabilistically assigning turns, etc. Such are the settings in which real economies, firms and agents compete. For example, the artificiality of knowing both the stopping rule and the resource forfeited may be replaced by a measure of relative rates of resource use and replenishment, adding nature as a third, unpredictable and unaccountable party. Also, for agents within multi-sector economies, structure, besides volume is significant, so games or experiments that accommodate structure and not just scalar (typically monetary) rewards may provide more relevant information. A game with a little more interactive uncertainty than the centipede is the ultimatum.

The ultimatum game

A player is picked at random and given an amount of money that he must divide as he chooses between himself and another player, a stranger, who also knows the size of the endowment. If the second player accepts the split, the money is shared in this way. If not, they both get nothing. The entire amount is lost to them.

In repeated applications of the game it has been observed that player B routinely accepts offers between one third and one half, but rejects offers less than one third, even when there is no room for retaliation and the loss is great. It has also been observed that player A often makes offers between 40 and 50 per cent. Since such conduct departs from the short-sighted pay-off maximization that is expected of *Homo economicus* under neoclassical assumptions, various interpretations have been proposed, and *Homos* such as the *reciprocans* have been entertained who are encouraged by social norms to share in fairness. Explanations based on naïveté, love, altruism, indignation or other 'visceral factors' (see Rabin, 1993) describe such behaviour as non-calculative and not relating, or only loosely relating to the players' self-interest.

Emotions enter even the most cold-blooded calculations of agents. An act is selfish only in the sense that, and to the extent that it also takes into account a variety of social considerations, and this is done subjectively. These help obscure the motivation and the goals pursued by economic agents. In particular, the said blending of the self with its social context, this dialectical, irreducible association of two opposites, helps obscure for an observer the foremost ambition of every agent, which is to be in control over his own circumstances. This at the same time means dominance over nature through joining of forces and dominance over the participants in such union. An agent does his best to attain a dominant position in his niche, under constraints and in the face of uncertainty, by demanding income and by inventing ways to expend it which are most effective to this end. But every agent has a different perception of constraints, of the degree and kind of uncertainties associated with conditions and outcomes (anticipative variety), of discount rates, etc. Thus, for example, players may behave differently according to whether they consider the sum to be split in a game as small or large, based on their standing in their wider social niche. If player B, for example, considers the sum to be large, he may accept small offers, since his gain in the game may considerably improve his social position. If the gain is trivial for player A, he may in principle offer it all to his opponent or, as responder, he may reject even an offer of nine-tenths of the total amount.

In view of a host of such considerations, if theories with broad explanatory power based parsimoniously on a few universals are going to help us grope through the mist of social relations and individual behaviour, it must first be confessed that economic behaviour of real people is calculative and grounded on antagonistic spirits that inform through the brain's associative capacity each player of his own position relative to others, associating, through his personal prism, his gains with his perception of fitness in some appreciated social domain. If these were not so, there should be observed frequent 'uninformed' offers of more than one half in a game like the ultimatum, which is not the case. Given that B is reactive, he can do no more than subvert the position of A, not allowing him to gain a great pair-wise or social advantage. And he obviously does that, as experimental evidence shows. But this is done under B's simultaneous consideration of the relocation his gains may secure for him in the wider context, which is itself modified dynamically. This is why the ratio measure discussed about the centipede provides poor base for interpretations and is not unequivocally supported by experimental evidence. Accepting 'fair' offers may significantly improve B's position in his social domain outside the game, and since players are often selected among people who, due to relatively low incomes, are more likely to accept to participate in such games (e.g. students), such effects are obscurely confounded in these experiments.

Speculative demand formation

After this excursion we return to our main theme, which is to make as precise as we can the process through which vector y is shaped as a resultant of individual demand vectors in the economy, emphasis being placed on compositions rather than on aggregate magnitudes. This admits that structure enters equally decisively from the consumption side, as it does in Sraffian analyses through technology. Such structure concerns the way individuals allocate their income to the n available goods in order to stretch their purchasing power, as is commonly said, or so as to promote their time-space expansion goal, as we visit things here. In our notation, we study how individual i structures his expenditures $\|y_i\|_1$ into a vector (basket) composed as y_i, but with $x_i = (I - A)^{-1} y_i$ actually in mind, and what this implies about the composition y of total consumption expenditure $\|y\|_1$ in relation to the technological eigenstructure, through which is determined output x, structural index λ and efficiency index ε.

These decisions are based on a continuous process of knowledge accumulation, whereby more information is made available to the participants to possess, process and appropriate per time unit, and thus more gross value is produced. Rules and connectives between consumption, production and income distribution are constantly created and destroyed, generating consuming-knowledge capital that complements production-type knowledge, namely, productive capital, which are both embodied in commodities as these are produced and consumed, and both of which stand for creative human time-space applied on material inputs, giving them form (informing them) so as to become fit as tokens for the said expropriation contest. These take place within adaptive institutional set-ups such as markets, which provide testing ground for the economic viability of new connections, that is, constellations of restructured A matrices and y vectors, engaging also factor and commodity prices, care of relation (4.1′).

Without consumption innovations attached to and complementing changing production conditions and commodities, only suicidal producers would risk innovating. Production innovations modify the qualities of produced items, requiring a favourable response by consumers in order to find their place in the market, at prices that yield monopoly profits. Lacking such response, an innovation will confront an indifferent or hostile market and will yield no such profits, accruing losses to the innovator. Even when qualitative differences between commodities are not easily discernible, consumers must adapt to the new conditions of production that entail increased capital intensity, changing work patterns and general living and social conditions. Thus, not only telecommunications services and cars change the entire social situation in this direction, but even simple products and processes such as milk making and cattle growing for meat, and an infinity of others, even though much less conspicuously. The inputs that went formerly into these latter processes were drawn from nature, say by grazing. They were not system produced and they made for lean cows that took years to grow, produced higher quality, more lean, better-tasting but less meat and milk. Today, cattle growing and almost all food production brings products to the family table in more ready-to-use forms (ground, pasteurized, packed, precooked, etc.), with much that that implies for family and general living conditions and other important aspects of social life. Production involves more system-produced inputs (grain feeding, facilities, transportation, refrigeration and so on) in a highly mechanized, industrial-production process that extends its consequences to the entire socio-cultural domain beyond nutrition, into the spheres of health, utilization of time out of work (leisure time?)

and general consuming habits, family relations, etc. It would not be too gross an exaggeration to consider the milk-making cows themselves as man-made, milk-making 'factories', in view of the quantities of milk they can produce per day (often more than 40 kg).

Being repetitive, we may say that congruence and conflation between consumption and production dynamics has received unfairly little attention, with standard theory constricting thought to static market clearing, through coincidence of unreal aggregate demand and supply relations. Agents being producers and consumers at the same time, self-interested, rational and non-schizophrenic, there must be some underlying regularity and coherence to what they pursue through all their economic activities, and none such is provided by assuming many kinds of commodity-based utility, or some such motive to consumption, while assuming profits as motivating production. As a matter of fact, housing all consumption-motivating sensations under a single *utility* rubric betrays that even reductionist standard theory is obliged to admit in an oblique way that there is some kind of regularity in motives, as is of course confessed through profits on the production side. So, why the remaining inhibition towards an overall unity of motive?

Lacking such unity it cannot be explained convincingly how the system can demonstrate cohesion, co-ordination and orientation amidst so much economic freedom, regardless of what institutions may be set up. Actually, it would be meaningless and wasteful to try to increase x for the sole purpose of reaping any given y. Exactly the opposite is happening: Agents try to expend on y in such ways as to reap a greater x, inventing production techniques and arranging income distribution to the same effect. This is accomplished at system level through each consumer's trying innovatively to determine the structure of his or her y_i so as to claim back the maximum possible x_i.

If consumption demand were shaped in arbitrary, dissonant ways according to freely changing tastes, with the technological regime having to keep up reactively with them or, conversely, if consumers were obliged to find what they pursued in whatever commodities producers happened to crank out, that would make for a coerced-performance situation in extreme wastefulness of social knowledge, where any kind of inefficient technology could be made to fit a random (or randomly set) purpose, without cohesion. Efficiency, as a notion, and especially efficiency *improvement* would hardly make any sense with things changing in such a way, and there would be nothing *organic*, that is, socially complete and inclusive about all this, or about the composition of capital. The state of knowledge in society, reflected most eminently through the level of mental division of labour on all fronts, would not be reflected in society's performance.

Marx thought that the driving force behind economic growth expresses the continuous pursuit of capital accumulation through the rising organic composition of capital. For the historical reasons discussed, consumption demand did not get seriously involved in this organicism. Today, the energetic participation of consumers, that is, of the entire society, makes imperative that in the notion of 'organic' be included a consumption dimension. The social mode of production is fully complemented with an accordingly social mode of consumption. Neither production knowledge nor consumption knowledge can be abstract. They can only be made to fit interactively a particular modus of social and economic development, as part of a more general culture. 'Use' knowledge and 'make' knowledge acquire reciprocal semantics. There is no mode of production alone, but an integrated mode of production *cum* consumption. Structural growth is two sided. In the physical analogue terms around Figure 4.1(d), if forces get dissonant, then motion will go out of tune and the system will wobble. For stable performance, tandem development of the two kinds of knowledge is required.

Cohesion is due to the fact that consumers compete for the same capital resource as do producers, and in the same speculative way. When human time-space is embodied in socially produced capital, it takes on material substance. But although the physical part of production may be complete, the valuation part is never finished before commodities leave the system as waste. As a commodity goes through its use-ful cycle, use-type knowledge is attached to and embodied in it. But all knowledge is human capital and all capital is human knowledge. As Potts (2001) notes, 'the concept of capital should have its primitive aspect in human capital, which is otherwise termed labour or work. All economically valuable work is knowledge work. All economic systems are knowledge-based and this knowledge is based in the human mind.' But it is false and misleading to consider as knowledge only that which pertains to production. Through industrial production, and through exchange and use, the sublime agent infuses knowledge to commodities, and it is this, nothing else, that agents appreciate and appropriate by purchasing. So, utility for consumer i should not be associated simply with purchased commodities, y_i. It should rather be understood as a claim over both direct and indirect inputs and associated with the whole of x_i.

Through knowledge, the system economizes on direct human inputs (work) considered as sacrifice from a life in leisurely bliss. Since it is in everyone's interest to stretch the buying power of their income, which is remuneration for the personal time-space they put in production, all try to economize on their own labour by making its remuneration command through purchasing as much as possible of the overall socially divided labour that was put into commodities. This is what production innovations also aim at, where a given profit income is made to exert control over more capital resources, that is, over more previously embodied labour. The notions of command and control thus take on specific meaning. Given any amount of basic intake requirements or, more generally, anything that may be defined as *de rigueur*, the remaining part of consumption (or at least this) is decided to the end of 'gaining control'.

These are not new, except maybe in the way of their expression here. Schumpeter (1947: 175) considered it to be an 'elementary proposition that consumers in evaluating ("demanding") consumers' goods *ipso facto* also evaluate the means of production which enter into the production of these goods'. From this proposition, he argued, follows for the theorist the possibility of a rational calculation for the factors of production, even in the absence of markets.

The second part of Schumpeter's thesis could be construed as alluding to some kind of equilibrium, which is not very...Schumpeterian in logic, and contrasts with Hayek's (1945) general thesis that only markets can process widely dispersed information; not a theorist, a planner or any other system component. This raises the following issue: Adam Smith attributed wealth to specialization of knowledge from division of labour *as determined by the extent of the market*. Subsequent theory interpreted this rather narrowly, as excluding knowledge from all other sources except production, although 'the extent of the market' clearly reaches into consumption as well. And one may invoke Ashby's Law of Requisite Variety again, cited in the previous chapter: Since markets compose producing *and* consuming activities (in markets participate agents in both capacities), there must also be consuming-type knowledge that monitors and cushions the knowledge shocks that originate from production. So, our theory concurs with the first part of Schumpeter's thesis and with Hayek's objection to the second, albeit in a more forceful way: The point is not that markets alone can process dispersed information, but that markets facilitate the generation of new information, in all spheres of activity. Therefore, no theorist can determine the factors of production in any meaningful sense, except in some kind of least interesting, statically optimal way. But, as Kalman who was cited in Chapter 2 argued, we must reserve limited appreciation for optimization principles. Any rationally optimal calculation would be lacking in (or it would suppress) interesting variety in both the production and consumption spheres, since both sources of variety operate within markets.

Markets are effervescent because they effect application and growth of knowledge from every source, from all participating parties, in all their capacities, knowledge being by definition *reduction of incessantly renewed uncertainty*. It is not so much the volume, type, or dispersion of information that causes handling difficulties, as is the fact that information is constantly destroyed and renewed, which means that economics is not about information, but about knowledge. As Potts (op. cit.) explained, if information were given, a closed mechanism would obtain, not an evolving system that reorganizes itself. And a crucial component of what can be called economically relevant knowledge relates to the way each agent shapes his or her consumption basket y_i, given his or her income.

The embodied-time-space concept of utility makes it possible to answer both questions, being free of the conceptual weaknesses associated with the standard notion. In spite of first appearances, it is less hazy or abstract, other than honestly admitting the indisputable fact that economic value (as all value) is not objective or commodity based, but (inter-) subjectively assessed and acquiesced. It does not dispute that, *ceteris paribus*, more is better than less. Rather than viewing the economy as choosing a production structure *given* consumers' preferences concerning what to consume, it gives consumers the right to choose their own income–consumption combination and thus to participate in determining the structure of the system, including production techniques, prices and their own real wages.

The difference between structure-enhancing command over some resource that expands vital space and enjoyment, self-esteem, or other such that may be drawn from consumption is easy to discern in some cases, as when one subscribes to a communications network. Power is conferred to the holder of the right to use, and in this sense to control such resources and affect structure, regardless of what actual use he or she makes of them. This is also easy to discern in general, once the social nature and the function of economic activity to communicate information is appreciated. Indeed, it should be worth visiting the economic issue from an information-theoretic point of view, whence it could be made clear that, as Norbert Wiener explained, what is important in communicating networks is not so much the information that is submitted for transmission (in our case, y) but the amount of information that is actually received and results in action (in our case, x). In other words, it is not the coding (the language) that determines the reach and content of a communications system and keeps unwanted noise in check, but the semantics which are communicated through its channels and the action, feelings, or other that are activated by it. It is not the utility, under whatever guise, that is drawn from purchasing and enjoying y, but something that is somehow latent to x. And that can be nothing but human time-space: x is nothing but such.

About how consumption expenditures are structured endogenously and how consumption skills emerge in the first place, Loasby (2001a), Metcalfe (2001), Potts (op. cit.) and others have offered valuable insight. But the idea of a single cause, of some underlying universal still eludes economic thinking, which is haunted by the same old idea of a gallery of natural desires. Witt (op. cit.) argues: 'Consumption activities change over time as a result of learning. . . . new ways of satisfying innate wants, and, in particular, satisfying them in new combinations, become feasible through cognitive learning.' But 'innate wants' speaks of natural tastes and of a variety of natural, hence exogenous desires. And if wants are set by nature, discretion and endogeneity become void. This stops short of taking the last critical step. Although recent consumer-oriented research has properly disputed the notion of a commodity-based utility, it has failed to get rid of the multi-wants idea and fix its attention to a single underlying cause. Of course, one may choose to retain for convenience the usual multiplicity, since this is how things appear to the eye. But sight must not be lost of the actual situation, which is that these are simply variegated outward expressions of a single inner urge.

The reductionistic, variegated-wants fallacy that legitimizes the pursuit of happiness and, insidiously, the ideology of capitalism, carries over to other contexts also, confusing both history and the reciprocal interaction between agency and structure. Nations have always been at war or preparing for war, supposedly for a variety of reasons that make it easier to convince naïve native populations on both sides of the divide that they are on the right side. War is always advertised to the masses as defensive, or for some moral or spiritual value among many that can be invoked to drum up its victims. Such are national pride, honour, faith, freedom, democracy, civilization, etc. It is never from prejudice, never aggressive, and never for conquering or securing vital time-space. Thus, it becomes easier to conceal its single cause and goal. But we do know better, and science should not give backing with its prestige to bigotry.

So, a self-respecting theory of consumer behaviour must be based on a single motivating concept of reference, an inner urge or guiding pole that explains the conduct of restive consumers who strive energetically to break away from competitive conditions, resisting natural forces that pull things down to a slumbersome, complacent, statically optimal equilibrium state. Consumers are antagonists, as are producers. Both need to change their strategies, conduct and image continuously, to expend effort in order to stay in the game and gain ground. If they do not, they lose ground. Outside physics, this is the essence of the entropy law, which demands that effort be expended for any type of social asymmetry to appear and be maintained. In the case of consumers, only through innovative effort may status, distinction, power, recognition or even mere survival be attained.

Prices

So, let us expound on the creative role of prices in such restive world. As said, they undertake a more substantive role than that of Hayekian transmission of dispersed and diverse information. They do not help markets clear by matching producers' profit-seeking ambitions with consumers' exogenous preferences. Their role becomes vital in promoting the system's development by the fact that *changes* to relative prices inform the system about newly discovered knowledge. The difference between a prevailing price, or a price at which a transaction is actually made, and the value that an innovator actually appropriates through the transaction in a speculative way, as things will be determined according to the future conduct of the totality of agents, is a price differential that is always on the making, with every transaction conferring monopoly or monopsony gains, depending on which of the two parties has speculated correctly on future market conditions. This difference between price and value is a lively entity, born to the sublime agent, and it is the only component of price that matters dynamically, while the 'overlapping' part reflects *past* knowledge about the value of goods, knowledge that is already diffused and shared by many (including the two trans-acting parties), representing those forces that pull towards equilibrium. If there were no innovative speculation, then exchanges would soon become exchanges of equivalents made under the overlapping part, which would stand for the right (fair, market-clearing) price. The said disparity reminds of Mengerian exchanges of unequal values (Menger, 1976 [1871]), but Menger ascribed such disparity to the costs of the process of exchange, not explicitly to the newness of knowledge and to its rewarding.

Price changes play a similar role to that of polarity, voltage or inductance changes in the transmission of bits of information through communication networks. Under openness, the future is constantly created, with the past informing it but not being forced upon it, and with the present *being* only by way of its *becoming* future. These are kin to Kaye-Blake's (2006) idea about 'linguistic economics' where all that exists is semiological contingencies of the mind. Speculative transactions take place at specific prices that can never be up to date with values, which means with all the knowledge, past and new on which value is based, because such knowledge and hence values, are constantly on the making according to consumer-behaviour semiological contingencies. And the present, or the price at which a transaction is made, cannot encompass the future.

The dynamic contribution of this non-observable price differential affects the system's development and upsets its static performance as the knowledge increment that it carries becomes diffused. With time, its effect, that is, the concomitant value increment becomes noticeable through the price changes it sets in motion, but it never becomes measurable because many such knowledge-effected changes are always confounded, in real time. The system reorganizes itself, shaping actively not only the path of its own development but also the social and environmental context within which it itself develops. And the actual size of this price differential, the actual value increment, is not anything that is preset or inherent to the knowledge increment itself, but something which the market will decide through its conduct, that is, through the pieces of knowledge that it will add, along the way. Thus, in the market, knowledge evaluates knowledge, meaning that it determines its economic relevance, that is, its time-space equivalent. No innovative knowledge is complete in itself. It is rather constructed little by little by those to whom it is submitted. Their conduct appends new nuggets to the original contribution. Followers are creative in the sense that their conduct determines the value of knowledge infused to commodities, in a wagering-like, speculative environment where each agent tries to anticipate average market behaviour. Diffusion, therefore, is as important as is innovation. Or, which makes it more obvious, innovations that fail to be diffused are white elephants. As Rosenberg (1982: 19) noted: 'Although the availability of a name and a date may simplify the writing of elementary histories, they add very little to our appreciation of the economic consequences of an invention. From the point of view of their economic impact, it is the diffusion process that is critical.'

Real-time uncertainty and non-linearities abound in all this, precluding any formal description with measurable magnitudes. Uncertainty that surrounds activities, decisions and calculations makes precarious all equating on the margin and undermines all optimization. For example, postulating any relationship between the utility of the wage with the disutility of labour (as is often done for deriving labour-supply schedules in a theory of employment, or in theories of taxation) assumes more than can be conceivably known. Even if we suppose that there is such a thing as a measurable utility of wages, this must be determined through the use made of all these wages in terms of present and deferred consumption, neither of which is available for any serious calculation at any one point in time, with any degree of confidence. The amount of human time-space to be appropriated from expending one's income (the real wage) is a developing entity, in whose development takes part the income disposer's innovativeness.

Keynes's (1936: 9) visiting of this indeterminacy was very similar. As he argued, 'the supply curve for labour will shift bodily with every movement of prices'. Therefore, the classical theory of employment 'leaves the question of what the actual employment will be quite indeterminate' (ibid.: 8 and Appendix to ch. 19). Moreover, the general level of real wages is not determined directly by the bargain on money-wages: 'For there may be *no* method available to labour as a whole whereby it can bring the wage-goods equivalent of the general level of money wages into conformity with the marginal disutility of the current volume of employment' (ibid.: 13, original emphasis). But where our theory shares much more intimately with Keynes's is with his explication of the process of making investment decisions, in chapters 11 and 12 of *The General Theory*, where he placed emphasis on their speculative nature and on the precariousness of the knowledge upon which they are based. As he marked: 'It is of the nature of organized investment markets [to be] under the influence of purchasers largely ignorant of what they are buying and of speculators who are more concerned with forecasting the next shift of market sentiment than with a reasonable estimate of the future yield of capital-assets' (ibid.: 315–16) and 'the entrepreneurs...will find it financially advantageous, and often unavoidable, to fall in with the ideas of the market, even though they themselves are better instructed' (ibid. Footnote 1). Indeed, most professional investors and speculators 'are, in fact, largely concerned... with forecasting changes in the conventional basis of valuation a short time ahead of the general public. They are concerned... with what the market will value it, under the influence of mass psychology, three months or a year hence' (ibid.: 154–5).

At the base of such speculation is an anticipation of demand for consumption commodities, however removed from the real economy an investor's interests may appear to be. His ultimate concern is to foresee the future appraising of commodities by consumers. Thus, consumption itself must be explained as a battle of wits; as a contest to 'outwit the crowd, and to pass the bad, or depreciating, half-crown to the other fellow' (ibid.: 155); as a contest 'to guess better than the crowd how the crowd will behave' (ibid.: 157); as 'a game of Snap...a pastime in which he is victor who says *Snap* neither too soon nor too late...These games can be played with zest and enjoyment, though all players know that...when the music stops some of the players will find themselves unseated' (ibid.: 155–6).

These may be likened to those competitions in which the competitors are asked to pick out the six prettiest faces from a hundred photographs, the prize being awarded to the competitor whose choice most nearly corresponds to the average preferences of the competitors as a whole; so that each competitor has to pick, not those faces which he himself finds prettiest, but those which he thinks likeliest to catch the fancy of the other competitors, all of whom are looking at the problem from the same point of view. In consumption, as in this game, we try to anticipate what average opinion expects the average opinion to be.

If economic fluctuations, slumps and booms as explained by Keynes depend strongly on: 'A conventional valuation which is established as the outcome of the mass psychology of a large number of ignorant individuals' (ibid.: 154), then this must be true to an even greater extent about consumption. The forecasting psychology of consuming masses is vital to the system's performance. Therefore, all this solemn concern with what is lately called 'consumer sentiment' is quite justified. With advance, where everything is speeded up, including innovative decision making, there is increased likelihood of a clogged consumption mechanism whose operation depends heavily on the whims of purchasers largely ignorant of the qualities of what they are buying, and of speculators who are concerned with forecasting correctly the next shift of such not perfectly informed market sentiment, that is, with forecasting what the average consumer will forecast the average consumer to be buying next. For these tasks, an 'average' consumer may not be too competent, as it is required that his consuming mood be always high and playful.

Besides short-term consumer psychology, what may be called *consumer sociology*, which looks into a broader horizon, is also critical for the long-run performance of an economy. With opening up of economies, congruence of long-term consumption behaviour to an economy's evolving technological idiosyncrasies may not be guaranteed. Given the ease of transmission and picking up of consumption-related information and the difficulties and slowness associated with the development of a congruent technology, it may so happen that the native population may construe the niche in which it tries to position itself as a time-space claimer and power holder in such ways that do not coincide with the boundaries of the national economy. Then, people may consume in ways that are resonant with the production capabilities of some other economy, one which is either less or more advanced, in which case there may emerge all kinds of unusual situations, depending on how the output of the native economy is disposed of. For example, the native economy may grow for a while by exporting its product to other markets, but if native consuming patterns are more advanced than native production capabilities, this growth may well obscure the fact that the said economy is falling back technologically, which means it may be falling back in terms of coupling and co-ordination of the twin knowledge process.

Therefore, for increasing output through increased roundaboutness – as the latter is reflected through increasing λ and ε, which are indicators of the above-said congruence – an appropriately sized *and structured*, that is, *effective* demand y organically meshed with supply is required. Speaking of effective demand, Keynes claimed that 'The ultimate quantity of *value* will not increase indefinitely, relatively to the quantity of labour employed, as the processes adopted become more and more roundabout, even if their efficiency is still increasing' (ibid.: 214, original emphasis). This is not supported *prima facie* by our theory, unless the marginal innovative yield of consumers is diminishing and consumption innovations (which determine how effective in the above sense demand will be) fall persistently out of tune with production innovations. But then it is hard to see how processes may become more roundabout and how their efficiency may be increasing.

And as our concern in this section has been with the role of prices in the speculative process, it is worth noting that prices as discussed earlier meet the requirement set by Ashby's Law of Requisite Variety. Or, as Hayek (1952: 185) also noted, 'the capacity of any explaining agent must be limited to objects with a structure possessing a degree of complexity lower than its own'. This means that if prices are to orchestrate conflict, not resolve or wipe it out, there must be degrees of freedom available so that they can usher to productive employment all individual urges to break away from competitive regimes, into the realm of monopoly and monopsony margins.

To explain these we may start by assuming that physical technology R is fixed, as also market demand relations specified by a vector relation $d = f(p)$. Assuming statically that a certain income $\overline{Y}$ is consumed, the standard perspective would be to view the system as tending to come to rest at the equilibrium solution of the following maximization problem:

$$\max_{p} k = \frac{\|P(I - R)^{-1}d\|}{\|Pd\|}$$

$$\text{s.t. } d = f(p)$$

$$p^T d = \overline{Y}$$

Such type of system lacks variety-generating behaviourism, which makes it analytically tractable, but this 'comes at the price of abstracting completely from the specific existence of connections and from the fact that they may change' (Potts, op. cit.). Fixing R assumes producer innovations out, so it entertains only reactive producers and lack of entrepreneurship. Fixing f reduces consumer behaviourism to a datum. No search goes on either by producers or by consumers for new connections to exploit in order to get an edge over competitors, no knowledge process is in progress. The same amount and type of information x is transmitted in each period, repetitively, amidst complete certainty. For being about fully revealed and evenly distributed information, this is in essence a 'no-information' type of situation. The market is reduced to a computational mechanism or a cyborg. The system settles in an optimal, no-missed-production-opportunity, minimum-cost-of-output state, exhausting all productive capacity. However: 'Knowledge can be ignored... when it does not change. But if knowledge does not change, then how can an economy ever grow?' (ibid.). Still, 'the market process is an experiment in knowledge: the creation of unforseen compounds out of ephemeral elements that become perfectly obvious only after the event. This is what innovation is and does and is why it is not and cannot be a closed mechanism' (ibid.). And:

> Rules originate as building blocks from within the market process, but this cannot possibly occur in a completely connected or integral market space. ... If everything is simultaneously determined, then complete preferences will operate through complete markets to completely structure production and thereby organize all knowledge, and vice versa. But it is meaningless to refer to this as a system of knowledge. If everything is already connected then nothing new, or original and generic, can ever occur endogenously.
>
> (Ibid.)

So, theorizing must deepen our understanding of the process of knowledge generation, instead of getting us mentally trapped with the mechanics of cybernetic forms. Wiener, a founder of cybernetics, explained that feedback is a method of controlling a system by means of re-registering in it the results of previous behaviour. If such data are used only for evaluation and adjustment, we get a closed, in terms of its design (although not necessarily in terms of its inputs and outputs) control or cybernetic mechanism. But if such information can affect the system's general method and mode of operation, that is, if the system is learning (through its constituting agency, of course), then there is what we can safely call a *knowledge process*. Coding agent behaviourism and innovativeness through prices affects not only the message, but also the system as such, by acting on its connectives through everyone's conduct in the market.

Thus developing p–d–R connections undermine all attempts at coming up with some type of objective prices [such as Seton's 'eigenprices', as pointed out by Steedman. (See Seton, 1992, Section 3.9.)] And stated in this report's expropriative terms, we can say that there is nothing like a proper price for acquisitive generativeness, since what is 'proper' will obtain from everybody else's future conduct, in the market. Prices feed information back and forth between physical demand d and the physical production mechanism R, coding messages in such ways as to maximize information $x = (I - P R P^{-1})^{-1} P d$ communicated through the channel (through the market) and so as to allocate system resources, especially the sublime one, efficiently. In simple terms, prices help increase money velocity. Given that information available for transferring is increased through innovation, it is unreal to set prices, or to determine them in any particular way, or to see them as coming to rest at any one stable position, such as at market-clearing equilibrium. The only meaningful way to interpret prices is as vehicles and catalysts for an information-transferring process, as outcome to the fact that every agent pursues innovative advantage, introducing new information into the system expressed as a value and price differential.

Consumer behaviourism creates irremovable uncertainty that is endlessly renewed, by generation of new knowledge that later spreads and becomes generally available information. Adding to consumer-generated uncertainty, and in adaptive response to it, technical innovations change R. These are outcome to the fact that the Production System in Figure 4.1(a) is open to the Human System, which constantly generates knowledge. The economically relevant part of such knowledge consists of innovations that change R, p and d, in a chain of cyclical causal relations. Abstracting from these amounts to locking the system in to some statically optimal state, condemning it to retard and fall behind while other systems move on. In principle, such a system could eventually be eliminated by selection. So, a real system is a flux of connections and variable interactions and economic evolution through markets is 'the stabilization ... of these interactions into complex systems' (Potts, op. cit.).

Performance improvement through conflict

Consumer behaviourism generates this flux by inventing ways to evade established price regimes, stretch the purchasing power of incomes and provide comparative advantage. 'Comparative' invokes goal uniformity, which is to relieve a single *felt* scarcity, not to satisfy different desires. This does not contradict the rich variety of sensations associated with the flows to which life is open. There are different tastes, sounds and other sensations that attract us differently and affect our mood, some pleasant and some not, and we prefer the former. But all this diversity is underwritten by a single desire: the desire to preserve and extend life which is, after all, a precondition for enjoying those pleasant arousals.[1] This helps establish competitive connections between individuals through purposeful interference with the system's normal flux; connections that would be hard to establish otherwise, if different individuals cared for different desires.

A zero-sum conflict invents rules, unsettles *status quo* and organizes the diffusion of successful routines through markets, establishing new connections towards more complex systems. According to Potts (op. cit.): 'The signature of innovation is diffusion' which, according to Dupuy (1996), *creates* a 'position' of the fittest (cleverest) party, from which one sees what others do not see, and: 'Far from immunizing one against the infinite play of intestine rivalry, this position inevitably precipitates one into the whirlwind of conflict', so that there is not 'a true form of exteriority in place, a position from which the truth of the system could be perceived' (ibid.: 83). *Position*, however, is a misnomer, since it is not some state that awaits to be reached, but a condition and an exploration. At the level of individuals, the goal is to increase $\lambda_i = ||x_i|| / ||y_i||$, and this causes λ to be increased, at the system level.

So, consumer i faces a set of prices and seeks ways to allocate his income $||y_i||_1$ on a bundle of goods y_i, so as to improve his position by gaining monopsonistic advantage, claiming as much back as he can of the gross value x he helped produce with his labour. He thus engages in a process of cognition that includes learning what others already know, plus discovering new value-enhancing ideas by inventing new combinations of commodities, or new uses of combinations of commodities that others will later come to appreciate; that is, by discovering new wants that can be satisfied by produced commodities. Or, as Loasby (1999: 61) put it: ' "Knowledge that" may be a public good, but the capability of making sense of it, in any one of the ways that are conceivable, is not'. In this way, consumers keep in step with technology, extending its range of application. They substitute wants for needs, much like producers substitute capital inputs for labour, making the former relatively cheaper, in the process. When successful innovations get diffused (their frequency of occurrence is increased), new connections are made and the system evolves in the direction of increasing λ.

Borrowing from the language of communications theory and neuroscience, we may say that, given price vector p, consumer i tries to transmit coded signal y_i in such a way as to transfer a message of maximum informational content $x_i = (I-A)^{-1}y_i$, under noise that is inherent to organically imperfect processes. The value x_i is to be determined by the market, whose behaviour determines what 'message' was received and acted upon, that is, its informational content. Matrix $(I-A)^{-1}$, known as the multiplier matrix, appears under this prism as an amplifier matrix. Knowledge processes in social systems are extensions of cognition processes in individual organisms. The term 'organically imperfect' relates to neurophysiological transmission and diffusion of knowledge through neural networks, where stimuli may or may not arouse the proper synapses, depending on a variety of noise-introducing factors. One such factor here is that the encoder matrix A is fuzzily known to transmitters and responders, and therefore they cannot adjust their consuming behaviour to any particular technological eigenstructure with any degree of certainty, so as to expropriate the maximum possible time-space, even if incessant generativeness were to be assumed out. Collectively, the above performance by each individual agent yields market demand vectors (signals) y as ensembles of individual signals which aim at (but never succeed in) maximizing total information $x = (I-A)^{-1} y$. The degree of amplification is thus seen to depend on the degree of structural coupling between signal and amplifier, between transmitters and responders, according to the degree of their resonance.

The normal mode of all animate systems is to economize on their own resource, and this is also designed into artificial or cybernetic systems. For example, a telephone switching system or computer memory keeps a record of frequency-of-connections data (demand) and allocates resources accordingly, rather than allow at the same cost all possible connections. Similarly, rather than genetically coding within the genome every single pattern of connections for each neuron in the brain, only a limited amount of genetic information is coded, thus economizing on the genes. And the signal recorded on a sound source is of very low energy level. In the same way, every economic system should try to economize on value added, that is, on the cost of the human input, which is the only 'own cost', while trying to increase output.

In view of the fact that economics is a knowledge activity, that is, one of generating and processing information, it should not be surprising that the above perspective to x_i and y_i and, by extension, to x and y, which is in a sense opposite to the usual one, is kin to the basic concepts in information theory. There, the notion of 'algorithmic complexity' or, from a roughly opposite view, the notion of 'algorithmic information content' (AIC) is defined as follows: Given an idealized all-purpose computer with infinite storage capacity (given, in our case, a limitationless environment), the AIC of a particular message string x is the length of the shortest programme that will drive the computer to print out that string. In our context, this corresponds to a small y, saving on the own resource. The smaller the programme, the smaller is the AIC of the string, in the sense that it exhibits a high degree of regularity. (Highly industrialized, roundabout production.) Alternatively, given the randomness characteristics of the string, the greater the complexity of the algorithm the greater is the saving. Information theorists are concerned with how the AIC behaves as the length of similar bit strings is increased, approaching infinity.

Dependence of algorithmic complexity on the language and on the number system employed (binary, decimal, etc.) may be paralleled with the dependence of λ on the sector-disaggregation scheme, which determines the degree and kind of heterogeneity retained and that which is forfeited, and the degree of structural coupling between demand and technology. Much as with the uncertainty that surrounds the maximal λ that could unequivocally decide the degree of an economy's advance (uncertainty about the convex hull of maximal x's), the AIC is not computable (decidable) either, given the impossibility of knowing the degree of randomness in any given string x. Most of the time, it is reasonable to suspect that there is more regularity in any given string than an algorithm can discern and exploit, so we can also safely assume in our context that there is always a better p–d–R arrangement that could have produced a greater λ, given everything about consumers.

We may also note that the attainment of increased informational content x for any given sacrifice y, that is, growth so highly prized in capitalism, may involve trivialization where, as Gell-Mann (1995: 49–50) explained, the AIC of a string typed by a chimpanzee that is equal in length to Shakespeare's literary work has greater informational content, due precisely to its randomness associated with the monkey's trivial punching of keys, at little expense of own (mainly mental) energy. So, the only meaningful complexity is that which Gell-Mann calls 'effective complexity' and concerns the description of a string's *regularities*, excluding trivial randomness, by means of a complex adaptive system that is observing it. In our case, as observing system may be considered the theorist or society at large, and we did distinguish lots of such regularity in the form of alienating trivialization of the tasks involved in the production of increased x by means of advanced industrial methods; a production in which we saw consumers, too, to be engaged. In Gell-Mann's (1995: 59) words, the normative concern this raises can be stated by saying that 'a grammar of pure gibberish ought to have zero length'. Translated, this means that no sacrifice is worth putting into the making of junk. 'At the other end of the scale of AIC, when it is near zero, ... [t]he effective complexity ... should be very close to zero' (ibid.). In our context, this would correspond to a pure-labour mode of production with zero (or minimal) round-aboutness and capital. 'For effective complexity to be sizable, then, the AIC must be neither too low nor too high' (ibid.). This means that a sense of proportion must guide mankind's campaign to sustain itself where people will neither be killing themselves to earn their day's bread, nor will they be wasting their lives into massively producing and consuming garbage.

There are places where one can look for drawing such balancing insight that includes a modest approach to life. This is where things have had enough time to instil wisdom to people, or where the second law has forced them to fall back on the defence. Frugality has been the rule in many old cultures, and elderly people may supply an example of the second kind. Besides the discussed aggressive way of going about increasing λ and ε-efficiency by increasing x for any given y, there is also the opposite one, of reducing y under any given technology. Notice that the direction in which the arrow of time points remains the same, but antagonistic incentives are reduced and so the rate at which λ is increased should be slower. Elderly people do not relinquish their right to life, nor to the conveniences made possible by capitalism. But they pursue the same objectives rather conservatively, reducing their consumption, saving on their own and on the system's resources. Instead of striving to increase x_i (and hence x), they reduce y_i (and thus y). The relevant question then is: Given technology (R, L), disposable income $\overline{Y}$ and two pairs (p, d) and (p', d') such that $\sum_{i=1}^{n} p_i d_i = \sum_{i=1}^{n} p'_i d'_i = \overline{Y}$, which pair is preferable, and why?

Each such pair determines an instance of relation (4.1). Given the purpose of economic systems as value-generating mechanisms, the logical answer to these questions under a growth-bound ideology is that that pair should be selected which leads to a greater x, so that no production opportunities will be left unexploited and no historically accumulated knowledge that has shaped R will be wasted. Alternatively, if we assume p to be given as well, A is determined uniquely and consumers are asked to choose d under income constraint $\sum_{i=1}^{n} p_i \, d_i = \overline{Y}$. Then, that d which maximizes λ is behaviourally consistent with maximizing purchasing power. But things are not as clear if one compromises the said ideology, and one does not have to be a Buddhist or very old these days, in order to raise such concern.

Restoring symmetry

Pasinetti (1993: 107–8) argued that, although 'the classical economists did sense the importance of knowing the direction of the evolution of consumers' demand, and made the well-known distinction between necessaries, demanded by the poor, and luxuries, demanded by the rich (who have already reached a saturated demand for necessaries)' and although there has been observed 'a fundamental statistical uniformity...that demand for food generally decreases as a proportion of total expenditure, as wages increase', still 'one must admit that all these remarkable hints and observed statistical findings, though coming indeed from the observation of a too overwhelming reality, have yet to be systematically and satisfactorily fitted into a comprehensive theory of consumers' behaviour in a dynamic context.'

These clearly speak of the concerns that we raised in the beginning of this chapter, and earlier. Under normal circumstances, the claim that there is an ideological reason for not even trying to resolve such counterfactual, provocative discrepancies between a discipline and its object of study should be dismissed as simple paranoia. But obstinate refusal to bridge such basic gaps makes for abnormal circumstances that even students in this discipline have revolted against, signing petitions and initiating what has become known as 'post-autistic' economics, not to mention the frequent remorse voiced by patriarchs in the profession (after they reach the apex of their careers, of course). There is hardly any such precedent in other sciences. So, we insist that the blatant asymmetry in the treatment of production and consumption is ideological, meant to conceal what the real object of consumption is. If the consumers' discretionary expenditures were put under scrutiny, it would be hard to evade the viciousness of their greed and the enviousness of their antagonism, or to hide that these are *sine qua non* for capitalism. It has been acknowledged, of course, that rivalry guides the choices and permeates the conduct of producers, thanks to the (once unorthodox) approaches of Joseph Schumpeter, after capitalists had been disgraced with Marx's charges about their exploiting workers. (And through this glass, despite his conclusions, Hayek supplied more useful material for waging criticism against capitalism than many of its critics.) But by neglecting consumer rivalry, producers' rivalry was made to appear as being to good effect: as aiming at satisfying consumers' desires. As long as those desires were not scrutinized, by considering them to be exogenous, there was none to accuse as aggressive, niggardly or malevolent, except nature, maybe.

Be this as it may, Pasinetti's observation suggests the way to go in order to systematize the 'overwhelming reality' about consumer behaviour, and that is by treating it in a way analogous to the one used for explaining producer innovations, which supposedly alone decide the distribution of income into wages and profits, classically associated with necessities and luxuries, respectively. But this requires that we shed the Marxic idea about all surplus being usurped by the capitalists and wages as being possible to expend only on necessities. Overwhelming reality suggests that, as an economy becomes technologically advanced and dominant, its members may rise *en masse* above bare survival, allowing part of wages to be expended in discretionary ways. This is actually why capitalism has found general approval. Discretionary expenditures can deceive consumers into thinking that they may soothe their angst, fill their void and defeat their fear by consuming.

We must acknowledge, while theorizing about present-day capitalism, that wages generally allow for consumption above basics, which provides room for discretion as to how wants can be dealt with. Relatedly, Shackle (1972: 157) argued that 'Those who must consume or exchange what they have in their hands in order to live through the day or the week cannot concern themselves with the notion of getting a better price next week.' And

> Poverty and urgency *demand* a price, and convention supplies it. The more nearly the economic society is confined to a hand-to-mouth existence, the more nearly, in principle, can its operations approach the rational. For when the goods dealt in on the markets are perishable and ephemeral, they must be exchanged at once and therefore find a price at once, and there will be no considerations bearing on the price except the immediate need, tastes and momentary endowments of the members of a society. ... It is the introduction of 'wealth', of assets which promise and represent permanence or persistence, that must destroy the basis of rationality.
>
> (Ibid.: 157–8, original emphasis)

Such 'assets' being real to consumers, we assume next an agent's income to be sufficient so as to permit also expenditures beyond necessities, allowing us, in turn, to decompose y in two components, associated with two different types of pursuit and two different degrees and kinds of discretion: One component, to be termed *needs*, denoted by N and associated with basic requirements for socially decent survival, and another, to be termed *wants*, denoted by U, and seen as fully subject to discretion, both being sensitive to social context and varying with time and other factors. That is, $y = N + U$, analogously as $VA = W + \Pi$, on the production and income distribution side.

Expenditures on needs bring consumers up to par with a social minimum or average, or up to a level and type of consumption considered minimally admissible. The physical base of such consumption may be set by nature (e.g. calorific content), but the means, that is, the particular commodities through which these will be satisfied are to a large extent socially determined, and so consumers can apply expropriative ingenuity and discretion. Thus, one may choose between different kinds of bread (or bread and cereals, etc.) for a sufficient intake of bran fibres or other nutrients. The overwhelming reality is that the path of development of capitalistic consumption follows closely that of capitalistic production. In the example, consumers tend to replace 'old-fashioned', labour-intensive, once even home-baked bread with capital-intensive cereals, other foodstuffs or even junk substitutes. And same goes on with soaps, cars, hairstyles and just about everything else.

Conceivably, we could pursue symmetry down to a technical level, treating N like W by assuming a $n \times s$ (or n by anything) matrix $V = \{v_{ij}\}$, $i = 1,2,\ldots,n$ $j = 1,2,\ldots,s$, where v_{ij} would stand for the amount of 'natural intake' j (nutrient j, for example) deemed appropriate for decent survival that a consumer would receive by consuming one unit of sector i output. This would correspond to matrix L of labour-input coefficients, on the production front. Then, one could repeat the arguments in Chapter 4, envisaging N in the way of the classical interpretation of W, as minimum-expenditure requirements for physically reproducing the consumer force, and describing substituting innovations analogously as with those of type (b), etc. But these would do violence to consumers' generativeness, reducing their angst and passion-guided innovations to frigid technical relations. Consumer innovations are more of a felt condition, an urge through fuzzy sensing of one's social environment, not a technical, cost-reducing matter. Therefore, since we are concerned with the logical part of the argument anyway, we choose to describe things more generally, as follows.

We denote the physical base of N with $\vec{v}$, whence $V = diag\{\vec{v}\}$ and $N = P\vec{v} = Vp$. In other words, we assume a single vector of minimally required intakes, one from each sector. This admits that there is a material underbase to sustained existence and reproduction of the consuming force and of the population in general, but the often made connection between wages and basics, in the sense that $\|N\|_1 = \|W\|_1$, and between profits and luxuries is abandoned. In modern capitalism, it is $\|W\|_1 > \|N\|_1$, as shown also in Figure 5.2(b). Thus, consumers can participate energetically in deciding the path of the economy's development through discretionary consumption, as part of an overall participatory engagement that includes also the political and general social process.

It is certainly more realistic today to associate needs and wants with *levels* of income, rather than with sources of income, and even then rather flexibly, since it is now culturally acceptable for lower-income groups to expend income on frills and luxuries, competing with the wealthy. Moreover, since the development of social forces on which Marx placed emphasis obtains from the mutual interaction between agency and structure, acting also on the general culture, analysis must take into account the reality and the consequences of agent mobility through occupations, income-level thresholds and behavioural protocols. In Pasinetti's (1993: 108) words, the discretionary margins of economic agents are continuously widened, and this contextualizes 'the necessity of learning in consumption activity, when income increases'. In terms of the kind of behaviour which bears on socio-economic dynamics, the relevance of social divisions by *source* of income is thus diminished. In our early language, dreams are getting more and more same. In whatever way one may draw social taxonomies, there will be social osmosis and diverse behaviour within each group. We are all, after all, very similar and very distinctly individual when it comes to spending our income, and income from all sources avails for all kinds of consumption. These have an impact on the system's evolutionary dynamics, as behavioural diversity alongside with motivational homogeneity supplies stamina to capitalism. It supplies both the requisite variety and the needed cohesion for selection to take place in an effective way.

So, as $\|N\|_1 < \|W\|_1$ and $\|W\|_1 < \|VA\|_1 = \|y\|_1$, the remaining income, $\|y\|_1 - \|N\|_1$, is spent on excess consumption U speculatively and purposefully, as no *natural* restrictions are placed upon it. Such consumption provides the extras in life through which is mainly decided one's status, social recognition or esteem, all of which reduce down to dominance. In a way analogous to the production innovations discussed in Chapter 4, the final structure of overall consumption y is determined and continuously updated through innovative substitutions of components of U for one another, and for components of N. The internal logic of these substitutions is to maintain a favourable relationship of y with the eigenstructure of A, so as to make component U command more of the capital content that is present in Ax by better aligning with it. This is what determines the time-space value of purchased commodities, their social worthiness and that of their owners. These kinds of innovation are the only proprietary ones that may yield monopsony gains, much as in the case of production innovations where monopoly profits could obtain from suitable substitutions of capital inputs r_{ij} for one another or, even more effectively, from substitutions of some r_{ij} for some l_{kj}, which we called type (b) substitutions.

So, consumers search for ways to replace physical components (commodities) of $\vec{v}$ with newer commodities, produced with modern, capital-intensive techniques that net more human time-space. They discover, for example, that fast food works better than home-cooked meals to this effect and gradually abandon the latter, 'because everyone else does the same' as the usual empty argument about fashions and imitation goes, but the truth is that they do so because they cognitively 'sense' that socially productive time-space is present in larger doses in industrial fast food than in home-cooked meals. So, they care less and less about the real relative *nutritional* characteristics and qualities of the two kinds of food, they accept becoming obese, etc., so long as 'others do the same', so long as by following such behaviour they avoid becoming weirdoes who fall behind in the race for socially recognized social presence.

Such innovative determination by consumers of component U complements and gives substance to entrepreneurship that produces production innovations. Without the former, the latter is meaningless. Junk-food businessmen could experiment as much as they liked with artificial tastes or worm-burgers to tempt the most jaded palate, but if consumers did not reckon that through the greater junk-food *culture* (remember to look around as you bite, leaning a bit forward, etc.) they could expropriate more time-space and thus mark and expand their social presence, junk-food businessmen would be eating mountains of worms.

Much as with Π, which obtains as reward for the accomplishment of possessing and employing capital, U may be seen as reward for accumulating and through successful speculation exploiting social knowledge that relates to consumption and is reflected in continually renewed diversification of consumption baskets. This knowledge is gathered in a similar catch-up, forge-ahead, or fall-behind type of contest as takes place among producers. Shaping U is not just a matter of increased spending, but also a matter of one's cognitive capacity and foresight, because what counts in U as a signifier of power is not just its volume (in vector terms, its L_1 norm), but also its composition in relation to the prevailing technological structure, which goes along with the sociological and cultural ones. This technological congruence between U and A is reflected in the degree of its alignment with Ax, and the evolutionary dynamics of U form part of the structural development of the system, complementing the innovative restructuring of productive capital K. Goods composing U are displayed, rather than consumed, and what is displayed through them includes also the capital Ax that is embodied in them, which means the human resources that went into their making, appraising and using.

So, the relationship between U and Ax is similar to that between Π and K, where the dynamics of building up these relationships are more important than all statics. Yet, as is often the case, a steady-state assumption may help communicate some of the points made, but this analytical and conceptual convenience is fraught with snares, not the least of which is its allusion to optimality. In steady-state, all relevant knowledge has been fully or partially but conclusively diffused and no new knowledge is entertained. So, for each agent and for the system as whole, the situation is knowledge-wise closed. The only thing that rational agents can do then is to perform optimally, upon whatever information each may happen to possess. But such optimality is as fictitious and impossible in real time as is the said closure on knowledge.

These having been said (which hold also about the already discussed relation between Π and K), we may envisage a basic consumption basket of fixed composition as $\vec{v}$ for decent individual survival that is the same for all κ members of an economy, imposed by nature and not updated by new knowledge. Each member's expenditures are then decomposed as follows: One part is expended on purchasing $(1/\kappa)\vec{v}$ at prices p, whence obtains $N = P\,\vec{v} = V\,p$, shown bold in Figure 5.2(b). Any income left over after purchasing these basics should be expended according to Ax, so that each individual consumption vector y_i that includes some excess consumption above and beyond $(1/\kappa)\vec{v}$ will have the largest possible Ax component. This will make value $x_i = (I-A)^{-1}\,y_i$ appropriated in total by individual i also maximum, given his or her income. Moreover, the market demand vector y will be such as to make vectors Ax and U align: $U = u\,A\,x = u\,P\,R\,q$, where the proportionality constant u will stand for a uniform rate of time-space expropriation, which we may call (for economy, and as a concession to tradition) 'utility rate'. This is, more precisely, a uniform rate at which any bundle y_i composed like y will embody capital composed as Ax. In a way analogous to producers, consumers will have been fully informed about all the conditions in the market, including the behaviour of others and their social appraisals of value, that is, of the time-space content of the various commodities, so that competitive equilibrium will have prevailed on the consumption side as well. Implementation of

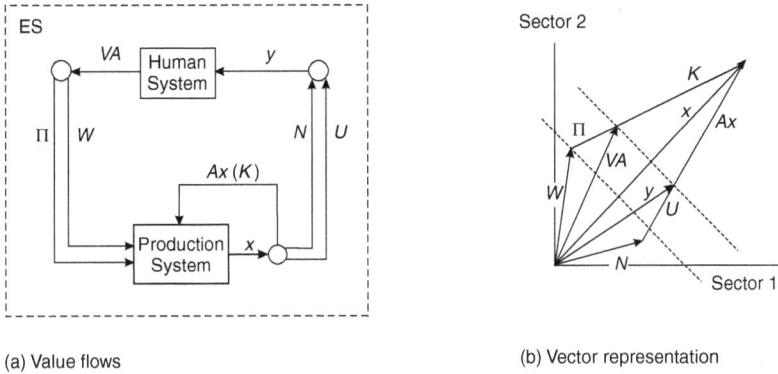

(a) Value flows

(b) Vector representation

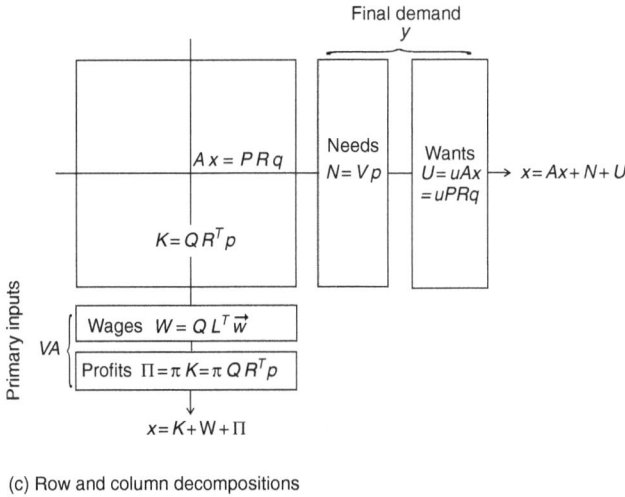

(c) Row and column decompositions

Figure 5.2 The economic system: a Sraffian representation with symmetric treatment of consumption.

this consuming prescription will be silently effected through society's ceding power (status, recognition, etc.) to those who succeed in the contest. Under such imaginary conditions, only the size of one's income will matter in terms of possessed power, since all time-space related knowledge will be equally available to everyone and they will all be buying the same consumption-basket compositions, all being assumed to be equally rational.

Given all, in steady-state it must be $y = N + U = P\vec{v} + uAx = P\vec{v} + uPRq$, much as $VA = W + \Pi = QL^T\vec{w} + \pi K = QL^T\vec{w} = \pi QR^Tp$, where it is easy to note a technical asymmetry in the expressions for N and W due to our reluctance to particularize things further. Once again: Simultaneous collinearity of Π with K and of U with Ax would be outcome to a full deployment of all interactions in the two spheres, that is, to full diffusion of all economically relevant knowledge, and a theoretical steady-state should be such that both these alignments are established. In reality, neither of these can materialize, because new knowledge is always produced.

As shown also through parts (b) and (c) of Figure 5.2, these restore logical symmetry in the two spheres, as mandated by our assumption of uniform motivation. Going in the other direction, we can start from a steady-state. Dynamical motion then obtains from equilibrium-disrupting, resonating motion of vectors on either side of x. If we allow ourselves to break-up circular causalities in order to be able to give a simplified picture, we may reason as follows: Production innovations aim at securing monopoly profits. This is achieved by introduction of new commodities or by qualitative changes to existing ones. Appended to these are complementing consumption innovations, as consumers acknowledge and exploit the value-generating potential of the said production innovations, in pursuit of privately owned knowledge that secures a utility differential at higher than uniform rate u. This requires successful speculation about how other consumers and the market in general will behave in the near future in relation to the newly introduced production innovation, predicting price changes and expending individual income in more effective, that is, more *economical* ways. These should destroy steady-state alignment, while competitive diffusion forces should tend to restore it. Required diffusion of proprietary knowledge undermines its exclusiveness, making it gradually banal, and thus prompting further innovations. However, non-diffusion entails losses to the innovator.

These readjustments of vectors to the developing eigenstructure of A gradually stretch out the quadrilateral in Figure 5.2(b), accelerating the roundabout flow in part (a) of Figure 5.2 and, through this, money velocity x. To these contribute also expansionary forces, which augment y and are also welcome. Efficiency-wise, λ and ε are increased. The time-space expropriating power $x_i = (I-A)^{-1} y_i$ of individual i is augmented by appropriate adjustment of his individual expenditures, y_i, subject to any given income constraint, $\|y_i\|_1 = c$. Such individual behaviour then gathers up through intermediate levels all the way up to system level, so that there is no structure-versus-agency inconsistency.

Let us repeat before closing that analytical timelessness through closure misses the time asymmetry induced by knowledge. One may see this as Keynes's revenge on mathematical technicalities and as vindication for Shackle who argued that 'In order to achieve demonstrative proof, the economic theoretician must reject time' Shackle (op. cit.: 255, cited earlier), as also for his claim that there is an incompatibility between time and logic. (To Keynes's 'revenge' we will refer in the next chapter.) In the above logical and technical restoration of symmetry, little distinguishes K from Ax, both of which appear indiscriminately as capital, that is, as embodiments of human time-space. But although the real object of consumer behaviour is something that looks into the future, consumer expenditures *deceive* consumers into thinking that they may soothe their angst, fill their void and so on. So, K is essentially different from Ax, in that the former looks forward, into the future, through the productive potential remaining in the capital forms associated with it. In contrast, *Ax* looks into the past, since the time-space contained in it is not further exploitable, in principle and in general. In other words, *K* and *Ax* appear as if they project onto the same sector-labelled axes, but these are not time-labelled.

We may say, therefore, that all this feverish consumer ingenuity is about crap. We have argued throughout that economics is about expropriating life. And we have argued that life is in capital of all kinds, since capital is knowledge and knowledge is time-space. But a capitalist's capital, which is speaking about *K*, is...live life, that looks forward, into the future, whereas consumers' capital, *Ax*, is life past; life gone, or lost. It can look forward no further. So, one may say that what capitalists catch and stock is live prey, whereas consumers only scavenge. Now, if consuming commodities were about pleasure, this would make some sense. But all indications are that this is hardly the case. Consumers buy commodities at bulk rate for fighting their angst, but they seem to be drawing little real satisfaction. What they accomplish is that, by spending their income like maniacs on consumption commodities, they supply capitalists with the kind of capital that looks into the future, which means they offer them their own lives on a plate, voluntarily, even though unwittingly. And 'consumers' includes those who are (really or supposedly) exploited. This is why we have claimed that, in affluent societies, where hunger has been defeated and the grim spectre of life loss due to it has been extinguished, those exploited are exploiting themselves. Stated in a picturesque way, smart birds are caught from the nose, as a Greek saying goes, and consumers think they are smarter than they really are. If they want to go pecking, let them learn *how* to peck.

6 Some issues revisited

In this chapter we revisit briefly and expand on a few issues, and we visit others from the viewpoint of the theory in the preceding chapters. These include the meaning of GDP growth and the ways people go about it, as well as an allusion made by Keynes to the relation between two different compositions of income and involuntary unemployment.

Growth economies

With very little in the way of convincing explanation, the mass media, politicians and economists alike have implicitly associated growth with welfare, so that the general public sees no other dimension to the latter than what national statistics tell us about the former. Roughly speaking, the argument is that if an economy grows, there will be more to divide among agents and so there will be less social tension. Or, from another angle, increasing transactions will come to meet increasing demand. So, if we take the existence of any type of demand to imply satisfaction by its meeting, then the increased volume of transactions summing up to a growing GDP will imply increased agent satisfaction. Surprisingly, instead of being eased social tensions have mounted, as has aggressiveness, at all levels and in all spheres. The way things stand, for humans and nature growth looks more like a menace, or like a forceful imperative; a distressful, coercive situation rather, than a joyous occasion.

We have placed emphasis on the distinction between net and gross output and between expansionary (balanced, steady-state, proportional) growth, on one hand, and structural growth, on the other, with the former being measured by GDP and the latter being reflected through λ. Innovations tend to increase λ through increased roundaboutness, expanding the set of available routines $\mathfrak{R}$, and increasing output per unit of labour input. This does not necessarily imply that net output is increased, except if there is also expansionary growth and/or capital accumulation that call for increased employment of current labour inputs. And even then, the population parameter dictates that proper concern should be with *per capita* income, which may or may not be rising. Even if we assume, in materialist fashion, that increased per capita net income implies welfare improvement, GDP may grow with innovation and structural advancement without net gains necessarily accruing to consumers. As already discussed, restrictions to the distribution of income tend to be relaxed, in principle, as vectors K, VA and x tend to stretch out and become better aligned, in Figures 4.1(b) and 5.2(b), which raises equity issues. But the association between GDP growth and welfare remains dubious.

Let us visit things from a considerably different angle. In general and abstract terms, things may be stated as follows: Of the past (and of past genius) nothing remains, other than a legacy that is either stored in the minds and hearts of the living, in the form of social capital, memories, values and norms, or becomes embodied in man-made commodities, as material capital. Therefore, in final analysis everything is about human capital. As we build our future upon the past and proceed to it through the present, we can experience the transition by means of all kinds of knowledge that relate to life, whether of a base or of a noble kind. Capitalism, which we have chosen as our way *to* life, is a world view and attitude towards life based on knowledge of a speculatively acquisitive kind. It values only that kind of knowledge which can be embodied in artefacts and possessed privately. So, it speeds up generation of knowledge which carries economic value, which means it speeds up GDP growth.

In more precise terms, what each tries to make private is $x_i = (1-A)^{-1} y_i$, because this is what asserts his or her relative power and control. It is not y_i, as appears to the eye, and as is commonly thought. And this causes the resultant vector x to grow, making individual and collective goals coincide, showing that it is gross output rather than net output that an economy pursues, because it is gross value that each agent tries to make private by expending income. These join consistently structure with agency and prove that growth is an imperative, a distressful or coercive situation rather, than something that relates to real, fulfilling welfare. Instead of easing tensions, the opposite comes through: As it is the pursuit of power and, hence, conflict that increases each x_i, so it is conflict that drives x up. Therefore, there is conflict in growth: conflict between agents, conflict with other economies whose resources are usurped, and conflict with nature, which is plundered; a position of the fittest party, in an aggressively Darwinian sense.

To repeat: We increase gross produced value and then fight amongst us in the final commodities market to snatch as much of it as we can. But so as to conceal the involved enviousness from ourselves and from others, we somehow manage to convince ourselves that if output grows, there will be more *worthwhile fighting for*, thus confusing conflict with happiness. Since there is only human life in x, which embodies time-space-related knowledge – knowledge which is economic, that is, of practical importance for the conduct of life – it is for human life that we fight, and this shows as violence against our own species in ways that no other species is capable of, since no other species appears to be possessed by the same anxiety and apprehension. This unappeased anxiety shows on our faces, which are anything but serene and composed, and on the way we behave, which is aggressive throughout, with calculated doses of other-regard for deception. Our angst in the face of cosmic time-space and imminent death makes us unassured, generating knowledge ever faster in order to speed up time and enjoy more experiences, which makes us look smarter than other species but also more violent.

So, GDP growth is not a measure of common welfare, but of the degree of collective distress and aggression let out by participants on each other. Such growth becomes an imperative for each capitalist economy because, to the extent that it fails in the above knowledge race, it is bound to fall behind technologically, lose markets and thus eventually lessen its net output as well and hence its material welfare. Antagonism between economies produces the same expropriative effect at a global scale, where not only energy sources but also clean air, the ozone layer and everything common risks being depleted at frighteningly fast, historically unprecedented rates.

Now, there may be a degree of linguistic exaggeration, by conventional standards, to speaking about economics as life-taking, but there is a host of *factual* exaggerations and overwhelming evidence that our life project is basically a conflict for life which are dismissed or denied by deductive economics. Actually, death itself sells, and it is *us* who buy it. Television shows trailers of deadly violence or accidents, before showing infinite replays of it. (Recall Hume: '*His pain… augments the idea of our own happiness, and gives us pleasure*'.) Economic theory, if it is to be realistic and social, must be informed by the fact that people trample over each other, killing each other as they stampede to get into a department store where there is a sale. It must be informed by the fact that capitalists 'kill themselves' working harder than workers, losing family, real enjoyments and everything that could reasonably constitute happy life; and by the fact that there was an immense redistribution of wealth in the 1990s in favour of professional speculators, not through any class struggle, war, or otherwise, but through the globe's stock markets as laymen blinded by greed dreamed of becoming thus capitalists by speculating. Theory must be informed by obvious but neglected facts. Guided by his celebrated 'animal spirits', a self-respecting modern entrepreneur is known to consider an Aristotelian society as placid and defunct. But this has become the firm view of all; not just of the businessmen. And what else is in the animal spirit than Life?

Technologically advanced commodities fail to appease our thirst for life. One may actually get more depressed by discovering that life is not man-made, after all, and thus impossible to grab hold of through man-made commodities. Only past (and gone) life through past knowledge is possible to embody in artefacts, while true life is in the way the future *becomes* a reality through the infinite succession of present moments, and in which commodities cannot share. So, the present is lost to those who waste their lives going after consuming illusions. The *economic* counterpart of these *creative* moments is in the value that is added in each period as VA, which relates only to current labour and maybe, but certainly to a lesser extent, to productive capital form K, as expectation of future yields of power-asserting artefacts. In contrast, y, by means of which the many as consumers fancy to taste life, is capable of appropriating only capital in its already exploited form Ax. According to which of the two one has access to, it is decided whether he is a capitalist or a wish-to-be capitalist. (We will return to these next, along with Keynes's revenge against maths.) To the extent that some are capable of usurping surplus from others, no matter how much income these others may have at their disposal to expend on consumption, they are bound to be on the loser's side of a negative-sum game, and there is bound to be a mismatch and conflict. This Marx saw in class-struggle terms that have largely been psychologically overcome by an individualistic contest of every one against every other.

Roundaboutness can be increased in various ways, all of which can be placed under a knowledge rubric. Finding out how to control the quality of produced commodities so that they do not last and how to design obsolescence into them, or even how to make them self-destruct, all constitute economically relevant knowledge, as does depriving others of knowledge. Mobile phones come loaded with games. These are considered to provide a service to the buyer, but they also wear out screens and key conductivity in a jiffy. [The first key that goes sends the entire gadget to the trash can, and the happy – for being stupid (recall the Bible) – consumer to the next phone model.] Even instances such as the following should inform theory: In departments of dentistry in universities all around the world, a core part of the students' training and job ethic taught is their obligation to inform patients about the details of preventive dental hygiene. However, this social obligation goes against the dentists' *private* interest, so when they later practice their *trade* they often 'neglect' to inform their patients. Such instances abound and are quite informative, revealing obliquely a rather distressful general situation that passes largely unnoticed because it has become commonplace.

Increasing λ, or other means towards growth, constitutes a social convention with evolutionary stamina that increases information processed per unit of time and reduces uncertainty; *an uncertainty that is created artificially, in order to be reduced.* (Suffice it to compare the volumes of information that need to be processed under the two contrasting situations in the relation between dentist and patient.) Economic evolution promotes the interaction and structural coupling between agency, structure and environment, the latter seen as a superstructure and as context, by means of cognitive and intentional, goal-seeking component action. The system evolves through an endless conversation that encourages action which promotes both component self-interest and system adaptability, according to a particular interpretation of the environment. Success reflects the appropriateness of this interpretation and the responsiveness of the system. Whether the prevailing interpretation is by normative standards wise or unwise is beside the point.

All this comes under the guise of a flourishing materialism and lavish accumulation that delivers commodity value in increasing volumes, so as to promote social stability, as is falsely claimed. But what is not false is that this helps legitimize an established social order. So, growth is an ideology. It is fear that keeps the system together and addiction to a commodified lifestyle that nourishes illusions. Although the contrivance of an omniscient and hyper-rational *Homo economicus* has been imposed on the discipline, there is considerable knowledge from cognitive sciences, psychology and behavioural economics concerning the boundedness of real people's rationality and memory. Previous welfare states are less easy to recall and less decisive with respect to whatever one derives from present welfare, than are comparisons with the states others are presently in. 'Utility' can only be in relative gains. Hence, it is non-satiable, whence the S-shaped (diminishing sensitivity) of gain and loss curves relating happiness with changes in material well-being. (For a review of such mental accounting literature, see Thaler, 1999.) No optimization is involved. Improvement is relative, goods are positional and changes to wealth matter more than its absolute level.

From a technical point of view, advance expands the use of capital, making it cheaper by embodying in it productive knowledge, skills and dexterities, thus displacing current labour from old tasks and making it appear as relatively more costly. Consumers are prompted to direct their ingenuity at inventing ways to consume, so as to claim back this human-knowledge content of commodities. Driven by socially fabricated preferences, they speculate against each other for positional gains, trying to anticipate correctly each other's future market conduct. The capital embodied in consumption commodities is not directly observable by consumers as they make purchasing choices, but it is reflected in the dynamics of relative prices, which register the relative technological prominence of the various commodities, conferring social prominence to their possessors, according to the gross value x_i they manage to expropriate through consumable commodities y_i. Circularity is plain to these: y_i is decided according to the x_i it expropriates, but p, A and x, hence also value x_i, are determined according to the preferences declared through these individual y_i's.

These get society intimately involved. As Hollis (1991) noted: 'Economics is ... no more a self-contained discipline than the economy is an isolable realm of social life.' And in order to answer its salient questions, economists must not isolate themselves from those disciplines that study the same system from various sides, in parochial quest for the glory of deductive sciences, or sciences which study inert systems. A dear price has been paid for approaching economics mechanistically, as a closed system on which control can be applied by the modeller, even on such macroeconomic magnitudes as is national income. The history of economic theorizing is a history of gross discrepancies between such descriptions and predictions, on one hand, and economic reality, on the other, for failing to analyse economies as open, self-organizing systems whose evolution is permeated by knowledge indeterminacy and reciprocal causal relations.

Loasby (2001b) has supplied strenuous arguments for openness: The system (and our theories) 'are embedded in time – and therefore in uncertainty – and [we should] take seriously the selective development of connections over time as a result of fallible human action'. The whole process is 'exercise[s] in Knightian uncertainty, for which there are no correct procedures, but the possibility of rewards for skill'. Therefore, 'we must switch our emphasis from closed to open systems, and from proofs to process.' And: 'though uncertainty gives rise to serious problems, ... it also provides abundant opportunities. For ... uncertainty is the precondition of imagination and creativity: it makes space for the growth of both theoretical and practical knowledge' (ibid.). The trouble is that knowledge processes are difficult to model or to classify. Their difference from mechanisms and from processes that transform inputs into outputs in pre-specified ways 'is that brains use *processes that change themselves* – and this means we cannot separate such processes from the products they produce. In particular, brains make memories, which change the ways we'll subsequently think. *The principal activities of brains are making changes in themselves'* (Minsky, 1986: 288, original emphases).

Another reason why economists shirk from approaching economics as a knowledge process is noise. Noise works to the detriment of information communicated through prices, much as in physical communication systems, where this becomes the cybernetic expression of the second thermodynamic law. For example, monetary, public finance, income distribution and other policies or interventions may compromise the informational effectiveness of prices. Thus, the ensemble of feasible $x = f(y)$ relations is determined in the light of limited and corrupted information, because the cost of perfectly noiseless information about possible outcomes is infinite, which is another way of saying that the future is unknown, and so the search for relative gain by each agent is groping, unsure and speculative on all counts and fronts.

Because this urge for snatching vital time-space stems from an inner distress, not from a pleasurable fulfilment of harmless and legitimate desires, growth of flows of individual wealth and by extension economic growth at the system level become forceful imperatives. Thus, economic growth is a collective outcome of a deplorable individual condition. This outgrowth of an inner coercion which develops into malignant capitalistic growth is becoming more visible with time as capitalism advances, gnawing not only at resources, as the usual environmentalist argument goes, but also at the inner world of humans who become alienated, stupefied, deprived and aggressive. There is agreement in the nefarious nature of forces which underlie both structure and agency. Even mainstream theory obliges to this, except that for ideological reasons it makes it appear as benign, by associating growth with utility seeking. As a result, welfare collapses down to simple GDP growth. Such coincidence, however, has been persuasively disputed by a number of investigators, some of whom have already been cited. Hirsch (1977) gives an eloquent account of disputing arguments. Ryan and Deci (2001) summarize an extensive literature documenting that the relation between happiness and material wealth is indeed very strained. To make a long story short, neither utility, as an individual pursuit, nor the social-welfare-promoting qualities of GDP have been proved or explained to the satisfaction of even those who put forward such arguments. Instead, they are taken for granted, as obvious, transmuted into high-calibre metaphysics. The underlying cause of such misconceptions and of the impossibility of explaining things out is the lack of all meaningful ontology for the mainstream agent.

In contrast, our theory contends that agents succumb to an existential anxiety, which induces them to struggle for positional advantage through consumption commodities as surrogate life. At a collective level, this promotes growth, which in turn promotes the chances of the economy against others. That is, at every level, from the individual all the way up to the economy and to the global situation, this anxiety ignites a struggle for gaining comparative advantage over others, through faster than average expropriation of valuable resources. Such an agreement was set early as a fundamental requirement, when we demanded of any self-respecting theory of consumer behaviour to find non-contradicting systemic expression in some kind of quasi-additive way. (No common good may obtain from personal evil.) Thus, through the prism of our theory, a capitalistic economy seen as an entity demonstrates a macroproperty that is in agreement with individual pursuits and marks a preferred direction in its development, in the sense that its performance relative to competing economies is improved by a similar preferred mode of individual conduct which promotes some selfish personal objective. This is complemented in the political arena with contentious behaviour between states, through war and other aggression, with which history is replete. In spite of pretexts and excuses, wars have always been appropriative, promoting aggressive national interests. In purely economic terms, capitalism, more than any previous system, places people, economies and nations against each other in a contest for dominance through growth at each and every one of the above levels. Expropriation is privatization of otherwise common resources. Resource scarcity is an apparent source of antagonism, but our explanation reverses the picture: Resource scarcity is contrived, to the end of promoting power, this desire stemming from a single universal scarcity: the scarcity of life. The deeper the sense of such scarcity, the more each unit will try to control resources for present use and for growth strategically, over time.

Resource allocation is a prime determinant of the relative performance of viable systems, in general. Driven by this imperative, such systems build, maintain and increase structure in out-of-equilibrium self-organization, exhibiting a privileged direction that depends on internal and external parameters which orient their evolution in time. In such open, dissipative ways they interact with their environment, striving against the second thermodynamic law, importing energy and exporting entropy. Life itself can be identified with the building up and maintaining of structure. As stated by Laborit (1996): 'The only reason for being is to be i.e., to maintain structure/information in relation to a less-organized environment.... In other terms, the goal is to combat the second principle of thermodynamics, the increase in entropy.'

Selection among imperfect replicates (non-identical copies) provides a random source of evolution. Competing systems evolve also through increased metabolism by autocatalytic feedback towards increased energy flows, appropriating commonly available resources and gaining competitive advantage. This is known as Lotka's principle (Lotka, 1926). According to Adams (1981), 'natural selection will so operate as to increase the total mass of the organic system, to increase the rate of circulation of matter through the system, and to increase the total energy flux through the system, so long as there is presented an unutilized residue of matter and available energy.' According to Thoben (1982): 'This evolutionary principle ... explained the fundamental process whereby natural selection worked and evolution continuously searched for new forms of life. ... It makes clear that life not only conforms to the entropy law but also, at the same time, accelerates its operation.... those life forms that give rise to a more extensive degrading of energy have a selective advantage over others and will outstrip their competitors.'

So, *ceteris paribus*, nature appears to favour systems that speed up its predilection for homogeneity and equilibrium at lower potential, and this predilection is served in the economic domain by growth.

A connection between antagonism, entropy, economic growth and dominance has been firmly established. Adams (op. cit.) claims that 'Culture provides human beings with the potentiality for extra-human extensions that allow them to capture energy and degrade it more rapidly and effectively. Thus, the societies that will be favoured by natural selection are those that have cultures that so operate as to increase the total mass of the organic system.' Thoben (op. cit.) marks: 'Complex social organizations have provided better and better ways of doing this, just as have the technological inventions that have provided the means by which energy could be at least consistently and, better, increasingly captured.' According to Foster (2000), the energy/information processing capacity reflects the efficiency of the novelty and variety generation mechanism upon which competitive selection operates: 'through the acquisition of new information and the exploitation of attendant new energy sources, … the expansion of organized complexity of culture in a highly developed species, such as our own, diminishes the impact of natural selection on its genetic make-up and increases its ability to pressure other species at a lower level of cultural development.' Abramovitz (1989: xvi) explicitly connects with rivalry: 'There are international rivalries for power that carry fears of losing in a growth race.' Also: 'nations viewed their security and power as resting on an economic base. To ensure their independence and safety, they concluded they must grow; if ahead, stay ahead; if behind, catch up' (ibid.: 11). And: 'Engaged in fierce international rivalries for mortal stakes, growth is the basis for an adequate national defense' (ibid.: 347).

Economic activity is thus clearly connected with a desire for dominance, avarice and greed. As we have already discussed, Smith, Marx, Keynes and many others had discerned such a relationship. For Smith, the driving sentiment of human behaviour is greed, while cooperation is used as expedient for the same purpose, namely, acquisition. Marx (1906: 649) argued that 'the development of capitalist production makes it constantly necessary to keep increasing the amount of capital laid out in a given industrial undertaking, and competition makes the immanent laws of capitalist production to be felt by each individual capitalist, as external coercive laws. It compels him to keep constantly extending his capital, in order to preserve it'. Laborit (op. cit.) elaborated on the co-evolution of capital ownership with the dominance trait as the latter developed historically and was promoted through acquisition of information. By considering such information from the viewpoint of its generation, as knowledge, its true essence is revealed to be in the human time-space invested to it.

In all, an expansionary, elbowing-others-out imperative has been definitively associated with capitalistic advance, where each contestant, agent or economy, is struggling to gain an upper hand over others. Thus must be explained the dominance of growth economies over others (which are disapprovingly considered as backward), the flourishing of materialism in modern societies and the importance of accumulation and of delivering goods in large volumes, *to the end of legitimizing a particular social order*. The prevailing culturally fabricated and institutionally promoted economic Darwinism – which orthodox theories dress up in harmless attires, as legitimate utility seeking, pleasure seeking or some such – presupposes *willing, participative and submissive agents* who adopt the conditions, values and relations proper to a society of pervasive power exhibition, enforcement and application, from an initial convention of well-guarded ownership rights over human time-space through the commodities it produces, all the way up to its environmental consequences and social ramifications. Such agents are fully accountable for their choices, and this is not meant in any indictive sense, but in the sense that no theory can be realistic and meaningful, unless it examines the social situation in the light of psychological motives and goals.

This wilful individual participation makes evolve economic systems which appear as if they were separate entities that display choice of means and ends. In reality, they contain active parts that perform different functions (they have a division of functional labour), being themselves parts of larger systems that are environment to them. So, they can be conceptualized as three-level systems which, according to Ackoff (1991, original italics), 'can try to increase the effectiveness with which they serve their own purposes, the *self-control* problem; the effectiveness with which they serve the purposes of their parts, the *humanization* problem; and the effectiveness with which they serve the purposes of the systems of which they are a part, the *environmentalization* problem.' These predilections trickle through every subsystem down to the individual, promoting selfishness which stems from apprehension and from a sense of vulnerability against future occurrences. Eventually, at all levels, survival is understood as being in the conquest of vital time-space by outpacing competitors in appropriating resources and increasing throughput. Capitalism inflates the self-control goal, subdues environmentalization to it and promotes creative destruction of resources and technologies, capitalizing on devaluation.

Creative destruction involves assessment of what is created relative to what is destroyed, and this decides the type of efficiency that is improved while the system evolves in the said ways, in the said direction. Progress along any preferred direction is a mixed outcome of a galore of human behaviours, all of which are perceived by the acting agent at the time he or she makes the relevant choices as personally valuable (profitable), although these may prove with time to have been short-sighted. Although not as transparently selfish as is the profit-making incentive, these modes of behaviour can always be placed under a selfish light. Conversely, change patterns that are advantageous for the system relative to other systems may be passed on to individual members, even though they may not be of immediate, direct or obvious benefit to them, which often makes them appear as non-selfish. Such 'group selection' reflects the need of individual members for a viable system entity (society) through which, and only through which, they can promote their personal interests. Therefore, *personal interest is in society*. This collective entity must adapt to exogenous impacts or external constraints in order to secure favourable conditions for its members. In general, successful system modes of operation are those which are beneficial also for the individuals, that is, sufficiently resonant with individual modes of conduct (the divisibility requirement). Preferred directions obtain from behaviour that is valuable to individual agents, after it is diffused because it is also valuable to the group, in a way similar to that of gene selection.

Going back for a moment to the conclusions drawn in Chapter 4, we see that in order to increase its fitness relative to competing economies, each one of them tries to increase the rate of flows that go through it, appropriating more resources. Structure provides the requisite leverage. Through change of technique and adaptation of prices, matrix A may be structurally advanced so that, with parallel adjustment of physical demand d to the evolving technological regimes, greater output is produced per unit of direct human input and per unit of time, through more intense use of intermediate inputs. In other words, the resource-expropriating power of VA is increased by stretching the leverage of capital K through proper deployment of mental human inputs from HS that are increasingly infused to it. Thus, the system economizes on its own, current human input, which is the source of all value. Kuznets (1972) referred to the supply part of this when he spoke of innovation which, 'through changes in sources of power, materials or major tools, ... permits a larger final output with the same or a lesser input of resources.' Since, by the first thermodynamic law (the principle of conservation), this is impossible about material inputs, such generally agreeable statements can make sense only in value terms. So, the final output must be understood as *value* output, and the expression 'lesser input of resources' must be understood as referring not to any material inputs, but to ones that are both valued and immaterial. And the only socially and personally valued (and indeed highly so) immaterial input is the mental input to the process of all those involved, through all economic activities, meaning the creative generativeness as experienced, informed, knowledgeable, current time-space. The more such time-space is stored in productive capital forms the greater the value output by each unit of it. In our notation, the greater is K, the more value x is produced by each unit of VA.

The importance of structure as a streamlined topology of interconnections that enhances a system's capacity to process information flows with minimum use of its own resources has been recognized in various contexts. For example, in explaining how Western science originating from the ancient Greek mode of thinking dominated Eastern science, despite the latter's earlier advance, Georgescu-Roegen (1966: 5–11 and *passim*) compared the process with the evolution of a living organism, attributing this dominance to a distinguishing feature of Greek science: its classification of knowledge already conquered not taxonomically, but in logically structured ways. Thus was economized thought, so that an ever-increasing knowledge content could derive from an as small as possible set of basic propositions or logical foundations. He termed this 'compressibility' and emphasized that it is a *structural* attribute: 'theoretical science['s] ... growth is organic, not accretionary. Its anabolism is an extremely complex process which at times may even alter the anatomic structure' (ibid.: 15). So, systems are efficient and effective in attaining their goals only to the extent that they succeed in economizing on their own resources. But, whereas in the science analogue *thought* is the obvious and acknowledged such resource, this is provocatively ignored in economics, which is indisputably a thoroughly mental activity. So, it strikes as odd that currently employed cognitive input valued as *VA* has not been interpreted in a similar manner, and that the orientation of the system has not been explicitly understood in a structural, λ-type sense, but rather in the accretionary sense of GDP growth, over which there has been conducted such extensive accounting.

To sum it all up: Nature's predilection for low-potential states is served by anything that speeds up transformation of available energy (negentropy) into non-available forms (entropy). This carries over to social systems, mental processes and to the sublime human resource that produces value. Increasing velocity of circular, Sraffian flows (producing commodities by means of more and more commodities) is precisely to such an effect, increasing output per each input unit. The kind of welfare associated with capitalistic growth is extremely dubious and other-disregarding. It is gambling, with a good dose of bad intent and exercising of power. Time-space-expropriating shrewdness counts at all levels and he (or that system) wins, which proves to be more effective in this contest. As in all battle (and as Nietzsche maintained), *he* is *condemned* to win who can sink lower, be more ruthless, less reserved or inhibited: in a word, less humane. Letting shrink one's life to pursuing material or pecuniary gains makes it more likely that one can actually succeed in making such gains. Same is true for economies. By gaining comparative advantage over other economies *by all means* (and non-forged, non-counterfeit history has recorded the most heinous national crimes), an advanced one can expropriate more global resources and increase also its *net* output, which is the material benefit and enticement that accrues to its agents. These then increase its chances to advance even further, through positive feedback. But capitalistic benefits being zero-sum, they are always at someone else's expense. If one adopts a parochial stance, one may be impressed by such success, (dis)missing the other half of the global condition, which is pithily contained in Stafford Beer's (1994: 389) comment about a 'true and not spurious compassion for the real and not imagined plight of mankind [where] one third of society is undernourished and three thirds are under the threat of extinction'.

Money wages and the investment–goods ratio

One should raise fewer eyebrows by claiming that ideology is involved in the virtual omission by mainstream theory of issues relating to distribution of income or wealth and unemployment, so that just his keen concern with unemployment would suffice to set Keynes apart. In what follows, we take a brief excursion into an allusion made by him about the relationship between income distribution, the structuring of expenditures made under any particular such distribution, and employment.

We took the edge off the sharp class dichotomy into workers and capitalists by focusing on motives, which we found to be common, stable and uniform. We saw all as trying to appropriate human time-space embodied in capital. Universal participation in this quest prompts our title, *Consumer Capitalism*, but this is not to dispute totally with Marx, since we told forms K and Ax of capital apart and concurred that it is only through the former that 'live life', meaning current human inputs that come under VA, can be usurped. Form K is productive, while Ax is the non-reusable capital content of consumables, which soon go out of the system as waste. But we underscored the importance of the historical developments under which W (or whatever is left over after Π is appropriated by the capitalists) is more than enough to maintain the work force in advanced capitalist economies. Such excess income has enticed consumers to learn how to consume, how to expend it aggressively in an effort to snatch as much as they can of x, corroding their consciousness and making alienation organic and global, seducing them into supporting the system of their own exploitation with their everyday market and general conduct, or attitude to life. Because of this, we argued that exploitation is partly self-inflicted.

In his *General Theory*, Keynes investigated the logical possibility of involuntary unemployment and explained it on the basis of the matching, or lack thereof, of saving with investment, where involuntary unemployment was meant in the sense that the existing volume of employment may be lower than the aggregate supply of labour willing to work for the current money wage, and also lower than the aggregate demand for it. His explanation made implicit reference to the structure of intended expenditures by income disposers in relation to the composition of the real-wages producers were willing to provide, in the sense of the relation of decisions about the mix of current consumption and saving, on one hand, and decisions about investment based on the prospective yield of it, on the other. In chapter 17 of *Epistemics and Economics*, Shackle revisited Keynes's ideas from the viewpoint of the implications of real time in economic theory and practice, suggesting an *ex post*-versus-*ex ante* explanatory frame as being appropriate for the occasion and placing emphasis on the uncertain nature of the future yield of investment (*ex ante* uncertainty), as opposed to the certitude with which decisions about the mix of present consumption and saving are made.

This issue is of interest to us, in view of the interplay between time, knowledge and the formation of structure. But we must mention that Keynes's explanation also acknowledged a good dose of conflict and malevolence between workers, by his maintaining that 'any individual or group of individuals, who consent to a reduction of money-wages relative to others, will suffer a *relative* reduction in real wages, which is a sufficient justification for them to resist it'. And 'the struggle about money-wages primarily affects the *distribution* of the aggregate real wage between different labour-groups' (Keynes, 1936: 14, original emphases). In our language, reductions to one's money wage lower *the scale* of his relative reach into the time-space contributed collectively, and this is hard for a wage earner to accept, given the zero-sum nature of the contest in which he participates, for which participation he actually contributes his own measure of sacrifice by supplying socially divided industrial work. But given his scale, the *composition* of what a worker buys with that income matters also in our theory, since time-space value depends on the capital content of the various commodities, being not same for two different baskets of the same total expense.

Keynes borrowed from Pigou the term 'wage goods' for those commodities 'upon the price of which the utility of the money-wage depends' (Keynes, 1936: 7). Then, early on, in Chapter 2, he underscored the importance of the mix of present and deferred consumption that income disposers desire, and its matching or mismatching by the willingness of producers to borrow and invest the saved money, that is, their willingness to provide workers *with the product composition of income* the latter desire, in the sense of its investment-goods content. Keynes thus placed emphasis on explaining involuntary unemployment upon a certain two-dimensional resonance (or lack thereof) in the behaviour of producers and consumers. This kind of resonance could not have been included in the analytical frame that we employed, since the latter involved the comparison of steady-states, where neither net saving nor net investment take place. All generated income is expended on capital replacement and on consumables. As a consequence, employment dynamics could not be visited from an accumulation viewpoint. But our theory outside the necessarily constrictive mathematical frame does share with Keynes's and Shackle's and it actually reaches into more detailed decision spaces, of higher dimension.

Keynes maintained that while money wages may be high relative to the prices of wage goods, so that unemployment may result from producers' unwillingness to hire more labour under such terms, at the same time, even if workers accepted a reduction in their money wages the problem would still remain, since reduced spending might push commodity prices down, keeping real wages high as before. But: 'If the workers were willing to spend on consumption a larger proportion of their incomes, then the contraction of quantities of product sold, due to a lowering of money wages, might be avoided' Shackle (1972: 169). And

> [w]hat hovers elusively on the threshold of perception ... is the idea ... that the discrepancy between offered and demanded product wages is not one of size but of composition. Wage-earners, or rather, the whole body of suppliers of productive services including even the business men themselves in their capacity as income-receivers and disposers ... desire a wage, or other pay, which in product terms consists partly in provision for the future rather than enjoyment in the present.
>
> (Ibid.: 169–70)

And Shackle went on to explain that 'the *real provision for the future* [are] the industrial facilities and equipment which alone enrich society as a whole' (ibid.: 170, original emphasis). And, a little further down,

> money, for society as a whole, for the body of income-earners all taken together, is no use as a provision for the future; only equipment, real tools and facilities, can constitute such provision. However, these tools and facilities will have to be formally and legally the property of the business men. The business men, when they invest with borrowed money, become hostages to an incalculable technological and *fashionable* future.
>
> (Ibid.: 174, emphasis added)

These allude to the asymmetry of time, which in this instance distinguishes the present decision by those lending money to businesses, about the mix of present and deferred consumption, from the future yields to the lender and to the borrowing businessman of the saving and of the investment, respectively. But on what does this yield or, more relevantly, on what does the prospective investors' current speculation about this yield depend? Keynes (for whom: 'All production is for the purpose of ultimately satisfying a consumer', etc., as we quoted him early in Chapter 1), based his answer on what he called 'effective demand', implicating it mainly through its aggregate magnitude.

For us, in view of the indissolubility of p, d and R effects inside a n-dimensional space (because of the integrated and socially organic nature of all involved processes), the worlds of the lenders and borrowers above cross at consumption choices made in such space, along the way, involving the future. The coalition of technological and consumption dynamics (the 'fashionable' component) within the sector-disaggregation scheme employed determines the yield of investment. Neither dynamics can stand on its own feet, or even makes any sense by itself. Decisions made by income disposers about present consumption at every present moment, concerning the dynamic allocation of consumption expenditures on the products of the n sectors, affect the decisions about how much to borrow in order to invest, and hence the level of employment. They also affect the *structure* of employment and its dynamics, that is, its developing temporal distribution over the various activities as was discussed, trivializing tasks, embodying some into capital and introducing new ones, which are highly paid, initially. That is, they affect L. Intimately connected with these is also the issue of the real wage.

In every case, the issue concerning capital ownership and future provision is perfectly settled only in steady-state, where all net income is expended on consumables and income disposers cannot purchase any more of the productive capital K (the highly valued 'real provision for the future') than they already possess, through saving and lending to the businessmen. Their unquenchable thirst for it is by necessity channelled towards the only form of capital that is available to them: the non-productive form, Ax. This is better than nothing since, although it does not constitute provision for the future, it still provides power in the present, being a commodified form of human time-space, as is K, which they would certainly prefer because it looks also into the future.

One might object that, outside steady-state, which is unreal anyway, consumers – which includes workers – can save and lend so as to lay their hands on bundles of high investment-goods content, and thus really reach into the future, precisely as capitalists do. But this is not so. The essence of time lies in its creative construction through ideas, and so it matters *who* makes the choices that constitute the time-ticking creative contributions. To the extent that investment decisions are in the jurisdiction of the capitalists, savings, too, provide consumers with the same kind of income (in the form of interest, this time) that their labour also provides (in the form of wages), simply setting a little higher only the *scale* of their temporal expenditures, all of which are still on consumables. In other words, it is about who decides expenditures on productive capital and who controls (decides the uses of) it, rather than who owns it, in the saver's case as a lender. It is about controlling the flows that derive from it.

Keynes toppled the static Investment-equal-Saving identity ($I \equiv S$), opening up an investigation of their relation in a dynamic context, in the light of decisions made by agents in real time, under the prism of knowledge generation through speculation, hence under uncertainty, even though, as usual, in one-sided terms. Income disposers and businessmen determined through their behaviour the value of the difference $I - S$, and thus also the unemployment rate and other macroeconomic magnitudes. The basic decisions were made on two fronts: Income disposers decided the mix of present consumption and saving, so as to provide for future consumption as well. Businessmen decided how much of the offered savings to borrow and invest, as also how to invest it so as to provide for future productive investments. The usual handicap was that, whereas the consumer's decision was just a dichotomous one (with dichotomy constituting the simplest kind of structure) and seen by theory as based entirely upon desires, with little in the way of real new knowledge generation and in the way of a time profile worth speaking of, investors' decisions were structured, time-dimensioned, and made through a genuine knowledge process. (Production innovations, financed by investment, etc.) It was through these that the future became involved, capturing Shackle's keen interest.

Our theory appends a consumption component to the above knowledge process, paying analogous attention to consumer motives and goals. Keynes did not delve into these in any considerable detail, essentially adopting the usual hypotheses about profits and utility. His interest was with outcomes and in particular with that of a disturbing and challenging kind: involuntary unemployment. So, it was enough for him to refer to the proportions of income that income disposers and business people wished to allocate to the present and to the future, at each point in time, largely sidestepping *why* they wished to do so, *what* they aimed at, what goal they pursued, and any details about how they tried to attain it, through more detailed (de)compositions, in particular as concerns their present consumption patterns. But it was already a contribution that he associated capitalist dynamics with the future, which implicates life as a vital concern, thus making it into an obvious next step to implicate also the consumer. It is through consumption, after all, that Keynes himself maintained that we pursue our final goals, as comes through many passages in *The General Theory*. This is how should be understood ultimately Shackle's 'provision for the future'.

In summary, consumers decide what part of their incomes to expend now, and what to save. Then, they decide how to allocate on the n available commodities that part of their income that they decided in the first stage to allocate on present consumption, and they enter this decision-making process in the same, capital-seeking frame of mind as in the first stage, when they decided about the mix. If there is any difference between these two income components that must be that, whereas saved income *could* conceivably look into the future in a capitalist way, namely, through securing control over productive capital, the same is impossible for consumption, which is 'final', and for which there is no prospect whatsoever for going after *K*, but only after *Ax*, which is the accumulated effect of past provision by businessmen. Actually, materialization of the above possibility can make a labourer into a capitalist, which may not be too common, but not entirely fictitious either. It presupposes, however, that a saver goes beyond the dichotomous reasoning about the said mix, into the same kind of speculative, forward-looking knowledge process that producers go through when they are called upon to particularize (structure) their investment strategies, based on expectations concerning yields. That is, they must undertake the same kind of cognitive burden as undertaken by investors. Profits may be seen as reward for this particular kind of creative mental contribution.

This extension challenges Keynes's view that it is fallacious to suppose that there is a nexus which unites decisions to abstain from present consumption with decisions to provide for future consumption; whereas the motives which determine the latter are not linked in any simple way with the motives which determine the former' (Keynes, op. cit.: 21). It also disagrees with Shackle (1972: 173), who concurred: 'there is "no nexus" between those figments, which we call expectations, invented by one person or group of people, and those invented by another, except the tenuous and delusive indications which are perhaps available to both persons, or both groups, in common, in the record of the recent past, in so far as they happen to make use of the same parts of it.' Our theory identifies this nexus as being in the underlying, time-space appropriating motive that is common to agents as they make all decisions concerning expenditures with an eye at the future, as this is constructed through a succession of (decisions made at) present moments. This connects what may appear at first glance as figments, or tenuous and delusive indications.

Keynes's concern with the impact of present effective demand downplayed that of the *structure* of expenditures on the level of employment, focusing mainly on its *volume*. From our viewpoint, everything is closely knit with the degree of resonance between the structure of the final demand vector and the eigenstructure of the technological matrix. But the sperm of such reasoning can be traced in Keynes's theory. It should be recalled, for example, that Keynes attributed 'the onset of a "crisis"' not so much to a rise in the rate of interest, and hence, to the cost of capital, but to 'a sudden collapse in the marginal efficiency of capital' (op. cit.: 315) relative to expectations as to its future yield, which at the later stages of the boom are characterized by excessive, unjustified optimism. In particular, he considered the basis of such investor expectations to be extremely precarious, because of their dependence on the consumers' propensity to consume. So: 'Being based on shifting and unreliable evidence, they are subject to sudden and violent changes' (ibid.). This appends to earlier statements of his, such as that 'The outstanding fact is the extreme precariousness of the basis of knowledge on which our estimates of prospective yield have to be made' (ibid.: 149). But what else could be so dangerously precarious about the basis of knowledge than the knowledge about how to consume, that is, about how to *structure* one's consumption expenditures? Undoubtedly, learning how to spend any *volume* of income does not take much genius.

So, our approach to consumption makes Keynes's argument about the precariousness of expectations more convincing, concrete and forceful. Deciding the precise structure of the n-dimensional vector y as a resultant of all the individual y_i's is in itself an extremely demanding speculative process, where choices are based on consumers' expectations about the consuming behaviour of other consumers and thus, indirectly, also about their decisions concerning the consumption-versus-saving mix. This complicates immensely the decision making by agents and increases the precariousness of all bases of calculation. Basing everything, and in particular the shaping of current consumption expenditures on knowledge, rather than on information, implies that everything is eventually a matter of knowledge generation and of its characteristics. In view of these, Keynes's all too important concept of effective demand should be understood not as a scalar (scale) parameter, but as structure. And in view of the relatively unco-ordinated way in which consumption-related knowledge is generated, as also in view of its relative flimsiness, compared with the other half of the cognitive process that takes place on the supply side largely through organized and directed research and development effort, the risk of maladjustment always lurks there for capitalism. And as we explained, dangers are greater for the more complex, highly advanced and more vulnerable economies: The coalition of forces on the two sides may at times be so poor as to rock the entire edifice.

Social considerations

We placed emphasis on personal constitution, which we considered as appropriate basis for examining the social condition. Societal characteristics, though, exhibit great inertia and impressive tenacity and they are sensitive to historical context. In its physical aspects, the economic activity cannot escape natural laws, and social processes are irreversible in the sense that the paths of socially accumulated knowledge cannot be retraced. Therefore, beautifying the past is perfectly meaningless. However, there is a degree of autonomy in choosing means, setting goals, and thereby picking what laws will govern the process, what the relation with the environment will be, what knowledge will be procured and what society will be shaped. There is qualitative choice. The search for alternatives is a search for what are perceived to be improved techniques in conscious pursuit of specific individual goals, which gather up force to become social choices with increased impact due to large numbers. This search is a mute exploration which, in the case of success, leads to mute affirmation. Societal choices are made at every stage, especially at where each member and the society as whole affirm such success. The way things stand with today's capitalism, affirmation documents and establishes itself as personal power at one level and as expansionary or growth potential at a higher. Concerning production, there is no need to invoke convincing arguments about this. After Schumpeter, entrepreneurship is understood in antagonistic terms, which Keynes characterized explicitly as animalish. But one still needs to explain that consumption, too, is an antagonistic engagement for power by expropriation of human time-space through behavioural patterns that develop in this direction: from natural soap to allergy-causing cosmetic soaps, from tap water to bottled water of often dubious quality and at a price far greater than that of gasoline, from home cooking to junk food, etc.

Given this congruence of intent, capitalistic advance may be unspecifiable in its details, but it is neither accidental nor arbitrary. It is a creative activity aimed at appropriating vital time-space through monopolistic *and monopsonistic* advantages deriving from two kinds of innovation. It is based on the human capacity to generate knowledge for private advantage, increasing as it becomes diffused and socially exploited our control over the environment, which includes other humans, through our relation with whom we interpret the content of our lives within this expanded environment. In the post-industrial world, exclusive knowledge has become a strategic resource for the individual and for society. Under such circumstances, a publicly financed education system appears as an anachronistic contradiction, which is why these are currently replaced by privately financed training camps, letting those who can pay get better training in the art of expropriating time-space.

Innovation impulses change flows, inducing structure changes that expand growth potential, which is a potential of increased expropriation from nature, from other economies, from other firms and from other individuals. These impulses promote qualitative changes to products, methods and types of work, and flexibility in the distribution of income. But how do they affect people? Quickness of change makes it difficult to assess all impacts, in time. Psychological effects, disruption of social cohesion, reduced diversity caused by globalization and increased vulnerability due to integrated complexity or due to globalized homogenization of methods, commodities, cultures, etc., are modern causes of concern that have not been adequately explored. Selfish behaviour induced by an accentuated perception of scarcity results in a type of human that dodges its fears, compromises its self-awareness and progresses in a direction which makes social systems more vulnerable to environmental or other perturbations and more dependent on continued availability of the types of entropy on which it relies and uses up at increasing rates (e.g. fossil fuels). At the other open end, entropy of wastes (worn out means of production and wasted consumer items) becomes increasingly difficult to cope with. (The assimilation problem.)

The above suggest that among requisite entropy forms should be included also what could be called *social entropy*. Social capital – in the form of family, neighborhood and other bonds, norms, traditions, etc., which enhance trust, mutual concern, solidarity, honesty, transparency in relations and participation in social values – is used up into labour-divided production and solipsistic techno-conformant consumption in a stampede for time-space through coincidence of antagonistic interests. This is a conditionally binding pact: Being a positive feedback one, it is potentially self-defeating in the long run, by malignantly consuming its own diversity. In complex adaptive schemata constituted by many different subsystems, every change to one of those induces changes to the environment of all others. So, the type and speed of changes to any one component may affect the integrated performance of the others and thus reduce overall system fitness, affecting adversely its prospects. The speed of capitalistic changes in the economic sphere puts under pressure all components of the evolving social structure and may jeopardize social homeostasis. The pendulum in the international fora on sustainable development, where relative emphasis swings between environmental and social concerns, is indicative of this. It acknowledges the fact that HS is an integral part of ES, but it is environment to PS (from which the latter draws a sublime flow) and a bearer of its consequences. Thus, a disruptive process is currently taking place in the political and general cultural (which includes religious) arena, internationally. So, through consumer solipsism, we may run out of social entropy, lapsing into war of all against all.

However, as far as relates to material aspects, it needs to be stressed that structural growth concerns *economic value*, which does not stand in any straightforward or fixed relationship with the material inputs employed. In fact, technological advance constantly changes this relationship, often reducing material inputs, as when communications services reduce transportation requirements. But there is always a material underbase for value so that, overall, and in the long run, the expansionary aspects of growth work to increase system thermodynamic negentropy by processing more material resources, thus increasing pressure on systems at a lower level of organization and increasing environmental entropy. Norbert Wiener termed this avaricious depletion of resources such as lumber, metal ores or environmental quality 'the Traditional American Philosophy of progress' and warned about its consequences. As we noted in Chapter 1, he saw reduction in labour requirements as a result of competition with machines, which have the economic properties of slave labour, and warned that people will either become slaves themselves by accepting the conditions of such competition, or free time will be invested to broadening their personal development.

This is a challenge that technological advance places upon modern societies and its resolution ties up with the efficiency criterion that will be selected, since it is here that is decided what the desired outputs and valuable inputs are. The basic choice is between labour intensity versus capital intensity, which means between ε'-efficiency and a contrasting ε one. In view of the consequences of our having strenuously pursued ε efficiency for a long time, more and more people are coming out arguing for a reversal. Global unemployment conditions and exhaustion of natural resources, especially on the assimilation end of the process, prompt us to consider reversing our historical view of efficiency, towards pursuing modes of production and consumption (modes of life, ultimately) in which labour intensity will not be seen as disgrace or anathema. This seems to provide a sustainable way of conserving the earth's resources while, at the same time, giving content to labour, so as to become less alienating. It may also heed Schumpeter's (1947) warning that capitalism may, by its very success, generate the forces (attitudes and preferences) that undermine the moral foundations of the market process. Actually, it is a homeostasis game inside a narrow preservation band, socially, environmentally and otherwise, where disruptive forces are easy to build up from prolonged excursions outside its limits. And ubiquitous violence, depression and alienation all indicate that social limits may be presently violated at rates comparable with those at which environmental limits are also exceeded.

Now, how does self-awareness, which we have invoked, enter the selection spoken above, and how does its absence enter the Aristippean domination of people by wants that capitalism makes flourish? Lawson (1997: 279) gives the answer:

[T]he possibility of emancipatory social change requires not merely shared real needs or interests but, equally, a self-awareness of these needs and interests. Needs and rights can be formulated as goals or wants or demands, and treated as legitimate or illegitimate, only under definite historical conditions. As such they may be poorly, and even misleadingly formulated. Specifically, real needs can be manifest in a variety of historically contingent wants, which may then be met by any of perhaps a multitude of potential satisfiers. ... To assume that either actual satisfiers, for example specific commodities purchased, or expressed objectives, such as owning more than others, are defining of human needs is to commit the epistemic fallacy all over again, albeit this time in an ethical form – to reduce needs to wants and wants to the conditions of their being satisfied or expressed. ... But the two, real needs and expressed wants, should not be conflated. Yet in contemporary orthodox economics the individuals' needs and rights are precisely collapsed onto preferences, tastes and wants, and measured by the purchases made or whatever.

Epilogue

Faith helps one find peace of mind, but science is Odyssean. And for Odysseans it is the journey that counts, not any reachable destination. Ours was a journey into self-awareness, a most scary of places. So, we sought support early on, citing Hume's view that an opinion is not certainly false 'because 'tis of dangerous consequences', and then continued in a provoking manner to contend that economics in general and consumption in particular are about life-taking. Still, few will concur that they take life when they buy a washing machine, hamburger or automobile, or that they are thus trying to be capitalists, or that private property is about depriving others of time-space. These seem strange to be frank, but reality is strangest. In the citadels of capitalism one risks being shot point blank for ignoring this grave warning: PRIVATE PROPERTY. NO TRESPASSING!

When the findings of a thinker are such as to enrage society or to clash with its interests, it is so much the worse for the thinker. And it was so much the worse for Hobbes who maintained that

> It may seem strange to some man, that has not well weighed these things; that Nature should thus dissociate, and render men apt to invade, and destroy one another: and he may therefore, not trusting to this Inference, made from the Passions, desire perhaps to have the same confirmed by Experience. Let him therefore consider with himselfe, when taking a journey, he armes himselfe, and seeks to go well accompanied; when going to sleep, he locks his dores; when even in his house he locks his chests; and this when he knows there bee Lawes, and publike Officers, armed, to revenge all injuries shall bee done him; what opinion he has of his fellow subjects, when he rides armed; of his fellow Citizens, when he locks his dores; and of his children, and servants, when he locks his chests. Does he not there as much accuse mankind by his actions, as I do by my words? But neither of us accuse mans nature in it. The Desires, and other Passions of man, are in themselves no Sin. No more are the Actions, that proceed from those Passions, till they know a Law that forbids them: which till Lawes be made they cannot know: nor can any Law be made, till they have agreed upon the Person that shall make it.

(Hobbes, 1991: 89)

Given the nature of the things Hobbes said, the neglect his theories met with attests more to their truth than to their falsehood. But he was not alone. In more genial but no less unequivocal terms, Hume distinguished similar traits in the behaviour of people and insisted on the usefulness of underlying uniformities. Since this sits at the basis of our argument, we quote him extensively, as excused also by our finishing:

> [A] traveller wou'd meet with as little credit, who shou'd inform us of people exactly of the same character with those in *Plato*'s *Republic* on the one hand, or those in *Hobbes*'s *Leviathan* on the other. There is a general course of nature in human actions, as well as in the operations of the sun and the climate. There are also characters peculiar to different nations and particular persons, as well as common to mankind. The knowledge of these characters is founded on the observation of an uniformity in the actions, that flow from them; and this uniformity forms the very essence of necessity.
>
> I can imagine only one way of eluding this argument, which is by denying that uniformity of human actions, on which it is founded. As long as actions have a constant union and connexion with the situation and temper of the agent, however we may in words refuse to acknowledge the necessity, we really allow the thing. Now some may, perhaps, find a pretext to deny this regular union and connexion. For what is more capricious than human actions? What more inconstant than the desires of man? And what creature departs more widely, not only from right reason, but from his own character and disposition?... Necessity is regular and certain. Human conduct is irregular and uncertain. The one, therefore, proceeds not from the other.
>
> To this I reply, that in judging of the actions of men we must proceed upon the same maxims, as when we reason concerning external objects. When any phænomena are constantly and invariably conjoin'd together, they acquire such a connexion in the imagination, that it passes from one to the other, without any doubt or hesitation. But below this there are many inferior degrees of evidence and probability, nor does one single contrariety of experiment entirely destroy all our reasoning. The mind balances the contrary experiments, and deducting the inferior from the superior, proceeds with that degree of assurance or evidence, which remains. Even when these contrary experiments are entirely equal, we remove not the notion of causes and necessity; but supposing that the usual contrariety proceeds from the operation of contrary and conceal'd causes, we conclude, that the chance or indifference lies only in our judgment on account of our imperfect knowledge, not in the things themselves, which are in every case equally necessary, tho' to appearance not equally constant or certain. No union can be more constant and certain, than that of some actions with some motives and characters;
>
> (Hume, 2000: 259–60)

In this report we sought the foundations of the said uniformity in Kierkegaardian Existentialism. But as Kierkegaard's was not a cheerful message and his subjectivism asserted that only what we construe and construct with our minds is there, we invited the reader with a gesture by Terentianus Maurus to improve or correct our gloomy findings before rushing to dismiss the entire argument with repugnance, for its being despicable or 'of dangerous consequences'. However, bold lines were drawn that may not be crossed, without lapsing back into empty theorizing. And the boldest of those is that no theory of economic systems in general and of capitalism in particular can make sense, which does not entertain honestly consumers with a realistic ontology. Barring this, it's all beating about the bush.

In the 1960s, hippies chanted: 'Eat it up, wear it out, make it do or do without'. Had they put this into effect, capitalism would be a memory now. But in flowery confusion they added an Aristippean clause: 'We want it ALL, and we want it NOW!' One cannot have it both ways, though, and the road from Lucy in the Sky with Diamonds to diamonds proved to be a short one. Same with sludging 'C'est pour toi que tu fait la revolution' with battle cries like: 'Nous sommes le pouvoir'. As it turned out, without self-awareness, these were excellent recipe for anything between perfect resignation and extreme neo-liberalism. Discontent places power against power. Which one will win may be uncertain, but the gain has always been with certainty nil. After a period of improving work, pay, and living conditions won through struggle, populations in the West became placid, indulging in feverish consumption. These made it appear as if capitalism were a final stage. Some even came to speak about the end of all history.

But one may visit the matter from an opposite angle. According to legend, Nezredin Hodja was a wise man in the East, and when a tyrant ruler who was facing discontent by the impoverished masses asked for his advice, he admonished: 'Levy more taxes.' 'But,' objected the ruler, 'they already complain about the ones they have to pay now!' 'Levy more taxes!' insisted he. So, the ruler increased taxes, and these went on for three consecutive years, until people stopped complaining, apparently subdued and resigned to their fate. Arrogantly, in the fourth year, the ruler increased taxes once more, without bothering to ask Hodja this time. When Hodja heard about it, he rushed to the palace yelling: 'Why did you do this?' 'Well', the tyrant exclaimed in surprise, 'you advised me to increase taxes when they complained and you chide me now for doing so when they don't?' To which Hodja replied: 'It is *now* that you ought to be concerned, not when they complained!'

The story does not tell us what happened next, and we will shun making prognoses about the future of capitalism, as we refrained from prescribing, or making poignant appeals to right, justice, or sentiment, since capitalism dilutes moral considerations into a vulturous ethic, so that they can no longer be invoked against it. So, we do not, in all good faith, subscribe to the hope that 'Possibly the model of the world as a great organization can help to reinforce the sense of reverence for the living which we have almost lost in the last sanguinary decades of human history' (Bertalanffy, 1969: 49). But if we were to follow Hodja, we should not find many good omens for capitalism, in today's blissful resignation of placid consuming populations.

To repeat: Discontent may ignite social revolt, but it cannot promote emancipating change. Such change takes enhanced self-awareness, which presupposes overcoming metaphysical fear, a fear which is in final analysis fear of our own selves and of others. With such self-awareness, Schumpeter's cited prognosis about the overcoming of capitalism may turn out to be an emancipating development. Without it, one metaphysical absurdity will be lined up against another, as it seems that we are witnessing these days. The ultimate test of dignity and excellence is in the way we face death, which means in the way we treat life. All power is founded upon fear, and at the base of all fear sits the fear of death. This is why religious obscurantism was never defeated and remained at the service of power, including that of the supposedly secular, democratic capitalist state.

Fear ignites aggression for control through power over things, over nature, and over humans. Having never come to terms with existential fear, our aggression keeps historically mounting. Under normal circumstances, capitalism channels aggression institutionally towards devouring each other's time-space through speculative innovation, by reaping from the commons, within an economy and between economies. But brute force is also employed, as fits the occasion. This makes us falter between all-out individualism and fighting jointly against what we consider to be nature's hostile power: the power to wear us out through its second law, which gnaws on our physical presence. Thus, we wear ourselves out, trying to make *private* what belongs to all, alienating ourselves from each other and from the product of our labour, that is, from ourselves, ending up to roam lonesome among alien, hostile crowds, gulping antidepressants and burying ourselves under mountains of industrial garbage. It is worth visiting words and noting that 'private', whose Latin root we saw to be in 'deprive', is ἰδιωτικός, in Greek, from which derives ἰδιωτεία, the medical term for a mental disorder commonly known as idiocy. In every case, we may call this *shameless capitalism*, for it is in shameless wastefulness that we behave towards each other and towards nature: a rapacious religion.

Social criticism is criticism of society. It is not an act of incriminating a few in order to vindicate the many, siding and weeping with the victims for having failed, for the time being, that is, to become victimizers. (If this were not so, it would heal patients if doctors sat and wept beside them.) A more just world cannot be grounded on pity or sympathy, which are disgracing sentiments. Social advance and personal elevation above cattle grade take compassion and self-awareness. To understand the world we must first understand language. Compassion must not be confused with pity. Compassion is a personal disposition of being able to share in another's equally personal emotional state. Pity bears the stains of disgrace, insidious calculativeness and despicable arrogance, of one who is spared of some harsh condition. It is the vestige of a lost innocence, reminding of the bookshelves in petty bourgeois houses, as decorative reminiscences of the lost intellectuality of the bourgeois class; as displays of social atavism. When the capacity for compassion withers, philanthropy flourishes. Then, we can fight AIDS, famine, drought, child abuse and any calamity that we ourselves help inflict upon others by sending our celebrities on tours through Africa, with lots of cameramen. That works for the celebrities, who cash in on thus gained publicity, but not for the victims. The trouble (for us) is that now everyone knows (except us).

Wherever one may turn, one can find specimens of intentional linguistic confusion. The first victim of such confusion is freedom: *our* freedom, which has come to be construed as one's right to disagree, as long as one does not put to risk the interests of those who hold the power to decide how free others can be.

The misconception, due to the imperceptibility fallacy, is that those are only some bad few, who control power. The truth, as anyone who happens to differ or dares to dissent knows, is that anonymous masses ('silent majorities', etc.) insidiously have great such powers.

But linguistic confusion harms also theorizing. One may think of neoclassicism as being unrealistic, autistic or irrelevant, which it may actually be. But there is more than what such language shows. Actually, there is much that such language helps obscure. And it obscures that neoclassicism is pure ideology. At a minimum, social critique must make sure that the use it makes of language does not make it confuse its own vision as fact. Critics need to confront that people have been charmed by capitalism, promoting it with their deliberate conduct, in resigned ignorance. But ignorance is no excuse, no loss to some bad luck, or an alibi. Ignorance is a choice. People are not willing to jeopardize their relative material affluence, wasting their time in search for any loftier kind of knowledge than the practical one about how to get the most out of the present capitalist set-up. What obstructs lofty explorations is so deeply rooted that the search for better social arrangement is far more demanding and precarious than critics have been willing to admit.

These make searching an urgent priority. Disillusionment is setting in with people, as the net yield from capitalistic growth is little more than growing depression and aggression. On the faces of ordinary people, acquisitive conflict paints no elation, but moodiness and tenseness that put to doubt its benefits. Social welfare, which advocates of capitalism claim is promoted, must be some strange kind of good. But if such disillusionment finds vent with reduced self-awareness, without adequate knowledge about motives, causes and effects, little good may obtain, and there is good chance that society may even lapse back into some new kind of obscure slavery.

As far as pedestrian Marxism is concerned, there are many questions remaining unanswered by assuming, in oblivion to Marx's other (lesser?) writings and through a glass of misplaced materialism, that material affluence is unconditionally desirable, once exploitation is abolished; that it becomes a legitimate claim on nature, to which we may all share without limits. It is hard to dispute that freedom has material preconditions, as maintained by Marx. But it also has immaterial ones, and they can all be subverted by materialistic extravagance caused by metaphysical fear. With all scarcities stemming from a single one, namely, that of life, affluence will remain zero-sum, conflictive and vain, unless cultural changes intervene that advance our perspective to life and death, the ways we pursue affluence, and the use we make of it.

Historical events and everyday social developments have taken over economic theory, which can no longer go by with skirmishes between competing descriptions. Social dynamics can no longer be adequately explained or described by means of rigid social divisions, where some exploit some others or, contrarily, some provide through their creative entrepreneurship jobs and income to others. Social relations are more integrated, intertwined, complex, volatile and dynamic, and globalization has raised issues which set new investigative requirements that need crossing into fields formerly treated as foreign. The Freudian method has called attention to the fact that history has also a psychological underbase, which Marx largely evaded as, in spite of his acclaimed historicism, he refrained from explaining what 'control over nature' really meant and implied. He chose to base his theory not on psychological forces that drive people to behave as they do, but on the social forces that develop upon those. He considered explanation at lower levels as immaterial or vulgar and chose to initiate his search not from emergence, but from a stage where there has already developed a particular *mode of production*. Given the industrial mode, Marx's conclusions were hard to dispute. But at issue is the *genesis* of such modes, none of which may be considered as final. Without knowing about such *geneses* we cannot anticipate or understand future developments, make less partial judgements and better predictions.

For our part, we observed people as they pursued capital, that is, knowledge *past*, while minimizing their *present* expenditure trying to expand their presence into the *future*; into experienced time-space. Over the two sides of the economic process in tandem, this promotes roundaboutness, picturing consumers as capitalists, albeit in a way that misses on their part the all too important distinction between productive capital (reusable knowledge) and capital used up. In terms of theorizing, these fail a number of standard conventions, by radical reinterpretation of the notions of scarcity and self-interest.

Such newness at the level of basics entails the risk of confusion, or of negative emotional reaction that can throw the baby out with the bathwater. But Michael Polanyi has explained the anthropocentric commitment and tacit dimension of knowledge. By 'discovery of rationality in nature' he meant that 'the kind of order which the discoverer claims to see in nature goes far beyond his understanding; so that his triumph lies precisely in his foreknowledge of a host of yet hidden implications which his discovery will reveal in later days to other eyes' (Polanyi, 1958/62: 64). And he added:

> It is the act of commitment in its full structure that saves personal knowledge from being merely subjective. Intellectual commitment is a responsible decision, in submission to the compelling claims of what in good conscience I conceive to be true. It is an act of hope, striving to fulfil an obligation within a personal situation for which I am not responsible and which therefore determines my calling. This hope and this obligation are expressed in the universal intent of personal knowledge.
>
> (Ibid.: 65)

And this is the kind of hope and obligation that Nietzsche, whom we put up front, bequeathed us, as he despised, along with Hesse, the wolf sinking low in his angst to survive. Thus, he wrote in a letter he addressed to Kaiser Wilhelm II in December of 1888:

> *Es giebt neue Hoffnungen, es giebt Ziele,*
> *Aufgaben von einer Größe für die der Begriff bis jetzt fehlte ...*
> *There are new Hopes, there are Goals,*
> *Tasks of an Excellence which still seeks its Content ...*

Notes

1 Theory, society and consumption

1 Cattle life: βοσκημάτων βίος, in Greek. Sardanapallus (Assurbanipal) was a mythical Assyrian king, the epitome of capricious, frivolous conduct.
2 Before they had time to realize what was happening, those who pressed modern China to open its doors to foreign trade rushed panic-stricken to seal off their houses from the beehive. And before long, the Chinese, too, will go through the same experiences.
3 What distinguishes this type of democracy from the aristocracy inspired by Aristotle is not that it is the rule of the many, but that it is the rule of the mean. If the mean were not many, if the many were noble (Greek: ἄριστοι), then these systems of governance would coincide.
4 In early AD 2005, the US Senate had to legislate against use of cruel and inhumane methods in the interrogation of 'detainees' held for years without charges. In November of that year, the Director of the CIA confirmed that no torture is used; only 'enhanced interrogation methods.' These include refusing to disclose relevant data, upon the argument that that would infringe upon the victims' privacy rights. The courts did not uphold such insolence and ruled against it. So, on 6 September 2006, The President himself named them 'alternate interrogation techniques.' Yes! Now, we can rest assured.

2 Critical overview

1 Fifth century BC Athenian philosopher, pupil of Socrates, founder of the Cynic school of philosophy.
2 The dynamic Leontief equation provides a good example of such failure. Although technical, its original dynamics aspirations were far more ambitious. Its 'complete instability' and 'causal indeterminacy' were debated for about 40 years by a large number of top economists, often in a heated way. Yet, as noted by Steenge (1990): 'A wide variety of explanations has been given, … none of which has been convincing. In practice, the problem was circumvented by developing alternative structures'. In the end, further discussion was repulsed, although, as Steenge again pointed out, understanding what went wrong should in itself be valuable in terms of the broader issue of economic dynamics. Nevertheless, the model was not displaced entirely from textbooks, providing a panoramic display of the strained relationship of economic theory with time.
3 For instance, he argued that 'So little are men govern'd by reason in their sentiments and opinions, that they always judge more of objects by comparison than from their intrinsic worth and value' (op. cit.: 240). This Hume considered to be 'an *original* quality of the soul, and similar to what we have every day experience of in our bodies' (ibid., original emphasis), which may well be seen as alluding to existence. And beyond that, Hume also asserted that 'as we seldom judge of objects from their intrinsic value, but from our

notions of them from a comparison with other objects; it follows, that according as we observe a greater or less share of happiness or misery in others, we must make an estimate of our own, and feel a consequent pain or pleasure. The misery of another gives us a more lively idea of our happiness, and his happiness of our misery. The former, therefore, produces delight; and the latter uneasiness' (ibid.: 242). And: 'The direct survey of another's pleasure naturally gives us pleasure, and therefore produces pain when compar'd with our own. His pain, consider'd in itself, is painful to us, but augments the idea of our own happiness, and gives us pleasure' (ibid.). Finally, 'envy is excited by some present enjoyment of another, which by comparison diminishes our idea of our own: Whereas malice is the unprovok'd desire of producing evil to another, in order to reap a pleasure from the comparison. But even in the case of an inferiority, we still desire a greater distance, in order to augment still more the idea of ourself. When this distance diminishes, the comparison is less to our advantage; and consequently gives us less pleasure, and is even disagreeable. Hence arises that species of envy, which men feel, when they perceive their inferiors approaching or overtaking them in the pursuits of glory or happiness' (ibid.: 243).

4 One may say with the Catholics that 'Every man is for himself and God is *with* all' or, with Werner Herzog, that 'Every man is for himself and God is *against* all.' But more to our point, to Hobbesian 'warre ... of every man, against every man' (Hobbes, 1991: 88), which he saw outside the power of a Civil State construed as an arbitrary and all-powerful sovereign, this report's undeclared 'war' drives the performance of the most civil of all known states: the capitalist states.

3 The life project

1 For someone who lives in a place where schooling or the threat of the law have curbed noise making, littering on public places or parking on sidewalks, the life-scorching fascism of such habits may be difficult to comprehend. But there are places with a 24-hour noise culture (a honking culture) that one may visit, if one wants to find out. (This time, if I show you around one such place you must pay me a fee.) Even music intrudes and violates the time-space of others when imposed on them at high volume.

2 Exchanging unequal values has been an issue in theories like Coase's, where transaction costs are acknowledged as: 'costs of acquiring the knowledge which is necessary to make transactions or the costs of making arrangements to counteract the irremediable lack of knowledge about the future' (Loasby, op. cit.: 76). In the presence of knowledge-acquisition costs, Hayek was interested in how a market can function as a well-co-ordinated mechanism, when each agent acts according to his particular and incomplete knowledge.

3 Cattle, too, walk in line while grazing, but they always look for new green patches, at the same time, while also keeping an eye on each other. Only, they would not be offended by the analogy with people.

4 Production innovations

1 Fixity of A implies fixity of R and p and, by extension, of d and of factor prices. These are extremely unlikely. Steady-state (4.1) is fictitious and should not be seen as a long-period position or as an attraction point. It is only made use of here for expositional purposes and for facilitating understanding of some of the propounded ideas.

2 With respect to our further decomposition of (4.1) into (4.1'), these vectors align if d is along v_F^R. Similarly, K, VA and x align when vector p is along v_F^{RT}. So, all vectors K, VA, y, Ax and x align when d is along v_F^R and p is along v_F^{RT}.

3 For a discussion of issues relating to heterogeneity, see Cantner and Hanusch (op. cit.). Here, we restrict to the observation that our discussion assumes no change to the

disaggregation scheme, if comparisons are to be valid. But other heterogeneities between two economies, even assuming the same sector scheme for both, makes comparisons between them rather precarious.

4 In biological terms, these, along with outdated and abandoned routines, correspond to conditionally neutral alleles, which provide a potential source of genetic flexibility, if they can be stored. They add variability that enhances a system's adaptability in the face of unpredictable changes to its environment. Thus, progressive evolution: (a) reduces the need to generate random variance by exercising control over the system's environment, (b) enhances capacity for generating polymorphic variance and (c) stores such variance in temporarily ineffective but readily recoverable forms.

5 This guarantees that, for every non-negative final demand vector, there are non-negative solutions to both the physical output system and to the system of prices.

6 This is a simplified, strictly economic description, but the actual process has widespread ramifications. Overwhelming of social life by the dictates of the market for the purpose of dominance, along with job requirements of a narrow scope for each working person, need alienated specialists and technocrats rather than socially aware and sensitive scientists and citizens.

7 So, maybe Protagoras's practice to let his students decide the value they set upon the knowledge he offered them and to accept a fee of that amount was much truer to the real situation, than any of the later theories of value.

5 Consumption innovations

1 One may view these pleasant arousals as incentives for guiding conduct towards the life-expanding (or just life-preserving) goal more effectively. (Pleasing the palate so as to entice someone to eat food, enjoying warm clothing so as to avoid freezing to death, etc.) But real explanation must reach to the root. Besides, all that could be drawn from higher-level incentives has already been drawn by orthodox theories.

Bibliography

Abramovitz, M. (1989) *Thinking About Growth*, Cambridge: Cambridge University Press.

Ackerman, F. (2002) 'Flaws in the foundation: consumer behavior and general equilibrium theory', in E. Fullbrook (ed.) *Intersubjectivity in Economics: Agents and Structures*, London: Routledge.

Ackoff, L. R. (1991) 'Science in the systems age: beyond IE, OR, and MS', in G. J. Klir (ed.) *Trends in General Systems Theory*, New York: Wiley-Interscience.

Adams, R. N. (1981) 'Natural selection, energetics and "cultural materialism"', *Current Anthropology*, 22 (6): 603–24.

Addleson, M. (1995) *Equilibrium Versus Understanding: Towards the Restoration of Economics as a Social Theory*, London: Routledge.

Alchian, A. A. (1950) 'Uncertainty, evolution and economic theory', *Journal of Political Economy*, 58: 211–21.

Allen, P. M. (2001) 'Knowledge, ignorance and the evolution of complex systems', in J. Foster and J. S. Metcalfe (eds) *Frontiers of Evolutionary Economics: Competition, Self-organization and Innovation Policy*, Cheltenham, UK, Northampton, MA: Edward Elgar.

Antonelli, C. (2003) *The Economics of Innovation, New Technologies and Structural Change*, London: Routledge.

Aristotle (1934) *Nicomachean Ethics*, Cambridge, MA: Harvard University Press, Loeb Classical Library. (First published 1926.)

Arnsperger, C. and Y. Varoufakis (2006) 'What is neoclassical economics?', *Post-autistic Economics Review*, Issue no. 38.

Ashby, W. R. (1954) *Design for a Brain*, New York: John Wiley. (Revised edition 1960.)

Becker, G. S. and C. B. Mulligan (1997) 'The endogenous determination of time preferences', *Quarterly Journal of Economics*, 112: 729–58.

Beer, S. (1994) *Platform for Change*, Chichester: John Wiley & Sons Ltd., reprinted in Stafford Beer Classic Library. (First published 1975, correct reprint 1978.)

Bertalanffy, L. von (1969) *General System Theory: Foundations, Development Applications*, New York: George Braziller.

Bianchi, M. (ed.) (1998) *The Active Consumer: Novelty and Surprise in Consumer Choice*, London: Routledge.

Blaug, M. (1997) 'Ugly currents in modern economics', *Options Politiques*, September: 3–8.

Boulding, K. E. (1966) 'The economics of knowledge and the knowledge of economics', *American Economic Review* (Papers and Proceedings), 56: 1–13.

Bowles, S. (1998) 'Endogenous preferences: the cultural consequences of markets and other economic institutions', *Journal of Economic Literature*, 36: 75–111.

Caldwell, B. (1982) *Beyond Positivism: Economic Methodology in the Twentieth Century*, London: George Allen & Unwin.

Canterbery, R. E. and R. J. Burkhardt (1983) 'What do we mean by asking whether economics is a science?', in Alfred S. Eichner (ed.) *Why Economics Is Not Yet a Science*, London: Macmillan.

Cantner, U. and H. Hanusch (2001) 'Heterogeneity and evolutionary change: empirical conception, findings and unresolved issues', in J. Foster and J. S. Metcalfe (eds) *Frontiers of Evolutionary Economics: Competition, Self-organization and Innovation Policy*, Cheltenham, UK, Northampton, MA: Edward Elgar.

Carter, A. (1970) *Structural Change in the American Economy*, Cambridge, MA: Harvard University Press.

Coddington, A. (1972) 'Positive economics', *Canadian Journal of Economics*, 5 (1): 1–15.

Crafts, N. (1999) 'Economic growth in the twentieth century', *Oxford Review of Economic Policy*, 15 (4): 18–34.

Daly, H. E. (1989) 'Steady-state and growth concepts for the next century', in Archibugi, F. and P. Nijkamp (eds) *Economy and Ecology: Towards Sustainable Development*, Dordrecht: Kluwer Academic Publishers.

Desai, M. (2002) *Marx's Revenge: The Resurgence of Capitalism and the Death of Statist Socialism*, London and New York: Verso.

Dietzenbacher, E. (1990) 'Seton's eigenprices: further evidence', *Economic Systems Research*, 2 (2): 103–23.

Di Ruzza, R. and J. Halevi (2004) 'How to look at economics critically: some suggestions', in E. Fullbrook (ed.) *A Guide to what's Wrong with Economics*, London: Anthem Press.

Dobb, M. (1972) [1937] 'The trend of modern economics', in E. K. Hunt and J. G. Schwartz (eds) *A Critique of Economic Theory*, Harmondsworth: Penguin. (Originally in *Political Economy and Capitalism*, London: Routledge and Kegan Paul.)

Dopfer, K. (2001) 'History-friendly theories in economics: reconciling universality and context in evolutionary analysis', in J. Foster and J. S. Metcalfe (eds) *Frontiers of Evolutionary Economics: Competition, Self-organization and Innovation Policy*, Cheltenham, UK, Northampton, MA: Edward Elgar.

Dopfer, K. (2005) 'Evolutionary economics: a theoretical framework', in K. Dopfer (ed.) *The Evolutionary Foundations of Economics*, Cambridge: Cambridge University Press.

Duesenberry, J. S. (1967) *Income, Saving and the Theory of Consumer Behavior*, Cambridge, MA: Harvard University Press.

Dupuy, J. P. (1996) 'The anatomy of social reality: on the contribution of systems theory to the theory of society', in E. L. Khalil and K. E. Boulding (eds) *Evolution, Order and Complexity*, London: Routledge.

Easterlin, R. (1972) 'Does economic growth improve the human lot?', in P. A. David and M. W. Reder (eds) *Nations and Households in Economic Growth: Essays in Honor of Moses Abramovitz*, Stanford, CA: Stanford University Press.

Edney, J. (2005) 'Greed (Part I)' and 'Greed (Part II)', *Post-autistic Economics Review*, Issues no. 31, 32, http://www.paecon.net/PAEReview/issue31/Edney31.htm (accessed 26 June 2006).

Eichner, A. S. (ed.) (1983) *Why Economics Is Not Yet a Science*, London: Macmillan.

Einstein, A. (1954) *Ideas and Opinions*, New York: Wings Books.

Feuerbach, L. (1957) *The Essence of Christianity*, New York: Harper and Row.

Foster, J. (2000) 'Competitive selection, self-organization and Joseph A. Schumpeter', *Journal of Evolutionary Economics*, 10: 311–28.

Franke, R. (2000) 'An integration of schumpeterian and classical theories of growth and distribution', *Structural Change and Economic Dynamics*, 11: 317–36.

Friedman, M. (1953) *Essays in Positive Economics*, Chicago, IL: University of Chicago Press.

Fromm, E. (2004) *Marx's Concept of Man*, London and New York: Continuum.

Fullbrook, E. (2002) 'An intersubjective theory of value', in E. Fullbrook (ed.) *Intersubjectivity in Economics: Agents and Structures*, London: Routledge.

Fullbrook, E. (2005) 'The rand portcullis and PAE', *Post-autistic Economics Review*, Issue no. 32, http://www.paecon.net/PAEReview/issue32/Fullbrook32.htm (accessed 26 June 2006).

Gell-Mann, M. (1995) *The Quark and the Jaguar: Adventures in the Simple and the Complex*, London: Abacus.

Georgescu-Roegen, N. (1966) *Analytical Economics*, Cambridge, MA: Harvard University Press.

Georgescu-Roegen, N. (1971) *The Entropy Law and the Economic Process*, Cambridge, MA: Harvard University Press.

Giddens, A. (1984) *The Constitution of Society*, Cambridge: Polity Press.

Gifford, A. Jr (2002) 'Emotion and self-control', *Journal of Economic Behavior & Organization*, 49: 113–30.

Gordon, J. M. and J. S. Rosenthal (2003) 'Capitalism's growth imperative', *Cambridge Journal of Economics*, 27: 25–48.

Hage, J. (ed.) (1998) *Organizational Innovation*, Aldershot: Dartmouth/Ashgate.

Hargreaves Heap, S. P. (2004) 'Living in an affluent society: it is so "more-ish"', *Post-autistic Economics Review*, Issue no. 26, http://www.paecon.net/PAEReview/issue26/Heap26.htm (accessed 26 June 2006).

Hayek, F. A. (1945) 'The use of knowledge in society', *American Economic Review*, 35 (4): 519–30.

Hayek, F. A. (1952) *The Sensory Order*, Chicago, IL: University of Chicago Press.

Hicks, J. (1932) *Theory of Wages*, London: Macmillan.

Hirsch, F. (1977) *Social Limits to Growth*, London: Routledge and Kegan Paul Ltd.

Hobbes, T. (1991) *Leviathan*, Cambridge: Cambridge University Press. (First published in 1651.)

Hodgson, G. N. (1988) *Economics and Institutions: A Manifesto for a Modern Institutional Economics*, Cambridge: Polity Press.

Hodgson, G. N. (1993) *Economics and Evolution: Bringing Life Back into Economics*, Cambridge: Polity Press.

Hodgson, G. N. (1999) *Economics and Utopia: Why the Learning Economy is Not the End of History*, London: Routledge.

Hodgson, G. N. (2002) 'Reconstitutive downward causation: social structure and the development of individual agency', in E. Fullbrook (ed.) *Intersubjectivity in Economics: Agents and Structures*, London: Routledge.

Hollis, M. (1991) 'Penny pinching and backward induction', *The Journal of Philosophy*, 88: 473–88.

Hollis, M. and R. Sugden (1993) 'Rationality in action', *Mind*, 102: 1–35.

Holub, H. W., G. Tappeiner and V. Eberharter (1992) 'The iron law of important articles', *Southern Economic Journal*, 58 (2): 317–28.

Hong, H. V. and E. H. Hong (ed. and trans.) (1967) *Søren Kierkegaard's Journals and Papers*, Vol. 1, Bloomington and London: Indiana University Press.

Hume, D. (2000) *A Treatise of Human Nature*, Oxford: Oxford University Press.

Jorgenson, D. W. (1995) *Productivity*, Cambridge, MA: MIT Press.

Kahneman, D., E. Diener and N. Schwarz (eds) (1999) *Well-being: The Foundations of Hedonic Psychology*, New York: Russell Sage Foundation.

Kalman, R. E. (1980) 'A system-theoretic critique of dynamic economic models', *Journal of Policy Analysis and Information Systems*, 4 (1): 3–22.

Kardiner, A. (1945) *The Psychological Frontiers of Society*, New York, London: Columbia University Press.

Kasser, T. (2002) *The High Price of Materialism*, Cambridge, MA: MIT Press.

Kaye-Blake, W. (2006) 'Economics is structured like a language', *Post-autistic Economics Review*, Issue no. 36, http://www.paecon.net/PAEReview/issue36/KayeBlake36.htm (accessed 26 June 2006).

Keynes, J. M. (1936) *The General Theory of Employment, Interest and Money*, London: Macmillan.

Kincaid, H. (1996) *Philosophical Foundations of the Social Sciences: Analyzing Controversies in Social Research*, Cambridge: Cambridge University Press.

Kindleberger, C. (1975) 'Germany's overtaking of Britain, 1860–1914', *Weltwirtschaftliches Archiv*.

Knight, F. H. (1923) 'The ethics of competition', *Quarterly Journal of Economics*, 37: 579–624, reprinted in Knight, F. H. (1935) *The Ethics of Competition and Other Essays*, London: George Allen and Unwin.

Kornai, J. (1971) *Anti-Equilibrium: On Economic Systems Theory and the Tasks of Research*, Amsterdam, London: North-Holland Publishing Company.

Krugman, P. (2000) *The Return of Depression Economics*, London, New York: Penguin Books.

Kuznets, S. (1972) 'Innovations and adjustments in economic growth', *Swedish Journal of Economics*, 4: 431–51.

Laborit, H. (1996) 'Neurological and social bases of dominance in human society', in E. L. Khalil and K. E. Boulding (eds) *Evolution, Order and Complexity*, London: Routledge.

Lachmann, L. M. (1959) 'Professor Shackle on the economic significance of time', *Metroeconomica*, xi: 64–73.

Landes, D. (1969) *The Unbound Prometheus*, Cambridge: Cambridge University Press.

Lawson, T. (1997) *Economics and Reality*, London: Routledge.

Lawson, T. (2004) 'Modern economics: the problem and a solution', in E. Fullbrook (ed.) *A Guide to What's Wrong with Economics*, London: Anthem Press.

Layard, R. (1980) 'Human satisfaction and public policy', *The Economic Journal*, 90: 737–50.

Layard, R. (2003) 'Happiness: has social science a clue?', Lionel Robbins Memorial Lectures 2002/3, delivered on 3, 4, 5 March 2003 at the London School of Economics.

Layard, R. (2005) *Happiness: Lessons from a New Science*, London: Allen Lane.

Leibenstein, H. (1950) 'Bandwagon, snob, and Veblen effects in the theory of consumers' demand', *Quarterly Journal of Economics*, 64: 183–207.

Loasby, B. J. (1999) *Knowledge, Institutions and Evolution in Economics*, London: Routledge.

Loasby, B. J. (2001a) 'Cognition, imagination and institutions in demand creation', *Journal of Evolutionary Economics*, 11: 7–21.

Loasby, B. J. (2001b) 'Time, knowledge and evolutionary dynamics: why connections matter', *Journal of Evolutionary Economics*, 11: 393–412.

Losman, D. and Shu-Jan Liang (1987) *The Industrial Sector*, Washington National Defense University.

Lotka, A. J. (1926) *Elements of Physical Biology*, Baltimore: Williams and Wilkins.

Louçã, F. (1997) *Turbulence in Economics: An Evolutionary Appraisal of Cycles and Complexity in Historical Processes*, Cheltenham: Edward Elgar.

Lucas, R. E., Jr (1981) *Studies in Business Cycle Theory*, Cambridge, MA: The MIT Press.

McKenzie, L. W. (1963) 'Turnpike theorem for a generalized Leontief model', *Econometrica*, 31 (1–2): 165–80.

Marshall, A. (1920) *Principles of Economics*, 8th ed., London: MacMillan.

Marx, K. (1906) *Capital*, Chicago, IL: Charles H. Kerr & Co.

Marx, K. and F. Engels (eds) (1939) *German Ideology*, New York: International Publishers, Inc.

Mason, R. (2002) 'Conspicuous consumption in economic theory and thought', in E. Fullbrook (ed.) *Intersubjectivity in Economics: Agents and Structures*, London: Routledge.

Mayhew, A. (2002) 'All consumption is conspicuous', in E. Fullbrook (ed.) *Intersubjectivity in Economics: Agents and Structures*, London: Routledge.

Menger, C. (1976) [1871] *Principles of Economics*, translated by J. Dingwall and B. F. Hoselitz, New York: New York University Press.

Mesarovic, M. D. (1972) 'A mathematical theory of general systems', in G. J. Klir (ed.) *Trends in General Systems Theory*, New York: Wiley-Interscience.

Metcalfe, J. S. (1998) *Evolutionary Economics and Creative Destruction*, London: Routledge.

Metcalfe, J. S. (2001) 'Consumption, preferences, and the evolutionary agenda', *Journal of Evolutionary Economics*, 11: 37–58.

Metcalfe, J. S. (2002) 'Knowledge of growth and the growth of knowledge', *Journal of Evolutionary Economics*, 12: 3–15.

Michéa, J. (1999) *L' enseignement de l'ignorance, et ses conditions modernes*, Paris: Éditions Climats.

Mill, J. S. (1972) [1843] *A System of Logic*, 8th ed., London: Longmans.

Mills, C. W. (1963) *The Marxists*, Harmondsworth: Penguin.

Minsky, M. (1986) *The Society of Mind*, New York: Simon and Schuster.

Mises, L. von (1949) *Human Action: A Treatise on Economics*, London: William Hodge.

Mitchell, W. C. (1937) *The Backward Art of Spending Money and other Essays*, New York: McGraw-Hill.

Mokyr, J. (2005) 'Is there a theory of economic history?', in K. Dopfer (ed.) *The Evolutionary Foundations of Economics*, Cambridge: Cambridge University Press.

Myrdal, G. (1978) 'Political and institutional economics', The Eleventh Geary Lecture. Dublin: Economic and Social Research Institute.

Nelson, R. R. (2001) 'The coevolution of technology and institutions as the driver of economic growth', in J. Foster and J. S. Metcalfe (eds) *Frontiers of Evolutionary Economics: Competition, Self-organization and Innovation Policy*, Cheltenham, UK, Northampton, MA: Edward Elgar.

North, D. C. (1990) *Institutions, Institutional Change and Economic Performance*, Cambridge: Cambridge University Press.

Odum, H. T. (1983) *Systems Ecology: An Introduction*, New York: John Wiley.

Ortmann, A. and G. Gigerenzer (2000) 'Reasoning in economics and psychology: Why social context matters', in M. E. Streit, U. Mummert and D. Kiwit (eds) *Cognition, Rationality and Institutions*, Berlin, Heidelberg, New York: Springer-Verlag.

Pack, H. (1994) 'Endogenous growth theory: intellectual appeal and empirical shortcomings', *Journal of Economic Perspectives*, 8 (1): 55–72.

Pareto, V. (1916/35) *Mind and Society*, 4, New York: Harcourt Brace. (English edn. 1935.)

Parsons, T. (1937) *The Structure of Social Action*, 2 vols, New York: McGraw Hill.

Pasinetti, L. L. (1977) *Lectures on the Theory of Production*, London and Basingstoke: The MacMillan Press Ltd.

Pasinetti, L. L. (1993) *Structural Economic Dynamics*, Cambridge: Cambridge University Press.

Pelikan, P. (2001) 'Self-organizing and Darwinian selection in economic and biological evolutions: an enquiry into the sources of organizing information', in J. Foster and J. S. Metcalfe (eds) *Frontiers of Evolutionary Economics: Competition, Self-organization and Innovation Policy*, Cheltenham, UK, Northampton, MA: Edward Elgar.

Pettit, P. and R. Sugden (1989) 'The backward induction paradox', *The Journal of Philosophy*, LXXXVI (4): 169–82.

Pfouts, R. W. (2002) 'On the need for a more complete ontology of the consumer', in E. Fullbrook (ed.) *Intersubjectivity in Economics: Agents and Structures*, London: Routledge.

Platt, M. L. and P. W. Glimcher (1999) 'Neural correlates of decision variables in parietal cortex', *Nature*, 400: 233–8.

Polanyi, K. (1944) *The Great Transformation*, New York and Toronto: Rinehart & Company, Inc.

Polanyi, M. (1958/62) *Personal Knowledge: Towards a Post-critical Philosophy*, Chicago, IL: The University of Chicago Press.

Polanyi, M. (1966/83) *The Tacit Dimension*, Gloucester, MA: Peter Smith.

Potts, J. (2000) *The New Evolutionary Microeconomics: Complexity, Competence and Adaptive Behaviour*, Northampton, MA: Edward Elgar.

Potts, J. (2001) 'Knowledge and markets', *Journal of Evolutionary Economics*, 11: 413–31.

Pribram, H. K. (1996) 'Interfacing complexity at a boundary between the natural and social sciences', in E. L. Khalil and K. E. Boulding (eds) *Evolution, Order and Complexity*, London: Routledge.

Prigogine, I. (2005) 'The rediscovery of value and the opening of economics', in K. Dopfer (ed.) *The Evolutionary Foundations of Economics*, Cambridge: Cambridge University Press.

Prigogine, I. and I. Stengers (1984) *Order out of Chaos: Man's New Dialogue with Nature*, New York: Bantam Books.

Rabin, M. (1993) 'Incorporating fairness into game theory and economics', *American Economic Review*, 83: 1281–302.

Repetto, R., Magrath, W., Wells, M., Beer, C. and F. Rossini (1989) *Wasting Assets: Natural Resources in the National Income Accounts*, Washington, DC: World Resources Institute.

Robbins, L. (1935) *An Essay on the Nature and Significance of Economic Science*, 2nd ed., London: Macmillan. (First published, 1932.)

Rosenberg, N. (1982) *Inside the Black Box: Technology and Economics*, Cambridge: Cambridge University Press.

Ryan, R. M. and E. L. Deci (2001) 'On happiness and human potentials: a review of research on hedonic and eudiamonic well-being', *Annual Review of Psychology*, 52: 141–66.

Rymes, T. K. (1989) *Keynes's Lectures, 1932–35. Notes of a Representative Student: A Synthesis of Lecture Notes Taken by Students at Keynes's Lectures in the 1930s Leading up to the Publication of The General Theory*, London: Macmillan (in association with the Royal Economic Society).

Saari, D. (1995) 'Mathematical complexity of simple economics', *Notices of the American Mathematical Society*, 42 (2): 222–30.

Salter, W. G. (1960) *Productivity and Technical Change*, Cambridge: Cambridge University Press.

Schlicht, E. (2000) 'Patterned variation: the role of psychological dispositions in social and institutional evolution', in E. M. Streit, U. Mummert and D. Kiwit (eds) *Cognition, Rationality and Institutions*, Berlin, Heidelberg, New York: Springer-Verlag.

Schmookler, J. (1966) *Invention and Economic Growth*, Cambridge, MA: Harvard University Press.

Schumacher, E. F. (1967) *Des Voeux Memorial Lecture*, National Society for Clean Air.

Schumacher, E. F. (1973) *Small is Beautiful*, New York: Harper & Row, Publishers, Inc. (Originally published by Blond & Briggs Ltd., London. Perennial Library edition published in 1975.)

Schumpeter, J. A. (1934) *The Theory of Economic Development*, Cambridge, MA: Harvard University Press.

Schumpeter, J. A. (1947) *Capitalism, Socialism and Democracy*, New York: Harper & Bros. (First edition 1942.)

Scitovsky, T. (1976) *The Joyless Economy: An Inquiry into Human Satisfaction and Consumer Dissatisfaction*, New York, London, Toronto: Oxford University Press.

Seton, F. (1992) *The Economics of Cost, Use and Value*, Oxford: Clarendon Press.

Shackle, G. L. S. (1958) *Time in Economics*, Amsterdam: North Holland Publishing Co.

Shackle, G. L. S. (1972) *Epistemics and Economics: A Critique of Economic Doctrines*, Cambridge: Cambridge University Press.

Simon, H. A. (1969) *The Sciences of the Artificial*, Cambridge, MA, London: The MIT Press.

Smith, A. (1869) *Essays by Adam Smith: The Theory of Moral Sentiments*, London: Alex. Murray & Son.

Smith, A. (1937) *The Wealth of Nations*, New York: Random House Inc., Modern Library.

Smith, A. (1980) 'The principles which lead and direct philosophical enquiries: illustrated by the history of astronomy', in W. P. D. Wightman (ed.) *Essays on Philosophical Subjects*, Oxford: Oxford University Press.

Solnick, S. J. and D. Hemenway (1998) 'Is more always better?: a survey on positional concerns', *Journal of Economic Behavior and Organization*, 37: 373–83.

Steenge, A. E. (1990) 'On the complete instability of empirically implemented dynamic Leontief models', *Economic Systems Research*, 2 (1): 3–16.

Stigler, G. and G. S. Becker (1977) 'De gustibus non est disputandum', *The American Economic Review* 67 (2): 76–90.

Stock, G. B. and J. H. Campbell (1996) 'Human society as an emerging global superorganism – a biological perspective', in E. L. Khalil and K. E. Boulding (eds) *Evolution, Order and Complexity*, London: Routledge.

Strassmann, D. L. (1994) 'Feminist thought and economics; or, what do the Visigoths know?', *The American Economic Review* 84 (2): 153–8.

Thaler, H. R. (1999) 'Mental accounting matters', *Journal of Behavioral Decision-Making*, 12: 183–206.

Thaler, H. R. (2000) 'From homo economicus to homo sapiens', *Journal of Economic Perspectives*, 14 (1): 133–41.

Thoben, H. (1982) 'Mechanistic and organistic analogies in economics reconsidered', *Kyklos*, 35: 292–306.

Tsukui, J. (1966) 'Turnpike theorem in a generalized dynamic input-output system', *Econometrica*, 34 (2): 396–407.

Ulanowicz, E. R. (1996) 'The propensities of evolving systems', in E. L. Khalil and K. E. Boulding (eds) *Evolution, Order and Complexity*, London: Routledge.

Van den Bergh, C. J. M. J. and J. M. Gowdy (2003) 'The microfoundations of macroeconomics: an evolutionary perspective', *Cambridge Journal of Economics*, 27: 65–84.

Varela, F. J., E. Thompson and E. Rosch (1991) *The Embodied Mind: Cognitive Science and Human Experience*, Cambridge, MA: MIT Press.

Veblen, T. B. (1912) *The Theory of the Leisure Class: An Economic Study of Institutions*, New York: Macmillan. (First published 1899. Mentor edition, 1953, by the New American Library, A Division of Penguin Books USA Inc.)

Vickers, G. (1970) *Freedom in a Rocking Boat*, Allen Lane: The Penguin Press.

Weber, M. (1978) *The Protestant Ethic and the Spirit of Capitalism*, 1st ed., 1904–5, London: Allen and Unwin.

Weisskopf, W. A. (1971) *Alienation and Economics*, New York: E. P. Dutton.

West, T. G. and G. S. West (trans.) (1984) *Four Texts on Socrates: Plato's Euthyphro, Apology, and Crito and Aristophanes' Clouds*, Ithaca and London: Cornell University Press. (Revised Edition 1998.)

White, L. (1963) 'What accelerated technical progress in the Western Middle Ages?', in A. Crombie (ed.) *Scientific Change*, New York: Basic Books.

Wiener, N. (1948) *Cybernetics: Or Control and Communication in the Animal and the Machine*, Cambridge, MA: The MIT Press. (First paperback edition, 1965.)

Witt, U. (2001) 'Learning to consume – a theory of wants and the growth of demand', *Journal of Evolutionary Economics*, 11: 23–36.

Wolff, R. D. (2004) 'The riddle of consumption', *Post-autistic Economics Review*, Issue no. 27, http://www.btinternet.com/~paenews/review/issue27.htm (accessed 26 June 2006).

Young, A. (1995) 'The tyranny of numbers: confronting the statistical realities of the East Asian growth experience', *Quarterly Journal of Economics*, 110: 641–80.

Index

For Product Safety Concerns and Information please contact our EU
representative GPSR@taylorandfrancis.com
Taylor & Francis Verlag GmbH, Kaufingerstraße 24, 80331 München, Germany

www.ingramcontent.com/pod-product-compliance
Lightning Source LLC
Chambersburg PA
CBHW061144220326
41599CB00025B/4343